# Changing Work, Changing Workers

SUNY Series, Literacy, Culture, and Learning: Theory and Practice
Alan C. Purves, editor

# Changing Work, Changing Workers

## Critical Perspectives on Language, Literacy, and Skills

EDITED BY

*Glynda Hull*

State University of New York Press

Published by
State University of New York Press, Albany

© 1997 State University of New York

For information, address State University of New York Press,
State University Plaza, Albany, N.Y., 12246

Production by Marilyn Semerad
Marketing by Nancy Farrell

**Library of Congress Cataloging-in-Publication Data**

Changing work, changing workers : critical perspectives on language,
    literacy, and skills / edited by Glynda Hull.
        p.    cm — (SUNY series, literacy, culture, and learning)
    Includes bibliographical references and index.
    ISBN 0–7914–3219–X. — ISBN 0–7914–3220–3 (pbk.)
    1. Workplace literacy—United States.    2. Literacy programs–
–United States—Case studies.    3. Working class—Education—United
States.    I. Hull, Glynda A.    II. Series.
LC149.7.C53    1997
374′.0124—dc21                                                        96–39209
                                                                              CIP

10  9  8  7  6  5  4  3  2  1

To the memory of Charles Scott Benson
(1922–1994)

# CONTENTS

# List of Illustrations

# List of Tables

# *Preface*

To introduce the major themes of this edited collection on language, literacy, skills, and work, I want to offer an excerpt from a conversation with Sook Yoo, a Korean-American woman who works at a circuit-board assembly factory in the Silicon Valley of northern California. This conversation took place in a run-down, inner city apartment complex near San Jose, where a community activist had set up a literacy and labor education program for Asian immigrant women. Sook Yoo, two other Korean-American women workers, the community activist, and I sat around a folding table on a hot afternoon, just after the women had finished their shift at the factory, discussing what it is like to work in the electronics industry in the Valley. I asked questions, the activist translated, and the three women workers responded in Korean, which the activist then translated back into English for me. We had talked at length, covering a range of topics—the women's educational histories, how they had heard about and gotten jobs in the industry, health and safety problems at the plant, the literacy requirements of work, and so on. Then the conversation had turned from serious to light-hearted, as one woman described a recent company picnic and the dunking booth that had been set up for managers. Suddenly, Sook Yoo, who had been the quietest during the conversation, interrupted our laughter with the following pensive observations, spoken in Korean. She returned us to what I later realized was the overriding problem facing virtually all of the considerable number of Korean-American workers in the plant, that of language:

> I think there is a reason why we don't speak English that well. When we started working at EMCO [pseudonym], our starting pay was so little. But since we didn't speak much English, we just took the starting pay. We started working and stayed for a while, but since the pay was so little, there was no time for us to study, realistically, because the pay was so minimal. . . . And we were so busy trying to survive. Since we came up that way, even now, we don't have a lot of money, and we are leading a hard life.

Sook Yoo and the others went on to explain that members of their cultural community generally don't like to get help from the government, that they want to earn the little that they get; this, plus the value they place on higher education for their children often necessitates their taking two jobs. The result is too little money, too little time to learn English. Not being able to speak English means not being able to defend yourself in the workplace when you're accused of a mistake, and most importantly, it means a greatly reduced chance of promotion, even when you do your current job very well. There are no Korean supervisors, they observe, in this high-tech workplace where international certification standards require that manufacturing process instructions be written, read, and communicated in English. They wish the company had provided English classes an hour before or after work. Sook Yoo concludes: "So we lost the chance to learn English, and now we are too old."

The stories of Sook Yoo and her friends and the stories of many other workers in the United States (and elsewhere) are rarely represented in the public discourse on literacy, language, skills, and work. We do hear from newspaper and magazine articles, from blue-ribbon panels and commissioned reports, that workers in the United States are "illiterate" to a disturbing extent, that higher levels of literacy and numerous other skills and competencies are needed increasingly for many types of work, that literacy tests, "audits," and instruction are, therefore, necessary phenomena in the workplace. We are told of fears that the U.S. workforce, increasingly comprised of women, immigrants, and people of color, can not measure up to the demands of international competition and increasingly sophisticated technologies. There are numerous calls for programs which train, retrain, or retool workers and potential workers who are dislocated, unemployed, or low-skilled, and federal panels are being formed to set national skills standards for jobs across the nation.

Despite an increasing interest in preparing people well for the jobs of the future, and an ever-present concern about workers' skills or the lack thereof, the public discourse on skills and work is rarely informed by research which actually attempts to describe the knowledge and know-how required in today's workplaces, including the ways in which language and literacy-related activities are embedded in work. Nor do we often document in helpful detail the successes and failures of education and training programs designed to prepare or repair workers, or to explore the intersection of the desire to acquire skills with the opportunity to acquire and to use them in the workplace.

We don't know much about, to return to the above example, the considerable literacy and language requirements of jobs at a place like EMCO, or how the language performances required there can best be taught in vocational programs or at work. We don't understand the relationship between literacy, skills, and the constraints imposed by the growing contract manufacturing industry, such as international certifications, that EMCO represents, though they are considerable. We very rarely explore what workers like Sook Yoo can do, what their lack of English or their accents mask. We don't know Sook Yoo's story, her educational and work history, her desires for the future.

There is a great need, I am arguing, to understand how people experience instructional programs and how they accomplish work; to document with care the kinds of things people are expected to know and be able to do in different work contexts; to critically examine the role that literacy and other valued practices can and cannot play in promoting economic productivity or in facilitating personal empowerment; and to discover the incentives and disincentives that people perceive and experience for acquiring and exercising literate skills. These are the sorts of themes that are explored in this edited volume. The collection brings together researchers and educators from a variety of fields and disciplines who have made contributions to understanding literacy, language, skills, and work through ethnographic or field-based studies of classrooms, workplaces, and training programs; through analyses of policy and public discourse; or through close and detailed examinations of texts and curricula. The selections draw their strength from fine-grained analyses rather than anecdote or diatribe, but most bring their analyses to life by representing the voices and stories and situations of people like Sook Yoo or the materials, methods, and texts of actual programs or work sites.

The book is divided into three sections, the first an introduction adapted from an article that I originally published in the *Harvard Educational Review*, and is reprinted here with that journal's kind permission. In this chapter I argue that current popular discussions about the role of literacy in the workplace are often based on largely unquestioned beliefs that workers are deficient in basic literacy skills and that there are clear links among illiteracy, poor job performance, and the declining economy. These assumptions have lead to demands for school-based, skill-driven literacy programs tied to the workplace. In the chapter I attempt to challenge these demands and characterizations, and I argue that we need to look with a critical eye at how work gets accomplished and to examine what roles literacy plays within work as well as the relationships between skills at work and the rights of workers. In essence, I call for the kind of research and reflection that is offered in the remainder of the book.

Part I, "Perspectives from the Classroom," begins with a chapter by Katherine Schultz, an analysis of the discourse of new workplace literacy programs. Despite the fact that there is much interest in establishing such programs, many of which have been sponsored by the U.S. Department of Education, and despite the fact that we know a lot now about literacy and learning, there have been few attempts to look at the new programs critically, to test them against the best of current theorizing and exemplary practice. Through her examination Schultz lays bear a "new orthodoxy," a dominant and not particularly helpful way of envisioning instruction, and she cautions us not to rush to accept this single way of thinking about and structuring workplace literacy programs.

Schultz's chapter is followed by three field-based studies of actual workplace literacy programs. Kalman and Losey documented a joint effort by a community college and a union to develop a literacy program for entry level hospital workers—ambulance drivers, maintenance workers, nurse's aides. All involved had great hopes for this program, for its organizers were aware of the pitfalls of the approach Schultz termed "the new orthodoxy," and they were knowledgeable about alternative approaches as well. Kalman and Losey's work is distinctive for its focus on the difficulties that can accompany pedagogical innovation and for their fine-grained examination of classroom interaction. Though such studies have been frequent in K–12 schooling, they are quite rare in adult education. Kalman and Losey's analysis of the teacher's interaction with her students and the students' interaction with each other lay bear for us some of the problems that plague even well-intentioned, well-organized, well-funded efforts, and also suggests some of the factors that must be considered if we want pedagogical innovation to take hold.

The second case study of a workplace literacy program is D'Amico and Schnee's examination of another federally funded demonstration project, this one for garment workers in New York City. The intent of the project was to prepare people for alternatives to work in the rapidly downsizing garment industry, specifically as bilingual paraprofessionals in education, for which there was a great need in the city and which would take advantage of the bilingual abilities of the participants. In a detailed history of this project, D'Amico and Schnee document the many successes of the students in terms of their experiences in the program, but ultimately conclude that the program failed in its aim to offer viable employment opportunities. Four years later, most of the participants still worked in non-professional jobs in the garment industry and other sectors. D'Amico and Schnee discuss the structural factors which intervened—gender, class, immigration status, local politics—and in this instance prevented education from leading to jobs. This account is singular in offering a longitudinal look at a literacy program and in its analysis which ranges far beyond the classroom door.

If D'Amico and Schnee challenge commonplace notions of program developers and policymakers, Gowen and Bartlett challenge widely held beliefs by educators about why and how women learn and what they prefer to learn about. This is a study of a literacy program in a university, a program offered in lieu of raises to the African-American maintenance and groundskeeping staff, and it is a story of how the authors as two white middle-class academics were forced to rethink their notions of women and literacy. Contrary to the literature on the preferred learning styles of women and African-Americans, many of the participants in this study did not enjoy cooperative learning; and contrary to ideas popular in critical pedagogy, they were offended by attempts to politicize them through literacy learning. Most startlingly, Gowen and Bartlett discovered that some of the women in the class had been or currently were victims of domestic violence, and they then began to understand the relationship between this abuse and their students' silence in the literacy class. This moving chapter not only reminds us to beware pedagogies and ideologies which pigeon-hole groups of people and suggest that students prefer or should prefer this or that in our classrooms, it also brings to light the fact that women abuse survivors are likely to be participants in worker education programs and that we must take into account how literacy's power to change lives has different consequences for different people.

The remaining three chapters in Part I keep our attention on classrooms but situate them within vocational education and current efforts to help students make the transition from school to work. To begin, Grubb examines the current intersection of three concerns in the history of American education: the occupational uses of schooling or the "New Vocationalism," as Grubb labels the most recent manifestation of this long-standing concern; literacy and illiteracy and the preparation people need for the reading and writing requirements of work; and innovation in teaching or the reform of curriculum and pedagogy. Grubb demonstrates the current confluence of interest in these three areas, but he argues that the programs that have been created to promote occupational literacy do not unfortunately employ new and improved approaches to teaching and learning. Rather, they follow an approach to teaching that Grubb calls "skills and drills," notable for being teacher-centered and skill-driven. Grubb helps us understand why federal policy has tended to neglect issues of pedagogy, and finally he gives us reason to be hopeful that current efforts to develop literacy programs will also incorporate innovative pedagogies. Of all the chapters, this one provides the broadest historical and political backdrop for understanding how programs are shaped, and it best helps us understand the relationship between our classrooms and federal and state policy.

As part of what Grubb calls the "New Vocationalism," there have been several kinds of efforts to improve work-related literacy instruction, including attempts to integrate academic and vocational education. Jury provides a critique of one type of integration called "Applied Communications," courses or lesson sequences that are supposed to help high school students develop job-related communication skills. Jury describes a popular commercially available package, testing it against current literacy and learning theory, and he finds that it comes up short. Designers of applied communication curricula typically view communication as a neutral package of skills, whereas Jury suggests an alternate view of it as engaged linguistic activity and negotiated understanding which will be influenced by ideology, social relationships, and culture. To conclude his chapter, Jury examines alternative ways for teachers to help students who are about to enter the world of work to reflect critically on language use.

Castellano reports an ethnographic study of a training program designed for women interested in getting jobs in the skilled trades, such as plumbing, carpentry, and machining. This training program was sponsored by the federal Job Training and Partnership Act, which in collaboration with local private industry, funds a range of training programs for the unemployed. Castellano demonstrates the ways in which a particular kind of literacy—the reading, writing, and thinking necessary for negotiating written tests about sentient activities—served to derail women's efforts to work in the skilled trades. She likens the use of standardized testing in education to its similar use for employment selection purposes and, in reviewing the literature in this area, argues that such tests shut out minorities and the disadvantaged while failing to accurately predict how people will actually perform on the job. Castellano concludes her chapter by proposing several ways that the skilled trades can avoid the problems associated with such testing.

Part II, "Perspectives from the Factory Floor," presents research about work processes and new technologies, about the relationship between literacy and language use and different forms of work organization, and about how people experience work and deal with unemployment. Some of these chapters introduce us to workers and workplaces where new ideas about work organization and worker empowerment have turned out to be hollow promises, but others look more optimistically at such efforts, documenting or envisioning occasions when skill development and literacy and language requirements can help to create new, more positive work identities.

Darrah begins this section by complicating our understanding of the common term "skill requirements," which is often adopted as a label for what jobs require and what people need to know and be able to do in order to perform them. Drawing on his ethnographic research conducted on the production floor of a manufacturer of computer work stations in the Silicon Valley, Darrah explodes a lot of the common assumptions we have about skills. For example, this particular company had recently instituted the "team concept" and had reorganized the workforce into cross-functional work groups which were compared to separate companies where each team member was a vice-president. When the team concept failed, management simply blamed the workers' skill deficits, but Darrah's examination revealed a complex set of influences—the incentives and disincentives employees felt about whether to invest themselves in this program, the opportunities or lack thereof to take part, employees' suspicions about managerial intentions, and management's responses to their attempts to take action—all these played a part in whether workers acquired and exercised the skills their employers recognized and valued.

Ziv's chapter returns us to the electronics factory that I introduced earlier where Sook Yoo and her friends and others assemble circuit boards. Ziv explores the beliefs, attitudes, and intentions of a manager as he interacts with front-line workers in a training session. Carrying out a pragmatic analysis of an audio-recording of the manager's speech, he shows how this manager was able to assert his authority through subtle discourse moves, including the use of social deixis or choice of pronouns, irony, and the alternation of restricted and elaborated codes. Ziv argues that if a workers are going to be able to participate in complex discourse situations that characterize restructured workplaces—environments where lines of authority are supposedly blurred—they will need finely-tuned oral language abilities. It is important to note, however, that such abilities are rarely called for in discussions of needed workplace skills and competencies.

The electronics industry is notorious for being low-wage and non-union and, some would argue, for taking advantage of a newly arrived immigrant workforce. Merrifield takes us to Blount County, Tennessee, and the closure of a pants factory, and in so doing provides an analysis of another industry with different patterns of exploitation. This factory, like many U.S. firms, had chosen to downsize its manufacturing in the United States and to open new plants abroad. With help from the Job Training Partnership Act, the company offered retraining as the answer to the shutdown: its former workforce, 92 percent female, would take part in job training classes that would prepare them for non-manufacturing jobs. Merrifield's research tracked a group of displaced women workers for a two-year period in order to find out what difference job training made in their ability to find a good job. In fact, she joined forces with the women, involving them in planning and carrying out the research. This research demonstrated that the job training the women took part in did not make a big difference in subsequent employment, and Merrifield has suggestions about how to transform job training so that it has the potential to be more helpful. However, Merrifield and her advisory committee also point to the importance, to the necessity, of job creation, arguing that a focus on the kinds of jobs that are being created in our economy makes job training look much less relevant.

In the last half of Part II we examine case studies in industries where new technologies, new forms of work organization, and new skill requirements have had or an have a more positive impact on workers.

Cook-Gumperz and Hanna explore the impact of new technologies—bedside computers—on hospital nursing practice. Taking an historical look at the development of nursing as a career, the authors demonstrate how nursing both became professionalized and stayed largely "women's work, which is an unusual pattern. With the introduction of increasingly sophisticated technology, which gives greater access to patient decision-making, nurses have a new, even more skilled image. Thus, by examining textbook accounts of nursing observation and documentation and by interviewing hospital nurses and nursing educators, Cook-Gumperz and Hanna show how recent changes in the technological practice of nursing have also brought changes in the professional identities. The considerable literate activity involved in bedside computing, where nurses record patient observations and develop a nursing care plan, highlight the central role of documentation in professional practice. Cook-Gumperz and Hanna point out that while some nurses in their study didn't welcome the new technology, finding it difficult to use as well as threatening, it nonetheless had benefits, not the least of which was allowing nurses greater responsibility as professionals who influence the flow of information and play an important part in decision-making.

Jolliffe takes us to the precision metalworking industry in Chicago, where workers stamp, mill, and fabricate a variety of small metal objects. Like many industries, this one claims that its employees must be able to respond quickly and adaptively to changing customer demands, to interact with computer technology, to absorb instructions and information of all sorts from print, and that such demands are increasing all the time. In a neat twist on the now familiar refrain of the growing literacy demands of the new workplace, Jolliffe argues that the leaders of American business, industry, and service—if they truly desire workers who are committed and involved—need to pay close attention to the ways in which work-related documents do or do not help workers to take on these characteristics. Jolliffe critiques the tried and true method of analyzing the grade-level readability of workplace documents and goes on to offer a discourse analytic framework for analyzing workers' "identify formation" in the documents. He also demonstrates the analysis of a workplace document that entry-level workers in a metalworking shop were expected to read and understand, and he uncovers the rhetorical and stylistic features which he believes would make it off-putting to workers. One of Jolliffe's interesting solutions is for workers to be involved in writing their company's documentation, a practice that seems as yet to be quite rare.

Finally, in their long-term ethnographic study of a "high performance" auto accessory factory, Hart-Landsberg and Reder illustrate how literacy practices evolve in tandem with the social settings of which they are a part. In this workplace where management had recently instituted self-directed work teams and a compensation system based on demonstrated knowledge and skills, Hart-Landsberg and Reder found literacy demands to be prodigious. New responsibilities for tracking quality, making decisions, and acquiring a variety of new skills put demands on workers to develop a range of literacy practices. Hart-Landsberg and Reder also learned, however, that while many workers were energized by the chance to improve skills, others felt put upon and pressured to give more than they believed the company had a right to ask. This study stands out as one of the first attempts to determine whether particular high performance work environments actually increase skill requirements, and to document how workers respond to reorganized workplaces and to companies' demands that they develop new proficiencies.

Although I've organized this book according to whether chapters have to do mostly with research in the classroom or research in the workplace, other patterns are salient and worth noting here. Several chapters focus on the experiences of women (Gowen and Bartlett, Castellano, Cook-Gumperz and Hanna, Merrifield), and this emphasis calls attention both to the gendered nature of work and the ways in which literacy learning is entwined with and shaped by the gendered identities and experiences of students and teachers. Practically all of the data-based chapters draw their strength from ethnographic or qualitative research methods and perspectives (Castellano, Darrah, Hart-Landsberg and Reder). In doing so, they fulfill a major goal I had for this book, illustrating and modeling the role that field-based studies can play in helping us to rethink the skills crisis. Several chapters rely on fine-grained linguistic analyses—of talk to understand and explore beliefs, attitudes, and intentions (Ziv) and to explore how participants interact and participate (Kalman and Losey)—and of writing to explore the formation of social identities and relations through the reading of texts (Jolliffe)—all unusual in the literature on adult education. And several demonstrate untraditional roles for researchers in participatory research or collaborative efforts with educators (Merrifield, D'Amico and Schnee, Gowen and Bartlett, Cook-Gumperz and Hanna), relationships that I hoped this book would illustrate and endorse.

My best hope for this book is that it will complicate and challenge current discussions about what workers need to know, about the skills they are expected, hoped, required to possess. The chapters illustrate again and again, in different contexts, with different people, different classrooms, different programs, different jobs, and different working conditions , the ways in which skills are not decontextualized, autonomous, individually owned and operated competencies that are always available for display and use. Rather, the skills that people acquire depend on who people are, on their backgrounds and cultures and opportunities. The ways that people use and demonstrate skills in a workplace depend on how work is organized and the incentives and disincentives that people perceive for displaying them, as well as their rights and responsibilities as workers. This book demonstrates how important it is, in addition to worrying about what workers should know and how best to determine what they must know, for policymakers, government and labor leaders, corporate people, educators, and activists to turn their collective attention to charting those various conditions and structures which best enable diverse working people to learn and to work.

# Acknowledgments

I'm grateful for the chance to have worked with the authors in this volume, some of whom are long-standing colleagues, some of whom have been my students, and all of whom I've come to know better and to appreciate greatly through working with their texts and their ideas.

This book grew out of my research in workplaces, and that research got its start through a collaboration a number of years ago with Jenny Cook-Gumperz. I appreciate her willingness to revisit that collaboration by writing a chapter for this volume. Another long-time collaborator has been Mike Rose, with whom I studied the teaching of writing in schools and with whom I began to think about sociocultural research; his helpful influence followed me into my research on work and this book. A more recent collaborator has been Kathy Schultz, research partner *par excellence*.

Over the years that I have studied literacy in the context of work, my own work as a researcher has been made immeasurably richer by the work of graduate research assistants, and for their energy, enthusiasm, commitment, irreverence, and intellect, I am very grateful. Thank you Marisa Castellano, Lynn Coddington, Margaret Easter, Meg Gebhard, Stan Goto, Pablo Jassis, Mark Jury, Mira Katz, Kay Losey, David Mullen, Brian Reilly, Susan Thompson, Craig Wilson, and Oren Ziv. Special thanks to Oren Ziv, who helped greatly with the preparation of this manuscript and the editing of individual chapters.

Norton Grubb made much of the research reported here a reality through his support as the Berkeley site director for the National Center for Research in Vocational Education. This center funded the research on which a number of the chapters are based—in fact, all those by written by authors at Berkeley. Both Norton Grubb and the late director of the center, Charles Benson, to whose memory I have dedicated this volume, helped to make space on the center's agenda for qualitative research on literacy and work. Similarly, Sarah Warshauer Freedman, director of the National Center for the Study of Writing and Literacy, recognized the need to tie studies of literacy to studies of work; I am grateful for her center's sponsorship of the research reported in my own and Oren Ziv's chapters. I am indebted as well to the Spencer Foundation, which has supported both my own research and the preparation of this manuscript through a Spencer Mentor Grant.

And last, thanks to Ed Warshauer for continuing to help me to think about changing workplaces and workers' rights and responsibilities.

*Introduction*

# ONE

## Hearing Other Voices: A Critical Assessment of Popular Views on Literacy and Work

### *Glynda Hull*

*Interviewer*: What about reading and writing? People are always saying that you need reading and writing for whatever you do. Do you need reading and writing skills in banking?

*Jackie*: I don't think so, 'cause, say, if you don't know how to spell somebody's name, when they first come up to you, they have to give you their California ID. So you could look on there and put it in the computer like that . . . push it in on those buttons.

*Alma*: But you still gonna have to look at it and read and write. . . . You've got to read those numbers when you cash their money; that's reading and writing. . . . If you can't read and write, you're not going to get hired no way.

*Jackie*: That's true.

Jackie and Alma, students in a vocational program on banking and finance, disagree about the nature and extent of the reading and writing actually involved in being a bank teller. But they do not doubt, even were such skills unimportant in carrying out the job itself, that literacy (or some credential attesting to it) would be a requirement for getting hired in the first place.

From what I can tell by examining a popular literature that is noteworthy for its doomsday tone, Jackie and Alma are right: There is consensus among employers, government officials, and literacy providers that American workers to a disturbing extent are "illiterate"; that higher levels of literacy are increasingly needed for many types of work; and that literacy tests, "audits," and instruction are, therefore, necessary phenomena in the workplace.

I find most current characterizations of workplace (il)literacy troublesome and harmful, and in this chapter I hope to show why. To begin, I will illustrate some widely held, fundamental assumptions about literacy, work, and workers—the debatable though largely uncontested beliefs which turn up again and again in policy statements, program descriptions, and popular articles. Most troubling is the now commonplace assertion, presented as a statement of fact, that because they apparently lack literacy and other "basic skills," U.S. workers can be held accountable for our country's lagging economy and the failure of its businesses to compete at home and internationally. I want to give space to this dominant rhetoric—the calls to arms by leaders in business, industry, and government to educate American workers before it is too late—for efforts proceed apace to design, implement, and evaluate workplace literacy programs largely on the basis of these notions.

The remainder of this chapter (and the subsequent chapters in this book) is spent complicating and challenging these views. Drawing on recent sociocognitive and historical research on literacy and work, I will suggest that many current characterizations of literacy, literacy at work, and workers as illiterate—as deficient—are inaccurate, incomplete, and misleading. I argue that we have not paid enough attention, as we measure reading rates, design curricula, and construct lists of essential skills, to how people experience instructional programs and to how they accomplish work. Nor have we often or critically examined how literacy can play a role in promoting economic productivity or in facilitating personal empowerment in the context of particular work situations and training programs for work. Nor is it common, in studies of work or reading and writing at work, to acknowledge the perspectives of workers—to discover the incentives and disincentives they perceive and experience for acquiring and exercising literate skills.

Alternate points of view and critical reassessments are essential if we are ever to create frameworks for understanding literacy in relation to work; if we are ever to design literacy programs that have a prayer of speaking to the needs and aspirations of workers as well as employers; and, most importantly, if we are ever to create structures for participation in education and work that are equitable and democratic. The main point of this introductory chapter is that we must allow different voices be heard, voices like those of Alma and Jackie. We must see, as we will in the remainder of this book, how different stories and other voices can amend, qualify, and fundamentally challenge the popular, dominant myths of literacy, skills, and work.

# Current Views on Workplace Literacy

In the following sections I present some widespread, popular conceptions of literacy and its relationships to work. To illustrate what I will call the "popular discourse" of workplace literacy—the common values and viewpoints reflected in currently dominant ways of talking and writing about the issue—I quote directly from policy documents, newspapers, magazines, and interviews.[1] In this way I hope to capture the voices and suggest something of the ideologies that dominate current debates about education and work. I view these voices and ideologies as a specific instance of what Giroux and McLaren (1989) have described more generally as "the conservative discourse of schooling" (p. xiv), wherein public schools are defined as "agents of social discipline and economic regulation" (p. xv), being valued only insofar as they turn out workers with the skills, knowledge, habits, and attitudes thought essential in terms of today's economy. I label the discourse on skills and work "popular" rather than "conservative" to suggest how persuasive and omnipresent and, well, popular these ways of thinking and talking about workers and literacy have become. Not only do died-in-the-wool conservatives or right-wingers adhere to this discourse, but concerned teachers and committed literacy specialists, well-meaning business people and eager students, interested academics and progressive politicians, worried parents, and a host of others as well—many people, I want to suggest, who don't necessarily think of themselves as conservers of the status quo.

### "Workers Lack Literacy"

The most pervasive and unquestioned belief about literacy in relation to work is simply that workers do not possess the important literacy skills needed in current and future jobs. Here are examples:

"Millions of Americans are locked out of good jobs, community participation and the democratic process because they lack adequate reading and writing skills," said Dale Johnson, spokesman for the Working Group on Adult Literacy. "Only leadership from the Presidential level can assure that the literacy needs of all Americans will be met." (Fiske, 1988, p. 12)

Anyone who has hired new employees or tried to retrain veteran ones is painfully aware of the problem. As much as a quarter of the American labor force—anywhere from 20 million to 27 million adults—lacks the basic reading, writing and

5

math skills necessary to perform in today's increasingly complex job market. One out of every 4 teenagers drops out of high school, and of those who graduate, 1 out of every 4 has the equivalent of an eighth-grade education. How will they write, or even read, complicated production memos for robotized assembly lines? How will they be able to fill backlogged service orders? (Gorman, 1988, p. 56)

The Department of Education estimates that there are about 27,000,000 adult Americans who can't really read. Almost all of them can sign their names and maybe spell out a headline. Most aren't totally illiterate the way we used to define illiteracy. But they can't read the label on a medicine bottle. Or fill out a job application. Or write a report. Or read the instructions on the operation of a piece of equipment. Or the safety directions in a factory. Or a memo from the boss. Maybe they even have trouble reading addresses in order to work as a messenger or deliveryman. Certainly they can't work in an office. (Lacy, 1985, p. 10)

Such accounts are exceedingly common: The shocking illustrations of seemingly basic, taken-for-granted skills which current workers and recent graduates lack; the apparently "hard" evidence that these illustrations apply to large numbers of people; and the frightening implication that, given the severity of the deficits, it is almost too late to solve this enormous problem. Notice the constant emphasis on deficits—what people are unable to do, what they lack, how they fail—and the causal relationship assumed between those deficits and people's performance at work.

Articles reporting worker illiteracy often specify as well which groups among the American population will dominate in future work—that is, women, minorities, and immigrants—and then make the point that, since these groups are likely to have the poorest skills, literacy-related problems in the workplace will likely worsen:

The years of picky hiring are over. Vicious competition for all sorts of workers— entry-level, skilled, seasoned—has begun. Employers must look to the nonmale, the nonwhite, the nonyoung. There may be a push for non-citizens as well: Over the next 10 years . . . only 15% of work force entrants will be native-born white males.

Building a new, more diverse work force and making it tick will be one of corporate America's biggest challenges in the decade ahead. (Ehrlich & Garland, 1988, pp. 107–108)

A growing share of our new workers will come from groups where human resource investments have been historically deficient—minorities, women, and immigrants. Employers will increasingly have to reach into the ranks of the less advantaged to obtain their entry-level work force, frequently those with deficient basic skills. (Former Secretary of Labor Ann McLaughlin quoted in *The Bottom Line*, 1988, p. ii)

Ehrlich & Garland, 1988, p. 107, decry as "the nonmale, the nonwhite, the nonyoung"). I will argue that the popular discourse of workplace literacy tends to underestimate and devalue human potential and to mis-characterize literacy as a curative for problems that literacy alone cannot solve. Such tendencies obscure other social and economic problems that literacy alone cannot solve. They also provide a smokescreen, covering up certain key societal problems by drawing our attention to other issues that, while important, are only symptomatic of larger ills.[7]

### Rethinking the Effects of Literacy and Illiteracy

It is ironic that, at a time when the value of literacy has been rediscovered in public discourse, theorists from many disciplines—history, psychology, anthropology, literary theory, critical theory, feminist theory—are engaged in questioning the grand claims that traditionally have been made for it. There was a time when scholars talked of literacy as essential for cognitive development or as transformative in its effect on mental processes (for example, Goody & Watt, 1968; Olson, 1977; Ong, 1982). Others have also put great stock in the social, economic, and political effects of literacy— UNESCO's adult literacy campaigns in so-called "developing nations" being a prime example (see UNESCO, 1976).

Graff (1979, 1986), however, has called the tendency to associate the value of reading and writing with socioeconomic development and individual growth "the literacy myth." He has pointed out that, contrary to conventional wisdom, at many times and in many places there have been major steps forward in trade, commerce, and industry without high levels of literacy—during, for example, the commercial revolution of the Middle Ages and the eighteenth-century protoindustrialization in rural areas (1987, p. 11). Conversely, higher levels of literacy have not always, in modern times, been the starting place for economic development. Claims about the consequences of literacy for intellectual growth have also been tempered by recent sociocognitive research. For example, in one of the most extensive investigations of the psychology of literacy, Scribner and Cole (1981) scaled down the usual generalizations "about the impact of literacy on history, on philosophy, and on the minds of individual human beings" to the more modest conclusion that "literacy makes some difference to some skills in some contexts" (p. 234).[8]

Contemporary claims about the connection between the economic difficulties of business and industry and the literacy and basic skill deficits of workers thus stand in sharp contrast to current revisionist thinking about literacy. Popular articles repeat stories of individual workers at specific companies who fail to read signs or perform some work-related task involving literacy, and thereby make costly errors; these stories then rapidly become an unquestioned part of the popular discourse on workplace literacy. But there are alternate ways to interpret such events, as Darrah (1990) illustrates in his ethnographic study of a computer manufacturing company where the workplace was temporarily reorganized. (See also Darrah's chapter in this volume.)

In the company Darrah studied, workers with the same job title had labored together, moving around the production floor at the direction of lead workers and supervisors. Under the "Team Concept," new work groups were formed, consisting of workers with different specialties, and these groups were ostensibly given total responsibility for producing a line of computers. The management expected that product quality would improve when workers, now with a greater say in decision-making, felt a greater commitment to the company's fortunes. In fact, the team concept failed, and when it did, the management blamed the workers. They claimed that these employees, many of them Southeast Asian immigrants, were deficient in oral and written communication skills and lacked the abilities to self-manage, to "see the big picture," and to analyze production flow.

Darrah acknowledges that it would have been possible to find instances of workers who did not have the skills the managers mentioned. He goes on to demonstrate, however, that the demise of the Team Concept had little to do with workers' skills, present or absent; rather, it grew from contradictions inherent in how this concept was introduced and experienced. From the beginning workers were skeptical about management's intentions. For example, the production manager and his supervisors announced the team concept on Thursday, scheduled team discussion for Friday, and instructed workers that beginning on Monday they should "act as if you're the vice-president of your own company" (p. 12). One repair technician commented dubiously to his coworkers after the initial meeting, "They never asked us anything before, but what can we do? We have to do what the company says" (p. 12). Further, workers feared that putting everyone at the same level on a team was a not-so-subtle attempt to eliminate job ladders and hard-won status. They felt shut out from particular kinds of information, even though the team concept was supposed to open communication and encourage workers to understand the totality of production (p. 22). Moreover, they did not believe that they had control over work processes that mattered. For example, they were asked to identify mistakes made by people outside the floor—such as improperly specified cables or faulty work by subcontractors—but when they did so, they were a little too successful: The people at fault complained, and the feedback was stopped.

Historical and sociocognitive studies of the consequences of literacy like Graff's (1979, 1987) and Scribner and Cole's (1981), as well as ethnographic accounts like Darrah's (1990, 1992) should make us question some of the facile claims found in the popular discourse of workplace literacy. They ought to make us think twice, for example, before we assume that increasing the grade level at which someone reads will automatically improve his or her performance on a literacy-related job activity (cf. Mikulecky, 1982). Further, they ought to at least slow us down when we reason that, if only people were literate, they could all get jobs. Research on the consequences of literacy tells us that there are various complex forces—political, economic, social, personal—that either can foster or hinder literacy's potential to bring about change, as can the variety of literacy that is practiced (Lankshear & Lawler, 1987; Sahni, 1992; Street, 1984). As Graff (1986) concludes in his historical look at the relationship between literacy and economic and social progress, "Literacy is neither the major problem, nor is it the main solution" (p. 82). And in the words of Maxine Greene (1989), "The world is not crying out for more literate people to take on jobs, but for job opportunities for the literate and unlettered alike."

It is hardly credible, given the complexities of work, culture, and ideology in this country, that worker illiteracy should bear the burden of causality for a lagging economy and a failure at international competition, or that literacy should be the solution for such grave problems. According to the World Competitiveness Report (1989), human resources, which include education and training, is only one factor among ten which affect a country's international competitiveness. Others include the dynamism of the economy, industrial efficiency, state interference, and sociopolitical stability. Some have argued (see, for example, Brint & Karabel, 1989; Sarmiento, 1989), in fact, that claims of illiteracy and other deficiencies make workers convenient scapegoats for problems which originate in a larger arena.

### Rethinking Workers' Potential

The popular discourse of workplace literacy sets up a we/they dichotomy. It stresses the apparent failures of large numbers of people—disproportionately the poor and people of color—to be competent at what are considered run-of-the-mill daily tasks. Exaggerated and influenced by race and class prejudice, this dichotomy has the effect of separating the literate readers of magazines, newspaper articles, and scholarly reports on the literacy crisis from the masses who, we unthinkingly assume, are barely getting through the day. As Fingeret (1983) has aptly commented, "It is difficult for us to conceptualize life without reading and writing as anything other than a limited, dull, dependent existence" (p. 133). Thus, in our current accounts of workplace literacy, we are just a step from associating poor performance on literacy tasks with being lesser and qualitatively different in ability and potential. This association has, of course, been common throughout the history of schooling in this

13

country (Zehm, 1973; Cuban & Tyack, 1989; Fingeret, 1989; Hull, Rose, Fraser, & Castellano, 1991) and is carried into the workplace. We have tended to think of children, adolescents, and young adults who have done poorly at English and math as intellectually and morally inferior and have used these labels to segregate them in special classes, tracks, programs, schools, and jobs.

When applied to workers, the stigma of illiteracy is doubly punitive, for it attaches further negative connotations to people whose abilities have already been devalued by virtue of their employment. There is a long-standing tendency in our society and even throughout history to view skeptically the abilities of people who work at physical labor (cf. Zuboff, 1988). Shaiken (1984) illustrates the recent history of this tendency in his account of skilled machinists in North America. Before the turn of the century, these accomplished workers had pivotal roles in production and considerable power on the shop floor; they lost their status with the advent of scientific management in the workplace—à la Frederick Taylor and others of a like mind. According to Shaiken, Taylor wanted to insure that "production workers [were] as interchangeable as the parts they were producing and skilled workers as limited and controlled as the technology would allow" (p. 23). The centerpiece of Taylor's approach was to monopolize knowledge in management. To justify this strategy he claimed that ordinary machinists were incapable of understanding the "science" underlying the organization of work processes.

The effects of Taylorism are still with us in the workplace and beyond, both in terms of how work is organized and in terms of how we view workers. The trend is still to break complex work into a multitude of simpler, repetitive jobs—95 percent of U.S. companies still organize work this way (Sarmiento, 1991). We still harbor suspicions, even when choosing to introduce new forms of organization, that our workers won't adapt to or thrive in these new work environments (see Darrah, 1990). Such an orientation provides fertile ground on which any criticism of workers can grow like kudzu, including claims of illiteracy and its effect on productivity.

As demographics shift and workers increasingly are minorities, women, and immigrants—"groups where human resource investments have been historically deficient" (*The Bottom Line*, 1988)—the tendency to view as deficient, different, and separate those who are not or do not appear to be conventionally literate is likely to grow. However, there is also an increasing research literature that can be used to counter such tendencies. Some of this work documents the uses of literacy in non-mainstream communities and thereby helps to dispel the common myth that certain populations have no contact with or interest in print (e.g., Heath, 1983). This kind of scholarship also demonstrates that there are other literate traditions besides school-based ones, and that these promote different practices with print. Other work shows how people get along without literacy—through the use of networks of kin and friends, for example (e.g., Fingeret, 1983)—without the feelings of dependency and self-degradation that we sometimes assume are the necessary accompaniment to illiteracy. From the military have come interesting experiments, some unintentional, in which recruits whose test scores fell below the cut-off point were allowed to enter the armed forces; those recruits performed 80 to 100 percent as well as "average-aptitude" service members on a variety of indicators (Sticht, Armstrong, Hickey & Caylor, 1987). Other studies have focused on the reading and writing of underprepared adults in school settings, showing that literacy performances that appear flawed on the surface do not necessarily imply a lack of intelligence or effort by the writer (e.g., Shaughnessy, 1977; Bartholomae, 1985; Hull & Rose, 1989, 1990). This work by Shaughnessy and others begins with the assumption that people can acquire whatever literacies they need, given the right circumstances. In Heath's (1986) words, "all normal individuals can learn to read and write, provided they have a setting or context in which there is a need to be literate, they are exposed to literacy, and they get some help from those who are already literate" (p. 23).

McDermott and Goldman (1987) provide a work-related example of the benefits of assuming that all people can learn to read and write, given the need and the support. They describe their encounters with a group of New York City workers who needed to pass a licensing exam. These ninety men were pest exterminators for the city's public housing units; half of the group had only a conditional license, which left them with lessened job security, lower pay, and zero access to promotions and extra jobs. To be licensed these men had to pass what amounted to a literacy test using job-related materials and a test of factual knowledge of exterminating. These tests were rumored to be tough. Some men had been on the job for twenty-five years without even attempting the licensing exam, and others had been thwarted by not being able to fill out complex preliminary forms.

McDermott set about organizing an instructional program based on the belief that "all the men knew more than they needed to know for passing the test, and that we had only to tame their knowledge into a form that would enable them to take and pass the test" (p. 6). He arranged peer teaching situations by pairing a group of ten students with two exterminator/instructors who had already passed the exam, and he also relied on the union's promise to provide whatever instruction was needed until everybody passed. McDermott and Goldman report that most men passed the test on their first try, and all passed the second time around. They go on to raise some important questions: "Why is it that school degrees and literacy tests are the measures of our workers? Whatever happened to job performance?" (1987, p. 5).

15

When we do look at job performance—when we pay close attention to how people accomplish work—we come away with quite different views of both workers' abilities and the jobs they perform. There is a relevant research tradition growing out of an interest in and respect for everyday phenomena that attempts to understand and study knowledge and skill in work (cf. Rogoff & Lave, 1984). Instead of assuming that poor performance in school subjects necessarily dictates poor performance on related tasks at work, researchers have used various qualitative strategies to investigate actual work practices (Lave, 1986). What this kind of research has tended to show is that people carry out much more complex work practices than we generally would expect on the basis of traditional testing instruments and conventional assumptions about the relationship between school-learning and work-learning.

Kusterer (1978), for example, studied the knowledge that workers acquire and use in jobs pejoratively labeled "unskilled," documenting the "working knowledge" acquired by machine operators in the cone department of a paper-container factory and by bank tellers. He illustrated how operators did not just master the procedures for starting and stopping the machines, cleaning them properly, packing the cones, and labeling their cases—routine components of the job that were officially acknowledged. These workers also had to acquire the know-how necessary to accomplish work when obstacles arose that interrupted habitualized routine, such as "how to keep the machine running, overcome 'bad' paper, diagnose the cause of defects, keep the inspectors happy, [and] secure the cooperation of mechanics and material handlers" (p. 45). Kusterer points out that we usually recognize the basic knowledge necessary to do even highly routinized work, but we are much less cognizant of how much supplementary knowledge is also necessary. The need for such knowledge, I would add, belies the common perception of much blue-collar work as unskilled and routinized and workers as deficient, incapable, and passive.

Research such as Kusterer's valorizes the abilities and potential of human workers, and rightly so. So do the later, related studies by Wellman (1986) on the "etiquette" of longshoring, by Wenger (1991) on the "communities of practice" constructed by claims adjusters at an insurance agency, and by Scribner (1985, 1987) and her colleague (Jacob, 1986) on the knowledge and skills of workers at a dairy. The promise of this kind of research is that it will bring to light the literate events—the situated writing, reading, talking, and reasoning activities—which characterize the work that people do in particular job and job-training settings, and that it will cast workers in a different light, one that gives their expertise its due.

## *Rethinking the Nature of Literacy*

The popular discourse of workplace literacy centers on the skills that people lack, sometimes "basic" literacy skills and sometimes "higher order" thinking skills. These skills that workers need but do not possess are sometimes determined by experts on blue-ribbon panels (e.g., SCANS, 1991), and they are sometimes based on opinion surveys of employers and round table discussions of business executives and educational experts (e.g., Carnevale et al., 1988). But startlingly, such judgments are almost never informed by observations of work, particularly observations which incorporate the understandings of workers.[9] Instead, skills are listed as abstract competencies and represented as context-free and universal. At best, the skill lists are skimpily customized—for instance, a job requires that a worker "signs forms appropriately," "uses listening skills to identify procedures to follow," or "speaks face to face coherently" (Hull & Sechler, 1987, p. vii).

I am sympathetic to the impulse to understand the knowledge and skills needed in particular jobs. But an uncritical acceptance of the skill metaphor—that is, of the belief that literacy as a skill is a neutral, portable technique—can lead to problems in how we conceptualize literacy and literacy instruction. Bundled with the notion of skills are notions of generality and neutral technique. We think of reading or writing as generic, the intellectual equivalent of all-purpose flour, and we believe that, once mastered, these skills can and will be used in any context for any purpose. This view of literacy underlies a great deal of research and teaching, but of late it has begun to be challenged (cf. Street, 1984; de Castell, Luke, & MacLennan, 1986; de Castell & Luke, 1989). The questioning generally focuses on the ways in which it seems erroneous to think of literacy as a unitary phenomenon. On one level, this could simply mean that literacy might be viewed as a set of skills rather than one skill—that a person can perform differently at reading or writing in different situations, that a person will read well, for example, when the material is job-related but less well when it's unconnected to what he or she knows, a point that Sticht makes in his research on the reading performance of military recruits (e.g., Sticht, Fox, Hauke, & Zapf, 1976), and that Diehl and Mikulecky (1980) refer to in their work on occupation-specific literacy.

A related implication is that, not only will the literacy performances of individuals differ on various tasks, but the uses that people in different communities find for reading and writing will vary too, as Heath (1983) demonstrates in her research on the uses of literacy among non-mainstream communities in the North American South. In a later work, she described literacy as having "different meanings for members of different groups, with a corresponding variety of acquisition modes, functions, and uses" (1986, p.

25). A notable instance of these differences occurs among biliterate populations, in which people have a choice of languages in which to speak or write—English and Spanish, for example, or English and Hmong—and choose one or the other based on the social meanings associated with their uses.

But there are other implications of viewing literacy as a multiple construct that offer a different, more sobering critique of the skills metaphor. Consider the following commentary about "what is suppressed in the language of skills":

> Skill in our taken-for-granted sense of the word is something real, an objective set of requirements, an obvious necessity: what's needed to ride a bicycle, for example. It is a technical issue pure and simple. However, what is forgotten when we think about skills this way is that skills are always defined with reference to some socially defined version of what constitutes competence. (Simon, 1983, p. 243)

Simon reminds us that particular activities, characteristics, and performances are labeled "skills," depending on which activities, characteristics, and performances are believed to accomplish particular purposes, to serve certain ends, or to promote special interests—usually the purposes, ends, and interests of those in the position to make such judgments. "Listening" in order to "identify procedures to follow" is a valued skill because employers want workers who will follow directions. "Sign[ing] forms appropriately" is a valued skill because supervisors need to keep records and to hold workers accountable. Conversely, Darrah (1991) discovered in his ethnographic study of a wire and cable company that there are skills that supervisors don't acknowledge but workers recognize and develop—such as learning to represent their decisions in such a way as to "establish their plausibility should they later be challenged" (p. 21; cf. Wenger, 1991). "The concept of skill," Simon (1983) argues, "is not just a technical question but is also a question of power and interest" (p. 243).

This point is driven home by Gowen (1990), in her study of the effectiveness of a workplace literacy program serving African-American entry-level workers at a large urban hospital in the southern United States. Gowen examined, among other things, the program's classroom practices and participant structures, the social relationships among workers and management, and this history of race relations in the region. The program was based on a "functional context approach" in which literacy instruction was linked to job content. Thus, instructors developed a series of lessons based on the memos one supervisor regularly sent his housekeeping staff. These memos were called "Weekly Tips," and the supervisor thought they were important, although he suspected that employees did not read them. The tips covered such topics as "Dust Mopping, Daily Vacuuming, Damp Mopping of Corridors and Open Areas, Damp Mopping of Patients' Rooms, and Spray Buffing Corridors" (p. 253), and lessons devised on the basis of this material asked students to discuss, read, and write about the information in the Weekly Tips.

Gowen found that the employees disliked this instruction. For one thing, they felt they knew a lot more about cleaning than did their supervisors, and they developed "tricks"—Kusterer (1978) would call this "supplementary working knowledge"—to get the job done efficiently. One worker commented, "I've been at King Memorial for 23 years, and I feel like if I don't know how to clean now, I will not learn. . . . That's not going to help me get my GED I don't think" (Gowen, 1990, p. 261). Another explained in an evaluation of the curriculum: "I didn't like rewriting things concerning mopping, cleaning, and dish washing. I felt I already knew that" (p. 262). Workers reacted to the functional context curriculum by resisting: They stopped coming to class, they finished the work as quickly as possible, or they lost their packet of "Weekly Tips." Said one student at the end of the unit, "So we off that Weekly Tips junk? I don't want to know nothing about no mopping and dusting" (p. 260). Gowen interpreted such classroom resistance as arising from several factors, including the long-standing African-American tradition of resisting control by the dominant class and the use of the functional context approach to literacy training to exercise control. Another factor was the disparity between the workers' goals for taking part in the literacy program and the goals that employers and literacy educators had for employee participation.

Gowen's research throws open the doors of workplace literacy programs, letting us examine reading and writing instruction within one such setting in its many layered complexity. (See also the chapters in this volume by Kalman & Losey; D'Amico & Schnee; and Gowen & Bartlett.) As we plan literacy programs for the North American workforce, we would do well to keep her portrait in mind, allowing it to remind us of the ways in which learning to read and write involves something other than acquiring decontextualized decoding, comprehension, and production skills. Literacy can more appropriately be defined as "literacies," as socially constructed and embedded practices based upon cultural symbol systems and organized around beliefs about how reading and writing might be or should be used to serve particular social and personal purposes and ends (see Cook-Gumperz, 1986; Dyson, 1992; Lankshear & Lawler, 1987; Levine, 1986; Scribner & Cole, 1981; Street, 1984). Thus, to understand literacy, to investigate its effect upon people, to construct situations in which it can empower, is to ask what version of literacy is being offered, and to take into account the sociocultural, political, and historical contexts in which that version is taught and practiced.

## Rethinking the Literacy Requirements of Work and the Nature of Work-Related Training

There is much worry recently that the changing nature of work—the shift toward high-technology manufacturing, service-oriented industries, and new forms of organization such as self-directed work teams—will bring changing literacy requirements, both in basic literacy skills and advanced or higher literacy skills for workers previously termed blue-collar (Sum, Harrington, & Goedicke, 1986). There is, of course, some disagreement over just how quickly work is changing and whether such changes will indeed result in jobs which require different, additional, or more complex skills (e.g., Levin & Rumberger, 1983; Bailey, 1990; Barton & Kirsch, 1990). But the uncertainties that are sometimes expressed in the research literature rarely make their way into the popular discourse on workplace literacy. The descriptions I have seen of recent workplace literacy projects—I have examined descriptions of and proposals for approximately sixty of them—regularly take as a given that literacy is a requirement for everything and anticipate benefits from a literacy program, both for the worker and the company, that are numerous and wide-ranging, such as productivity, promotions, accuracy, on-time delivery, self-esteem, and job retention. There are almost no attempts at qualifying this rhetoric. The requirements and benefits of literacy, however, are certainly much more complicated than this.

A case in point is a recent *Los Angeles Times* story about the relocation of a large part of one California-based technology firm to Bangkok (Richards, 1990). The chairman of the company reported that there he had access to cheap labor—Thai women who are "conscientious and compliant." "In Thailand," he said, "there is a lot of close work under microscopes," whereas "it is pretty tough to find people in the U.S. to do that kind of work" (p. D3). So his most highly paid and educated employees—about one-fourth of the company—stayed in the United States, while he looked to Asia for the low-cost portion of his workforce. The women in the Bangkok factory speak only Thai (no mention is made of whether they read and write it), as do most of the native-born managers. It seems, then, that being able to converse or write in English is not crucial for most of these workers. Nonetheless, the company provides instruction in English as a Second Language (ESL), during which the young women also acquire, according to an account oblivious to stereotyping, "a sense of urgency," being "asked to set aside a typically gentle, easygoing nature that would rather avoid than confront a problem" (p. D3).

We should keep such stories as this in mind. The relocation of the California high-tech firm to Thailand was a move, not to seek out a more literate population, but to take advantage of a cheaper one, whether it is literate or not. In light of economic policies favoring "free trade" agreements with countries such as Mexico, we are likely to hear many more such reports. We need to listen with a skeptical ear when blanket pronouncements are made about literacy and its relations to work—when we are told, for example, that high-tech employment necessarily means increased demands for literacy, that foreign workers are illiterate and therefore only too happy to work for peanuts, or that most workers in industries that are non-information-based lack literate competence. We should be skeptical not in order to deny literacy instruction to anyone nor to disparage efforts to create workplace literacy programs, but to appraise more realistically what literacy as it is defined and practiced in a given context can offer, and to assess what else we need to be concerned about if our sights are set on improving the conditions as well as the products of work.

Another case in point is provided by Zuboff (1988), who has studied, among other industries, several pulp and paper mills, where experienced workers are trying to make the transition from older craft know-how to computer-based knowledge. Instead of walking about the vats and rollers, judging and controlling the conditions of production by touching the pulp, smelling the chemicals, and manually adjusting the levers of machines—relying, that is, on what Zuboff calls "sentient involvement" (p. 60)—workers are now sequestered in glass booths and their work mediated by algorithms and digital symbols, a computer-interface, and reams of data. Here is how one worker expressed the sense of displacement he felt as a result of this change in his job:

> With computerization I am further away from my job than I have ever been before. I used to listen to the sounds the boiler makes and know just how it was running. I could look at the fire in the furnace and tell by its color how it was burning. I knew what kinds of adjustments were needed by the shades of color I saw. A lot of the men also said that there were smells that told you different things about how it was running. I feel uncomfortable being away from these sights and smells. Now I only have numbers to go by. I am scared of that boiler, and I feel that I should be closer to it in order to control it. (p. 63)

Zuboff's research demonstrates in riveting detail how some jobs are changing because of new technologies and how some workers will, as a result, be faced with losing those jobs or retooling by acquiring new work practices and skills. To be sure, finding the best means we can to ease the way for workers in such situations is a worthy goal. I believe it is a mistake, though, as we try to understand what skills are needed, to focus all our attention on technology per se, to assume that once we understand Zuboff's "intellective skills"— those capabilities involved in information-based knowledge—that we are home free. When we think of a worker in front of a computer, we do tend to focus on the individual abilities that a person needs in order to interact with a program. Wenger (1991) points out, however, that if we view intellective skills only as individual abilities, we will overlook important social components in work, such as membership in work-based communities through which particular work practices are generated and sustained (see also Lave & Wenger, 1991).

Wenger (1991) studied the claims processing center of a large insurance company where workers, mostly women, received claims by mail, "processed" them—determining whether and for what amount a claimant's policy would cover specific medical costs—and entered them into a computer system. He found that there are crucial differences between the institutional setting that an employer provides and the communal setting that workers themselves construct, and he assigns great importance to the latter: "The practice of a community is where the official meets the non-official, where the visible rests on the invisible, where the canonical is negotiated with the non-canonical" (p. 181). If the objectives of the institution are somehow at cross purposes with the ways of functioning that are developed in these communities of practice— as happened in Darrah's (1990) computer company and as was often the case in this insurance company—serious problems occur. For example, Wenger noted an aggravating mismatch between how workers were evaluated and the work their jobs required. Although workers needed to spend time and energy answering telephone calls from irate, puzzled, or misinformed claimants— and this service was a necessary interface with customers—the company evaluated the claims processors only on the basis of their speed and accuracy in production. Such mismatches between community practice and institutional demands resulted in what Wenger called "identities of non-participation" (p. 182). That is, workers thought of themselves as only peripherally involved in the meaning of their work, and this disengagement seriously limited the success of the business. It is worth noting, too, that although the insurance workers were evaluated on literacy-related tasks, much of their work involved interpersonal communication, which did not, in contrast seem to count.

Wenger's research alerts us to the fact that difficulties will arise when competencies and tools are defined and developed in isolation from workers' communities of practice, and this holds as much for Zuboff's mill workers as for the insurance adjusters. As we imagine the training and literacy programs that will greet technological transformations in the workplace, we might question whether the intellective skills we teach are in any way anchored in the practice of the workplace community, and if they are not, what difference our instruction will make. This is simply another reminder that—contrary to the popular discourse—neither all the problems nor all solutions will reside in illiteracy and literacy. Management and workers have a history, and that history more often than not is one of conflicting interests. Among others, Shaiken (1984) argues that the history of machine automation has been the history of deliberate de-skilling—the effort to reduce reliance on workers' knowledge and thereby to eliminate workers' control. Thus, rather than welcoming advanced technology with open arms, Shaiken wants to see its development proceed in what he views as more socially responsible ways—creating or maintaining jobs and improving the conditions of work.

In like manner, we might be vigilant against uses of literacy in the workplace that are socially irresponsible. Increasingly, businesses and corporations are beginning to employ literacy-related tests and assessment instruments to determine whether workers are qualified for hiring and promotions; to certify workers (as with the exterminators' exam); and to determine whether workers are proficient at the skills their current or future jobs require. These tests and assessment devices may be administered with good intentions. Literacy audits, for example, are supposed to result in a customized curriculum. There are several issues worth worrying about, however. Although the courts have ruled that literacy cannot legally be used as a screening device unless the literacy skills required on the test reflect actual job demands (e.g., *Griggs v. Duke Power Company*), such tests may still eliminate qualified job-seekers through literacy-related demands that do not reflect job performance. Others fear a more deliberate discriminatory use of literacy tests and audits (cf. Carnevale et al., 1988). "I am concerned that workplace literacy programs will be used to admit a few and eliminate many," writes Añorve (1989, p. 40), a workplace literacy specialist. Añorve goes on to predict that high-tech positions may be used as excuses to get rid of employees with low reading skills, and he also worries that new communication criteria such as accentless speech will be used to discriminate against immigrants.[10] For similar reasons, the AFL-CIO's *Union Guide to Workplace Literacy* (Sarmiento & Kay, 1990) looks on the use of literacy audits in the workplace as potentially abusive, a too-handy rationale for management to justify decisions which jeopardize workers' earnings and even their jobs. (Cf. Castellano, this volume.)

Understanding the literacy requirements of work is not, then, so simple an issue. Some jobs that are coupled with new technologies may not require much literacy at all (which is not to say they do not require considerable working knowledge). Other, more traditional occupations may involve surprisingly frequent literacy-related activities (see Scribner, 1985; Jolliffe, this volume). And radically altered and reorganized jobs may require radically altered literate capabilities (see Hart-Landsberg & Reder, this volume), yet the development and exercise of those capabilities will depend on more than literacy alone (see Cook-Gumperz and Hanna, this volume). Similarly, the complexity that characterizes literacy, literacy learning, and the literacy requirements of work ought to spill over into our conceptions of workplace or work-related literacy programs. It would be needlessly naive to assume, for example, that in order to design a workplace program, one need only collect representative texts used at work and then teach to those documents (one variant of the "functional context approach"), or that whatever is learned in a literacy program will translate directly to promotions or productivity, or even that work-related literacy is something that all workers want to acquire (see Gowen, 1990, and Schultz, this volume).

Again, the point is not to argue against work-related literacy projects, but to speak in favor of a serious rethinking of the nature of the instruction we imagine for workers (cf. Jury, this volume). As we rush headlong to design curricula and programs and to measure reading rates and writing quality, we pay precious little attention to how people experience curricula and programs and for what purposes they choose and need to engage in reading and writing. We steer our ships instead by what corporate and government leaders think they want in a workforce and by our own enculturated notions of what teaching is about, even when our students are adults rather than children. Schooling is a bad memory for many adults who are poor performers at literacy, and workplace instruction which is school-based—that relies upon similar participant structures, materials, and assessment techniques—will likely be off-putting by association. I am dismayed, then, to see how frequently proposals for and descriptions of workplace literacy programs rely upon school-based notions of teaching and learning (cf. Grubb, this volume). Categories for instruction tend to follow traditional models: ESL, basic skills, GED preparation, or commercially available computer-based programs. Basic skills instruction may be dressed up with occupationally specific materials—hotel workers might practice reading with menus, for example—but the format for this instruction is a teacher in front of a classroom of students with workbooks and readers. Perhaps this approach grows out of the commonplace deficit thinking concerning workers' abilities described earlier. If adult workers lack the literate competencies that we expect children to acquire, then the temptation is to imagine for workers the same instructional practices believed to be appropriate for children.

This is a good time to recall Reder's (1987) research on the comparative aspects of literacy development in three American communities—an Eskimo fishing village, a community of Hmong immigrants, and a partially migrant, partially settled Hispanic community. In these communities, Reder found that adults often acquired literacy spontaneously, without participating in formal literacy education classes, in response to the perceived needs they had for literacy in their lives. They acquired literacy because they needed to, and they did so in collaboration with others. Reder points out that individuals participated in collaborative literacy practices in a variety of ways. Some were "technically engaged"; that is, they were proficient with paper and pencil and other media. Others were "functionally engaged," helping with literacy practice by providing specialized knowledge and expertise such as political savvy.

Others were "socially engaged," lending background knowledge and approval and thereby certifying the literacy practice.

Perhaps such research can help us rethink traditional conceptions of adult literacy instruction in the workplace.[11] Like Lauren Resnick (1990), Reder proposes an "apprenticeship" model for literacy learning:

> Participant structures that provide opportunities for individuals to be function-ally engaged in the practice before they have the requisite technological know-ledge and skills may be a very successful means of socializing functional knowledge and knowledge of social meanings essential to accomplishment of the practice, stimulating individuals' acquisition of literacy even as they may be just learning basic technological skills. (p. 267)

Instead of or in addition to pull-out programs in which workers are sequestered in classrooms, we might imagine apprenticeship arrangements whereby workers who need to carry out a task involving complex literacy skills learn on the job with someone who can already perform that task and, in this way, acquire the requisite technological, functional, and social knowl-edge. It may be that if we study the workplace to see how literacy learning occurs "naturally," in the absence of formal instruction provided through lit-eracy programs, we may see something similar to this kind of participant structure. We might also find distributed literacy knowledge, where workers typically carry out certain tasks which involve literacy in collaboration with each other, with one person supplying one kind of knowledge and others, dif-ferent proficiencies. Rather than assuming that structures and practices for learning literacy must be imported from school-based models of teaching and learning, we might do well to study workplaces and communities to see what kinds of indigenous structures and practices might be supported and built upon. What we learn may enrich our school-based versions of literacy and instruction as well.

## Different Voices and Other Stories

At the time I knew Alma and Jackie,[12] the students whose comments on literacy at work provide the headnote for this introductory chapter, they were both enrolled in a short-term vocational program on banking and finance in a community college. Both of these African-American women said that they needed and wanted to work and that they longed to get off public assistance. They dreamed of professional, white-collar jobs in banks. Before she enrolled in the banking program, Jackie had been out of high school only two years

25

and had held several short-term jobs in addition to working at McDonald's: She had been an aspiring rapper, a janitor at an army base, and a food helper at a park and recreation facility. Alma, on the other hand, was in her forties; she had grown up in Arkansas, raised several children, and had worked only at a convalescent home and as a teacher's aide. I don't think either of these women thought of themselves as having a literacy problem, but, as the quotations that begin this chapter suggest, they expected to do reading, writing, and calculation at their future bank jobs as a matter of course. I do think, though, that they would be *viewed* as having a literacy problem, and that this problem would be seen as an impediment to their success at work.

Both women said they expected to do well in the banking and finance program and at work. "All you have to do is try," said Jackie. "I think I can master it, whatever it is," said Alma. And both did well in the program, coming to class regularly, participating in the "simulated" bank-telling exercises, practicing the ten-key adding machine, and taking their turn at doing proofs—feeding debit and credit slips through a machine the size and shape of a refrigerator lying on its side. Two months into the semester representatives of a local bank came to test students' ten-key skills, administer a timed-written exam, and carry out interviews. Jackie did just fine and was hired right away, but Alma failed the written exam, which consisted of visual discriminations and problem-solving.

The instructor got a copy of the test and asked me to practice with those who, like Alma, had not passed it. Students were amazed at the trickiness of the questions—the "matching" portion which asked you to discriminate quickly between items in two lists like "J. T. Addonis" and "J. T. Adonnis." The most troublesome part, however, and one students invariably fell down on, required the interpretation of a rather complicated visual display of deposit slips and checks as well as the selection of answers from a multiple choice list of the "A but not B" or "A and B but not C" variety—and all this under timed conditions. To the relief of everyone, Alma passed the test on her second try, though she confided in me that she had memorized the answers to the problem-solving portion during our practice sessions and then simply filled them in during the test rather than working the problems.

Jackie and Alma were hired part-time at $6.10 an hour at the same proof-operation center. This center takes up an entire floor of a large bank building and is filled with proof machines—a hundred or so are going at the same time when work is in full swing—most of them operated by women of color. Workers arrive at 4 p.m. and continue until all their bundles are "proved," which is around 11 p.m. except for the busiest day, Friday, when work sometimes continues until after midnight. Jackie worked at this proof-operation center for two months, until she was late three times, the third time for three minutes, and was asked to resign. She blamed her lateness on transportation problems; she had to drop her baby off at a distant, low-cost childcare center, she said, and then take the bus back to the subway stop, and sometimes she was late or the trains didn't arrive on time. Jackie claimed, though, that she liked working at the proof center: "I would have stayed. . . . I liked the environment and everything. . . . You have to even have a card just to get on the elevator." And she believed that if she could have held on to this job, and if her hours had been increased, she could have made enough money to support herself: "We was only working like six and four hours. If . . . I would have been working eight hours or something, I really could have bought food and everything, bought a car and everything. But it was enough. It would have been enough."

Being late was not a problem for Alma, but being left-handed was. To make production in the proof-operation center, workers have to process twelve-hundred items an hour—that is, they have to feed twelve-hundred credit and debit slips into a machine with one hand and enter calculations on a ten-key pad with the other. The machines all have the keypad on the right, so if you are left-handed you are at a distinct disadvantage. When I talked to Alma a few months after she lost her job, she said she felt good about having worked at the bank. "I was doing the work," she said. "I had no problem opening the machine and closing the machine. I was doing that work." She was adamant, though, about the lack of relationship between the test she had failed and the job she had performed.

Right now, both Alma and Jackie are at home taking care of their children. They are presently receiving Aid for Families with Dependent Children, but they both look forward to getting another bank job. Jackie has already applied for several bank jobs, she has also attempted to provide a day-care service at her apartment, and she now has dreams of becoming a firefighter. The vocational program in banking and finance thrived for a few years after Alma and Jackie completed it, but it has now fallen on hard times, the instructor being unable to place his students in proof jobs. Local banks are downsizing, and new technologies will soon replace proof operators all together.

Certainly there are skills that Jackie and Alma have not acquired; perhaps they even could have benefited from a workplace literacy program or from "academic" training integrated into their vocational program. But there are many other complex factors in their situations which push literacy from a central concern to the periphery. These factors include short-term, narrowly focused vocational training; the lack of childcare at work; part-time employment with no benefits, few rights, stressful tasks, and low pay; and workplaces where women of color inherit the most tedious jobs an industry can offer. To blame the problem on illiteracy in this instance, and I believe in many others, is simply to miss the mark.

We need to look from other perspectives, to hear other voices and the different stories they can tell. Many people from a variety of disciplines and perspectives are beginning to talk these days about honoring difference. Part of the impetus for these conversations comes simply from the increasing diversity of our country, where different cultures, languages, and orientations by virtue of their numbers and presence are forcing a recognition of North America's plurality. Part of it comes from educators who are pressed daily to find ways to teach in classrooms that are nothing if not richly diverse. Part of it comes, too, from a sense among many in academic communities that times are changing intellectually, that a "postmodern" age is now upon us, an age in which there is no widespread belief in a common rationality or a shared knowledge, but, rather, a growing conception of the world as "continuously changing, irreducibly various, and multiply configurable" (Greene, 1989).

In this age of difference, diversity, "otherness," and change, we are lost if we do not learn to admit other views, to hear other voices, other stories. This means, for those workers whose situations have been represented univocally in the popular discourse of workplace illiteracy, looking anew at training programs and workplaces, not simply by measuring reading rates, collecting work-based literacy materials, or charting productivity—the customary focuses of much previous research and even teaching (cf. Sticht, 1988; Grubb, Kalman, Castellano, Brown, & Bradby, 1991). We need, rather, to seek out the personal stories of workers like Jackie and Alma; to learn what it is like to take part in a vocational program or a literacy class and what effect such an experience has, really, on work and living. We need to look with a critical eye at how work gets accomplished and the roles of literacy and language within work and what relationships exist between skills at work and the rights of workers. We must ask what is meant by literacy, and in what contexts and under what circumstances, this literacy will be empowering. We need to ask, then, with Maxine Greene (1989), "How much, after all, depends on literacy itself?" What else must we be concerned with, in addition to literacy, if we want to improve the conditions and products of work (cf. Merriefield, this volume)?

In the popular discourse of workplace literacy and skill requirements, we seem to tell just a few stories. We are able to tell sad tales of people who live impoverished lives and cause others to suffer because they don't know how to read and write. Or we are able to tell happy, Horatio Alger–type stories of people who prosper and contribute to the common good because they have persevered and become literate. We have our dominant myths, our story grammars if you will, of success and work, from which it is hard to break free. Other stories, with their alternate viewpoints, different voices, and other realities, can help us amend, qualify, and fundamentally challenge the popular discourse of literacy and work. The purpose of the remainder of this book, then, is to tell those other stories.

## Notes

1. In addition to the articles and interviews mentioned in this paper, other recent examples of the popular discourse of workplace literacy can be found in *Basic Skills in the U.S. Work Force*, 1982; Bernstein, 1988; Cole, 1977; Holmes & Green, 1988; *Investing in People: A Strategy to Address America's Workforce Crisis*, 1989; *Job-Related Basic Skills*, 1987; Lee, 1984; *Literacy in the Workplace: The Executive Perspective*, 1989; Oinonen, 1984; Rush, Moe, & Storlie,1986; *The School-to-Work Connection*, 1990; Stone, 1991; "Workplace Literacy," 1990; and *Workplace Literacy : Reshaping the American Workforce*, 1992.

2. The popular view that unskilled minorities and women will increasingly dominate the work force while future jobs will require more highly skilled workers (see the next section of this chapter) is largely based on a widely disseminated report prepared by the Hudson Institute for the Department of Labor, *Workforce 2000* (Johnston & Packer, 1987). For a counter-argument, see Mishel and Teixeira's *The Myth of the Coming Labor Shortage* (1991).

3. See *Business Council for Effective Literacy: A Newsletter for the Business and Literacy Community*, published especially for the business community to keep employers apprised of developments in adult literacy and to encourage them to provide support in the field.

4. Given worries about workers' skills and the relationship assumed between those skills and a company's ability to compete, one might expect to see a great deal of corporate investment in the training and retraining of workers, similar to the efforts at Motorola. However, this has not been the case. Although various politicians, policy makers, and literacy specialists are applying pressure (see, e.g., SCANS, 1991), the percentage of companies that currently invest in training and retraining their workers remains quite low. See *America's Choice: High Skills or Low Wages!* 1990, Sarmiento, 1991, and Mishel & Teixeira, 1991.

5. For example, *The Bottom Line: Basic Skills in the Workplace*, 1988; *Workplace Basics: The Skills Employers Want*, Carnevale, Gaines, & Meltzer, 1988); *Upgrading Basic Skills for the Workplace*, 1989; and *Literacy at Work: The Workbook for Program Developers*, Philippi, 1991. Publishers are even beginning to produce customized materials for particular indus-

tries, for example, *Strategic Skill Builders for Banking* (Mikulecky & Philippi, 199).

6. The U.S. Department of Education has published a description of the National Workplace Literacy Program as it has been implemented in its first three funding cycles—*Workplace Literacy: Reshaping the American Workforce*, 1992.

7. Cf. Apple (1987), who writes: "It is possible to claim that by shifting the public's attention to problems of education, the real sources of the current crises are left unanalyzed. That is, the crisis of the political economy of capitalism is exported from the economy onto the State. The State then in turn exports the crisis downward onto the school. Thus, when there is severe unemployment, a disintegration of traditional patterns of authority, and so on, the blame is placed on students' lack of skills, on their attitudes, on their 'functional illiteracy.' The structural problems of poverty, of the de-skilling and elimination of jobs, of capital flight, of systemic racism and sexism, problems that are 'naturally' generated out of our current economic and political arrangements, are distanced from our discussions" (p. viii; see also Apple, 1985).

8. This extensive literature has been reviewed by Street, 1984, Bizzell, 1987; and Salvatori & Hull, 1990, and Walters, 1990. Even those scholars who support claims for the value of literacy at one time have more recently qualified their endorsements (see Goody, 1987; Olson & Torrance, 1991, Ong, 1988).

9. Despite the many and frequent claims concerning the skills, including the literacies, required in reorganized, technologically sophisticated workplaces, as well as what skills workers lack, little is known about the actual skill demands of these workplaces of the kinds of training new jobs might require. There have been studies of the "reading difficulty level" of job-related materials through the application of readability formulas (see Diehl & Mikulecky, 1980; Duffy, 1985; Mikulecky, 1982; Rush, Moe, & Storlie, 1986), as well as attempt to differentiate reading at school from reading at work (see Diehl & Mikuleky, 1980; Sticht, 1979; Sticht, Armstrong, Hickey, & Caylor, 1987; Sticht & Hickey, 1987). And there have been a handful of projects that examined literacy at work within larger ethnographic studies of knowledge acquisition in real-world settings (e.g., Jacob, 1986; Martin & Scribner, 1988; Scribner, 1985, 1987; Scribner & Sachs, 1991). However, for the most part, complaints about worker "illiteracy" arise, as Darrah (1990, 1992) points out, not from detailed observations of work, but from surveys and anecdotal reports (see also Baba, 1991).

10. His worries are realistic. In Massachusetts, parents recently objected to the transfer of a teacher who spoke English with a Spanish accent from a bilingual class to a "regular" one and drew up a petition to prevent anyone not demonstrating "the accepted and standardized use of pronunciation" from taking teaching jobs in elementary school. The petitioners claimed that they were attempting through their proposed ban to protect the quality of public education during a current period of budget cut (Canellos, 1992, p. 27).

11. For other attempts to rethink adult literacy instruction in the workplace, see Soifer et al., 1990 and Jurmo, 1989.

12. The stories of Alma and Jackie, reported below, come from a larger ethnographic study (Hull, 1992). I am aware that in presenting their stories so briefly here I increase the risk of oversimplifying the complexities of their situations and views. Interested readers are urged, then, to examine the longer report. See also Fine (1992), who provides some helpful cautionary comments on the use of personal stories and voices in qualitative research.

# References

Adult Performance Level Project. (1977). *Final report: The adult performance level study*. Washington, DC: U. S. Office of Education.

*America's choice: High skills or low wages!* (1990). The Report of the Commission on the Skills of the American Workforce. Rochester, NY: National Center on Education and the Economy.

Añorve, R. L. (1989). Community-based literacy educators: Experts and catalysts for change. In A. Fingeret & P. Jurmo (Eds.), *Participatory literacy education* (pp. 35–42). San Francisco, CA: Jossey-Bass.

Bailey, T. (1990). *Changes in the nature and structure of work: Implications for skill requirements and skills formation*. Berkeley: National Center for Research in Vocational Education, University of California at Berkeley.

Bartholomae, D. (1985). Inventing the university. In M. Rose (Ed.), *When a writer can't write* (pp. 134-165). New York: Guilford Press.

Barton, P. E., & Kirsch, I. S. (1990). *Workplace competencies: The need to improve literacy and employment readiness*. Washington, DC: Office of Educational Research and Improvement.

*Basic skills in the U.S. work force: The contrasting perceptions of business, labor, and public education.* (1982). New York: Center for Public Resources.

Bernstein, A. (1988, September 19). Where the jobs are is where the skills aren't. *Business Week*, pp. 104–106.

Berryman, S. (1989). The economy, literacy requirements, and at-risk adults. In *Literacy and the marketplace: Improving the literacy of low-income single mothers* (pp. 22–33). New York: The Rockefeller Foundation.

Bizzell, P. (1987). Literacy in culture and cognition. In T. Enos (Ed.), *A sourcebook for basic writing teachers* (pp. 125–137). New York: Random House.

*The bottom line: Basic skills in the workplace.* (1988). Washington, DC: U.S. Department of Education and the U.S. Department of Labor.

Brint, S., & Karabel, J. (1989). The diverted dream: Community colleges and the promise of educational opportunity, 1900–1985. New York: Oxford University Press.

Carnevale, A. P., Gainer, L. J., & Meltzer, A. S. (1988). *Workplace basics: The skills employers want.* Washington, DC: U.S. Department of Labor and the American Society for Training and Development.

Cole, G. (1977). The chains of functional illiteracy. *The AFL-CIO American Federationist, 84*(6), 1–6.

Cook-Gumperz, J. (Ed.). (1986). *The social construction of literacy.* Cambridge, England: Cambridge University Press.

Cuban, L., & Tyack, D. (1988). *Mismatch: Historical perspectives on schools and students who don't fit them.* Unpublished manuscript, Stanford University, School of Education, Stanford, CA.

Darrah, C. N. (1990). *An ethnographic approach to workplace skills.* Unpublished manuscript, San Jose State University, Department of Anthropology and Cybernetic Systems, San Jose, CA.

Darrah, C. N. (1991). *Workplace skills in context.* Unpublished manuscript, San Jose State University, Department of Anthropology and Cybernetic Systems, San Jose, CA.

de Castell, S., & Luke, A. (1989). Literacy instruction: Technology and technique. In S. de Castell, A. Luke, & C. Luke (Eds.), *Language, authority, and criticism: Readings on the school textbook* (pp. 77–95). London: The Falmer Press.

de Castell, S., Luke, A., & MacLennan, D. (1986). On defining literacy. In S. de Castell, A. Luke, & K. Egan (Eds.), *Literacy, society, and schooling: A reader* (pp. 3–14). Cambridge, England: Cambridge University Press.

Diehl, W., & Mikulecky, L. (1980). The nature of reading at work. *Journal of Reading, 24*(3), 221–227.

Ehrlich, E., & Garland, S. B. (1988, September 19). For American business, a new world of workers. *Business Week*, pp. 107–111.

Fields, E. L., Hull, W. L., & Sechler, J. A. (1987). *Adult literacy: Industry-based training programs* (Research and Development Series No. 265C). Columbus: Ohio State University, Center on Education and Training for Employment.

Fingeret, A. (1983). Social network: A new perspective on independence and illiterate adults. *Adult Education Quarterly, 33*(3), 133–146.

Fingeret, A. (1989). The social and historical context of participatory literacy education. In A. Fingeret & P. Jurmo (Eds.), *Participatory literacy education* (pp. 5–16). San Francisco, CA: Jossey-Bass.

Fiske, E. B. (1988, September 9). Policy to fight adult illiteracy urged. *The New York Times*, p. 12.

*Functional illiteracy hurts business*. (rev. 1988, March). Brochure. New York: Business Council for Effective Literacy.

Giroux, H. A., & McLaren, P. (1989). Introduction: Schooling, cultural politics, and the struggle for democracy. In H. A. Giroux & P. McLaren (Eds.), *Critical pedagogy, the state, and cultural struggle* (pp. xi–xxxv). Albany, NY: SUNY Press.

Gorman, C. (1988, December 19). The literacy gap. *Time*, pp. 56–57.

Gowen, S. (1990). *"Eyes on a different prize": A critical ethnography of a workplace literacy program*. Unpublished doctoral dissertation, Georgia State University, Atlanta.

Graff, H. J. (1979). The literacy myth: Literacy and social structure in the nineteenth-century city. New York: Academic Press.

Graff, H. J. (1986). The legacies of literacy: Continuities and contradictions in western society and culture. In S. de Castell, A. Luke, & K. Egan (Eds.), *Literacy, society, and schooling: A reader* (pp. 61–86). Cambridge, England: Cambridge University Press.

Greene, M. (1989). *The literacy debate and the public school: Going beyond the functional.* Talk given at the Annual Meeting of the American Educational Research Association, San Francisco, CA.

Grubb, W. N., Kalman, J., Castellano, M., Brown, C., & Bradby, D. (1991). *Coordination, effectiveness, pedagogy, and purpose: The role of remediation in vocational education and job training programs.* Berkeley: National Center for Research in Vocational Education, University of California at Berkeley.

Heath, S. B. (1983). *Ways with words: Language, life, and work in communities and classrooms.* Cambridge, England: Cambridge University Press.

Heath, S. B. (1986). The functions and uses of literacy. In S. de Castell, A. Luke, & K. Egan (Eds.), *Literacy, society, and schooling: A reader* (pp. 15–26). Cambridge, England: Cambridge University Press.

Holmes, B. J., & Green, J. (1988). *A quality work force: America's key to the next century.* Denver, CO: Education Commission of the States.

Hull, G. (1991). Examining the relations of literacy to vocational education and work: An ethnography of a vocational program in banking and finance. Technical Report. Berkeley: National Center for Research in Vocational Education, University of California at Berkeley.

Hull, G., & Rose, M. (1989). Rethinking remediation: Toward a social-cognitive understanding of problematic reading and writing. *Written Communication, 62*(2), 139–154.

Hull, G., & Rose, M. (1990). "This wooden shack place": The logic of an unconventional reading. *College Composition and Communication, 41*(3), 287–298.

Hull, G., Rose, M., Fraser, K. L., & Castellano, M. (1991). Remediation as social construct: Perspectives from an analysis of classroom discourse. *College Composition and Communication, 42*(3), 299–329.

Hull, W., L., & Sechler, J. A. (1987). *Adult literacy: Skills for the American work force* (Research and Development Series No. 265B). Columbus: Ohio State University, Center on Education and Training for Employment.

Hunter, C. S. J., & Harman, D. (1979). *Adult illiteracy in the United States.* New York: McGraw Hill.

*Investing in people: A strategy to address America's workforce crisis.* (1989). Washington, DC: U.S. Department of Labor, Commission on Workforce Quality and Labor Market Efficiency.

Jacob, E. (1986). Literacy skills and production line work. In K. M. Borman & J. Reisman (Eds.), *Becoming a worker* (pp. 176–200). Norwood, NJ: Ablex.

*Job-related basic skills.* (1987). New York: Business Council for Effective Literacy.

Johnston, W. B., & Packer, A. B. (1987). *Workforce 2000: Work and workers for the 21st century.* Indianapolis, IN: Hudson Institute.

Jurmo, P. (1989, January). How can businesses fight workplace illiteracy? *Training and Development Journal, 43*(1), 18–20.

Kozol, J. (1985). *Illiterate America.* Garden City, NY: Anchor Press/Doubleday.

Kusterer, K. C. (1978). Know-how on the job: The important working knowledge of "unskilled" workers. Boulder, CO: Westview Press.

Lacy, D. (1985, November). American business and the literacy effort. *PIA Communicator,* pp. 10–12.

Lankshear, C., & Lawler, M. (1987). *Literacy, schooling and revolution.* New York: The Falmer Press.

Lave, J. (1986). Experiments, tests, jobs and chores: How we learn what we do. In K. M. Borman & J. Reisman (Eds.), *Becoming a worker* (pp. 140–155). Norwood, NJ: Ablex.

Lee, C. (1984). Who, what, and where? *Training, 2*(10), 39–47.

Levin, H., & Rumberger, R. (1983). The low-skill future of high-tech. *Technology Review, 86*(6), 18–21.

Levine, K. (1986). *The social context of literacy.* London: Routledge & Kegan Paul.

*Literacy in the workplace: The executive perspective.* (1989). Bryn Mawr, PA: Omega Group, Inc.

Martin, L. M. W., & Beach, K. (1990). *Learning to use computerized machinery on the job.* Unpublished manuscript, Graduate School and University Center of the City University of New York, Laboratory for Cognitive Studies of Work.

Martin, L. M. W., & Scribner, S. (1988). *An introduction to CNC systems: Background for learning and training research.* New York: Graduate School and University Center of the City University of New York, Laboratory for Cognitive Studies of Work.

McDermott, R., & Goldman, S. (1987). Exterminating illiteracy. *Information Update: A Quarterly Newsletter of the Literacy Assistance Center,* 4(1), 5–6.

Mikulecky, K., & Philippi, J. (1990). *Strategic skill builders for banking.* New York: Simon & Schuster.

Mikulecky, L. (1982). Job literacy: The relationship between school preparation and workplace actuality. *Reading Research Quarterly,* 17(3), 400–419.

Morelli, M. (1987, October 29). Reading up on literacy: What USA businesses can do to educate workers. *USA Today,* p. 4B.

National Workplace Literacy Program: Notice inviting applications for new awards for fiscal year. (1990, April 17). *Federal Register,* 55(74), 14382.

Oinonen, C. M. (1984). *Business and education survey: Employer and employee perceptions of school to work preparation* (Parker Project No. 3, Bulletin No. 4372). Madison, WI: Parker Pen Company and Wisconsin Department of Public Instruction. (ERIC Document Reproduction Service Number ED 244 122)

Olson, D. R., & Torrance, N. (eds.). *Literacy and Orality.* New York: Cambridge University Press.

Philippi, J. (1991). *Literacy at work: The workbook for program developers.* Westwood, NJ: Simon & Schuster.

Reder, S. M. (1987). Comparative aspects of functional literacy development: Three ethnic communities. In D. Wagner (Ed.), *The future of literacy in a changing world* (Vol. 1, pp. 250–270). Oxford, England: Pergamon Press.

Resnick, D. P. (1990). Historical perspectives on literacy and schooling. *Daedalus,* 119(2), 15–32.

Resnick, L. B. (1990). Literacy in school and out. *Daedalus,* 119(2), 169–185.

Richards, E. (1990, June 25). Why an American high-tech firm recruits in Asian rice fields. *Los Angeles Times,* pp. D3–4.

Rogoff, B., & Lave, J. (1984). *Everyday cognition: Its development in social context.* Cambridge, MA: Harvard University Press.

Rush, R. T., Moe, A. J., & Storlie, R. L. (1986). *Occupational literacy education.* Newark, DE: International Reading Association.

Salvatori, M., & Hull, G. (1990). Literacy theory and basic writing. In M. G. Moran & M. J. Jacobi (Eds.), *Research in basic writing* (pp. 49–74). Westport, CT: Greenwood Press.

Sarmiento, A. R. (1989). *A labor perspective on basic skills.* Talk given at Workplace Conference, Columbus, OH.

Sarmiento, A. R., & Kay, A. (1990). *Worker-centered learning: A union guide to workplace literacy.* Washington, DC: AFL-CIO Human Resources Development Institute.

*The school-to-work connection.* (1990). Report on the Proceedings of "The Quality Connection: Linking Education and Work," a conference sponsored by the Secretary of Labor and the Secretary of Education, Washington, DC.

Scribner, S. (1985). Knowledge at work. *Anthropology and Education Quarterly, 16*(3), 199–206.

Scribner, S. (1987). Literacy in the workplace. *Information Update: A Quarterly Newsletter of the Literacy Assistance Center, 4*(1), 3–5.

Scribner, S., & Cole, M. (1981). *The psychology of literacy.* Cambridge, MA: Harvard University Press.

Shaiken, H. (1984). *Work transformed: Automation and labor in the computer age.* New York: Holt, Rinehart, and Winston.

Shaughnessy, M. (1977). *Errors and expectations.* New York: Oxford University Press.

Simon, R. I. (1983). But who will let you do it? Counter-hegemonic possibilities for work education. *Journal of Education, 165*(3), 235–255.

Stedman, L., & Kaestle, C. F. (1987). Literacy and reading performance in the United States, from 1880 to the present. *Reading Research Quarterly, 22*(1), 8–46.

Sticht, T. G. (1988). Adult literacy education. *Review of Research in Education, 15*(1), 59–96.

Sticht, T. G., Armstrong, W., Hickey, D., & Caylor, J. (1987). *Cast-off youth.* New York: Praeger.

Sticht, T. G., Fox, L., Hauke, R., Zapf, D. (1976). *Reading in the Navy* (HumRRO FR-WD-CA-76-14). Alexandria, VA: Human Resources Research Organization.

Stone, N. (1991, March-April). Does business have any business in education? *Harvard Business Review, 69*(2), 46–62.

Street, B. (1984). *Literacy in theory and practice.* Cambridge, England: Cambridge University Press.

Sum, A., Harrington, P., & Goedicke, W. (1986). *Skills of America's teens and young adults: Findings of the 1980 National ASVAB Testing and their implications for education, employment and training policies and programs.* Report prepared for the Ford Foundation, New York.

U.S. Bureau of the Census. (1982). *Ancestry and language in the United States: November 1979* (Current Population Reports, Series P-23, No. 116). Washington, DC: U.S. Government Printing Office.

U.S. Congress, House of Representatives. (1984). *Illiteracy and the scope of the problems in this country.* Hearing before the House Subcommittee on Post Secondary Education and Labor, September 21, 1982. Washington, DC: U.S. Government Printing Office.

*Upgrading basic skills for the workplace.* (1989). University Park: Pennsylvania State University, Institute for the Study of Adult Literacy.

Venezky, R. L. (1990). Definitions of literacy. In R. L. Venezky, D. A. Wagner, & B. S. Ciliberti (Eds.), *Toward defining literacy* (pp. 2-16). Newark, DE: International Reading Association.

Wellman, D. (1986). Learning at work: The etiquette of longshoring. In K. M. Borman & J. Reisman (Eds.), *Becoming a worker* (pp. 159–175). Norwood, NJ: Ablex.

Wenger, E. (1991). *Toward a theory of cultural transparency: Element of a social discourse of the visible and the invisible.* Palo Alto, CA: Institute for Research on Learning.

Whitman, D., Shapiro, J. P., Taylor, R., Saltzman, A., & Auster, B. B. (1989, June 26). The forgotten half. *U.S. News & World Report,* pp. 45–53.

Wiggenhhorn, B. (1989, January). How can businesses fight workplace illiteracy? *Training and Development Journal, 41*(1), 20–22.

Workplace literacy [Special issue]. (1990, October). *Vocational Education Journal, 65*(6).

# TWO

## Discourses of Workplace Education:
## A Challenge to the New Orthodoxy

*Katherine Schultz*

In a small factory conference room in Schaumburg, Illinois, a half dozen of mostly African-American and immigrant factory workers attended a course in grade-school arithmetic. They were instructed to solve a grocery store problem: How much would a pound of grapes cost if 2⅔ pounds cost $3.25? These workers are considered part of Motorola's "illiterate" workforce who need to be retrained to use statistical process control to monitor robots which assemble 11,000 computer chips an hour. In another class at the same plant, students used pictures of coffee makers in a catalogue to discuss the meanings of words like fewer, taller, smaller, fatter, and thinner (*New York Times*, September 26, 1989).[1]

At King Memorial Hospital (a pseudonym) in the South, a group of African-American hospital employees working in housekeeping, food service, and laundry puzzled over their assignment written on the board: "It is Wednesday afternoon February 15, 1989. You are the team leader or supervisor. Two of your workers are out sick with the flu. The Joint Hospital Commission is arriving in three hours. You have a problem to solve. What is it? List the steps you will take to solve the problem" (Gowen, 1992, p. 84). The workers reluctantly tackled the problem which seemed both obvious to them and at the same time irrelevant to their own desire to improve their literacy (Gowen, 1992).

Three long rows of tables were placed diagonally in the meeting room of a circuit board assembly plant in the Silicon Valley of California. Assembly workers attended classes to prepare them to participate in self-directed work teams. Their teacher, a U.S.-born Asian American, displayed a picture of two men. She asked the class to imagine that these are team members and their job is to build a bridge between them. She explained that English plays the major role in the success of building this bridge and asked them to consider the following question: "When management says you must use English at work, how do you feel?" Although most of the workers have been observed to speak their native languages during the class, the predominant response was that it is appropriate to be required to speak English on the factory floor (field notes, 10/7/94, Hull et al.).

In Virginia, workers identified as LEP (limited English proficiency) left their jobs as hotel workers after eight hour shifts, traveled to a learning center in a nearby high school, and sat in front of computer terminals to learn the proper way to interact with the customers they encounter when they make up beds. The videodisk training course led them through a self-paced lesson on the computer that taught each worker phrases that have been determined by management in conjunction with educational specialists to be useful and necessary to keep their jobs and have the possibility to be promoted. Each lesson was developed for a particular proficiency level. So, for instance, "beginners" were taught to identify hotel room furniture and bathroom fixtures, while the "high intermediates" were taught how to request room keys from guests. The computer pronounced the name of the vocabulary word to the trainee as the trainee looked at the visual cue and read the word on the computer screen (Final Report for REEP, Arlington Education & Employment Program, 1990/1).

Across the United States, education programs like these have been established in workplaces to retrain, or, in current business terms, to retool workers to meet the demands of the changing, more technological, "high performance" workplaces of the twenty-first century. Program designers and managers describe and anticipate a future "skills gap" due to the characteristics of the present and future workforce: including a increasing number of women, older workers and minorities who are thought to be both less (or more poorly) educated and less skilled (e.g., Berger, 1989; Dowling, W. D., Pritz, S. G., DeStefano, J. S., Puleo, N. F., Girkins, M., Collins, J. H. & Connor, P. M., 1992; Johnson & Packer, 1987).[2] While the workplace education programs vary in their content and mode of instruction, there are certain "self-evident truths" or what I have begun to call "new orthodoxies" that dominate the discussions about programs, the criteria for funding, and the evaluation and dissemination of curriculum. In this chapter, I want to suggest we interrogate the discourses of workplace education programs, the taken-for-granted ways of talking about these programs, in order to uncover their underlying assumptions and to allow for the possibility of imagining alternatives that might be more suitable for the workplaces of the next century.

In response to the perceived skills gap between the needs of businesses and companies and the qualifications of U.S. workers, the National Workplace Literacy Program was created in 1988 with the explicit purpose to fund projects designed to improve the productivity of the workforce through the improvement of literacy skills (P. L. 100-297, 1988).[3] As this chapter is being revised (in November 1994), hearings have begun in Congress on the Adult Education Act, which allocates funding for this program. Thus, it is a critical time to reconsider and reevaluate the premises on which this program is based. At the same time that attention has been focused on education programs or literacy classes in the workplace, there has also been considerable discussion and major advances in our thinking about literacy and learning by literacy researchers and practitioners. Yet despite all we now know about literacy learning, there have been few attempts to critically assess current workplace education programs in light of this new knowledge, in order to suggest future directions for research and practice.[4] Although educational research is more often directed at conventional classrooms located inside schools, it seems particularly important to assess and apply what we know about teaching and learning to workplace programs which are traditionally designed for individuals who have been unsuccessful in school.

In this chapter, I examine the discourse of workplace education programs to make explicit this new orthodoxy and to raise a caution to those who have rushed headlong into accepting a single way to envision and design effective programs. I suggest that more expansive notions and ways of speaking about language and literacy will allow us to imagine and put into place a broader range of programs. In order to focus on the discourse of workplace education programs, I chose to analyze the language used by programs funded by the U.S. Department of Education through the National Workplace Literacy Program. These programs are considered by the funders to be both innovative and exemplary. While many such programs operate under extreme financial and time constraints, with the bottom line or a push for evidence of concrete results or improvement dictating their decisions, these programs have none the less been given rare financial resources and additional time to develop a well thought-out course of action.

As I examined programs, it quickly became clear that while many promising programs exist in a wide variety of settings, in numerous critical areas, most of these programs were essentially identical. Nearly all had adopted a common lexicon. Although these programs were in existence for a relatively short time, a dominant ideology, or a single way to set up projects had emerged that was accepted, almost without question, by most programs. An analysis of assumptions about literacy, curriculum, teaching and learning helps to describe the current workplace education programs, points to what's missing in most descriptions and to new ways of both conceptualizing and enacting programs. While program developers have been quick to buy into a prescribed way of setting up programs, many have been slower to wrestle with questions of purpose, method, curriculum, pedagogy, and evaluation criteria. This chapter will begin this discussion, which I believe is critical to the long-term success of these programs.

## Method

Focusing on the language used in the written documents prepared by programs funded under the National Workplace Literacy Program allowed me to examine a full range of projects developed under this federal program so as to describe this relatively new field. I examined the language of the written materials available to educators and companies to set up these programs, including the wording of the requests for proposals in the *Federal Register* and the reports and booklets issued by the U.S. Department of Education in order to determine both what was included and that which was excluded. The brief visits to programs which frequently accompany reviews such as this one, while providing added details and perspectives, necessarily offer partial views of the programs themselves. Conclusions drawn from such visits can be misleading.[5] Longitudinal studies, close evaluations, and detailed ethnographies are needed to provide deeper, more nuanced pictures of programs.[6] My study of the discourse of workplace education—the language that is used to describe and promote, evaluate, and fund these programs, the writing and discussion about workplace programs, including the guidelines for proposals, the program and curriculum descriptions—allowed me to uncover the theoretical assumptions that underlie the choices program designers, managers, curriculum specialists, and instructors make when they set up workplace education programs. A focus on text, or discourse, highlights and enables me to make explicit these assumptions. My goal is to examine the ways in which people choose to represent their programs to a wide range of audiences to make explicit the paradigms that shape, and, I will argue, constrain them. As a first step, then, this paper reviews the discourse of workplace education programs in order to interrogate their assumptions and to provide a framework to conceptualize alternative models.

For this review I systematically examined nearly sixty descriptions of workplace education programs.[7] The descriptive materials I obtained from programs varied considerably—program directors sent letters responding to questions, promotional materials, conference handouts, handbooks, curricular materials and lesson plans, applications for funding, final performance reports and evaluations.[8] In an attempt to answer questions and fill in the skeletal pictures often provided by program descriptions, I had follow-up conversations or written correspondence with more than twelve of the programs, which allowed me to obtain additional detailed information about areas such as teaching, curriculum design, and assessment.

Once I had collected materials, I combed each program description for information about teaching, learning, and assessment. From this search I developed the following categories which were helpful in sorting the information: definitions of literacy and workplace literacy; assumptions about and descriptions of learners, teaching and learning, curriculum and assessment; program purposes or goals; and criteria for evaluation. As I gathered information I revised the categories, rereading the reports many times as I attempted to fill in the gaps. No program description contained information for each of the categories that I had developed, and frequently the reports included facts that fit in two or three of the categories. After gathering the initial data, I looked at all of the programs across each of the categories to find both similarities and differences. I used the information provided by the sixty programs to develop the arguments below.[9] The conclusions I have reached are necessarily tentative and are designed to provoke program designers, policymakers, companies, instructors, and researchers to carefully examine their own assumptions as they plan and evaluate new and existing programs. (See Table 2.1 for a summary of program characteristics.)

# Discourses of Workplace Education Programs

*Assumptions about Literacy*

Many discussions about literacy issues begin with a consideration of definitions of the term "literacy." I would argue that this exploration of literacy definitions is critical to an understanding of the underlying assumptions about language and learning issues in a workplace context. In this section, three types of definitions of literacy, in the context of workplace programs, will be described: literacy as skills; literacy as social practices; and literacy as critique (see Lytle & Wolfe, 1989). A typical final report for a workplace literacy program equated literacy with basic skills or reading, writing, speaking, and listening, or more simply put, communication skills. Out of nineteen federally funded programs that gave their definition of literacy in their written material, sixteen utilized a definition of literacy as skills. Indeed, the rules and

Table 2.1: Characteristics of Federally Funded Workplace Education Programs Reviewed for This Project (N=37)

*Type of business or industry*
    manufacturing—35% (13)
    service—35% (13)
    hospital/health care—14% (5)
    hotel/hospitality—8% (3)
    office—8% (3)
    maintenance—3% (1)
    other—3% (1)
    mixed (projects including both manufacturing and service—24% (9)
    other—5% (2)

*Number of participants*
    fewer than 100—24% (9)
    100 to 200—19% (7)
    200 to 500—41% (15)
    over 500—14% (5)
    not specified—3% (1)

*Union involvement*
    yes—30% (11)
    no (or not mentioned)—70% (26)

*English as a Second Language (ESL) classes*
    yes—57% (21)
    no—43% (25)

*General Equivalency Diploma (GED) classes*
    yes—33% (12)
    no—67% (25)

*Reorganized workplace*
    yes—14% (5)
    some of the workplaces within the project—16% (6)
    no or not mentioned—70% (26)

*Number of years funded by the federal government (in the first three cycles)*
    one year—78% (29)
    two years—11% (4)
    three years—11% (4)

regulations governing the National Workplace Literacy Program embrace this definition; the first purpose of the Adult Education Act is to assist states to "improve educational opportunities for adults who lack *the level of literacy skills* requisite to effective citizenship and productive employment" (*Federal*

*Register*, 1989, p. 34409, emphasis added). Note that while skills for citizenship are included in this definition of literacy, more programs choose to focus on the skills they believe are needed for "productive employment." These definitions of literacy and workplace literacy rest on the assumption that literacy is a set of universal skills disassociated from the individual and made specific by the functional context in which they are applied.[10] I would suggest that a focus on the skills for citizenship might push programs to choose a more critical or participatory perspective on literacy.

The term "functional literacy," originally developed by the U.S. Army to indicate the skills necessary to carry out basic tasks in the military, assumed to be at a fifth-grade reading level, has recently gained currency as the accepted way to set up workplace programs (de Castell & Luke, 1986; Harman, 1970; Sticht, Armstrong, Hickey & Caylor, 1987; Sticht & Hickey, 1987). A skills definition of workplace literacy ultimately leads to a competency-based model of education which rests on the assumption that literacy, or more accurately reading and writing skills, can be divided into discrete teachable and testable subskills (de Castell & Luke, 1986). A fundamental tension in this definition of literacy as tied to functional context rests in the notion that while the actual literacy skills taught change according to the context or work site, there is an implicit assumption that all individuals within that particular context should be taught the same skills in the same manner (Lytle, 1991).[11] This definition of functional context relies on a restricted definition of context as texts or more specifically the particular texts encountered on-the-job, and thus necessarily narrows the definition of literacy for any given workplace to the materials gathered in a "literacy audit." A more expanded notion of context would include the social relations that surround work with attention to the ways in which workers collaborate as a group.

Examples of functional context curricula abound. For instance, curriculum developers at an auto plant looked at a job description and briefly observed work to determine the particular tasks for one type of work—a "rework operator." They determined that these workers perform the following two tasks: count scrap and calculate the cost of the scrap.[12] The following "literacy tasks" were developed from this analysis: addition of whole numbers, location of information on a chart, and multiplication of whole numbers, decimals, and fractions. These tasks formed the basis of the lesson plans for the workers in this position.[13]

By way of comparison, a group of workplace programs established under the auspices of the Consortium of Worker Education, funded by a group of unions and the New York Education Department states that their purpose is to "help workers to understand that what they do in their every day lives *is based on literacy*. . . . These workers are *context literate*, that is, their reading and writing skills are related to specific survival or workplace needs. The work of the Consortium of Worker Education, therefore, is to expand those contexts" (Collins, Balmuth, & Jean, 1989, p. 458). In the curriculum for one of these programs designed for apparel workers, students discuss the conditions they face in their daily lives. Together with the learners, instructors choose pictures, stories, and vocabulary that reflect learners' actual experiences as workers, tenants, parents, recent immigrants, and residents of New York City. The approach assumes that vocabulary and grammar can be learned most effectively if they are connected to the critical needs and interests of the learners (Collins, Balmuth, & Jean, 1989).[14]

Although both of these programs are contextualized, each defines "context" differently. In the auto plant, workers are given job specific skills to enhance their productivity in their current job. In the course for apparel workers, program designers take a broader view of literacy and ground it in the everyday competencies and events of the learners' lives. Thus, learners, rather than the person who performs the task analysis to determine the skills required for the job, are the experts and architects of their own learning.

Numerous theorists and researchers who have studied literacy learning in a wide variety of cross-cultural settings have called into question the definition of literacy as skills (Cook-Gumperz, 1986; Heath, 1986; Street, 1984, 1987). Rather than a view of literacy as a universal set of discrete skills or bits of information, these researchers and theorists propose a definition of literacy as social practice, embedded in particular cultures, including, but not exclusively, the culture of the workplace. Szwed (1981), for example, urges that we consider a variety of "configurations of literacies, a *plurality of literacies*," rather than a single, universal notion of literacy which translates into a standard to measure and classify people as either literate or illiterate. In other words, Szwed and others claim that there are a range of ways in which literacy can be used—in many different kinds of social interactions and activities, for a range of purposes and in a variety of settings. Rather than applying universal principles to the understanding of literacy acquisition and use, literacy researchers and theorists suggest the need to discover local understandings of literacy as contextualized in a larger social, cultural, and historical framework (Heath, 1982; Scribner & Cole, 1978, 1981; Street, 1984, 1987).

The current economic and political climate necessarily shapes our understanding of literacy. In the context of a de-industrializing society in which traditional blue-collar jobs are rapidly disappearing, literacy takes on a new meaning. Fingeret (1988) emphasizes the political nature of literacy and suggests the importance of examining the social relations surrounding its definition when she writes:

> Literacy is not some naturally occurring object, like stone or soil or water or air. It is a social construct—it is defined and created by those in power in a society,

and those definitions change as conditions change. Thus, literacy is considered historically and culturally relative; definitions of literacy depend on time and place (although they always are decided upon by those in positions of power). As the definitions shift, membership in the categories of "literate" and "illiterate" changes, and the rewards and stigma attached to membership in each category change as well. (Fingeret, 1988, p. 1)

Contrary to the assumption that "functional literacy" is a neutral and ahistorical term without cultural, social, economic, or political meanings, Fingeret suggests that CEOs, and others with managerial or oversight responsibilities, are the individuals authorized to define functional literacy. In workplaces, this means that the employers set the standards by which some people are pronounced "illiterate" and determine the content and skills that define what it means to "become literate."

The notion of multiple literacies suggests that a single standard—whether it is a literacy test for a job, a placement test for a class, or a set of benchmarks (e.g., a fourth-grade reading level)—cannot be used fairly to judge whether someone is literate or not. Individuals and groups differ in their complex histories of using literacy in their daily lives—on their job, at home, and in their communities—and in their purposes for engaging in formal learning (Fingeret, 1989; Heath, 1983; Lytle, Marmor & Penner, 1986; Lytle & Schultz, 1990; Reder, 1987; Reder & Green, 1985). Furthermore, this perspective argues against the notion of literacy as an attribute of a person, emphasizing instead its essentially social nature and suggesting that literacy can be most accurately conceptualized as a social practice (Lytle, 1991; Lytle & Schultz, 1990, 1991; Reder, 1987; Scribner, 1984).[15]

As work changes and workplaces are reorganized, it seems likely that new literacies will be required of workers, although we do not know yet for sure what these literacies will be. On the one hand, programs such as the one in the auto plant described above claim to teach workers communication and team-building *skills*. On the other hand, the notion of literacy as social and cultural practices suggests that something more than isolated skills is needed. It seems likely that workers and managers will need to learn skills embedded in practices which, while they may include technical skills such as the math needed to utilize statistical process control, will also include new patterns of interaction and collaboration. Companies undergoing reorganization describe new roles and responsibilities that workers will be given in the reorganized workplace. As compared with many low-skilled factory jobs in companies organized according to traditional, mechanistic models, in these newly organized workplaces, workers may be required to take more initiative, make more judgments and communicate to a wider variety of people in a broad range of circumstances. While programs claim to be teaching interactional *skills* which

51

are designed to match these new requirements, if the classes operate under outdated assumptions about literacy—that workers need reading and writing, and possibly listening and speaking skills handed to them by their instructors—rather than with the understanding of literacy and learning as active, constructive processes which build on the knowledge teachers and learners bring with them, then the roles workers take in these new workplaces will remain fundamentally unchanged.[16]

In addition to looking at individuals as they work, this definition of literacy suggests the importance of looking at the ways in which individuals as members of a group accomplish work, especially as work changes. It includes an understanding of the variety of literacies required to do work. One implication from this understanding of literacy as more than the skills of decoding and encoding print, is that we need to closely examine literacy practices at work over time. Brief tours of companies, collection of documents, and interviews may not be sufficient. New methods are required for understanding the complex and changing processes involved in accomplishing work. In a project located in an electronics factory in the Silicon Valley, Hull and her colleagues (Hull, Jury, Ziv, & Schultz, 1994) have developed the notion of a "work event" to capture the complexity of the knowledge workers need to accomplish work in the new high performance workplace. Rather than an analysis of the texts workers read and write, this procedure for looking at work encompasses an analysis of the work environment, including the social interactions that shape the texts as they are produced and used. The social, historical, economic, political, and cultural contexts are viewed as central to an understanding of literacy at work. We define a "work event" as the set of interactions and activities that set work processes back into motion after the flow of work has been interrupted. For these work events, we analyze the strategies and rules—including reading, writing, talking and problem-solving—participants use to accomplish their tasks. (Hull et al., 1994)[17]

A third type of definition of literacy emphasizes its transformative potential. Labeled as critical literacy, critical reflection (Lytle, 1991; Lytle & Wolfe, 1989) or even the "new literacy" (Willinsky, 1990), this view emphasizes the role of the individual situated in the community as the site of knowledge and potential change (Gowen, 1990, 1992). Freire (1976, cited in Salvatori & Hull, 1990), a leading teacher and writer about critical literacy, describes the explicitly political nature of this meaning, focused as it is on power and structural relations: "It is not enough to know mechanically the meaning of 'Eve saw the vineyard.' It is necessary to know what position Eve occupies in the social context, who works in the vineyard, and who profits from this work" (Freire, 1976, p. 71).

In literacy programs which follow the model proposed by Freire and others, learners use literacy to gain insight into and power in the communities in which they live. Giroux (1988) emphasizes the potential of literacy to engender productive conflict rather than harmony. He writes, "To be literate is *not* to be free, it is to be present and active in the struggle for reclaiming one's voice, history, and future" (Giroux, 1988, p. 65). This stands in contrast to the notion of literacy as delivering economic or social freedom, a notion that is implicit in much of the current rhetoric which proclaims the benefits of becoming literate (Hull, this volume). A definition of literacy as critical literacy suggests that workplace education programs should have as their focus, not only the tasks of the workplace, but also an understanding of the historical, social, economic, and political relations that surround work and the possibilities for transforming both the workplace and one's position within it. At the same time, workplace education programs operate under the same financial constraints as the companies themselves and program managers are often asked to justify the time employees spend in a program against the bottom line or in relation to an economic gain. While this makes it difficult to enact the sort of program I have described, it is useful to develop the ideas as a model against which programs can be compared.

To summarize, in their narrow definition of literacy as functional literacy, programs limit their scope and thus their ultimate impact on both the workplace and on learners' lives. When learners are presumed to be functionally illiterate, the multiple ways in which they use literacies—both their native and second language literacies—in their daily lives, including in their work and community settings, are left unexplored.[18] The definition of literacy as functional literacy necessarily constrains both curriculum and instruction by tying teaching to the delivery of discrete skills and curriculum to a sequence of lessons in which competencies are mastered. As an alternative, more inclusive understandings of teaching and learning may be more appropriate to the new workplace. The changing workplace which requires new ways of interaction necessarily expands the definition of literacy beyond isolated skills to the notion of literacy as practices and critique.

### *Assumptions about Curriculum and Curriculum Development*

It has become common for programs to initiate discussions of curriculum with a description of how they "customize" their curricula. For this process, program developers conduct a job task analysis or literacy audit to identify the "literacy" (or skills) required for the job prior to the start of the program. The procedure generally involves: limited observations of work and workers; interviews with managers, supervisors, and "experienced" or expert workers; questionnaires; and an analysis of the written materials used in the workplace. The program developers use the information gained from this procedure to adapt the curriculum so that the skills taught are related to the context of the particular workplace. The abbreviated example below illustrates this process.

In one program designed for hospital workers, curriculum developers conducted a literacy audit of targeted jobs. They collected examples of texts—both specialized and generic—and observed the literacy practices of experienced workers. Once the artifacts were collected, staff members analyzed them to determine the literacy processes used to read and write them. These processes were then translated into the objectives of the curriculum as illustrated below:

| Job Task | Literacy Objectives |
|---|---|
| Follow the policy regarding needle disposal (The policy is attached to the lesson plan) | |
| 1. Check all needles in your assigned area. Seal the opening when the container is filled to the appropriate level which is indicated by the instructions: "Do not fill above this level." | 1. To read and summarize the policy. To paraphrase the information. To determine meanings of words in context. To use the dictionary to find word meanings. |

(Nurss, Final Evaluation Report, 1990, p. 23)

Most programs funded by the U.S. Department of Education report that they have customized their curriculum through the use of a job task analysis. Indeed, it is strongly recommended that some form of job task analysis be performed by a company before it submits an application for funding (*Workplace Literacy*, 1992). The concept of a job task analysis or literacy audit is directly tied to the concept of a functional context curriculum. Numerous manuals and workbooks (cf. Askov, Aderman, & Hemmelstein, 1989; Philippi, 1991) have been developed to explain how to conduct a job task analysis, often considered the linchpin to successful programs. The guidelines for literacy audit observations in a workplace program located in an auto plant are typical of these procedures and summarized below.

- Select priority tasks from a predetermined list. (Eliminate tasks with no basic skills content such as sweeping the floor; identify problem tasks; give weight for importance.)
- Observe employees performing the priority tasks to analyze the use of basic skills.
- Observe a competent performer and ask that person questions to obtain information about the mental processes she uses when she per-

forms the task. (Ask questions about reading, writing, speaking, listening, computing, measuring, decisions, and problem-solving.)
- Ask for copies of printed materials related to the task (including both filled in and blank forms).
- Orient yourself ahead of time to the activities, environment, tools, and equipment for the task.
- Screen the printed materials for "problematic tasks".
(Dowling, et al., 1992)[19]

The notion that teachers should conduct a job audit or collect materials used in the workplace as a first step to curriculum development is not in itself a bad idea, although there is some concern that it may lead to job-testing and discrimination (Añorve, 1989; Carnevale, Gainer, & Meltzer; 1988; Hull, this volume; Sarmiento & Kay, 1990). Job audits can be a vehicle for teachers to become more familiar with the workplace and a basis upon which to build a curriculum that is tied closely to the needs and interests of both the learners and the company. Too often, however, job audits are conducted by outsiders—educational specialists or curriculum developers—and used to generate lists of skills and to restrict the focus of a program to activities tied only to a worker's present job, not to the future or to the wider context of a person's life. In addition, job audits, as they are usually carried out, rarely give an accurate picture of work and the multiple and often complex roles that literacy, as broadly defined, plays in the accomplishment of work. While in theory the process of curriculum development using literacy audits or job task analyses frequently involves the participation of managers, supervisors, instructors and employees, in the program material that I examined, the nature of the participation of each party was rarely spelled out.

What is striking about literacy audits is that they almost always lead to lists of skills and subskills rather than to a broader understanding of literate practices. Furthermore, and perhaps even more importantly, the dominant ideology which supports this single way of conceptualizing the curriculum necessarily limits the possibilities for teaching and learning in these programs. If the content of teaching is defined by a list of skills, then instructors are limited in what and how they can teach, and learners are limited in what they are given the opportunity to learn. A sample from a typical list of skills generated from a literacy task analysis conducted for non-native-speaking workers in a housekeeping job at a hotel is given below.

*Work Goals/Language Skills*
Personal identification
Identify self
Ask and answer simple questions
Ask for clarification

Answer requests for supplies
Identify suppliers
Answer requests
Ask for clarification
Offer assistance
Apologize
Explain reason
Make a suggestion
(Kirby, 1989, p. A-6)[20]

The curriculum that accompanies this skill list explains the ways that lessons can be developed from the list. Each skill is considered a "function" and has listed beside three columns: language sample (e.g., "My name is _____); structures (simple present, who-questions); and resources (lists of texts, visual aids, video, etc.).

Contrast this conceptualization of curriculum to a Freirean model of worker education proposed by Auerbach (1990; Auerbach & Wallerstein, 1987). Auerbach characterizes this process of curriculum development as participatory; it involves learners in the co-investigation and codification or representation of themes into instructional materials, the extension of skills through critical dialogue, problematization, and action, and as its final step, evaluation and reflection (Auerbach, 1990; Freire, 1970). In the first example knowledge is seen as located outside of the learner, while in the second example learners are viewed as knowledgeable, and full participants in all aspects of their learning. The language and concepts about teaching and learning as reflected in curriculum are worlds apart.

A close examination of the materials which describe the guidelines for federally funded workplace programs, as well as the materials from the programs themselves, revealed a dominant way to conceptualize curriculum development and content. The statement—"researchers and practitioners are unanimous in recommending some form of job task analysis" (e.g., *Workplace Literacy*, 1992, p. 21)—occurred regularly in these reports. In addition, this apparent unanimity was reflected in a letter I received from a program director who described the instructional program of her project in the following manner: "Instruction is customized to each company with which we work, as I'm sure you've heard 1,000 times by now. And of course, everything is related to the "functional context", i.e. the job and the company." Further, the initial review of the National Workplace Literacy Program prepared for the U.S. Department of Education (Kutner, Sherman, Webb, & Fisher, 1991) used the presence of functional context curriculum as one of the criteria for their selection of exemplary programs. Thus, the presence of a functional context curriculum has become synonymous with a successful program. It is important to note the strengths and limitations of this single way of viewing curriculum development, and, perhaps most importantly, to recognize that it is only one of the many ways to conceptualize the construction of curriculum.

Conceptual frameworks for constructing a literacy curriculum are necessarily tied to definitions of literacy. If literacy is perceived as a set of skills, then the curriculum will be viewed as composed of discrete lessons based on the diagnosis of deficits and the assessment of competencies. In its isolation and drill of discrete, decontextualized skills, functional context curricula replicate the social organization of work in traditional, Tayloristic workplaces, factories where work is broken down into discrete and repetitive tasks. If, on the other hand, literacy is viewed as cultural practices, then a curriculum must necessarily emphasize those practices learners bring with them as well as the ones they need and want to learn. This implies that the communities of practice to which the learner belongs and will join should be taken into account when instructors or program designers determine the content and the instructional processes of a program (Lave & Wenger, 1991; Resnick, 1990). Thus, it is not only the individual's actual job description or the work that employees perform on a particular day that should determine the content of the curriculum, but the larger context in which the employee works, the various people with whom the employee interacts, and the larger milieu of the workplace. In addition, this definition suggests that the changing practices as well as the changing skills of newly reorganized post-Tayloristic workplaces should be included as part of literacy learning.

In contrast to functional context curricula, programs which are based on the notion of critical literacy often begin with the learners' own interests and goals and frequently include a critical examination of existing relationships and social or political action (Mezirow, 1985; see Auerbach, 1990, and Auerbach & Wallerstein, 1987, for examples in the context of ESL education). Rather than a focus on existing conditions, these programs focus on what a workplace might become.[21]

The choices that program designers make in their construction of programs are political ones and situate power and knowledge inside the learners, the instructors, and/or the texts (Apple, 1979). Thus, another way to conceptualize curriculum is to define it as both the selection and the organization of knowledge (Eisner & Vallance, 1974). Using this definition, the following pairs of questions can be posed:

- Whose knowledge is included? (And whose knowledge is excluded?)
- Who selected the knowledge? (And who was not included in the selection process?)

- Why is the curriculum organized and taught in a particular way? (What other possibilities are there? Who determined the present sequence?)
- Why is this knowledge being taught to this particular group of learners? (And who is not included among the learners?)

These questions might be used as a framework for eliciting the participation of multiple parties in curriculum development and for clarifying the roles and responsibilities of those people involved in the process.

For a variety of reasons, the taught curriculum often differs dramatically from that which is planned, an occurrence which the official discourse of workplace literacy programs rarely documents.[22] Goodlad and his colleagues (1979) proposed a typology that is helpful in analyzing how curriculum changes as it moves from conception to enactment. They suggest that there are five different curricula: the ideological curriculum which is based on ideas and emerges from the planning process; the formal curriculum or the officially approved curriculum which, for political reasons, often differs from the one initially proposed; the perceived curriculum or the ways in which the various parties including teachers, learners and, in the case of workplace education, program managers and supervisors perceive the curriculum; the operational curriculum or the curriculum that is actually taught; and finally, the experiential curriculum or the curriculum that the learners (and I would add, the teachers) experience. This analysis emphasizes that the development and implementation of a curriculum is not a neutral activity and that frequently many different curricula operate simultaneously. Reports on workplace education programs often limit their descriptions of curriculum development to the process of gathering workplace materials. The framework described above suggests the importance of examining the trajectory of the curriculum, comparing, for example, the ways in which it is conceptualized by planners and perceived by learners. It emphasizes the interactional processes involved in curriculum development as compared to the conception of curriculum development as a scientific and neutral process.

A continuum might more accurately represent the processes of curricula development available to workplace education programs. At one end of the continuum are prepackaged "teacher-proof" materials—often in the form of textbooks and computer programs—usually written by outsiders to the program *for* rather than *with* teachers and learners. At the other end of the continuum is a participatory program in which learners play a major role in the determination of the content of their learning at all stages of the planning process, including the actual classes. Although a participatory curriculum would most likely focus on the content of work, it might also include interests and goals from other parts of the learners' lives. Somewhere between these two end-points are functional context curricula; the content of these curricula is generally determined by instructors, managers and, frequently, outside experts with some input from the learners themselves.

In addition to commonly accepted understandings about the processes of curricular development, in the literature which describes workplace education programs there is a presumption that the content should only include material related to the specific jobs performed by the workers. The decision of what content to include in the curriculum is closely tied to the narrow range of purposes for workplace education programs and a legitimate concern for justifying the costs of a program. It is also tied to the notion that reading and writing "skills" are not transferable and therefore must be tied to job content.[23] A typical purpose for a workplace education program is reflected in the following statement from a statewide workplace literacy program which serves seven manufacturing firms:

> Employees . . . will be brought up to the level of competency of their present job (math, english [sic], communication, etc.) and they will also have a solid foundation of higher basic skills (team-building skills, interpersonal skills, etc.) in order to participate in a Total Quality Manufacturing work environment.

Note the implicit functions of workplace education contained in this statement—to produce competent workers by teaching them discrete skills. Thus, skills rather than practices or ways of participating, are emphasized. There is an assumption that only "illiterate" or "incompetent" workers need "higher basic skills," rather than an emphasis on teaching team-building skills to the actual teams that perform the work in the context of the workplace, and the inclusion of all members of the work team—supervisors and managers along with line-workers. This emphasis on the generalized goal of individual competency and the exclusive focus on job-related skills is illustrated in the U.S. Department of Education's own evaluation and blueprint for future programs:

> A curriculum is a conceptual system of related learning experiences. The curriculum developed helps the learner to progress from his or her level of job-related basic skills to a point of competency needed for the current or a future job, or for a new system such as team-based management. (*Workplace Literacy*, 1992, p. 22)

This understanding of curriculum is based on research which suggests that reading is more effectively taught in occupation-specific contexts (Diehl & Mikulecky, 1980; Mikulecky, 1982, 1993; Rush, Moe, & Storlie, 1986; Sticht, 1979, 1988; Sticht, Armstrong, Hickey & Caylor, 1987; Sticht &

Hickey, 1987). As a consequence, programs tend to define curriculum as a sequence of reading, writing or math exercises whose content is related to a specific job or workplace. The result is that despite their diversity of learners and the complexity of their contexts, many programs look nearly identical.

If programs are designed without taking into account workers' broader interests and purposes for reading and writing, in the long run they are likely to falter. Not only might learners stop attending classes, but the ultimate goals of the program may not be reached.[24] If programs claim to teach workers the new practices that will be required as work is transformed, both the content and the way in which teaching occurs must necessarily reflect the new workplace. That is, if workers are expected to do such activities as participate in teams, have flexible work assignments, solve new problems, and continue to learn on the job, they need to be taught both new content and new ways of learning. Once again, my concern is the unquestioning attitude that there is only one legitimate kind of program or way to develop curriculum as reflected in the language of functional context literacy that dominates the discourse of workplace education.

Another way to conceptualize workplace education programs is for a job-related focus to be one of the many options that a program considers. As an alternative to a single focus on basic skills related to specific jobs, programs might base the content of curricula on learners' own purposes, interests and needs. While programs often ask learners to state their interests, they frequently present employees with a checklist of predetermined goals. Furthermore, while the specific goals might be used to develop an individualized education plan, they frequently do not affect the actual curriculum of the program.[25] Brookfield (1986) suggests that programs incorporate both action and reflection as ongoing processes so that learners will become more proactive in assuming control over setting their own goals and establishing criteria for evaluating their learning (Lytle, 1991). As workers are asked to assume more control and responsibility in the modern, post-Tayloristic workplace, it seems even more critical that programs rethink the ways in which they hand workers the skills to adapt to these changes. If the restructured workplace requires new "thinking skills" (cf. Carnevale, Gainer, & Meltzer, 1988; the Secretary's Commission on Achieving Necessary Skills, 1992), then it seems reasonable that programs include more than the content of thinking skills in the curriculum (e.g., problem-solving activities). In customizing basic skills curricula to the workplace, then, programs need to adjust not only the content of the curriculum, but also the process by which it is constructed.

As a rare example of this different conception of curriculum, one program uses themes developed in conjunction with learners which address workers' language skills, needs and interests.[26] These themes are wide ranging and include more general topics such as "work" or "health and safety" and more specialized topics such as "signs in the workplace" or "tools, equipment and gauges," and integrate reading, writing, speaking and listening. At one site, the learners participated in the decisions about the content of their learning, how they were taught, the purposes of the instruction, and the ways in which learning should be documented.[27] Thus, the participation structures of the classroom—the roles and relationships of teachers and learners—were changed to more closely match those of a reorganized workplace.

In comparison with a prepackaged curriculum, there are apparent drawbacks to this method of curriculum development for the cost-conscious company. For instance, this way of setting up a program is likely to take longer and require more knowledge and expertise from the instructors, two concerns of cost-conscious companies. However, evidence from adult basic education (ABE) programs strongly suggests the benefits in terms of increased participation and learning from these learner-centered approaches (Fingeret & Jurmo, 1989; Grubb, Kalman, Castellano, Brown, & Bradby, 1991; Kazemak, 1988). Furthermore, alternative and broader conceptions of literacy are likely to encourage instructors to use a wider repertoire of teaching strategies.

If curriculum is seen as a predetermined sequence of skills designed to help learners master competencies which are tied to specific jobs, the result is a particular kind of program. Most often these types of curriculum are developed because of a reliance on standard forms of evaluation. It is relatively easy for a company to measure the success of a program designed to teach specified competencies. A quantitative indication of progress, whether or not it is accurate, is often needed to secure future funding for a program and is frequently tied to bottom-line concerns or the importance of financially justifying a company's investment in education. In contrast to a curriculum which responds to such "short term" concerns, Stein (1991) proposes that curricula can also be developed with long-term company goals in mind, such as education for increased participation.

When curriculum is perceived more broadly as including the numerous decisions detailed above; and when the content is viewed as negotiated and constructed rather than as determined by the context of the work, then a wider range of programs is possible. In addition, it is more likely that these long-term, less easily measured goals will be met. If this model of curriculum development is used, each program might vary not only according to the particular industry but also according to the individuals involved, their own histories, practices, purposes and goals.

### Assumptions about Teachers and Teaching

Most portrayals of workplace education programs describe the teachers and teaching in the program by giving the qualifications of teachers and facts about the instructional setting. In the materials I examined, few programs discuss pedagogy or their theories of teaching and learning, and the instructors are rarely mentioned. Most programs simply describe instruction as occurring. For example, *Workplace Literacy* (1992), the report issued by the Department of Education on the first three funding cycles of workplace education programs, states, "How workplace literacy instruction is provided is critical." Following this statement is the argument that basic skills should be taught in a job-related context. There is no mention of pedagogy or ways to think about how to set up learning environments. While I want to exercise caution in making assumptions from written materials, it is worth noting that what is (and is not) included in these reports reflects the priorities set by both the individual programs and the funding agencies. A careful examination of materials and subsequent telephone conversations suggested to me that despite good intentions, most programs have not focused on issues of pedagogy; they have chosen instead to devote their attention to techniques for gathering lists of new skills. Grubb and his colleagues (1991) found a similar pattern in their study of remedial programs which employed functional context literacy training methods. While the programs stated that their curriculum is adapted to particular work environments, Grubb discovered that in actuality, little was changed except the source of the text.

With few readily available models, programs often fall back on traditional ways of teaching, ones that replicate the ways children are taught in school: Teachers lecture in front of classrooms or use teacher-led and teacher-structured activities. As Hull (this volume) explains:

Schooling is a bad memory for many adults who are poor performers at literacy, and workplace instruction which is school-based—that relies upon similar participant structures, materials, and assessment techniques—will likely be off-putting by association. I am dismayed, then, to see how frequently proposals for and descriptions of workplace literacy programs rely upon school-based notions of teaching and learning. (p. 24)

The point is not that these techniques are necessarily bad, but that like the rusty, slow machines and old ways of organizing work, they may not be appropriate for preparing workers for newly organized workplaces. Further, as Hull points out, if workers were not successful in learning literacy at school, as is true for many, although certainly not all participants in workplace education programs, it does not make sense to use those same teaching methods to instruct them as adults.

The descriptions of workplace education programs list a variety of titles for teachers, including: instructors, "live instructors" (as compared with computers), project staff, process training specialists, curriculum developers, and instructional managers. Each of these titles reflects particular assumptions about the teachers' roles and relationships with learners and other project partners. For instance, the title "live instructors" is applied to the people who do the teaching, in contrast to the inanimate instructors—the computers. This title suggests a rough equivalence between the two, as if the choice between engaging in a process of learning with a person was a parallel or even similar experience to "working on" a computer. The terms "project staff," "process training specialists," "curriculum developers," and "instructional managers" have a similar tone. They all seem impersonal and emphasize the role of managing learners, their learning, and the knowledge they are taught. In contrast, Brookfield (1986) argues that teaching should be conceived of as facilitation, and teachers as facilitators. Rather than acting as transmitters of established skills, the teacher's role, according to Brookfield, is to make it possible for learners to experience varied ways of thinking and acting so that they can make informed choices about their purposes for learning (Lytle, 1991). By acting as a facilitator, teachers can join learners in the process of co-investigating the knowledge they bring to programs and their goals for literacy learning.

Programs assign teachers a range of jobs including: enhancing workers' skills, using a variety of techniques to meet the literacy needs of the employees, monitoring computer use, and in one instance reporting to company officials any "unexcused absence, excessive tardiness, lack of interest and/or horseplay or goofing off during class time." Again, each of these responsibilities implies a different set of roles and relationships with learners.

Most program descriptions do not mention the explicit roles and relationships between instructors and learners. Instead, they frequently emphasize what is taught (the curriculum or more specifically the process of curriculum development) and when it is taught (the schedule and number of contact hours).[28] Research on adult learning suggests that adult education teachers should pay particular attention to how learning occurs (Brookfield, 1986; Cross, 1981; Knowles, 1970, 1979).[29] Because, in so many cases, adults enrolled in workplace education programs were not successful in schools in a conventional sense (although, of course, this should not be assumed), it is particularly important that this relationship be reexamined and redefined in adult programs (Kazemak, 1988; Lytle, 1991). On the other hand, experience shows that adults often come to programs with particular expectations about the roles of their teachers and might react negatively if those expectations are violated.[30] This argues for a careful consideration of the instructor-learner relationship.

In addition to a discussion of where and when instruction takes place, most reports on workplace education programs detail techniques of specific activities rather than teaching methods or ways of organizing instruction. These techniques range from teacher-led discussions and worksheets to more "worker-centered" activities such as cooperative learning, role-playing, and the language experience approach. In their study of remediation in vocational education and job training programs which included some workplace education programs, Grubb and his colleagues (1991) found that most programs relied on what they termed "skills and drills" rather than "meaning making" methods of teaching. A review of federally funded workplace education programs suggests a similar pattern. While a few programs indicate that they use whole language or process-writing methods which emphasize the integration of reading and writing and the use of whole texts (rather than decontextualized words, sentences, or paragraphs), most programs rely on workbook-type exercises which use the job context to teach isolated skills. They frequently supplement these exercises with practice using role playing or dialogues.[31]

Because program descriptions rarely describe actual teaching interactions (whether they are in classrooms, union halls, or on the shop floor), it is difficult to know whether teachers use traditional, didactic teaching methods[32] or more participatory teaching methods[33]. While traditional methods tend to rely on what Freire (1983) has termed the banking model, in which learners are the passive receptacles of knowledge, more participatory approaches assume that learners are active collaborators in all aspects of their learning (Fingeret & Jurmo, 1989).[34] In an examination of workplace education programs, we need to ask questions not only about the background of instructors (although that may be important) and the numbers of students and schedule of their classes, we also need to look closely at how teaching and learning occurs, how lessons are constructed and the roles and relationships between and among teachers and students. The choice that many program directors make to omit this information from their program descriptions can be read as a conscious one, based on a lack of information or a decision that these issues are not a priority.

### Assumptions about Learners and Learning

Workplace education programs utilize a variety of labels for learners. Whether learner, student, trainee, client, participant, employee, or worker, each label implies a slightly different role and purpose for participation in the program. When a program labels its employees as "trainees," it conveys to the learner, to the instructor, and to the public that its purpose is to train the employees in particular skills to enhance their job, rather than to educate them in a broader sense. Similarly, programs which use the term "clients" seem to focus on short-term goals or primarily use computer-assisted learning with very specific and predetermined goals. Programs which label the learners as "workers" often seek to emphasize the social, historical, and political relationships in the workplace as integral to their curriculum.[35] In the material I surveyed, there were instances where employees were described as commodities who need to be upgraded, as in the following statement: "We improve our people, products, and services." A report from the ASTD (American Society for Training and Development) states: "In the new economy people must be treated as assets to be developed in order to add value, not costs to be reduced" (1990). These labels and ways of speaking often reflect and may even determine the roles and relationships of learners in programs and also the educational views and priorities of the program managers.

Following both school-based and traditional adult education models, the reports on workplace education programs frequently describe learning in terms of contact hours, with the added presumption that a particular number of contact hours will be equivalent to predictable advances in learning. For example, in the abstract for one of the currently funded programs, although the program claims a broad and far-reaching objective "to provide industry related information that will allow team members the opportunity to understand the diversity of the company, workplace, terminology, math and reading skills, problem solving skills, critical thinking skills and basic skills," the primary (and presumably most critical) outcome is that skill levels will be raised by two grade levels (National Workplace Literacy Program Abstracts, 1993). Programs which adhere to strict formulas which equate a particular number of contact hours with specified increases in grade levels in reading and math subscribe to the presumption that learning is linear and that standards used to measure the progress of grade school children (and are questionable in that setting)—grade levels—are appropriate for adults and for workplace education programs.

Funding agencies require programs to report the total number of contact hours to them, and in their reports program directors frequently make a correlation between numbers of hours and advances in learning. This method of quantifying learning has its own appeal to many companies—it can be used to put a price tag on learning that can be entered on a balance sheet. If a specific amount of learning can be said to occur in a predictable number of hours, then a company can calculate the cost of increasing the collective reading levels of workers. Unfortunately, the process of teaching and learning is not that neat. If reading and writing were simply the mastery of particular skills, then there might be a rough correlation between the number of contact hours and the skills acquired.[36] If, on the other hand, reading and writing are conceptualized as social and constructive processes and learning includes negotiation and collaboration, then it is impossible to put either a clock or a price tag on learning literacy.

Each of the federally funded workplace education programs includes a section in their final performance reports to the Department of Education that describes the characteristics of both the participants who completed and of those who did not finish the program, including the outcomes achieved by the completers. The reports most often describe these two groups of individuals through demographic characteristics (e.g., their age, gender, ethnicity, and education levels) and their scores on standardized tests. Outcomes generally include both standardized test measures and affective measures which are reported both in percentages and through brief anecdotes.

These are relatively narrow ways of describing learners and may actually misrepresent the complex histories and practices that adult learners both bring to and take away from programs. A much broader framework for understanding adult learners and their literacy development has been developed by Lytle and her colleagues in collaboration with literacy teachers and learners in an urban, community-based literacy program (Lytle, 1991; Lytle & Schultz, 1990, 1991; Lytle, Belzer, Schultz, & Vannozzi, 1989). This framework includes four dimensions of literacy: *beliefs* or learners' theories about language and literacy, teaching and learning; *practices* or learners' everyday uses of literacy; *processes* or how learners accomplish reading and writing including the products of these transactions; and *plans* or learners' short-and long-term goals and the ways they hope to accomplish these goals over time. This framework is not meant to be exhaustive. Instead, it suggests the range of information and knowledge that can be collected by the learners on their own and in collaboration with instructors. This ongoing compilation of information both gives a more complete picture of the strengths learners bring to programs and provides a basis for charting change or growth over time.

At the same time that most programs argue that standardized evaluation measures do not accurately measure either the knowledge employees bring to programs and, of greater concern, the knowledge they gain through participation in programs, nearly every program uses these measures and reports the scores to document their success as a program.[37] Recent research in learning emphasizes the social context of learning and suggests the importance of viewing learning as an interactional process which encompasses interactions with other people and with physical objects, symbols, and cultural and historical practices (Vygotsky, 1978; Rogoff, 1984; Erickson, 1984; Tharp & Gallimore, 1988). Likewise, recent studies of work emphasize the social context of work (Darrah, 1990, 1991; Hull & Schultz, 1992; Hull et al., 1994; Jacob, 1986; Kusterer, 1978; Scribner, 1985; Wenger, 1991; Zuboff, 1988). This research argues both for collaboration as a learning process and against individual measures of growth. An additional difficulty with using standardized tests, even if they are keyed to particular programs, is that learning becomes equated with scoring higher on tests. If literacy is to be viewed as more than the accumulation of isolated skills, then we need to develop more complex assessment measures, which account for a broad understanding of learners and diverse ways of describing learning.

A second method of reporting the progress of learners in programs is through testimonials given by managers, supervisors, instructors and the employees themselves. These reports usually focus on the ways in which employees have improved their performance at work and often include statements about punctuality, productivity, and self-esteem. While these measures have their value, I would suggest that longer, more in-depth and potentially open-ended interviews with diverse parties, especially the workers themselves, would give more insight into the changes or growth that programs are attempting to describe. For instance, Gowen (1992) used in-depth interviews to examine the underlying assumptions and beliefs of the learners, teachers, and program designers. In her study she reveals the ways in which employees were much more competent than they were assumed to be by their employers and literacy instructors. She argues that differences between workers and their supervisors were interpreted as deficits, with the result that people were defined as illiterate. Gowen used these interviews to illuminate the hidden complexities in and multiplicity of perspectives on how people learn.

In addition, the ways in which many programs judge their success reinforces an essentially Tayloristic view of work. This view, which is now thought to be outmoded,[38] introduced production methods which gave workers limited jobs requiring very specific skills that were endlessly repeated. Workers were to act like cogs in a machine without understanding or participating in production in the larger sense, thus making factories more efficient. New forms of work organization suggest the need for new ways of viewing learning and assessment as active, constructive processes rather than passive, receptive processes which involve the mastery of lists of skills. Flattened hierarchies in these reorganized companies are thought to require workers to perform a wider variety of tasks and take greater responsibility for their work (Appelbaum & Batt, 1993; Grubb, Dickinson, Giordano, & Kaplan, 1992; Hull & Schultz, 1992). While the organization of work is changing, for the most part the definitions of literacy, the conceptions of curriculum, and the means for teaching and testing at workplaces haven't been significantly altered. Simply put, those U.S. companies which are establishing workplace education programs are using the classrooms of yesterday to teach for the workplaces of tomorrow.

This analysis of the common assumptions of workplace education programs and discussion of alternative ways of conceptualizing literacy, curriculum, teaching and learning suggest the importance of taking a broad look at ways to set up workplace education programs. As workplace education programs become more prevalent across the country, it is critical that program designers explore and try out a wide range of possibilities, rather than accepting a single model for their design and implementation.

## Conclusion

### Moving beyond Common Assumptions

A drawing which accompanied an article in Time entitled "Literacy Gap" (Gorman, 1988) captures one perspective on workplace education programs commonly found in the media.

Fig. 2.1: Literacy Gap Drawing

Source: Time (1988, December 19, p. 56, Mirko Ilic, artist)

This drawing depicts a line-up of five European-American male workers wearing hard hats and overalls. The men are drawn without eyes. A sixth European-American man wears glasses and a suit. This professional man holds a pencil and is carefully drawing letters in place of the eyes of the blue-collar workers. He has drawn A and B on the first man, C and D on the second, and is in the midst of drawing the E and F on the third man. Beneath the drawing, under the article's title "The Literacy Gap," is the subheading: "To close it—and to open the eyes of millions of workers—U.S. companies are spending hundreds of millions every year as educators of last resort."

The drawing reflects many of the common assumptions about workplace education programs explored in this article. First, there is a presumption about who the workers are—in the drawing the workers are identical, both in their backgrounds and their needs. Second, embedded in the drawing are assumptions about teaching and learning. The men stand passively in a row to receive the knowledge which is literally imprinted on them by another man who is different and presumably wiser (and who not only has eyes with which to see, but also wears glasses). The "suits" are handing out their knowledge to the "hard-hats." Third, the knowledge given to (written on) the workers is in the form of letters—decontextualized bits of information devoid of meaning. The subtitle of the article declares that the workplace education programs established by U.S. companies will "open the eyes of millions of workers;" only after *he* has participated in some kind of program will the male European-American worker (there are no women or people of color in the picture) truly be able to see.

In fact, the programs that have been established in workplaces are somewhat better than the caricature in the drawing. None the less, the drawing can be seen as emblematic of a particular conception of a workplace education program. Many, although not all, of the components of most workplace education programs are contained in the picture: the workers, the instructor, and the giving and receiving of knowledge. The picture, in effect, enacts a commonly stated goal of many programs: "to upgrade the skills of workers." The irony of the drawing, and a point that is critical, is that while the prose of the article describes a "crisis" that has been caused by advancing technology and newly organized workplaces, the solution proposed by the drawing which leads the article is one entrenched in antiquated understandings of teaching and learning.

In this final section, I suggest some initial research questions which fall into the following categories: definitions of literacy, curriculum, teaching and learning, partnerships, and success. My hope is that these questions will be useful for: practitioners—to help present and future programs examine their assumptions as they make decisions about how to set up, operate and evaluate programs; for policymakers—to set new directions for research and development of workplace education on federal, state and local levels; and finally for researchers—to bring about new understandings of literacy theory, teaching and learning through close examinations of workplaces and their educational programs.

An examination of definitions of literacy suggests the need for a thorough study of existing workplace education programs to understand the range of definitions of literacy which guide these programs. It would be important to collect these definitions not only from published program reports, but also from the various participants including the instructors and learners in a range of programs, and from observations. Furthermore, there is a need to study how definitions of literacy change as workplaces themselves are transformed. Many workplace education programs are initiated on the premise that new forms of work require new literacies. We need to conduct in-depth qualitative studies of these new workplaces to understand what literacies are required for work, including the interactional as well as the technical practices.

Definitions of curriculum and curriculum development suggest the importance of developing several detailed models of processes for constructing curriculum, including how the curriculum is put together, who is involved, when various individuals or groups are involved, and the nature of their involvement. If curriculum development is conceived of as an ongoing process, then the ways in which curricula change as they are enacted, in addition to the perceptions that various people have about the curriculum, need to be documented.

The exploration of definitions of teachers and teaching leads to research questions which takes a close look at all aspects of teaching. As described above, programs rarely describe the actual teaching of workplace education classes. These questions are likely to be explored most effectively by teachers themselves.[39] Teacher-research, defined by Cochran-Smith and Lytle (1990; Lytle & Cochran-Smith, 1990) as "systematic, intentional inquiry," has been used effectively in a range of settings as a means for teachers to explore their own guiding philosophies and varied ways of interacting with learners. In addition, an examination of a range of programs would provide information about both the diversity of roles teachers play in workplace education programs and the variety of definitions of teaching used by the same programs. Descriptions of the instructional models that exist and might be used in workplace education programs could provide valuable information to program planners and policymakers.

A focus on learners and learning suggests questions such as: Who are the learners who participate in workplace education programs? What are their purposes and goals for participation? What knowledge and practices do they bring with them to programs and what new knowledge and practices do they take away with them? How do the participants go about learning on the job, at home, in their communities? What beliefs about teaching and learning do they bring with them to the program? How do these beliefs change during the course of the program? Researchers, practitioners, and policymakers interested in questions such as these might invite the learners in the program to participate in this research about themselves and their own learning.

This is only a preliminary list of questions for a research agenda. One recommendation is that programs begin to collect a broader range of material that includes information about their definitions of literacy, curriculum, teaching, and learning. Other research questions will require both surveys of a range of workplace education programs and in-depth and ongoing studies of a few programs. It is critical that these questions be explored and discussed among researchers, practitioners, and policymakers as the number of programs begins to proliferate across the country.

Current workplace education programs reviewed for this chapter seem to follow the outmoded model of education depicted in the cartoon and assumed by its accompanying article. This seems particularly ironic since many of these programs have been set up to respond to changes in technology and organization in today's workplace; they are responding to the "new" workplace with "old" teaching methods and limited conceptions of literacy and learning. I would like to issue a new call. This call is *not* simply for more worker education to meet the needs of today's changing workplace, but rather it is a call for radical rethinking of what workers need to know to work and live in today's society. Until programs include workers, their knowledge, and their own understandings of what *they* want and need to know, programs fall short of their stated goals of preparing tomorrow's workers for the new workplace. First we need to change the dominant discourse. More importantly we need to change the programs.

## Notes

1. This research was initially funded by the National Center for Research on Vocational Education. Special thanks to Glynda Hull, Norton Grubb, Susan Lytle, Rebecca Steinitz, and David Paul for their mentorship, reading, and constant education.

2. For a detailed analysis of this phenomenon, see Hull, this volume. See also Mishel and Teixeira (1991) and Gowen and Barlett, this volume.

3. The National Workplace Literacy Program was created in 1988 through the Hawkins and Stafford Elementary and Secondary School Improvement Amendments.

4. For exceptions see Gowen, 1992; Kutner, Sherman, Webb, & Fisher, 1991; Mikulecky, 1993; *Workplace Literacy*, 1992.

5. See Gowen, 1992 and Kalman & Fraser, 1993. For a similar point with respect to factory visits or "grand tours," see Darrah, 1990, 1991.

6. For examples of these kinds of reports see Gowen, 1992; Kalman & Fraser, 1992.

7. All 39 of the programs funded in the first cycle (1989) and the 73 programs funded in the third cycle (1991) of the National Workplace Literacy Program were contacted by letter and program descriptions were requested. Fifty-one programs responded to these two requests. Of these, 14 sent little or no information. Additional program documentation was found on the ERIC database.

8. This variety of information made it difficult to achieve a comprehensive sense of each individual program and argues for a more standard reporting format.

9. See Schultz, 1992, for a set of matrices to accompany the analysis I present in this chapter.

10. There are many comprehensive discussions of the definitions of literacy including, Bizzell, 1988; de Castell, Luke, & MacLennan, 1986; Salvatori & Hull, 1990; Street, 1984, 1987; Wagner, 1987. For a book devoted to exploring this issue, see Venezky, Wagner & Ciliberti, 1990. For a discussion of definitions with reference to workplace literacy, see Gowen, 1990.

11. Many programs have developed an educational approach which utilizes IEP's (Individual Educational Plans) or IDP's (Individual Development Plans) in an effort to individualize their programs. However, in these programs individuals choose from a predetermined list of skills that are constant for each participant and use teaching methods that are essentially the same for each individual. Thus the skills, but not the ways of teaching, are adapted to each learner.

12. Scrap is the material left over after the manufacturing process. A goal of most manufacturing plants is to reduce overhead costs by reducing the amount of scrap.

13. For an interesting contrast, see the description of problem-solving by workers in the rework position at an electronics manufacturing plant in Hull et al., 1993.

14. See D'Amico, this volume, for a description of one of the programs funded by the consortium.

15. Scribner and her colleagues have explored this notion of literacy practices in a variety of workplace settings (Jacobs, 1986; Scribner, 1985; Scribner & Sachs, 1991).

16. For an excellent discussion of the hazards of relying on the concept of skill in workplace education, see Darrah, this volume. Also see Lave & Wenger, 1991; Scribner, 1984, 1985; Scribner & Sachs, 1991, for a discussion of practices.

17. See Darrah 1990, 1991 for an argument for using ethnographic methods to study work. See also Baba, 1991; Hull & Schultz, 1992.

18. I want to acknowledge once again the difficulty of incorporating these ideas into a workplace setting. On the other hand, when programs fail to do this, it seems inevitable that their effectiveness will be diminished. (See, for instance, Gowen, 1992.)

19. This set of procedures was based on Philippi, 1990.

20. Auerbach (1987, 1990) provides the perceptive critique that the typical ESL curriculum teaches how to apologize, call in sick, and follow orders, but rarely how to complain, initiate grievance procedures, or give orders.

21. This critical perspective on the workplace also serves the goals of most "high performance" workplaces which often use the process of continuous improvement as a linchpin for their reorganized workplace.

22. For a description of an instance of the enacted curriculum differing substantially from the planned curriculum in a workplace literacy program, see Kalman and Fraser, 1992. See also Gowen, 1992.

23. See Mikulecky, 1993, for support of this argument, and Gowen, 1992, for another perspective.

24. In her critical ethnography of a workplace education program, Gowen (1990, 1992) uncovered the resistance by hospital workers to a functional context literacy curriculum. The instructors in this program had developed a series of lessons based on materials in the workplace, such as a weekly newsletter written by the supervisor for the housekeeping staff. The workers resisted the instruction; they felt that they already knew the information in the newsletter and that studying it wouldn't help them with their ultimate goals, e.g., obtaining a GED. Likewise, the designers of a program for hospital workers that Kalman and Fraser studied (1992) assumed that the topic of work would be motivating for the participants in the program. The workers interviewed by Kalman and Fraser disagreed.

25. Goals aren't a panacea, however, and participants of adult literacy programs often resist that kind of involvement in their learning.

26. Perhaps because of the stringent funding guidelines that advocate particular ways of setting up programs, there are relatively few examples of workplace education programs with "promising practices"—programs which have developed alternative conceptions of curriculum development. Rather than advocating a particular method of curriculum development, I am suggesting that programs should be encouraged to develop truly innovative practices. If the goal is to prepare workers for newly organized workplaces, programs will have to risk replacing traditional methods of teaching that have predictable, although limited results, with newer, more appropriate methods.

27. See also Auerbach, 1990; Auerbach & Wallerstein, 1987; Jurmo, 1989, 1991; Soifer, Irwin, Crumrine, Honzaki, Simmons, & Young, 1990; and

73

Stein, 1991, for other descriptions of learner-centered or participatory ways of teaching in workplace education programs.

28. The first review of the National Workplace Literacy Program (Kutner et al., 1991) gave as one of its recommendations that researchers should determine a standard number of hours of workplace literacy instruction required for participant literacy levels to improve. This recommendation assumes that learning literacy is a finite process (after $x$ number of hours a person will be literate), is the same for every individual (the $x$ remains constant across individuals), and equates teaching and learning with covering material.

29. For a critique of the studies of adults as learners, see Brookfield (1986), who raises the concern that these studies are primarily based on European Americans.

30. See Kalman & Fraser, 1992 for an example of this.

31. In other words, rather than recognizing that workers learn on the job with the support of social relationships and the work environment (e.g., the placement of machines and written materials), functional context curriculum tends to remove texts from this rich context, thus losing much of the benefit of using work-related materials in the first place.

32. Kazemak (1988) reports that most adult education classes use traditional teaching methods. It seems likely that most classes affiliated with workplaces would use these same methods.

33. See Fingeret & Jurmo, 1989 for a description and rationale in support of these methods.

34. Kalman & Fraser (1992) point out the difficulty of using more participatory methods without ongoing training and support.

35. See Kalman & Fraser, 1992, for an example of this.

36. However, this is easily confounded because people learn in very different ways depending on their interests and abilities.

37. For critiques of the use of standardized testing in adult education programs in general and workplace education programs in particular, see Kazemak, 1988; Lytle & Schultz, 1990; and Lytle & Wolfe, 1989.

38. See for example the Secretary's Commission on Achieving Necessary Skills (SCANS) report (1992) which suggests that this form of work organization is being replaced with a more participatory, team-based approach, often referred to as "high performance." See also *America's*

*Choice: High skills or low wages!*, 1990; Appelbaum & Batt, 1993; Grubb, Dickinson, Giordano, & Kaplan, 1992; Hull & Schultz, 1992; and Sarmiento & Kay, 1990.

39. See Lytle, Belzer, & Reumann, 1993, for a discussion of a new framework for staff development in adult literacy education.

# References

*Adult performance level study: Final report.* (1977, March). Austin: University of Texas. (ERIC Document Reproduction Service No. ED 185 113.)

*America's choice: High skills or low wages!* (1990). The Report of the Commission on the Skills of the American Workforce. Rochester, NY: National Center on Education and the Economy.

Añorve, R. L. (1989). Community-based literacy educators: Experts and catalysts for change. In A. Fingeret & P. Jurmo (Eds.), *Participatory Literacy Education.* San Francisco: Jossey-Bass.

Appelbaum, E., & Batt, R. (1993). *Transforming the production system in U. S. firms.* A Report to the Sloan Foundation. Washington, DC: Economic Policy Institute.

Apple, M. W. (1979). *Ideology and curriculum.* London: Routledge & Kegan Paul.

Askov, E. N., Aderman, B., & Hemmelstein, N. (1989). *Upgrading basic skills for the workplace.* University Park, PA: The Institute for the Study of Adult Literacy.

Auerbach, E. (1987). Competency-based ESL: One step forward or two steps back? *TESOL Quarterly, 20,* 411–428.

Auerbach, E. (1990). Toward a transformative model of worker education: A Freirean Perspective. In S. H. London, E. R. Tarr, & J. F. Wilson (Eds.), *The re-education of the American working class.* New York: Greenwood Press.

Auerbach, E., & Wallerstein, N. (1987). *ESL for action: Problem-posing at work,* Reading, MA: Addison-Wesley.

Baba, M. L. (1991). The skill requirements of work activity: An ethnographic perspective. *Anthropology of Work Review, 12*(3), 2–11.

Berger, J. (1989, September 26). Companies step in where the schools fail. *New York Times*, p. A1.

Bizzell, P. (1988). Arguing about literacy. *College English, 50*(2), 141–153.

Bowers, N., & Swain, P. (1992, June). *Education, training and skills.* Paper presented at the meetings of the Western Economic Association, U.S. Bureau of Labor Statistics and U.S. Department of Education.

Brookfield, S. (1986). *Understanding and facilitating adult learning.* San Francisco: Jossey-Bass.

Carnevale, A. P., Gainer, L. J., & Meltzer, A. S. (1988). *Workplace basics: The skills employees want.* Washington, D.C: U. S. Department of Labor and the American Society for Training and Development.

Cochran-Smith, M., & Lytle, S. L. (1990). Research on teaching and teacher research: The issues that divide. *Educational Researcher, 19,* 2–11.

Collins, S. D., Balmuth, M., & Jean, P. (1989). So we can use our own names, and write the laws by which we live: Educating the new U. S. labor force. *Harvard Educational Review, 59*(4), 454–469.

Cook-Gumperz, J. (1986). Literacy and schooling: An unchanging equation? In J. Cook-Gumperz (Ed.), *The social construction of literacy.* Cambridge, England: Cambridge University Press.

Cross, P. (1981). *Adults as learners.* San Francisco: Jossey-Bass.

Darrah, C. N. (1990). *An ethnographic approach to workplace skills.* Unpublished manuscript, San Jose State University, Department of Anthropology and Cybernetic Systems, San Jose, CA.

Darrah, C. N. (1991). *Workplace skills in context.* Unpublished manuscript, San Jose State University, Department of Anthropology and Cybernetic Systems, San Jose, CA.

de Castell, S. & Luke, A. (1986). Models of literacy in North American schools: Social and historical conditions and consequences. In S. de Castell, A. Luke, & K. Egan (Eds.), *Literacy, society, and schooling: A reader* (pp. 87–109). Cambridge, England: Cambridge University Press.

de Castell, S., Luke, A., & MacLennan, D. (1986). On defining literacy. In S. de Castell, A. Luke, & K. Egan (Eds.), *Literacy, society, and schooling: A reader* (pp. 3–14). Cambridge, England: Cambridge University Press.

Diehl, W. & Mikulecky, L. (1980). The nature of reading at work. *Journal of Reading, 24,* 221–227.

Dowling, W. D., Pritz, S. G., DeStefano, J. S., Puleo, N. F., Girkins, M., Collins, J. H., & Connor, P. M. (1992, May). Workplace literacy for world class manufacturing: Final report, the Ohio State University College of Education, and Inland Fisher Guide Division of General Motors and UAW Local 969.

Edelsky, C. (1986). *Writing in a bilingual program: Habia una vez.* Norwood, NJ: Ablex.

Edelsky, C. (1991). *With literacy and justice for all: Rethinking the social in language and education.* London: The Falmer Press.

Edelsky, C., & Draper, , K. (1989). Reading/"reading"; writing/"writing"; text/"text". *Reading-Canada-Lecture, 7,* 201–216.

Eisner, E. W., & Vallance, E. (1974). *Conflicting conceptions of curriculum.* Berkeley, CA: McCutchan Publishing Corp.

Erickson, F. (1982b). Taught cognitive learning in its immediate environment: A neglected topic in the anthropology of education. *Anthropology and Education Quarterly, 13,* 149–180.

Erickson, F. (1984). School literacy, reasoning, and civility: An anthropologist's perspective. *Review of Educational Research, 54*(4), 525–546.

*Federal Register.* (1989, August). *54* (159), p. 34409.

Fingeret, A. H. (1983). Social network: A new perspective on independence and illiterate adults. *Adult Education Quarterly, 33.*

Fingeret, A. H. (1988, November). *The politics of literacy: Choices for the coming decade.* Paper presented to the Literacy Volunteers of America Conference, Albuquerque, NM.

Fingeret, A. H. (1989). The social and historical context of participatory literacy education. In Fingeret, A. and Jurmo, P. (Eds.), *Participatory literacy education.* San Francisco: Jossey-Bass.

Fingeret, A. H., & Jurmo, P. (Eds.). (1989). *Participatory literacy education.* San Francisco: Jossey-Bass.

Freire, P. (1970). *Pedagogy of the oppressed.* New York: Seabury Press.

Freire, P. (1976). Literacy and the possible dream. *Prospects, 6,* 68–71.

Freire, P. (1983). The importance of the act of reading. *Journal of Education* [Special issue]. *Literacy and Ideology, 165*(1), 5–11.

Giroux, H. (1988) Literacy and the pedagogy of voice and political empowerment. *Educational theory, 38*(1), 61–75.

Gorman, C. (1988, December 19). The literacy gap. *Time*, pp. 56–57.

Gowen, S. G.(1990). *"Eyes on a different prize": A critical ethnography of a workplace literacy program.* Unpublished doctoral dissertation, Georgia State University, Atlanta.

Gowen, S. G. (1992) *The politics of workplace literacy: A case study.* New York: Teachers College Press.

Grubb, W. N., Dickinson, T., Giordano, L., & Kaplan, G. (1992).*Betwixt and between: Education, skills, and employment in sub-baccalaureate labor markets.* Berkeley: National Center for Research in Vocational Education, University of California at Berkeley.

Grubb, W. N., Kalman, J., Castellano, M., Brown, C., & Bradby, D. (1991). *Reading', writin', and 'rithmetic one more time: The role of remediation in vocational education and job training programs.* Berkeley: National Center for Research in Vocational Education, University of California at Berkeley.

Gumperz, J. J. (1971). *Language in social groups.* Stanford, CA: Stanford University Press.

Harman, D. (1970). Illiteracy: An overview. *Harvard Educational Review, 40*, 226–243.

Heath, S. B. (1982). Protean shapes in literacy events: Ever shifting oral and literate traditions. In D. Tannen (Ed.), *Spoken and written language: Exploring orality and literacy.* Norwood, NJ: Ablex.

Heath, S. B. (1983). *Ways with words: Language, life, and work in communities and classrooms.* Cambridge, England: Cambridge University Press.

Heath, S. B. (1986). The functions and uses literacy. In S. de Castell, A. Luke, & K. Egan (Eds.), *Literacy, society, and schooling: A reader* (pp. 15–26). Cambridge, England: Cambridge University Press.

Hull, G. (1993) Hearing other voices: A critical assessment of popular views on literacy and work. *Harvard Educational Review, 63*(1), 20–49.

Hull, G., Jury, M., Ziv, O., & Schultz, K. (1994, December). *Changing work, changing literacy? A study of skill requirements and development in a tra-*

*ditional and restructured workplace.* Interim Report Two. National Center for the Study of Writing and Literacy, University of California, Berkeley.

Hull, G., & Schultz, K. (1992). *Changing work, changing literacy? A study of skill requirements and development in a traditional and restructured workplace.* Proposal for the National Center for Research in Writing and Literacy and the National Center for Research in Vocational Education.

Jacobs, E. (1986). Literacy skills and production line work. In K. M. Borman & J. Reisman (Eds.), *Becoming a worker* (pp. 176–200). Norwood, NJ: Ablex.

Jurmo, P. (1989). The case for participatory literacy education. In A. Fingeret & P. Jurmo (Eds.), *Participatory literacy education.* San Francisco: Jossey-Bass.

Jurmo, P. (1991). Understanding lessons learned in employee basic skills efforts in the U.S.: No quick fix. In Taylor, Lew, & Draper (Eds.), *Basic skills for the workplace.* Toronto: Culture Concepts.

Kalman, J., & Fraser, K. L. (1992). Lost opportunities and lessons learned: Inside a workplace literacy program. Berkeley: National Center for Research in Vocational Education, University of California at Berkeley.

Kazemak, F. E. (1988). Necessary changes: Professional involvement in adult literacy programs. *Harvard Educational Review, 58*(4), 464–487.

Kirby, M. (1989). Perspectives on organizing a workplace literacy program, Arlington Education and Employment Program (REEP), Arlington County Public Schools, Arlington, VA.

Knowles, M. S. (1970). *The modern practice of adult education: Androgogy versus pedagogy.* New York: Association Press.

Knowles, M. S. (1979). Androgogy revisited part II. *Adult Education, 30*(1), 52–53.

Kusterer, K. C. (1978). *Know-how on the job: The important working knowledge of "unskilled" workers.* Boulder, CO: Westview Press, Inc.

Kutner, M. A., Sherman, R. Z., Webb, L., & Fisher, C. J. (1991). *A review of the National Workplace Literacy Program.* A report prepared for the U.S. Department of Education, Office of Planning, Budget & Evaluation.

79

Lave, J., & Wenger, E. (1991). *Situated learning: Legitimate peripheral participation.* Cambridge, England: Cambridge University Press.

Lytle, S. L. (1991) Living literacy: Rethinking development in adulthood. *Linguistics and Education, 3*(2), 109–138.

Lytle, S. L., Belzer, A., & Reumann, R. (1993). *Invitations to inquiry: Rethinking staff development in adult literacy education.* Technical Report TR92-2. National Center on Adult Literacy, University of Pennsylvania, Philadelphia.

Lytle, S. L., Belzer, A., Schultz, K., & Vannozzi, M. (1989). Learner-centered assessment: An evolving process. In A. Fingeret & P. Jurmo (Eds.), *Participatory literacy education.* San Francisco: Jossey-Bass, 1989.

Lytle, S. L., & Cochran-Smith, M. (1990). Learning from teacher research: A working typology. *Teachers College Record, 92*(1).

Lytle, S. L., Marmor, T., & Penner, F. (1986). *Literacy theory in practice: Assessing reading and writing of low-literate adults.* Unpublished manuscript, University of Pennsylvania Graduate School of Education, Philadelphia.

Lytle, S. L., & Schultz, K. (1990). Assessing literacy learning with adults: An ideological approach. In R. Beach & S. Hynds (Eds.), *Developing discourse processes in adolescence and adulthood.* Norwood, NJ: Ablex.

Lytle, S. L., & Schultz, K. (1991). Looking and seeing: Constructing literacy learning in adulthood. In S. McCormick, & J. Zutell, (Eds.), *National Reading Conference Yearbook.* Chicago: National Reading Conference.

Lytle, S. L., & Wolfe, M. (1989). *Adult literacy education: Program evaluation and learner assessment.* Columbus, OH: ERIC Clearinghouse on Adult, Career and Vocational Education.

Mezirow, J. (1985). Concept and action in adult education. *Adult Education Quarterly, 35,* 142–151.

Mikulecky, L. (1982). Job literacy: The relationship between school preparation and workplace actuality. *Reading Research Quarterly, 17,* 400–419.

Mishel, L., & Teixeira, R. A. (1991). *The myth of the coming labor shortage: Jobs, skills, and incomes of America's workforce 2000.* Washington, DC: Economic Policy Institute.

National Workplace Literacy Program Abstracts (1993), U. S. Department of Education, Office of Vocational and Adult Education, Division of National Programs, Washington, DC.

Nurss, J. R. (1990). *Hospital Job Skills Enhancement Program: A workplace literacy project*. Final Evaluation Report. U. S. Department of Education Workplace Partnership Program, Center for the Study of Adult Literacy, Georgia State University, and Grady Memorial Hospital, Atlanta.

Philippi, J. (1991). *Literacy at work: The workbook for program developers*. Part IV: Designing Instruction. New York: Simon & Schuster.

Reder, S. M. (1987). Comparative aspects of functional literacy development: Three ethnic communities. In D. Wagner (Ed.), *The future of literacy in a changing world*. Oxford, England: Pergamon Press.

Reder, S. M., & Green, K. R. (1985). *Giving literacy away*. Portland, OR: Northwest Regional Laboratory.

Resnick, L. B. (1990). Literacy in school and out. *Daedalus, 119*(2), 169–185.

Rogoff, B. (1984). Introduction. In B. Rogoff & J. Lave (Eds.), *Everyday cognition: Its development in social context*. Cambridge, MA: Harvard University Press.

Rush, R., Moe, A. & Storlie, R. (1986). *Occupational literacy education*. Newark, DE: International Reading Association.

Salvatori, M., & Hull, G. (1990). Literacy theory and basic writing. In M. G. Moran & M. J. Jacobi (Eds.), *Research in basic writing* (pp. 49–74). Westport, CT: Greenwood Press.

Sarmiento, A. R., & Kay, A. (1990). *Worker-centered learning: A union guide to workplace literacy*. Washington, DC: AFL-CIO Human Resources Development Institute.

Schultz, K. (1991). *Do you want to be in my story? The social nature of writing in an urban third-and fourth-grade classroom*. Unpublished doctoral dissertation. Philadelphia, PA: University of Pennsylvania.

Scribner, S. (1984). Studying working intelligence. In B. Rogoff & J. Lave (Eds.) *Everyday cognition*. Cambridge, MA: Harvard University Press.

Scribner, S. (1985). Knowledge at work. *Anthropology and Education Quarterly, 16*(3), 199–206.

Scribner, S., & Cole, M. (1978). Literacy without schooling: Testing for intellectual effects. *Harvard Educational Review, 48*, 448–461.

Scribner, S., & Cole, M. (1981). Unpackaging Literacy. In M. F. Whiteman (Ed.), *Writing: The nature, development, and teaching of written communication*. Hillsdale, NJ: Lawrence Erlbaum Associates.

Scribner, S., & Sachs, P., with DiBello, L., & Kindred, J. (1991). *Knowledge acquisition at work*. Technical Paper No. 22. The Graduate School and University Center of the City University of New York: Laboratory for Cognitive Studies of Work.

Soifer, R., Irwin, M. E.., Crumrine, B. M., Honzaki, E., Simmons, B. K.., & Young, D. L. (1990). *The complete theory-to-practice handbook of adult literacy: Curriculum design and teaching approaches*. New York: Teachers College Press.

Stein, S. (1991). *Tradition and change: The role of workplace education in the transformation of the workplace*. Presentation to AAACE, Montreal.

Sticht, T. G. & Hickey, D. T. (1987). Technical training for "mid-level" literate adults. In C. Klevenn (Ed.), *Materials and methods in adult and continuing education*. Los Angeles: Klevenn Publishers, Inc.

Sticht, T. G. (1979). Developing literacy and learning strategies in organizational settings. In H. F. O'Neil & C. D. Spielberger (Eds.), *Cognitive and affective learning strategies*. New York: Academic Press.

Sticht, T. G. (1988) Adult Literacy Education. *Review of Research in Education, 15*, 59–96.

Sticht, T. G., Armstrong, W., Hickey, D., & Caylor, J. (1987). *Cast-off youth*. New York: Praeger.

Street, B. V. (1984). *Literacy in theory and practice*. Cambridge, England: Cambridge University Press.

Street, B. V. (1987). Literacy and social change: The significance of social context in the development of literacy programmes. In D. A. Wagner (Ed.), *The future of literacy in a changing world*. Oxford, England: Pergamon Press.

Szwed, J. F. (1981). The ethnography of literacy. In M. F. Whitman (Ed.), *Writing: The nature, development, and teaching of written communication: Vol. 2. Variation in writing: Functional and linguistic-cultural differences*. Hillsdale, NJ: Erlbaum.

Tharp, R. G., & Gallimore, R. (1988). *Rousing minds to life: Teaching, learning, and schooling in social context.* Cambridge, England: Cambridge University Press.

*The bottom line: Basic skills in the workplace.* (1988). Washington, DC: U.S. Department of Education and U.S. Department of Labor.

The Secretary's Commission on Achieving Necessary Skills (SCANS). (1992). *Learning a living: A blueprint for high performance.* Washington, DC: U.S. Department of Labor.

Venezky, R. L., Wagner, D. A., & Ciliberti, B. S. (Eds.). (1990). *Toward defining literacy.* Newark, DE: International Reading Association.

Vygotsky, L. S. (1978). *Mind in society.* Cambridge, MA: Harvard University Press.

Wagner, D. A. (1987). Literacy futures: Five common problems from industrialized and developing countries. In D. A. Wagner (Ed.), *The future of literacy in a changing world.* Oxford, England: Pergamon Press.

Wenger, E. (1991). *Toward a theory of cultural transparency: Elements of a social discourse of the visible and the invisible.* Palo Alto, CA: Institute for Research on Learning.

Willinsky, J. (1990). *The new literacy: Redefining reading and writing in the schools.* New York: Routledge.

*Workplace literacy: Reshaping the American workforce.* (1992, May). U. S. Department of Education, Office of Vocational and Adult Education, Division of Adult Education and Literacy.

Zuboff, S. (1988). *In the age of the smart machine: The future of work and power.* New York: Basic Books.

# THREE

## Pedagogical Innovation in a Workplace Literacy Program: Theory and Practice

*Judy Kalman and Kay M. Losey*

This chapter concentrates on the concerns of teaching and learning in adult education and training. We examine classroom life in a workplace literacy program by looking at the interaction between adult students and their teacher. While there is a long tradition of classroom research in elementary and secondary classrooms, research of this type is virtually nonexistent in adult education. Our focus is primarily pedagogical, on issues of teaching and learning and the difficulties involved in accomplishing pedagogical innovations. We look specifically at one workplace literacy program and its planners' attempts to revise their ideas about teaching and learning as well as their practices. We believe that this program is a particularly relevant example because not only were the planners knowledgeable of the "new orthodoxy" in adult education (Schultz, this volume), they were also aware of some conceptual and practical alternatives to it. Because they were familiar with other approaches to adult education from their own professional experiences, they were very cautious about openly embracing the new orthodoxy as a whole. An important part of their effort was to question some of its proposals and to look for viable alternatives that would promote what they called "a different kind of learning."

84

The program we discuss is a workplace literacy program funded by the U.S. Department of Education. In response to the growing concern in the United States about the literacy level of its work force, the federal government has increased funding to adult education and literacy programs (Schultz, this volume). As a result, educational efforts designed to serve the adult population have proliferated. Despite a lack of explicit direction for creating programs, curricula, and classroom activities, there are several widely accepted approaches that constitute a "new orthodoxy" for teaching adult learners who seek to continue their education in job-related situations (Grubb, Kalman, Castellano et al., 1991; Shultz, 1992; Schultz, this volume).

In order to characterize and discuss what happened in this program and how it might help other teachers and learners, we begin by describing the new orthodoxy and some of its underlying assumptions. We also discuss an alternative approach to teaching and learning and some of its implications for transforming ideas into practice. We continue with a series of typical classroom scenes as a way of portraying how some of the most widely accepted teaching practices in traditional classrooms undermined this program's goal of pedagogical innovation.

While "how-to" manuals promoting the new orthodoxy in workplace literacy programs are in abundance (Carnavale et al., 1990; Harman, 1985; Phillippi, 1991; Taggart, 1986; Sticht, 1990; *The Bottom Line*, 1988), there are practically no in-depth studies of what actually occurs in these programs on a daily basis.[1] Current endeavors point more to the way programs and classes *should be* run and far less attention is paid to how they *are* being run, that is, to who the students in these programs are, what motivates them to enter such courses, how they experience these programs, how they participate in their classes, the effect (if any) that their educational efforts have on their lives on and off the job, what teachers do, what materials they use, how they use them, how they and their students interact, what they believe learning is, and what they consider to be evidence of learning. Instead, for the most part, the actors directly involved in these programs are left standing in the wings.

### Pedagogical Paradigms and Innovating Classroom Practice

Proponents of the new orthodoxy posit that a work-related curriculum is an important element for encouraging workers to improve their skills and for making materials relevant. The study of forms, manuals, instructions, and other printed matter from specific jobs provides the basis for such programs. These programs have become synonymous with "functional context training." Supporters of these programs believe that the immediate on-the-job application of newly acquired skills and the prospect of employment as a result of improved skills will motivate adults to seek literacy and training programs and to stick with them. Furthermore, they argue that job experience serves as a base for learning basic skills and provides a relevant context for developing exercises and drills. Ultimately, the goal of such educational programs is to enhance job performance and improve employment possibilities.

In the end, functional context literacy training is based on the assumption that learning is merely "information processing" (Carnavale et al., 1990; Chisman, 1989; Sticht, 1979). Through highly structured and hierarchical learning objectives (often ordered sequentially from "easy" to "difficult"), repetitive exercises, and individualized programmed learning, students are presented with subskills that they are to master. The implicit assumption of such an approach is that students will automatically reintegrate the predetermined and fragmented course content into a whole process, ability, or skill.

These types of programs are often teacher-centered, that is, the teacher initiates, directs, and monitors daily activities. Learners in such classrooms complete workbook-type exercises and demonstrate mastery of skills by successfully completing standardized tests. The notion of students' "previous experience" is limited to the skills mastered before arriving at the program as measured by standardized placement tests.

In this chapter, we wish to emphasize that the implicit conceptualizations about students, teachers, learning, practices and activities, and achievement found in this new orthodoxy are widespread at all levels of formal education.[2] Many of the learning activities and the assumptions about literacy, teaching, and learning they reflect are not new at all (except a few new features, such as content from specific jobs to teach basic skills and locating classrooms at worksites or simulating workplaces and jobs). On the other hand, practices such as repetitive exercises, the primacy of skills and subskills, and isolated and hierarchically organized content all suggest an approach to education that has been in existence in this country since at least the turn of the century (Cuban, 1993). Smith (1986) has pointed out that students in such programs may gain mastery of individual skills but what they learn is divorced from authentic use, understanding, or purpose. He emphasizes that learning is driven by students' desire to know and accomplished through meaningful engagement with materials and other learners. From his point of view, the teacher's job is to provide the context, experience, and support necessary for learning. Furthermore, educators (Edelsky, 1991; Trueba, 1987) have questioned the appropriateness of skill-driven teaching for ethnic and language minority students, many of whom attend adult education classes. Nevertheless, skill-centered teaching is common to remedial programs and curricula designed for "at risk" populations (Knapp & Turnball, 1990) and for adults or other learners who are often referred to as "disabled," "deficient," "handicapped," "low-ability," and "low-achieving," and who are thought to be "embarrassed" about themselves (Carnavale et al., 1990; Chisman, 1989; Sticht, 1990).[3]

A common variation of this deficit view of students can be found in an objective of many new orthodoxy programs, namely, that students need to "learn to learn." "Learning to learn" is vaguely defined as "learners increasing their awareness of their learning processes and their capacity for reflection" (Carnavale et al., 1990, p. 59). While there is nothing inherently undesirable about students being aware of what they know and what they are learning, the fact that this objective is singled out for this particular population reveals a belief that these adults do not know how to learn, despite their obvious abilities to cope and deal with the demands of everyday life.

In contrast to programs based on the new orthodoxy, an important emergent paradigm in workplace literacy programs places student interests—rather than skills or abilities—in the center of classroom life in an attempt to make learning meaningful. Educators working from this perspective advocate for increased student participation by building curricula (in the case of workplace literacy) related to adults' other potential needs and interests, not just work. They do not see adults in such programs as without skills, but as learners with a broad range of experiences and know-how whose goals are "to extend their knowledge of the world and their abilities to function more effectively in everyday life and work situations" (Soifer et al., 1990, p. 3). From this point of view, the curriculum of programs aimed at adults, including those located at work sites, must be student-centered, focusing on interaction and the exchange of ideas. Students should initiate, direct, and monitor their own learning with guidance from the teacher. From participation in meaningful encounters with others, skills and strategies are improved and competence is increased.[4]

In alternative workplace education programs, learners play a major role in selecting the content of instruction and planning all stages of their education, including what goes on in the classroom (Schultz, 1992). Most programs center on work and how to accomplish it but other topics may also be covered unlike the work-only approach of the new orthodoxy. From this pedagogical perspective, "work" is seen as a basis for reflective learning that "moves back and forth between [in-class] sessions and workplace experiences, the energy for teaching and learning flows continually in both directions: to the workplace for observation and application and from the workplace for description, clarification, judgment, and interpretation" (Simon, Dippo, & Schenke, 1991, p. 13), rather than as just a job or a place where one masters skills. The objective is to allow students to make connections between their own experiences, materials, and real-life situations with an understanding that work does not constitute the whole of an adult's interests or experience (Soifer et al., 1990).

87

Curricular proposals from this perspective posit that situations at work and away from it must be rendered problematic so that participants consider different aspects and solutions to problems and issues. The goal is for students to learn to communicate, to listen and to be listened to. In reading and writing about issues that they deeply care about, they fine tune some skills and acquire others. These activities are seen as the basis for developing critical, creative, and innovative thinkers. This approach does not claim to offer a short-term solution to a long-standing problem. Rather it views adult learning as a developmental process that occurs over time and through interaction with others. It envisions workplace programs as full-blown educational endeavors where intellectual challenge and development drive learning efforts rather than skills improvement or task mastery for a specific job.

These ideas are not easy to put into practice, and, as Cuban (1993) has pointed out, such innovative ideas and practices run counter to the history of teaching in the last century. Only in special circumstances and with special efforts can they be successfully enacted. Teachers who were trained to work in one way but have been convinced through their professional experience that they want to try another often find themselves "teaching against the grain" (Cochran-Smith, 1991; Simon, 1992), isolated from (and by) their co-workers and their supervisors and often overwhelmed by the task of trying to innovate their practice with little or no support from others (Alvine, 1987; Belzer, 1993). Furthermore, "richly developed portrayals of expertise in teaching are rare" (Shulman, 1987, p. 1), so there are few models to follow for teachers trying to transform their practice.[5] Teachers writing about their experiences in the classroom describe how difficult it is to put thoughts and beliefs into action and how sometimes apparently simple decisions in the classroom involve very complex choices (Cochran-Smith & Lytle, 1993; Goswami & Stillman, 1987; Lampert, 1985; Tharp & Gallimore, 1989).

The planners of the program that we studied faced many of the teaching and learning issues described above. As they set up their project, they sought to develop a curriculum that would be relevant and challenging to students in ways similar to student-centered or participatory teaching. At the same time they were concerned with helping their prospective students to develop skills and abilities that would enhance their job opportunities. Finding a way to meet both of these goals became a major issue for the educators involved in this program. The advisor, the program director, and the teacher all agreed to try to create their own approach, but the teacher, Deborah, an experienced adult educator, was left on her own to put these very new and complex ideas into practice. Once the students arrived, she had little support from her colleagues.

Later in this chapter we describe some crucial moments in the classroom in which the teacher, with differing degrees of success, attempted to enact some of these innovations. First, however, we give a brief description of the program.

## The Elmwood Program

In the summer of 1990, the International Brotherhood of Hospital Workers (IBHW) in conjunction with Elmwood Community Colleges[6] submitted a proposal to the U.S. Department of Education for a National Workplace Literacy grant to implement an innovative model for upgrading skills and promoting literacy at the workplace. The proposal targeted several entry-level occupation groups such as ambulance drivers, maintenance workers, nurse's aides, vocational nurses, and cafeteria workers as potential students for this program. Concerned with issues of recruitment and retention in adult education programs, the developers of this grant advocated the inclusion of social support and counseling services for working adults who were seeking to upgrade their skills.[7]

Like workplace literacy programs that follow the new orthodoxy described earlier, "work" was to provide the main content of the program's curriculum and to serve as a context for acquiring and improving skills. However, the planners questioned the narrow definition of work as completing job tasks. Instead they viewed "work" as a complex social setting that included not only accomplishing job assignments, but also relating to other people and dealing with management's demands. In short, they saw it as a situation requiring the use of a wide range of abilities and skills. Rather than a curriculum predetermined by an analysis of job-related reading and writing or mathematical tasks, they envisioned a curriculum shaped by students and the teacher together through dialogue and discussion. Students' interests were to be one of the most important criteria for choosing topics or skills to work on. As the teacher said in a planning session, "If the students want to do math, let's do math."

The program was to be student-centered to the extent that the planners expected students to raise issues, direct the class, and organize classwork. Furthermore, the program called for reflective, critical learning and stated that students should play an active part in their learning. The program staff often referred to this as "a new way of learning," where "what people think, what they feel, what they know can get brought out and put into (. . .) a new form." In this sense they also questioned making skill development (the mastery of individual abilities in a fixed sequence and hierarchy) the center of the curriculum. In the Elmwood program the focus of an activity was to be an issue (for example, "your rights on the job") and development would vary from student to student. Yet at the same time, they planned to teach "generic" skills (such as vocabulary building, memo writing, overviewing, and filling out forms) that they considered to be essential.

The program designers at Elmwood thought that locating the program at the workplace offered several advantages to potential participants, such as no transportation costs, easy access before or after shift changes, and familiarity with others in the class; but, they also had concerns about putting it there. One noted:

> Workplace projects are different than community-based projects. They're also different than community college projects. They're also different from ESL classes. Even though there are workers in all of those other settings, the fact that it is a work-based program makes it very different.(. . .) If we ask people to reveal something about themselves in the class (. . .) they are gonna be concerned about how that goes out into the workplace. So the kinds of things that people may feel free to talk about in a community college class where they're anonymous is very different than in a work-based [program].*

While it was assumed that conducting classes at the workplace would create special tensions for student participation, it was also believed that placing a program there and using work as the basis of the curriculum would guarantee student involvement because the subject matter would be relevant to their interests. The planners believed that learning new skills and procedures that could lead to job promotions would surely motivate students to complete the course. As they saw it, the key to success was to design a program that capitalized on students' shared experience and their knowledge of the workplace in a way that was non-threatening and validating at the same time. The difficult question, of course, was how to transform this idea into curriculum for the classroom.

When the program planners and the teacher discussed ideas for class sessions, they included ideas such as using pay checks to understand percentages and other calculations, creating a news mural or bulletin board for the hospi-

---

* We have edited the oral language of interviews to make reading less difficult. Excerpts of classroom interaction presented in later sections use standard punctuation to indicate tone and the following transcription code.

    / / / / = overlap, interruptions
    (sternly) = narrative and description to help explain dialogue
    [student's name] = researchers' comment added to clarify meaning
    (. . .) = pause; between sections, omitted data
    ((0)) = best guess at what was said

tal community, memo writing, and reading the contract between the employees' union and the hospital. However, not all of their ideas diverged from the traditional thinking found in new orthodoxy programs. For example, one staff member commented that the objective of student learning for the program should involve "being able to take a problem and break it down into a process so it's even more generic (. . .) it's really learning to learn." She defined learning to learn as "rais[ing] learners' consciousness about how they are learning and what they are using what they are learning for." Such an approach reveals underlying assumptions about the perceived cognitive needs of these students that are similar to those found in many new orthodoxy programs.

In summary, the Elmwood program planners sought to develop a program that redefined some long held practices and concepts about teaching, curriculum, and learning. They questioned some of the standard educational practices common to traditional education and "the new orthodoxy" such as the role of work in a workplace program, the focus of the curriculum, the role of students, and the special conditions created by holding class at the workplace. But they left several important and widespread notions about teaching and learning virtually untouched. While they questioned the wisdom of predetermining course content and shaping it in terms of sequenced (and fragmented) skills related to specific job tasks, they accepted making "work" the specific content of the class even if it was a broader view than simply job tasks. Moreover, they had certain beliefs about the workers which led them to conclude that some skills needed to be "broken down" for the class.

In the next section we look at several classroom situations in order to see how the teacher attempted to enact these tenets in the classroom. We focus our attention on the way the teacher interacted with her students and how students interacted with each other in the context of learning activities. We are interested in what this interaction reveals about how the teacher attempted to make pedagogical change a reality and how aspects of two approaches to the teaching of workplace literacy interacted.

## Scenes from the Classroom

Class met for eight weeks on Tuesdays and Thursdays from four to six in the afternoon in one of the seminar rooms located on the twelfth floor of the hospital. Although the hospital management had promised a classroom, a specific room was never assigned. Therefore, the meeting place changed from session to session, causing some confusion. The biggest seminar room had a sweeping view of Elmwood below and on late summer afternoons it was hard not to slip over to the window and take a look. Management provided refreshments for the first class, and the students, teacher and project staff took turns bringing in snacks for the rest of the sessions.

Deborah, the teacher, had planned several activities for the course, centered on writing and revising a memo (five classes), overviewing written texts (three classes), and medical terminology (two classes). In all of these activities she used the same methods. She consistently used reading aloud, paraphrasing ("say it in your own words"), defining words, and examining graphic display (e.g., use of bullets, italics, indentation, position of subtitles) as procedures for reading new material. To her, successful use of these subskills was evidence of learning. Isolating, defining, pronouncing, and breaking down words were tasks used for working with both oral and written language, and they constituted the most frequent activities in which the teacher and students engaged (80% of classes). One complete lesson was dedicated to teaching a procedure for reading in a group, which was described on a class handout as follows: "(1) Reader reads sentence 1; (2) Discuss unfamiliar words in a sentence; (3) Have the reader paraphrase the sentence he just said." Likewise, writing in class followed a clear format, whether it was filling out questionnaires, forms (registration form and writing folder form), or worksheets. While all of these activities included oral language, teacher-student talk was *not* used to promote active learning, although that had been one of the goals of the program. Rather, students were restricted to verbalizing written texts, giving short answers to teacher questions, and reading aloud handouts.

On the following pages we examine teacher-student and student-student talk which, although restricted by the structure of interaction imposed by the teacher, nevertheless constituted the most important activities in the class. Talk was used in all classroom situations for discussions, for "direct instruction," for organizational purposes, for group work, for support, and for personal interaction. Following the methodological suggestions of Hymes (1974), we center our attention on how social relationships in the class are enacted through talk: who talks, which topics are validated and talked about (and which ones are not), who chooses the topics, and who decides classroom procedure. Answers to these questions provide important evidence for understanding classroom practices.

Each of the three classroom situations we present is typical of the interaction that occurred in the classroom. To understand the range of interaction and participation in the classroom and to understand how different variables influenced student participation, we look at each situation in terms of three aspects of the classroom situation: (1) who initiated the topic, that is, who had the idea for the activity (teacher or student); (2) who initially directed the interaction, or who decided the procedures for the activity; and (3) who monitored the interaction, or who made decisions once the activity had begun.

We also consider the materials presented to the students, their origin, and how activities were planned and executed around them. In conducting this analysis, our goal is to discover the outcome of pedagogical planning that was based on two different and contradicting paradigms. The sequence of examples begins with a class where the teacher controls most of the interaction and is followed by classes where the students progressively contribute more and more to what goes on in the classroom.

### Memo Writing: A Teacher-Initiated,-Directed, and-Monitored Activity

The program planners decided in a curriculum meeting several weeks prior to the starting date that both reading and writing memos were important abilities for workers to have. Memo writing was announced as part of the course content on the flyer that was distributed among workers at the hospital and was also one of the writing skills listed on a questionnaire handed out to students in the third session to determine their educational interests.

The second of five classes devoted to memo writing began, as usual, by asking students if they had applied anything from the previous classes on the job. One of the students mentioned that a handout on health and safety had been a topic of conversation among several workers. This comment led to a more general discussion about health and safety issues. Deborah, the teacher, made the transition from the general discussion to her plans for the day by saying, "What I'd like to do today is start with some writing [by] taking advantage of this conversation. I've heard details and proposals (writes "details" and "proposals" on big pad in front of class). What were some of the details?" As students responded, the teacher wrote some of their words and phrases on the board. When they finished, the teacher had compiled a long list of problems (fumes, ventilation, noise, possibility of explosion, feeling short of breath, etc.) and possible solutions (masks, respirators, training, extra pay).

The teacher initiated a discussion about memos, including to whom students might address them, what information they might gather to include in a memo, and how they might obtain that information. She asked the students if there were any other topics that concerned them. Marie, a medical assistant in oncology, mentioned the budget debate in the state assembly and Lois, a single mother working part-time, started to bring up a medical issue, but the teacher instructed them to stick to health and safety issues and reintroduced the problem of vacuum cleaners and shampooers that gave workers electrical shocks. In the following exchange, note the way the teacher tightly controlled each step of the memo-writing procedure. This approach is of particular relevance to our discussion, as is her response to several important questions that students have about format and procedures.

Teacher: Let's stick to health and safety. People mentioned buffers and vacuum cleaners and shampooers giving electrical shocks. Each of you can write about something and share it and get information about this. Let me make a suggestion before you write. What I think makes sense to do is write a memo. But a long one, like a report. At the top of the page write the date. Then write "To" and if you know who you want to write to, put it there. You don't have to.

Lois: To Schafer [a personnel manager], I'm gonna send it.

Teacher: Could be union, management, *Evening Herald-Times*, whoever. (*Teacher walks around and looks at each student's paper.*)

Cathy: On top line or drop a line?

Teacher: It's just a draft. You can make those decisions later.

Yolanda: I need to write about San-I-Pac [the medical waste incinerator].

Teacher: Just wait now. OK now. Write RE: What's that?

Students: Regarding

Teacher: What's that? (*no response from students*) What was on the worksheet last time that tells you? (*no response*) What word in the reading?

Students: Notice? Regarding?

Teacher: No, no.

Marie: Topic?

Teacher: Yeah, that's what a topic is asking you for. What's your topic? (*As students say their topics, the teacher nods and repeats them.*) Incinerator, Health, Radiation, Respiration.

Students began to write about one hour into the two-hour class meeting. After twenty minutes, the teacher called out to them:

Teacher: Notice the writing process we're using.

Lois: Should I sign my name at the bottom?

Teacher: Well . . .

Marie: No, it's not going any place.

(*Connie points to the top where it says "From:" on Lois' page; Lois understands that she doesn't have to sign the memo.*)

Lois: Oh yeah.

Teacher: The reason is that your name is on top.

Cathy: Do I need to say "Sincerely"?

Teacher: No! Already there. Could you set your last thoughts down? I always hate to interrupt people when they are on a roll. Think about this: Notice what we've been doing as part of the writing process. What did we start doing?

Students: Talking?

Teacher: And as we were talking?

Students: Listening.

Teacher: More than listening . . .

Students: Writing . . .

Teacher: Writing what? What about?

Students: Notes.

Teacher: Some people call that jotting down ideas. Then a rough draft. What next?

Cathy: Review.

Teacher: Not quite yet.

Lois: Discuss it, talk about it.

Teacher: [We're going to] get the reactions to what you wrote. Share and respond. That's to get more detail. Learn from others. Give ideas. It's interesting to get and give. And, *then* revise and rewriting.

Program planners set out to allow students a voice in what they wanted to learn, but this example illustrates how their pedagogical approach undermined this goal. Most obviously, the planners, not the students decided memo writing was an appropriate activity. Moreover, the excerpt shows interactive sequences where several specific student requests concerning memo writing were either downplayed or ignored by the teacher. First, students were not allowed to write on topics of immediate interest other than those about health and safety. Then students' specific questions about the memo format (where to begin and if they should sign their memos) were minimized when the teacher did not answer or told them just to write it for the moment, it's only a draft.

Perhaps the teacher did not answer the students' questions because she was trying to avoid focusing on subskills and wanted students to think of the larger task at hand. But the best way to teach and learn such skills is in the context of situated activity, when students felt a need and desire to learn them. Moreover, the teacher did not hesitate to focus on other subskills, such as where to put the date on the memo.

The teacher attempted to contextualize the memo writing activity by linking it to an ongoing discussion about problems at work and eliciting student comments. She put student language (word choices and phrases) on the big pad in front of the class, thus using and validating student knowledge. However, in terms of the larger goal of contextualizing skill learning (or improvement) by embedding it in authentic communicative use, the memo was still only an exercise. The memo writing activity was divorced from the communicative use of memos, so while in theory it may be a form of written communication common at the students' workplace, it was not clear if it was one they encountered often or if they were ever in the position of sending memos. Also, students were well aware that the memos would not be sent, as evidenced both by Lois' memo with the phone number "976-Take-a-Walk" and Marie's comment regarding signing: "It's not going any place." But they nevertheless recognized the communicative purpose of memos. When questions were posed concerning whether or not to sign the memos, the teacher interpreted the question in formal terms while Marie answered in terms of its communicative purpose.

The teacher's view of memo writing included questions of form such as who to address it to and what type of specific information to include. However she ignored other important social and communicative issues (Kalman, in press) such as what the consequences of sending a memo such as this one might be, how a worker's position could be strengthened or jeopardized, who would be the most sympathetic recipient of such a memo (in terms of personal and institutional histories), whether memos that are critical of policies and practices should be individual endeavors or collective efforts, what role the union might play be if such a document were sent, and so on.

The teacher also called the students' attention to the writing process as a way of making student learning visible, but through her interaction with the students, she turned the consciousness-raising activity into a guessing game (Kalman & Fraser, 1992). She did not allow the participants to describe their own experiences. Instead, she had set answers to her questions about the writing process, rejecting all other responses even when they were synonymous with her preferred responses. Unlike the teacher, students Marie and Connie took the questions of their classmates seriously and attempted to answer them when the teacher would not. But because the teacher was monitoring the interaction, they had few opportunities to fully explain to their peers what they knew about memo writing. Student participation was stunted by her questioning. The one-word staccato answers illustrate this.

While this class work was oral, it was not truly a dialogue or a discussion. The teacher and students were not learning by listening and interacting with one another, nor were they sharing experiences, raising questions about facts or opinions presented in class, or constructing new interpretations of familiar ideas (Soifer et al., 1990). Students were looking for right answers to teacher questions. Rather than promoting student participation, this interactive structure was a vehicle for the teacher to assume authority in the classroom. She initiated, directed, and monitored the interaction and the organization of the activities. In this sense the teacher—her content and her procedures— were the center of the curriculum, not the students. In such an interactional framework, it is very difficult for students to break into the interaction and for teachers to break out of it (Losey, in press).

## Overviewing: A Teacher-Initiated, Teacher-Directed, Student-Monitored Activity

On several different occasions the teacher selected work-related reading materials and developed worksheets based on them to teach what she called "overviewing" or "looking at the shape" of texts before reading them in detail. In her words, the logic of this activity was to "combine reading and writing as skills and thinking with some content from the job."

After a class discussion on health and safety, the teacher handed out a short reading assignment and a worksheet for students to complete in class. As she distributed the assignment, she suggested a similarity between the worksheet and forms they might fill out on the job. She told students that doing worksheets would help them learn to fill out forms better and asked students to work together to find the worksheet answers. The class organized into pairs, students choosing their partners. In the next sequence, notice how the students discuss each item on the worksheet and how they support each other. Their non-linear procedures for completing the assignment are in contrast to the teacher-monitored activity in the previous section.

Wilma and Consuelo worked through the worksheet together (see Appendix B). When they reached number ten, "Does a hazard affect you?," Wilma commented, "If it's a hazard, it affects all of us." Their interaction continued:

Consuelo: (*reading from her paper*) Infections, exposed to diseases. It can be transmitted by skin punctures, by bacteria and virus . . .
Wilma: And blood.
Consuelo: Look (*reads from handout*) and fungi.
(*They move on to another question.*)
Wilma: Infectious linen.
Consuelo: Did you put page?
Wilma: Uh-huh. Twenty-one.
Consuelo: Now what do we put here?
Wilma: Stress and burnout. Every time you put it [bedding], roll it or it's airborne.
Lois: (*listening in from other side of table*) You're right.
Wilma: Ain't been on beds a long time, but I know that it's airborne. All this is yes [i.e., Does a hazard affect you?].

Although this activity was structured by the teacher's worksheet, the students monitored the activity themselves, working collaboratively on several questions simultaneously, rather than following the given order of the questions. They used a variety of resources—each other's experience, the written text, and previous answers—to answer the worksheet questions. When they turned to their own experiences, the curriculum became student-centered: Their language became expressive, self-presenting, and self-revealing (Britton, 1969/1990).

For example, when they got to question number ten in the exercise ("Does a hazard affect you?"), Wilma first defined "hazard" in a personal context ("If it's a hazard, it affects all of us"), to make her understanding of the question precise. Wilma then added "blood" from her own experience, and Consuelo, reading from the handout, added "fungi." Wilma relied on her own experience as a housekeeper at the hospital to include "airborne" diseases and "infectious linen." Consuelo agreed. Wilma then returned to the question of whether hazards affect them, and she answered it "Yes," a conclusion reached with knowledge gained from the handout and her own experience as a worker. Their participation was much more extended than the teacher-monitored activity of the previous section, although it was still constrained by the worksheet. Students taught and learned from each other as they combined their experiences into written responses to the worksheet, using information from the text and help from each other.

The teacher's purpose for using the worksheet was very different than that of the students. Her objective was to teach two skills: filling out forms and scanning a text. For her the point of this activity was not reading the text and understanding its content but filling out the form and learning to "overview." In an interview she explained:

> I wanted to teach overviewing. I wanted to get people not to sit down and read something real closely because I think they're accustomed to doing that rather than noticing the shape of something and then going back and reading something closely. And that's what I used it for.

But the students had a different understanding of reading and how it should be taught, which was clearly revealed in a different teacher-directed reading activity.

Students repeatedly asked to read the contract between the employees' union and the hospital after the teacher suggested it as a possibility in the first class meeting. The activity was postponed several times so that in the end only one session was allotted to reading the contract. On the day of the lesson, the students asked to carefully read a section of the contract together. But the teacher had prepared a worksheet that she wanted them to complete in pairs. She opened the lesson by announcing that the students needed to help decide if the class should "overview" the whole contract or read an article of the contract closely. Marie suggested that students look over the whole contract quickly, but spend most of their time doing a close reading of some part of it. Other students supported her suggestion. The teacher responded, "I really want you to use the worksheet." Another student, Yolanda, asked that students be allowed to work as a whole class, arguing that the group was very small and that it was better to discuss the contract together so that in the end they would "all know the same." But the teacher was adamant about working in pairs and doing the worksheet. She ended the discussion by asking people to choose partners. During an interview, Marie looked back on that day and commented:

> She [the teacher] gave us a choice but it was really like what she wanted us to do. It wasn't really a choice. She had two things up there, but then when Yolanda said well (. . .) since it's so few of us, can't we all (. . .) do something together and that way (. . .) you get more involved in it. We never did go into one specific thing; we just did the table of contents, the index, and these questions that she had. And I think that it helped, but I think that it would have been more beneficial to get one person's problem which would have helped all of us because if you can solve one person's problem then the solution to that problem helps somebody else maybe solve their problem.

The students' requests in class and Marie's comments reveal an understanding of reading that is driven by an authentic need or interest. Marie wanted to explore real problems and research real solutions. The students also indicated that they perceived reading as something that should be done collaboratively, something mutually engaged in and mutually benefited from. Furthermore, Marie's comments indicate that the students were aware that the teacher was not really allowing for student participation, although she paid lip service to it.

The teacher had difficulty combining student participation and decision-making with her notions about the skills students needed to acquire and how they should be taught. She realized that students had had a difficult time filling out the registration form for the class, and she also knew students were interested in learning how to complete job applications. She believed that her worksheets would help students with job applications. In fact, she saw a direct relationship between the worksheets that she prepared and all other forms. In an interview she explained, "The worksheet is a form that has text on it and has blanks and it asks questions and asks for information." Although filling out a form depends a great deal on its purpose, the type of information that it requires, and the status and relationship of the applicant to the institution and recipient of the form, the teacher believed that if students could fill out an overviewing worksheet, they could fill out a job application. This assumption was never made explicit to the students, however.

In the examples of overviewing activities that are teacher-directed but student-monitored, we see again how the teacher's desire to control not only *what* students learn but also *how* students learn conflicts with the program's plan for a less teacher-centered classroom. However, we also get a glimpse of what a class might look like when students are allowed to monitor themselves and work collaboratively on a worksheet. In the next section, we provide an example of a student-directed, student-monitored activity in which students garnered greater control over their learning, despite the teacher's attempt to maintain control.

### Response Groups: A Teacher-Initiated, Student-Directed, Student-Monitored Activity

As a way of creating opportunities for students to learn from each other, Deborah, the teacher, organized the class into response groups to help them get feedback for revising their memos. This activity is compatible with many of the premises of participatory classrooms in that it gives authority to the students to criticize and revise their own work, it takes advantage of student knowledge, it encourages student-student interaction, and it allows students to use their knowledge and skills in an authentic context. It is also in keeping with current practice in the teaching of writing which acknowledges that writing is a collaborative activity and deems response an important step prior to revision.

In the revision groups created by the teacher to further develop the memo assignment, students followed the teacher's initiative, but because of the nature of the activity, they were able to combine their own experiences and purposes with the teacher's. They were given guidelines for what a memo should contain (introduction, description of the problem, solution, and conclusion) as well as instructions for revising their memo. They were to answer the following questions about the memos in their revision groups: "(1) What was strong and clear about the writing? (2) What could be expanded, added, clarified?"

The group revision activities spanned two class sessions. In the second session, the teacher worked with one group of students while the other was left on its own. In the group without the teacher, Lois read her memo:

Date: 7-16-91
To: Jim Harris
From: Lois Weston
Re: Aids patient

1. Aids patient suffers harshly every day. The aids disease has become one of the world number one subjects. So far researchers has found no cure fo this deadly disease. While reasearchers or working very hard for answers and cures.

2. We will have to lern to work around our aidss patients. Accept our aids patients. Keep our aids patient. We keep our aids patient room clearn. They also notices cleaniliness ispite of tghere severe illness. Always clean room with germicide.

3. We also can use clorox but it could coause nausea, By the fume it carries. Its such a terrible disease. We have to be careful about the germ.

I feel when a aids patient has been discharge from there room, the rouum should be clean with germicide and windows ans well. And *new* curtains surrounding the bed bereplaced couse of illness that it surround.

The new patient should not have to use the same soiled (dirty) curtains.

Lois' memo could use improvement in several areas, from grammar, spelling, and punctuation to differing levels of commentary (AIDS as a world health problem to hospital hygiene). However, the format is correct. Her difficulty seems to lie in developing in writing the general ideas that she has about AIDS and connecting them to the reality of the hospital where she works. In the following dialogue, note how Lois' revising group helps her verbalize her many ideas and search for connections.

Lois: What I'm talking about is AIDS patients and that no cure like Tylenol or aspirin, taking aspirin, doesn't [make it] go away, can't say [there are any] drugs created that will cure AIDS. Number two will say I know who is here. (*Lois then explained that the curtain pulled around patients was rarely laundered and often soiled with blood, stool, etc. She proposed that it get changed between patients or regularly washed.*)

Marie: They ain't never gonna do that. What exactly is your point? Exposure to other patients? Acknowledging patient needs?

Lois: Our attention. Seein' their rights, not to deny their rights to our services.

Marie: (*starts to read from the teacher's list on the chalkboard*) What was strong and clear about the writing? What could be expanded, added, clarified? What //could you//

Lois: // Teacher's// way over there. Did you get all "A's? When I'm in the corner, I'm over here. You're so picky.

Up to this point in their conversation, Marie has allowed Lois to list her first two main ideas (how serious the disease is in general and how poor the care and hygiene of patients at Elmwood is) and has provided her with several possible central points for her memo. As long as the conversation seemed spontaneous, Lois interacted competently with Marie. However, when Marie returned to the teacher's questions, Lois (not so gently) rejected the teacher's topic ("When I'm in the corner, I'm over here") and called Marie "picky" for her use of the teacher's language. Lois did not reject other questions from Marie, however, that helped her see what could be "expanded, added, clarified" in her essay.

Marie: How often do they change those curtains?

Lois: They paint more often than they change them. Every patient is entitled to depend on us. They are in our hands. We're their loved ones.

Marie: Is there a checklist? I'm asking for myself.

Lois: It says spot clean curtains.

Marie: Oooo! (displeased)

Lois: Gross, huh. Any patient with respiratory or AIDS problems, chicken pox or any kind of these germs (*cough*). We're backed by a "quarter person" [someone who does halls], spend more time on halls than people.

Marie: How often do they change those drapes?

Lois: I've been here since 1989 [three years], as of now, none. Clorox is supposed to be "off" [no longer used] at hospitals. Not used as often, but it's a good cleaner for part of substances that I'm talking about, although we do have germicides.

Marie: Solution (*referring to memo*) would be to change curtains. Are they washable?

Lois: It's inexcusable. So my subject is AIDS and my conclusion was cleanliness of curtain.

One difference between exchanges guided by the teacher and the student interaction here is the amount of talking that students were allowed to do. In teacher-controlled situations, students often gave one word or short answers. Their participation was restricted by the teacher's questions and purposes. Once in a group without a teacher, students were able to determine which topics were valid and how they would relate to each other. In this exchange, the students directed and monitored their own interaction. They accepted and rejected topics ("Teacher's way over there. Did you get all "A's? When I'm in the corner, I'm over here. You're so picky"), asked each other questions ("How often do they change those drapes?"), made suggestions ("Solution would be . . . "), and drew conclusions ("It's inexcusable").

Through their interaction, they subverted the teacher's attempt to direct them with her handout of specific questions ("What was strong and clear about the writing? What could be expanded, added and clarified?").

Nevertheless, they gave each other feedback that would help them to revise their essays. They remained very much on task while at the same time contextualizing that task in their own experiences. As a result, the opportunities for learning were broadened. Marie learned from Lois about the curtains, their lack of cleanliness, and the hospital rules regarding cleaning them. And Marie helped Lois learn how she could revise her memo. Marie first tried to help her state what she meant with greater precision by asking, "What exactly is your point?" Lois restated her concern that patients receive appropriate care ("Seeing their rights, not to deny their rights to our services"). Marie then reintroduced the teacher's agenda by reading the directions and restating what the teacher said.

Unlike her experiences in other classroom situations, in this context Lois had the opportunity to use knowledge of her job by describing the standard of cleanliness, telling what the official checklist required, and displaying knowledge of the written materials associated with her job. She also described the source of the "germs" on the curtains, naming what she considered to be serious and contagious illnesses ("Respiratory or AIDS problems or chicken pox").

And Lois' topics were validated by her classmate. Time and again she was given the opportunity to verbalize what she knew, to describe what she believed was a major health problem, and to voice opinions about what she thought might be solutions ("I've been here since 1989, as of now, none. Clorox is supposed to be 'off' at hospitals. Not used as often, but it's a good cleaner for part of substances that I'm talking about, although we do have germicides"). The suggestions for improvement that Marie offered to Lois were given in the context of the discussion about the curtains. Lois participated competently throughout this exchange. Yet when she tried to use the staccato language of "answers" ("So my subject is AIDS and my conclusion was cleanliness of curtain"), the wealth of knowledge already displayed seemed lost.

Clearly, one revising group activity will not perfect Lois' writing. Her memo reveals several domains that need improvement. However, learning to write requires learning to produce language in certain ways. For that ability to develop, multiple and varied opportunities for language use are necessary. Discussing and exchanging ideas about what might be written, what kinds of details to include, how to order ideas, how to express and connect thoughts is invaluable for students learning to write. Moreover, such a critical examination of experience and ideas is crucial for promoting any learning experience.

The teacher, however, did not recognize the quality of teaching and learning that occurred in Lois and Marie's group. She commented in an interview:

The response group (. . .) I think that the other one [without the teacher] was not as successful. Lois is the only person from the other group who wrote a revision

(. . .) so it's possible that it didn't work. The need for a teacher or more instruction on how to do sharing with something like that is important.

Other factors that might have affected students' decisions not to revise, however, included the fact that no class time was given for writing revisions and, as mentioned earlier, no real audience—and therefore no real purpose—for the memo or its revision existed.

Throughout the course students were given very few opportunities to control class activities. Usually Deborah, the teacher, initiated, directed, and monitored all activities in class. Sometimes, if she initiated and directed, she would allow students to monitor. In this last example, we showed the class at its most participatory. We saw students teaching and learning about their jobs and about literacy as they were allowed to monitor the activity as well as usurp the teacher's attempts to direct it. Although they had not initiated memo writing or response groups, they were working collaboratively on topics they had selected, under the general theme of health and safety. We find the difference in the quality of student interaction impressive. But we also see a teacher that feels disappointed in the outcome of that participation and assumes that it is because there was a lack of a teacher or a lack of instruction—a lack of one sort of control or another.

## Discussion and Conclusions: Curious Combinations

The teacher's pedagogy included a curious combination of several practices from both student-centered and new orthodoxy (or traditional) paradigms. She also adapted job-related materials for teaching skills such as overviewing, memo writing, and filling out forms. She separated the skills she taught from their context of use, presenting them to students as generic, for instance, memos do not have to be signed, initialed, or addressed to anyone in particular, and reading long documents requires skimming and scanning first regardless of the reader's purpose. She presented a lock-step, one-skill-before-the-next approach in her interactions with the students, in her organization of activities, and in the materials that she prepared.

In instructional situations in which the teacher interacted directly with students, she retained control and authority, determining to what degree and under what circumstances students should participate in activities, how students should be grouped, what skills were the most appropriate ones for students to learn and what instructional tools were most effective—all activities indicative of a traditional approach to teaching (Cuban, 1993). At times, she implemented planned activities based on what she considered to be important and relevant (for example, overviewing), regardless of explicit student wishes to the contrary.

Overall, the teacher directed classroom time. While she allowed for some variation, she did not promote it. For example, although she allowed student-student interaction around worksheets and in response groups, she tried to direct and monitor their interactions with detailed oral and written instructions. The balance of her teaching methods tipped heavily towards traditional and new orthodoxy practices.

Why do teachers cling to certain practices even when they specifically intend to implement others? Deborah was a seasoned teacher with advanced degrees. She was a faculty member at the local community college teaching in renowned programs for adult students returning to school. She adhered, at least in theory, to notions of more student-centered, participatory classrooms and recognized the importance of student participation. Yet, in practice, she did not fully explore what "a new kind of learning" might be. She believed that the worksheets, surveys, overviewing, and planned lessons responded to student needs. She failed to pick up on important student cues—what they wanted to learn, how they wanted to read the contract, when they wanted to work together—that would have allowed them to participate and learn in a different way.

Part of the answer to this question is related to notions of "good teaching," notions that are tied directly to the teacher's authority in the classroom. The teacher is responsible for maintaining order and has the institutional power to do so. Cuban (1993) points out that "maintaining class control, an essential exercise in authority, is a fundamental condition for instruction to occur" (p. 257). Many of the actions of control are subtle, nearly hidden in the teacher's job: calling roll, assigning seats, grouping students, making assignments. Others are part of the teacher's interactive relationship with the students: praising correct answers, deciding on topics of discussion, selecting or ignoring student participation, calling on students to read aloud.

While the program espoused student-centered classroom practices, Deborah's colleagues' declarations were not enough to see her through the enactment of their ideas. Teachers trying to generate a different kind of teaching often "have more questions than answers" (Alvine, 1987, p. 108). Deborah revealed in her interviews that she had many questions about what to do in the classroom. She wondered how to connect some of the lively discussions about work at the beginning of class with the skills she wanted to teach, about when to insist on following a lesson plan and when to let go. She pondered how much follow-up an activity needed or should have, and how many times a memo could be written. She was uncertain about what were the best ways to proceed and, when in doubt, she turned to what was most familiar—a traditional approach. She looked for and found new materials to work

105

with, but her activities consisted of traditional questionnaires and worksheets. The question of how to build on student interests and concerns to teach specific subject matter is a difficult one for any teacher to resolve, even in the best of circumstances (Grimmet & MacKinnon, 1992). In those situations in which she took a risk and tried something new, such as revising groups, she expressed doubts about the outcome.

Deborah received very little support for making innovations in practice. She was left alone to sort out the general idea of a "new way of learning" and translate it into practice. The program director, who had a better understanding of student-centered practice, was virtually unavailable to her during the eight weeks of the course because he was absorbed in writing a new grant proposal, became ill, then took a two-week vacation. Without concrete participatory activities well-thought out in advance and without a support person who is familiar and experienced with such an alternative approach, it is understandable that a teacher might "default" to traditional methods with which she feels more comfortable. For Deborah to change her approach to teaching, she had to be able to resolve the tensions caused by new theoretical ideas and the complexity of classroom practice (Smylie, 1994). In her efforts to do just that, Deborah created a "hybrid" classroom, rooted in traditional approaches with a few new activities or superficial modifications added on to her teaching (Cuban, 1993). In the words of Bishop (1990), she used a *Something Old, Something New* approach in her teaching.

Students, too, sometimes worked against teacher change. They felt familiar with a traditional approach that they remembered from their earlier schooling experiences. They came into the classroom wanting and expecting to be taken seriously, and some saw letting students initiate topics as playing games and not taking their education seriously. Some complained that discussions about work were a waste of time and had nothing to do with the type of education they expected to receive.

One of the challenges to developing a different approach to teaching is to distribute authority in teacher-student relationships. While a well-managed classroom is essential to a supportive learning environment, there are several domains where the responsibility can be shared. How time is used, how students are grouped, what resources are used, what content to cover, and so on are all aspects that can be negotiated and where students can make a contribution. Deborah's interactive pattern was deeply ingrained in her relationship with the students. She thought discussions were important but often monitored them carefully around her chosen content. She advocated for student participation, but she sometimes insisted that they do what she had planned for them the way that she had planned it. She posed questions for the students to respond to, but only acknowledged the answers she was waiting for.

In an analysis of changes in classroom practice in U.S. schools during the years of 1890–1980, Cuban found few teachers made substantial, long-lasting changes because such changes involve much additional planning and hours of extra work to produce materials, think of new approaches, and imagine new ways to teach. Deborah may have run into similar problems because of a series of glitches in the project start-up. Due to last-minute problems organizing all of the parties (hospital, union, community college), planning time for the curriculum, and more so for its implementation in activities and pedagogical procedures, was extremely limited. In addition, in an attempt to be participatory, the teacher held off on finalizing her plans until after the course had begun so that she could get student input on the course content. This gave her very little time to think of innovations.

Cuban (1993) also describes several cases where teachers made deep and lasting changes in their teaching, and he poses the important question why these teachers transformed their classrooms. His answer is indeed thought provoking: He attributes the change in their teaching to a transformation of their beliefs about learning and education, which drove a desire to explore and devise new ways of teaching and learning. Similarly, Bishop (1990) found teacher beliefs the essential difference in college writing teachers who made lasting changes in their teaching methods. She calls those who make these changes "the converted" (p. 143).

To the extent that Deborah's preferred teaching practices were mostly those of the new orthodoxy, which in many ways reflect traditional teaching methods, they reflect a certain way of thinking about adult students and how they must be taught. Those ways of thinking can be best seen in the quotations we provided earlier in the chapter to describe the beliefs of proponents of the new orthodoxy. They find adult students "disabled," "deficient," and "handicapped" (Carnavale et al., 1990; Chisman, 1989; Sticht, 1990). When Deborah taught she sent the message that she considered her students unable to learn without her direct control of the situation. This message was doubly loud, since in planning she had indicated a desire to use an alternative, participatory approach. In the end, it appears that she did not believe (Cuban, 1984; Grimmet & McKinnon, 1992) that her students could benefit from a student-centered participatory approach. Because she was left to her own resources to reinvent her teaching, Deborah had few opportunities to reflect on her teaching in such a way that it was belief changing or practice transforming, beyond only a few superficial features (Grimmett & MacKinnon, 1992).

From Deborah's experience we can extrapolate an understanding of the kind of situation that might make teacher change in a workplace literacy program more likely to occur. First, the teacher must believe that the change is educationally sound and will benefit the students. Secondly, an adequate amount of time for preparation and sufficient support from those who have already changed is necessary. Also, students need to be sold on the approach as well. It must not appear that the teachers are flakey and unprepared when they ask for student input. Lastly, teachers must be willing to give up some control.[8] To the extent that Deborah did not question her notions of learning, her views about literacy, her beliefs about the students, or her role as a teacher, the only changes that she could make were purely ornamental.

The program Deborah taught in is typical of projects that have resulted from the increased interest in and availability of funding for adult literacy education. The IBHW program was anything but improvised: It had a grant, a program director, a consultant, a teacher, support from both the union and management, and an educational model. What seemed to be missing from this orchestrated effort was the realization that what goes on between teachers and students is essential to learning.

Deborah *was* able to innovate in her teaching in minute ways. While the changes she made could be the basis for future innovations, it is unlikely that she could accomplish further development without additional support. The availability of financial resources is critical for improving education, but money alone will not change teacher beliefs. If we desire more than cosmetic improvements in our classrooms, teaching and learning must be redefined, teacher training improved, institutional support provided, and guidance in curriculum development made available.

## Appendix A. Research Methodology, Data Collection, and Analysis

We became involved with the International Brotherhood of Hospital Workers' (IBHW) program as the project evaluators. Our participation resulted from the direct invitation of the program director, and we were assured full access to all participants as well as to his personal notes and a journal that he agreed to keep for the purpose of evaluation. The data reported has been selected from information collected during our seven-month relationship with the program that covered the start-up period, the summer pilot program, and the two months that followed. While the program continued for another nine months, we did not follow it through to completion due to circumstances discussed later in this section.

At the onset of the program, our efforts began without the hostility that often characterizes evaluation situations, and initially our dealings with the program director were completely cooperative. He endorsed our intentions to study the implementation of the program model from the perspective of those involved and saw our collaboration as a valuable resource that could inform their efforts to create an innovative workplace program. We—the evaluators and the program director—believed that the purpose of the evaluation would be both formative as well as summative. Through a careful and detailed accounting of the program's progress, a coherent internally valid understanding of how and why events occurred as they did could be reached and could aid the program staff in improving its implementation as they went along. In the end, we would also have a detailed history of the program rather than isolated statistics without explanation, as found in most program evaluations. Such a detailed evaluation would allow us to discuss cogently the project's successes and determine with precision those areas where improvement might be needed.

We viewed the evaluation as an unfolding process where all participants' views—student, staff, and partners alike—were equally important for determining its achievements and difficulties. We believed that in order to evaluate this program, it would be necessary to document its development as it progressed. We should stress that all of the names of individuals, places, and organizations used in this paper are pseudonyms. The following is a list of the methods that we used:

- Participant observation and field notes of classes: because taping was not allowed, two observers were present in fourteen out of sixteen classes. The remaining two class sessions were observed by one researcher only.
- Participant observation, field notes, and audio recordings of meetings: at least one researcher was present at advisory board and planning meetings.
- Interviews with students who stayed, students who left, classroom personnel, and with various partners (i.e., community college officials, management, and union representatives).
- Document collection: grant proposal and handouts from class, from meetings, and from student portfolios.

We participated in the class as note takers—during whole class and small group activities; as tutors in one-on-one interactions with students during reading and writing assignments; as occasional translators for Spanish-speaking students; and as participants, often doing the same assignments as the students.

Our analysis of the unfolding history of this project took several forms. We looked for the most frequent and continuous topics of discussion among the staff, teacher, and students. Topics such as concerns about teaching and

109

learning, about class content and activities, about attendance, and about the educational model became the themes that focused our examination of the data gathered inside the classroom and collected through interviews and in documents.

We documented classroom talk and then examined it, looking for inter-active patterns and the characteristics of teacher-led lessons and juxtaposed them to talk initiated and controlled by the students. Because taping was not allowed in the classroom, our analysis of student-teacher interaction is based on the handwritten field notes of two observers. We use as examples those episodes in our notes with considerable coincidence in turn taking, context, and wording. In a few incidents, the analysis was based on single notes taken during small group interaction where the researcher was able to take down most of what occurred. Because we were obviously handicapped without a tape recorder, our ability to capture other important paralinguistic cues was severely limited. Only the most obvious uses of emphasis, intonation, and gesturing were noted. As a result of the tape recording ban, many events were only partially recorded and others were missed altogether.

We examined the curriculum as it was developed; how it took shape; and what knowledge, events, or beliefs were taken into account when decisions concerning activities and sequencing were made. Finally, we chose focal students to follow in classes, to interview, and to have informal conversations with. We looked for clues that might help explain why students chose not to continue in the class or why they chose to participate in class as they did. We asked them for their opinions about the program, what they felt worked well, and what and how it might be improved upon.

As evaluators, we took a qualitative research approach to understanding the project that we were trying to learn about. This required "being there," and we never pretended that our presence did not effect what occurred. In the beginning, we collaborated harmoniously with program staff and received enthusiastic cooperation in our evaluation efforts. But as things began to go wrong in the program, tensions between the project staff and the evaluation team developed. The staff argued that our presence in the classroom and our choice of evaluation methods were responsible for students leaving the course. Ultimately, they put so many restrictions on our data collection meth-ods that we felt compelled to leave the project. Otherwise, we would have lost our status as independent evaluators.

While we found many problems in the pilot, we believed—and continue to believe—that the project was essentially a good idea. We tried to be very sensitive to the fact that the program was doing something innovative and that there was not much experience to build on. We saw the emerging diffi-culties as part of the process. For these reasons, the aspects of this project described in this chapter are based on only the first seven months (start up and pilot class) of an eighteen-month grant period.

# Appendix B

### GETTING AN OVERVIEW OF HEALTH AND SAFETY INFORMATION

1. How many health and safety topics are in the packet? _____

2. In what order are the topics presented? _____

3. How many pages are devoted to each health and safety topic?
   _____

4. What is the purpose of the horizontal lines near the top of every page?
   _____

5. How many paragraphs are used to explain stress and burnout?
   _____

6. Regarding Infectious Agents, how many suggestions are given for employees to get management to do? _____

7. Regarding Toxic Chemicals, how many suggestions are given for employees to do? _____

8. If a co-worker complains of skin irritations, which page would you consult? _____

9. If a co-worker complains of exhaustion, which page would you consult? _____

10. Complete the following chart for each health and safety topic discussed in the information packet:

| health & safety topic | page # | explain hazard briefly in your own words | does hazard affect you? |
|---|---|---|---|
| | | | |
| | | | |
| | | | |
| | | | |
| | | | |

11. What health and safety hazards NOT included in the informational packet affect you on the job? Please explain:

111

# Notes

1. Recent exceptions are Hull, 1991, Gowen, 1990, Kalman & Fraser, 1992.

2. Although the "new orthodoxy" shares many of the ideas and practices found in traditional education (and in that sense is not new at all), it is considered "new" because it is widespread among the emergent adult literacy programs. The pedagogical aspect of this approach is but one of several components: it also includes criteria for funding, evaluating, and organizing educational efforts. See Schultz, 1992, and Schultz, this volume.

3. For a different view of the self-image of working adults, see Fingeret 1983.

4. Interestingly enough, both approaches in adult education (the new orthodoxy and student-centered teaching) are anchored in a critique of Adult Basic Education (ABE). Authors and educators advocating "literacy training" argue that the problem with schools is that they currently promote a brand of literacy that could be characterized as "reading to learn" while what most jobs require is reading to accomplish specific and immediate tasks (Carnavale, et al., 1990; Sticht, 1979; *The Bottom Line*, 1988). Critics of this position, however, find schools guilty of teaching a brand of literacy that is narrowly restricted to the demands of the labor market (Aronowitz & Giroux, 1985; Simon, Dippo, & Schneke, 1991).

5. While there is ample research on teacher effectiveness (Brophy & Good, 1986), much of what has been written "has assumed that the relationship between teachers' actions and their observable affects is a linear one and is unidirectional" (Clark & Peterson, 1986, p. 257), leaving out the potential relationship(s) between teachers' thoughts and theories and their actions.

6. All names, places, organizations and other identifying information have been changed. We gathered this data as part of an ethnographic evaluation of the eight week pilot for this program. We attended all planning meetings, which were audiotaped; attended all class sessions, where we took copious notes (taping was not allowed by the staff); interviewed students and program staff; and collected relevant documents and student writing. For more details of our role in the program and our methodology, see Appendix A.

7. Using a mental health model, IBHW proposed the incorporation of a counselor into the program who would serve as support in the classroom and out. They also included in their program a "learning advocate," a

class member from the workplace who would act as a peer counselor for the other students. The teacher, the counselor, and the learning advocate were to work together on curriculum and classroom activities, forming a "teaching team." They theorized that this model would better meet the needs of working adults interested in upgrading their skills. While the model had important implications for the outcome of the project, it is not the focus of this chapter. For further discussion and analysis of the model, see Kalman & Fraser, 1992.

8. For additional recommendations for implementing a successful workplace literacy program, see Kalman & Fraser, 1992.

# References

Alvine, L. (1987). Buena Vista writing to learn: Teachers as agents for educational change. In D. Goswami and P. R. Stillman (Eds.), *Reclaiming the classroom teacher: Research as an agency for change* (pp. 107–123). Portsmouth, NH: Boynton/Cook Publishers.

Aronowitz, S. & Giroux, H. (1985). *Education under siege*. South Hadley, MA: Bergin & Garvey.

Askov, E., Aderman, B., & Hemmelstein, N. (1989). *Upgrading basic skills for the workplace*. University Park, PA: Pennsylvania State University Press.

Belzer, A. (1993). Doing school differently. In M. Cochran-Smith & S. L. Lytle (Eds.), *Inside/Outside: Teacher research and knowledge* (pp. 276–283). New York: Teachers College Press.

Bishop, W. (1990). *Something old, something new: College writing teachers and classroom change*. Carbondale, IL: Southern Illinois University Press.

Britton, J. (1969/1990). Talking to learn. In D. Barnes, J. Britton, & M. Torbe (Eds.), *Language, the learner, and the school* (pp. 89–130). Portsmouth, NH: Boynton/Cook Publishers.

Brophy, J. E. & Good, T. L. (1986). Teacher behavior and student achievement. In M. C. Wittrock (Ed.), *Handbook of research on teaching* (3rd ed.) (pp. 328–375). New York: Macmillan.

Carnevale, A., Gainer, L., & Meltzer, A. S. (1990). *Workplace basics: The essential skills employers want*. San Francisco, CA: Jossey-Bass.

Chisman, F. P. (1989). *Jump start: The federal role in adult literacy.* Final Report of the Project on Adult Literacy. Southport, CT: The Southport Institute for Policy Analysis.

Clark, C. M. & Peterson, P. L. (1986). Teacher's thought processes. In M. C. Wittrock (Ed.), *Handbook of research on teaching* (3rd ed.) (pp. 255–296). New York: Macmillan.

Cochran-Smith, M. (1991). Learning to teach against the grain. *Harvard Educational Review, 61,* 279–310.

Cochran-Smith, M. & Lytle, S. L. (1993). *Inside/Outside: Teacher research and knowledge.* New York: Teachers College Press.

Cuban, L. (1993). *How teachers taught: Constancy and change in American classrooms, 1890–1980* (2nd ed.). New York: Longman.

Edelsky, C. (1991). *With literacy and justice for all: Rethinking the social in language and education.* London: The Falmer Press.

Fingeret, A. (1983). Social Network: A new perspective on independence and illiterate adults. *Adult Education Quarterly. 33,* 133–146.

Fingeret, A. (1990). Literacy for what purpose: A response. In R. Venezky, D. Wagner, & B. Cilberti (Eds.), *Toward defining literacy* (pp. 15–18). Newark, DE: International Reading Association.

Goswami, D. & Stillman, P. R. (Eds.). (1987). *Reclaiming the classroom: Teacher research as an agency for change.* Portsmouth, NH: Boynton/Cook Publishers.

Gowen, S. (1990). *"Eyes on a different prize": A critical ethnography of a workplace literacy program.* Unpublished doctoral dissertation, Georgia State University, Atlanta, GA.

Grimett, P. P. & MacKinnon, A. M. (1992). Craft knowledge and the education of teachers. In G. Grant (Ed.), *Review of research in education* (pp. 385–456). Washington, DC: American Educational Research Association.

Grubb, W. N., Kalman, J., & Castellano, M. (1991). *Readin', writin', and 'rithmetic one more time: The role of remediation in vocational education and job training programs.* Berkeley, CA: National Center for Research in Vocational Education, University of California at Berkeley.

Harman, D. (1985). *Turning illiteracy around: An agenda for national action.* New York: Business Council for Effective Literacy.

Hull, G. (1991). *Examining the relations of literacy to vocational education and work: An ethnography of a vocational program in banking and finance.* Berkeley, CA: National Center for Research in Vocational Education, University of California at Berkeley.

Hymes, D. (1974). *Foundations in sociolinguistics.* Philadelphia, PA: University of Pennsylvania Press.

Kalman, J. (in press). *The literacy link: The practices of scribes and clients in Mexico.* Cresskill, NJ: Hampton Press.

Kalman, J. & Fraser, K. Losey (1992). *Opportunities lost and lessons learned: Inside a workplace literacy program.* Berkeley, CA: National Center for Research in Vocational Education, University of California at Berkeley.

Knapp, M. & Turnball, B. (1990). *Better schooling for the children of poverty: Alternatives to conventional wisdom.* Washington, DC: U.S. Department of Education.

Lampert, M. (1985). How do teachers manage to teach? *Harvard Educational Review, 55,* 178–194.

Losey, K. M. , (in press). *"Listen to the silences:" Mexican American interaction in the composition classroom and the community.* Norwood, NJ: Ablex.

Philippi, J. (1991). *Literacy at work: The workbook for program developers.* New York: Simon & Schuster Workplace Resources.

Shulman, L. S. (1987). Knowledge and teaching: Foundations of the new reform. *Harvard Educational Review, 57,* 1–22.

Schultz, K. (1992). *Training for basic skills or educating workers? Changing conceptions of workplace education programs.* Berkeley, CA: National Center for Research in Vocational Education, University of California at Berkeley.

Simon, R. I. (1992). *Teaching against the grain: Texts for a pedagogy of possibility.* New York: Bergin and Garvey.

Simon, R., Dippo, D., & Schneke, A. (1991). *Learning work.* New York: Bergin and Garvey.

Smith, F. (1986). *Insult to intelligence: The bureaucratic invasion of our classrooms.* Portsmouth, NH: Heinemann.

Smylie, M. (1994). Redesigning teachers' work: Connections to the classroom. In L. Darling-Hammond (Ed.), *Review of Research in Education*

115

*1994* (pp. 129–178). Washington, DC: American Educational Research Association.

Soifer, R., Crumrine, B. M., Honzaki, E., Irwin, M. E., Simmons, B., & Young, D. L. (1990). *The complete theory-to-practice handbook of adult literacy: Curriculum design and teaching approaches.* New York: Teachers College Press.

Sticht, T. (1990). *Functional context education: Policy and training methods from the military's experience with lower aptitude personnel.* San Diego, CA: Applied Behavioral and Cognitive Sciences.

Sticht, T. (1979). Developing literacy and learning strategies in organizational settings. In H. O'Neil & C. Spielberger (Eds.), *Cognitive and affective learning strategies* (pp. 275–307). New York: Academic Press.

Taggart, R. (1986, July). *The comprehensive competencies program: A summary.* Washington, DC: Remediation and Training Institute.

Tharp, R. G. & Gallimore, R. (1989). *Rousing minds to life: Teaching, learning, and schooling in social context.* Cambridge, NY: Cambridge University Press.

*The bottom line: Basic skills in the workplace.* (1988). Washington, DC: U.S. Department of Education/U.S. Department of Labor.

Trueba, H. T. (Ed.). (1987). *Success or failure? Learning and the language minority student.* Rowley, MA: Newbury House Publishers.

# FOUR

## "It Changed Something Inside of Me": English Language Learning, Structural Barriers to Employment, and Workers' Goals in a Workplace Literacy Program

*Debby D'Amico and Emily Schnee*

In this paper, the authors, a union education program administrator and an ESL teacher, present a longitudinal picture of a program that began as a federally funded workplace literacy demonstration project and has evolved over nearly four years in a variety of directions. The purpose is to examine the impact of instruction related to employment on workers, teachers and program development and to discuss the implications of these experiences for understanding the contested relationship between education and work. Specifically, the article seeks to unravel the connections among literacy, English language fluency, and structural factors such as immigration status, class, and political-economic context. A history of the program's development is supported by illustrative case studies of two workers; quotations from workers, workers' writings, and classroom discussions are interspersed throughout. Finally, conclusions and the questions these raise for adult education practice and related policies are discussed.

# Programmatic and Theoretical Context

The experience documented in this article is a programmatic one, and reveals the dialectic between practice and theory. Most of us who work in adult literacy, workplace literacy, or ESL instruction are aware of, and in many cases agree with, critiques of policy based on assumptions about the role of literacy in employment. However, our critical theory is tested by our daily work in programs structured by these very assumptions, as well as by the degree to which workers in our classes hope and believe that increased literacy or English-language fluency will positively affect their work, their goals, and their opportunities.

The workplace literacy program described here reflects these dilemmas. In the first year of the project, the curriculum and direction of instruction were tied to the demands of the funding. These were directed toward measurement of improvement in skills, or what Delpit would call acquisition of the codes for participating in the culture of power (1995, p. 25). Workers learned English and how to fill out applications for the jobs they sought. However, they also developed or discovered their own interests in education and over the years have come to merge their English-language mastery with their goals for their own communities and with their own forms of expression. At the same time, their experiences reveal the underestimation of the non-educational or structural limits to acquiring jobs for immigrants and non-native speakers of English.

The purposes to which workers in the program have put their education adds a new dimension to the ongoing debate over the relationship between increased education in a language alien to one's own linguistic, ethnic, cultural, or class background and identification with one's family and community of origin. In *Hunger of Memory*, Rodriguez describes his education as a working-class Chicano in terms of inevitable separation from his home and community, a separation he describes as necessary for participation in public life (1982). The opposition Rodriguez postulates between mastery of public life and ties to the immigrant community, however, is contradicted by research that suggests that community networks facilitate success in mastering the language and literacy demands of establishing one's self in the United States. For example, a two-year national study by Aquirre International found that experience in one's native country and support in the immigrant community in the United States determined the extent to which immigrants acquired legal status and secured jobs, social services, and education (Guth & Wrigley, 1992).

Debates about the politics of literacy, literate discourse, and pedagogy engage the opposition between the language of home and community and that of school and work as a conflict between primary discourses and those of an oppressive and alien power structure (Gee, paraphrased in Delpit, 1985, p. 153). Delpit addresses the determinism inherent in this position by summarizing the objections of educators, parents, and students of color to this polarization. She states that: (1) access to discourses of power are necessary to all members of society; (2) these discourses can be and have been acquired in classrooms; and (3) individuals can transform dominant discourses for their own liberatory purposes (p. 162). Supporting these premises, an analysis of immigrant education in the early 1900s and of the Highlander citizenship schools in the 50s and 60s concludes that cultural pluralism and political purpose can be incorporated into successful literacy initiatives (Rees, 1993).

In the case discussed below, ESL learners in union education programs formed a community within which workers studying about jobs in education and day care designed a way to meet the needs of immigrant parents, particularly women, for child care during times when they were in class (Office of Vocational and Adult Education, 1990). At the same time, they created jobs and work experience for themselves. Their experience is instructive in its fracturing of the polarization between learning English as spoken in workplaces and public arenas, on the one hand, and using English to respond to community needs, on the other. At the same time, their success in doing both starkly highlights the non-educational barriers faced in applying for jobs in public schools and day care centers. It instructs us to be vigilant against complicity with the assumption that unemployment can be solved by developing a more literate, English-speaking workforce without addressing the economic crisis and its political origins.

## Education for Education Careers: Background

In the summer of 1990, one of the authors (Deborah D'Amico), then a senior researcher at the Literacy Assistance Center (LAC), met with directors of three union education programs to discuss collaborating on a proposal for a federal workplace literacy demonstration grant. The Literacy Assistance Center is a not-for-profit organization that is funded to provide technical assistance, staff development, data collection, and research for publicly funded adult education programs in New York City. The three unions involved (the International Ladies Garment Workers Union [ILGWU], the Amalgamated Clothing and Textile Workers Union [ACTWU], and District Council [DC] 1707 of the American Federation of State, County and Municipal Employees) were all participating members of the Consortium for Worker Education (CWE). The CWE is a not-for-profit organization comprised of 29 New York City labor unions that offer education, training, and other services to workers.

At the time the proposal was written, there was a documented need for bilingual paraprofessionals in education and day care in New York City. Meanwhile, manufacturing jobs had declined from nearly 1,000,000 to 300,000 from the 1950s to the 1990s, with the apparel industry sustaining the largest job losses in this sector (O'Neill & Moss, 1992, 34, 35). Based on goals articulated by workers in the participating garment unions and on needs evident in classrooms throughout the city, the purpose of the grant was defined as follows: to provide advanced ESL instruction with content focused on work in bilingual education and day-care settings for workers in threatened industries, particularly garment workers. The intent was to provide alternatives to work in the rapidly downsizing garment industry that would meet the needs of immigrant communities and utilize the immigrant experiences and bilingual capacity of the participants. As the union representing day-care and Head Start staff, DC 1707 participated in the program in order to offer its members the opportunity to acquire additional knowledge about child development and pedagogical theories and methods.

### Year One

The project was funded and begun in April 1991. A total of 106 workers entered the program; they attended five separate classes, for a total of six instructional hours weekly (two were held during the week on evenings and three on Saturdays) from July of 1991 to August of 1992. Based on requirements for the targeted paraprofessional jobs, entry requirements included evidence of a GED or high school diploma, from the United States or another country. A number of participants held credentials from both, such as a GED acquired here in addition to secondary education or higher in their native country. Data collected by the project evaluator show that 93% of those reporting previous education data held a high school diploma or its equivalent; 83% had credentials from countries other than the United States. Of the 53% of those with GEDs, 81% had acquired them in Spanish and 16% in English. Participants came from 22 different countries. The largest contingent was Latino (64%). Eighty-three percent of initial entrants to the program reported speaking Spanish, or a combination of Spanish and English, at home. Eight percent spoke Chinese or Cantonese, or a combination of one of these languages and English, at home. Seventy-one percent were female and 29% male.

Year One was marked by struggles to implement the program and by the ways in which the goals of the funder and of the project partners diverged.

These are explored more fully in D'Amico and Schnee (1994). Essentially, these discrepancies centered around the following issues:

1. *Individual vs. community aspects of motivation and success.* The desires of immigrant adult learners to progress as individuals and to contribute to their communities were often expressed as interrelated goals by project partici-pants and by workers in the participating union education programs. However, a section of the proposed curriculum that outlined the community aspects of education had to be deleted in order to comply with revisions required by the funder. Under the terms of the grant, the curriculum was to be primarily concerned with language skills development and workplace spe-cific applications of acquired English language skills. Content was narrowly defined as related to forms, tasks and interactions associated with work in the school setting, as opposed to the problematic interaction between schools and communities. Yet it is precisely in this area that the experience of immigrants can make a contribution by culturally and linguistically bridging community and school.

2. *English language skills as the primary determinant of job acquisition and workplace competence.* The focus on skills as the route to jobs reduced the importance of the role of the counselor as a resource for addressing structural barriers to employment. Because the premise of the funding for the project was that English language skills were the critical factor governing access to jobs, the role of the counselor, specifically her role in job development and job counseling, was reduced from that outlined in the original proposal. Nevertheless, the counselor accompanied groups of workers to the board of education to be fingerprinted and to apply for jobs; years later, workers in the program still comment on how important this was for them.

3. *Evaluation, following from the assumptions above, emphasized the acquisition of discrete skills by individuals, rather than group achievements or jobs acquired.* We are not arguing for job placement as a performance measure, because this too assumes that education guarantees access to jobs. Rather, we are pointing out that the program goals were to develop "job readiness" as demonstrated by measurable gains in English language skills. In our experience, this is at most a necessary, but far from sufficient, indicator of the ability of participants to acquire jobs in education and day care. This created a tension between the project's outside evaluator and the curriculum developer; the former was bound to measure the program's success in the funder's terms, while the latter tried to develop critical awareness of education issues in ways that did not lend themselves to measurement. Many of the small group or whole class activities also lay outside the realm of assessment of individuals, although they were essential to the participatory pedagogy to which the program's staff was committed. The project developed, to start a child-care center in the third

year of the program, would have been difficult to measure by the standards of the original funding, yet it is an outstanding achievement representing remarkable progress for both individuals and the group.

During the first year, the project director (D'Amico for part of the year and then Fran Richetti of the LAC),[1] teachers and counselors met monthly to collaborate on curriculum, share project experiences and participate in staff development. The project director's job was a balancing act that required reconciling the goals of the funder with those of project participants and staff, despite the areas of contention outlined above. The teachers attempted to comply with demands of the project evaluation while creating space for a participatory dialogue with workers that itself modeled the experiential, "hands-on" pedagogy espoused in the curriculum and by most project staff. Workers struggled to learn and eventually to practice a variety of teaching methods and to understand the content and context of education in a multicultural city. Teachers strived to demonstrate the holistic, student-centered teaching methods we hoped students would embrace.

A unit on multicultural education, for example, began with teachers modeling whole language reading techniques through a lesson on slavery that used pictures to teach workers to "read" a computer generated symbol language. The rest of the unit revolved around independent research by cooperative learning groups on topics of their choosing related to the theme of multiculturalism. Workers were encouraged to do experiential research in order to prepare and present a lesson to their classmates on their topic. They interviewed friends and neighbors, screened videos, visited museums and the library to research topics as diverse as Jews and the Holocaust, the civil rights movement, and Native Americans, to name a few. Each cooperative learning group developed a lesson plan that emphasized participatory teaching techniques such as brainstorming, role play, collaborative story writing, and facilitated discussion. The methods chosen also aimed to connect the topic to the experiences of the participants as immigrant workers in New York. The lessons, which were presented to the rest of the class and videotaped for a follow-up critique, provoked deep explorations of prejudice and misconception and served as a catalyst for much future discussion. In the process, the workers honed their reading, writing, and speaking of English and made decisions about how they would use these skills and their knowledge of education.

The English for Education Careers (EEC) curriculum component that most challenged and excited workers were the mock-teaching experiences. Participants worked in small groups to research a topic, prepare a lesson plan and teach a model lesson to their classmates. These activities were tremendously rich language learning experiences as they engaged workers in using language for purposes of real communication and expression. They simulated the kind of "real-life" language use (and learning) that happens when immersed in an authentic English-teaching situation. In fact, we believe that it is only through real immersion in such simulations that workers will acquire the language facility and confidence they need to successfully do this work. Studies of workers on the job confirm that most of what they need to know to do their jobs is learned in the workplace itself (Garvey, 1992, p. 11; Young, 1994). Similar claims are made about training programs; in testimony before the Senate Labor and Human Resources Committee, Anthony Carnevale, chair of the National Commission on Employment Policy stated: "The best training is a job" (1995).

In journal writings at the end of the first year, workers expressed their opinions about the program. These reflect both their excitement about what they learned and their frustration with the lack of opportunity to apply their knowledge. One worker described the experiences of those who are professionally educated in their native language but who work in blue-collar and service jobs because they do not speak English, are undocumented, and/or lack professional credentials for the U.S. job market:

> there are many individuals prepared in different disciplines in their own language and they cannot succeed because there is not an entity who dedicates itself to capitalize those values and place them to function on the base of their preparation. In that way, they would have the opportunity to collaborate with their different communities. These people just need a little bit of help with English. If we make a survey of the system of "gypsy" cabs in the different boroughs of New York, we will find ourselves with the big surprise of the majority of the drivers are professionals, such as lawyers, doctors, accountants, pharmacists and others.

The dilemma this created for the EEC program was that, in the opinion of teachers and counselors interviewed after the first year, many of the best workers could not even apply for jobs because of their undocumented immigration status. In one typical class, roughly half (10 workers in a class of 19) were undocumented. A number had been teachers in their own countries and wanted to use their experience in the United States.

> I was a teacher in my country. I want to improve my English. I thought the best way was to take classes in the field I was involved in my country. I want to learn about education in this country. I learned a new methodology—participatory.

Others emphasized the contribution the class made to their ability to contribute to their communities:

I think this program is really important for all of us, not only because it gives us an opportunity for studying a career, and perhaps for getting a better job, but also because it helps us to develop as human beings. It allows us a broader vision about the differences existing between our countries of origin and the U.S., taking advantage of our experience and becoming not just immigrants who live and work here, but an aid through the direct participation as an integral part of the community which we belong to. In this way, we leave a very worthwhile cultural legacy for future generations.

When I came to this school, I felt insecure about my development as assistant teacher. Then, when I started to read about the problems of our community, the needs of bilingual education and the recognition of our cultural values, I thought that I had to do something to help our children and to get a good job. Now, as volunteer in the school, I see that I can do much more than I thought, and thanks to my teacher, I know how to do a good class. I also learned a lot about the education system. Now I feel that my English is better; I can express my ideas easily and of course my comprehension also.

Through volunteer experiences and jobs in education and day care, some workers exemplified the attainment of the goals of workers, funders, and staff. One worker in the program had volunteered at her child's day-care center and then was asked to work as substitute teacher. To qualify as a substitute, she had to get a medical exam, be fingerprinted and take a child-abuse detection training.

The "Education for Education Careers" program has been very helpful. . . .The knowledge I have gained in this program I practice at the day care center where I work. The teachers at work provide me with the opportunity to take control of the entire class. When the teacher leaves me alone with the kids I create fun and educational activities for them. In the teacher evaluation the teacher said I'm doing very well.

After taking this course I feel much more confident working with children. I have learned a lot from the experience. I really thank God that I found this program, because I needed it. . . . I have gained great knowledge. I now have the self-confidence to look for a job.

Others focused on the way in which the project helped them improve their English language skills:

When I first came to this country I was so young and my parents wanted me to go to school, but I have six brothers and sisters, and I knew my parents needed help. I refused to go to school; instead I started working in a factory where my mother used to work. I worked many hours every day, but I was happy. I was helping my parents!

I lived three years with them until I got married. It was then I started studying English two days a week for two hours each day. It was hard, because I kept myself working. After awhile I took the GED and passed it with a high score.

My goal for the future is to be a good teacher. At this time I speak English fluently, but many times it's difficult for me to find the exact word when I'm talking with someone. I know by experience that it's very hard, but I also know that I have to keep learning the language in order to be successful in the future.

These passages from worker writings reveal the complex relationship among English language, educational credentials, family needs, and community commitments that structure both worker experiences and their understanding of these. An eloquent description of structural barriers to success in the United States is expressed in the following workers' poem:

To be immigrants in New York is not easy. The growing number of immigrants who adventure to this cement jungle finish by suffering from homesickness sooner or later.

And how not to be like this?

Behind are the dear ones, habits, food, music, friends, and the homeland.

The lives of the majority of the immigrants here are very difficult. They came in search of better conditions than what their countries have.

They bring big hopes to save money, to help sisters and brothers, to finish school, to help the fathers not work hard, or construct a house that they promised to the family.

With that dream they cross the river or the sea, they hop the fence and try to get past "la migra."

Everything is fine until they collide with barriers.

When they try to get something here in the city of the Statue of Liberty, they see the reality. They only can find hard jobs and lost dreams.

At the end of year one, the project could be considered a success for the 60 participants who completed the program. As judged by a variety of assessment measures, including portfolios, self-assessment and teacher ratings, workers clearly improved in their facility with English—orally, in writing, and with print. Moreover, they acquired a genuine understanding of, and excitement about, the variety of classroom practices which were the subject of their reading, discussions, observations and practice.

*Year Two*

After one year of the program, focus groups with workers, meetings of staff, and advisory board members, and interviews with teachers indicated a need to continue the program. There were many EEC workers who wanted to work in education and day care but were unable to get jobs the first year and others who did not feel ready to apply for such work but who wanted to learn more about teaching and jobs in the field. For some, the class was an opportunity not only to learn and practice English, but also to be intellectually stimulated and to think about how they might apply what they were learning. Federal funding ended in December of 1992, and the ILGWU and DC 1707 offered to sponsor two classes that would accommodate those who wanted to continue in the program as well as new recruits. Union education staff and the former project director, now an administrator of CWE, met with teachers and workers and decided to try to develop ways workers could use their learning within CWE programs as well as to build opportunities for volunteering and visiting schools and day care centers into the program. In addition, a summer class for dislocated workers was offered that featured an accelerated version of the curriculum and emphasis on job placement activities. A packet of materials explaining the paraprofessional application process was prepared, and a consultant with years of experience within the New York City Board of Education was hired to assist with job development. The difficulty of breaking into an established system of access to jobs is evidenced by the fact that heavy networking within the UFT (United Federation of Teachers, the union representing paras), the CSA (Council of Supervisors and Administrators, representing day care directors and administrators), local districts where participants live and contacts at the central board generated only a single placement, although all six of the women attempting to get hired were qualified, dedicated and in two cases had been subbing regularly.

By the end of the second year, five of nineteen workers in an EEC class sponsored by DC 1707 were working in education and day care, while eight from a second class offered by ILGWU were now interested in looking for work in the field. Of these, five had college degrees from their own countries. Program staff agreed to continue to seek volunteer opportunities for workers, to learn more about the evaluation of foreign credentials and to provide information about college, including financial aid.

An important development during the second year of the project was the hiring of EEC workers as part-time paraprofessionals in the ILGWU education program. This practice fulfilled both the community service objectives of workers and a longstanding goal of the ILGWU program: to hire former and current garment workers to staff the program. A program director from the ILGWU described the benefits of the EEC worker teachers as follows:

Our experience with hiring workers has been an extremely positive one. They have been a boost to staff development. Their knowledge and personal experience with garment work and immigration has oriented other teachers. The skills and understanding of the program they have learned from the EEC class has helped new and experienced teachers. Because each of them has participated in the program as a worker for at least two years, they have often helped with "reality checks" for lesson preparation, assessment and evaluation. Their presence in the classroom has helped break down traditional roles of teachers and workers (and perceptions of these roles). Their bilingualism has been useful.

While paraprofessional positions within the union education program provided some EEC workers with jobs that used the knowledge and skill they had acquired in the program, for undocumented workers, these jobs were out of reach. Some of these workers began to develop their community involvement by deciding to work toward a day care center that would both serve their fellow workers and learners in CWE programs and provide opportunities to link their study of education with classroom practice on an ongoing basis. Thus, the Child Care Project was born. Workers in the program conducted research to document the need for child care among workers attending classes sponsored by the ILGWU, ACTWU, and DC 1707 at several CWE program sites. A total of 47 classes were visited during the conduct of the survey and close to 500 survey forms were collected. The documented need for child care among CWE workers attending classes echoes the need found among immigrant women in general as they pursue literacy in English (Office of Vocational and Adult Education, 1990). Workers used their knowledge of educational methods to design a dramatic role play illustrating problems associated with parenting, working, and studying to introduce the survey and its purpose. In a determined and professional manner, workers presented information about the survey, collected data, and analyzed the results over the summer of 1993. They participated in program planning for both the 1993/1994 year of EEC and for the Child Care Project. In all of these activities and accomplishments, EEC workers both fulfilled the purpose and demonstrated the accomplishments of the evolving EEC program.

### Year Three

During this year, workers in the program presented the results of their survey to the CWE community and to funders. Together with their teacher, three EEC workers applied for and were awarded a minigrant from the LAC to support their work in the Child Care Project. A proposal for funding was written, and in the spring of 1994, a commitment from the Robert Bowne Foundation for a matching grant of $15,000 was offered. This initiated a search for space for the child care center and an intensive effort to raise the matching funds.

EEC continued to be offered in 1993/1994, this time as one class sponsored by DC 1707 (a second class opened later in the same program year). In early October, a focus group with workers, many of whom had been with the program since its inception, indicated their assessment of their participation. Again, community goals were primary. For example, one worker, who was volunteering in the ILGWU Justice Center, said: "My goal is to reach knowledge—to read, write, and speak English and lose my fear of speaking English, because I want to help workers."

Another spoke about helping his co-workers practice English at lunch time. A worker working as a para in the ILGWU program described her experiences:

> I feel I am in the environment of education now. I work for the program as a teacher assistant. That was my purpose—to know the field of education and to improve my English. I think I achieved these.

Another worker said:

> I changed in my form of thinking. The classes gave me knowledge and support to participate in and contribute to the Child Care Project and now I feel comfortable when I talk to someone.

One worker emphasized the personal transformation that occurred among workers participating in the Child Care Project:

> This program changed something inside of me. Yes, it did. When I started to study I didn't expect to go as far as I did. . . . I didn't think of working in groups, being involved in my community—making an effort to contribute and to show to others we can be workers and productive and creative through the chance that these programs have given to me.

Another worker, who worked in an employment program for the disabled, described how the EEC class changed his understanding of his job:

> The change began when I started studying in the Education for Education Careers class, and I hear the word "facilitator." Immediately I realized that I was also a facilitator in my work, with the only difference that I was not teaching them literature or some other topic, but I was teaching them how to work, how to use

tools, how to improve their skills, and how to relate to each other, and that also I was an instructor, that I had the same responsibility in my work as a facilitator in the classroom, and if I use the method or the qualities that the facilitators use in their classroom, I can bring back a good relationship with the clients without losing the respect or the experiences and the qualities of a good foreman that I had gained in my work.

In a summary of the themes of the group discussion, one of the authors of this chapter, Emily Schnee, a teacher who has been with the program since its inception, indicated the tension between learning English as a primary motivation and as a perceived vehicle for getting jobs on the one hand and the actual experiences of workers with formidable structural obstacles to employment. The integral connection between individual achievement and contributing to the community was an equally salient theme, as was the desire to go to college.

### Year Four

The CWE continues to support the EEC program, now with two major directions: the implementation of the Child Care Project and the opportunity to enroll in two college classes with tuition paid by the CWE and a variety of support services provided. These included help with the formal application and testing process, counseling, and a study-skills component offered immediately following the college class. Six former EEC workers have been accepted into college and are attending these classes; another three are enrolled in a college prep class.

The Child Care Center opened in late September of 1994 and has operated during each program year since then. A matching grant was received from the Aaron Diamond Foundation and some funds were awarded by the Seth Sprague Foundation. Together with the Bowne grant and CWE in-kind contributions, these funds supported the center in its first year. The center operates on Saturdays, during the time CWE classes are held (10 a.m.–2 p.m.). (Because most students in CWE programs work, classes are held during weekday evenings, or Saturdays. During the week, most workers come straight from work, and thus would not be able to bring children in the evenings.) Recruitment of children for the center was done by participants in the Child Care Project, using a triumphant recruitment flyer that announced:

Don't stop coming to school because you don't have anyone to care for your child!! Our dream is a reality. The Child Care Center will open in September 1994.

129

Approximately 20 children from ages 4 to 12 attend the center regularly. The center is staffed by a teacher who herself began as a volunteer in a Head Start program and who went to college through the CWE—affiliated City College Center for Worker Education. Five of the EEC workers are paid teacher assistants, allowing the participating children to work in small groups according to age. Another four EEC workers work as family literacy facilitators, planning and conducting workshops that support the ability of immigrant parents to help children with their schoolwork and to advocate for their children within the New York City public school system.

## Case Studies

The following case studies of workers in the Education for Education Careers (EEC) program illustrate how factors other than language and literacy influenced individual "success" in this workplace literacy program. For most workers, the assumption of a match between formal job requirements on the one hand and qualified, trained, educated, and "literate" applicants on the other culminating in the happy outcome of employment was not borne out by experience. While two workers acquired positions early on in the first year of the program, this was due to the connections of their teacher, who was himself an administrator of bilingual education in a district office of the New York City Public Schools. Efforts to get jobs for other workers revealed a deeply entrenched, highly politicized system of access to these jobs. Despite the assistance of a counselor and classroom practice, the formalized application process for paraprofessional jobs confused and intimidated instructors, administrators, and workers alike. The application for paraprofessional is very extensive; some pages are written in obtuse "legalese." Fingerprinting, which during 1991–92 cost $73 and took at least three months to clear, was another requirement, as was a highly detailed medical exam. The applicant who successfully completed all of these aspects of applying to the Board of Education wins a place in the para substitute pool. This means being on a list of those who may be called at 6:30 in the morning to sub that day. Subbing can lead to a permanent hire if positions become available. Intense lobbying with local school and district office personnel is also necessary if a permanent position is desired; although applications are filed centrally, jobs are filled locally, often by elected community school district board members. To make matters worse, by the time workers were completing the first year of classes, jobs as bilingual paraprofessionals were no longer available in New York City, due to a series of budget cuts.

The identities of the workers described below have been changed for reasons of confidentiality. In some instances several workers' voices have been merged to form a composite picture of a particular type of EEC worker. Much of the information used to develop the case studies was gleaned through informal conversations over a period of many years. Our access to this information was due to the confidential and intimate nature of the worker-teacher relationship. We have tried to veil individual identities, as best as possible, for obvious reasons.

## *Angelica*

Angelica, a 40-year-old Ecuadoran immigrant, entered the EEC program in its first year. A cursory language placement process led her to one of the two more advanced ESL classes within the program, although Angelica was at the weaker end of the language proficiency spectrum in comparison with many of her classmates. Angelica's writing and grammar were adequate, though not expert, her comprehension weak, and she was hampered by a heavy accent that markedly limited her ability to express herself orally in English.

Angelica is married, the mother of two young boys and a former elementary school teacher. She has a bachelor's degree from a university in Ecuador and is a citizen of the United States. When she entered the EEC program, Angelica was working in the home. Her husband, Fernando, also an immigrant and ESL worker in CWE programs, was working long hours in a garment factory, including much overtime, while Angelica pursued the classes and volunteer work that would enable her to make the leap into professional work.

The EEC curriculum (as implemented by Angelica's teacher) combined information about jobs in education, learning and practicing specific teaching methods and techniques, and a whole-language approach to language learning. Angelica's contributions to class discussion, although cumbersome and slow, were valuable and insightful. Her sense of self and the value and importance of her ideas and experiences helped Angelica to overcome her difficulties in oral expression. Her ability to thoughtfully evaluate worker teaching experiences was evidence of her background as a teacher. Nevertheless, Angelica was quite cognizant of her new context and was eager to acquire new teaching skills and techniques (whole language, participatory methods, critical inquiry) and embrace pedagogical directions that were absent from her education and experience as a teacher in Ecuador.

While many workers were interested in the EEC curriculum components that focused on jobs in education (board of education forms and procedures, volunteer teaching opportunities, panel discussion with current paras), Angelica soaked up and made use of this information in a way that few others in the program did. Angelica visited her child's school and arranged a volunteer position for herself; she took an additional volunteer slot at an alternative school in another borough. Angelica was pro-active in seeking both the counselor's and her teacher's aid in filling out the paraprofessional application form and was part of the first team of workers who visited the board of education central offices to be fingerprinted. Angelica independently went and had her transcripts professionally translated (by one of the services recommended on the application form) at considerable expense, and before the end of the first year of the program had had all required medical exams, including a chest X-ray when she tested positive to TB.

While one-third of her classmates who returned to the program the second year, Angelica had no intention of remaining in the program beyond Year One. Although, Angelica completed the first year lagging behind most of her classmates in terms of language proficiency, she was one of very few workers to complete all the bureaucratic requirements for a job as a paraprofessional. Angelica was determined to use our connections and information to regain her former status as an educational professional. Angelica's perseverance paid off. By the beginning of the next academic year, she was enrolled in education courses at a community college near her home (to acquire obligatory credits for full transfer of her degree from home) and was working as a paraprofessional in her child's school. When I last saw Angelica she was enrolled in a National Teachers Exam (NTE) preparation course and was working towards getting her license as a teacher, not a paraprofessional. We believe that it was Angelica's vision of herself as a professional, her ability to rely, albeit temporarily, on a male wage earner, and her documented immigration status, *not* her language proficiency, that enabled her to pursue, achieve, and surpass the EEC program goals in so timely and efficient a manner. This interpretation is supported by the acknowledged influence of socioeconomic background and educational attainment on immigrant success (Portes & Rumbaut, 1994, pp. 71, 214, 175).

### Gabriela

Gabriela is an undocumented Colombian immigrant in her late 30s who entered the EEC program in its first year. Unlike other EEC participants, who were required to have their GED or high school diplomas, Gabriela was allowed to enter the program with only an 11th-grade education due to her facility with the English language and her apparent aptitude and readiness for professional work. Gabriela has always ranked at the top end of all EEC workers in terms of both oral and written language proficiency. From the start, she showed an unusual affinity for, and receptiveness to, the participatory educational methods the EEC program advocated, in contrast to many other workers who preferred the safety of more familiar, traditional educational models. Gabriela showed a keen understanding of how people learn and the politics and subtleties of education in the United States. While she was sensitive to the needs of other workers who focused on the curriculum components related to attaining employment, Gabriela seized upon the aspects of the curriculum that stimulated her academically and broadened her intellectual horizons.

At the time Gabriela entered the EEC program, she was working in a non-union garment factory during the day and studying in the EEC classes in the evenings. Mandatory overtime forced her to arrive late to class on many occasions. During the second year of the EEC program, Gabriela was fired from her job, because of a work-related accident, and after a period of unemployment, she found a job in a restaurant which she juggled with part-time domestic work. The long hours and unstable nature of this work also affected Gabriela's ability to attend class consistently in the third year of the program.

Aware that her undocumented immigration status would make it impossible for her to seek work as a board of education paraprofessional or in a licensed child-care facility, Gabriela approached the EEC counselor, in the first year of the classes, with the idea to open a child care center for the children of other adult workers in CWE classes. Though not a parent herself, Gabriela recognized that many of her classmates missed school because of problems with child care. She recognized a unique intersection of worker needs—her own and others—in the creation of a child care center that would provide jobs and practice for EEC workers and child care for workers with children. Gabriela was discouraged from pursuing this idea due to the many bureaucratic obstacles (insurance, space, money) involved in realizing such a project. The idea was put on hold, but not forgotten.

In the second year of the EEC program it became apparent that very few EEC workers had exited the program ready to apply for work in the field of education. Rather, there was a tremendous sense of identification with, and commitment to the continued existence of the classes. Workers, teachers, and administrators began to meet on a monthly basis to raise questions and seek answers to this dilemma. Early on, the idea of the child care center was mentioned again. This time the idea was received skeptically, but supportively, and Gabriela and several other workers began the two-year-long process of creating, distributing, and tabulating a survey of worker child-care needs and researching, seeking support, and raising funds for the center. Throughout the lengthy and, at times, arduous process of making the child care center a reality, Gabriela has been a driving force behind it. Nevertheless, her participation has been limited by the concrete realities of her life.

The limitations Gabriela confronts were cast in high relief, when midway through the second year of the program, the ILGWU opened several teaching assistant positions in their basic ESL and Spanish literacy classes, with the intention of employing workers from the EEC program. Gabriela, along with many of her classmates, updated her resumé and applied for the position. She was interviewed and offered the job, which she then had to turn down, because she lacked the proof of eligibility to work that the CWE, or any employer, is obliged to require. Gabriela's obvious disappointment was tempered by her vision of the interview process as a good learning experience (she was aware from the outset that proof of eligibility to work would be required to accept the job) and her realization that her full-time work in a garment factory would have made it extremely difficult for her to consistently arrive at this job on time.

Another limitation to employment in education that Gabriela confronts is not having a high school diploma. It is interesting to note that despite Gabriela's stated intention to get her GED, and the firm assurances of several of her teachers who know the quality of her academic work that she is ready to pass, Gabriela has never taken the exam. It is not until the fourth year of the program that Gabriela finally takes the step of enrolling in a GED prep course. There appear to be several, interrelated factors that contribute to Gabriela's delaying the achievement of what appears to be an easily realizable goal. Undoubtedly, Gabriela's time is sorely limited by her multiple jobs and erratic schedule. Her few free hours per week are dedicated to the EEC program, and its outgrowth, the Child Care Project (an arena in which Gabriela plays a leadership role and from which she derives a great deal of status and recognition). We believe that despite Gabriela's stated intentions, she must question the importance of attaining a GED diploma since her undocumented immigration status precludes the possibility of her doing paid professional work.

Gabriela has clearly chosen the Child Care Project as her venue for professional and personal growth and achievement. The factors that prevent her from attaining employment in education are not relevant in this volunteer initiative which Gabriela has shaped from the bottom up. It is here that Gabriela's true abilities (her "readiness for employment" in proposalspeak) shine through the web of structural limitations that exclude her from such work. Gabriela's multifaceted skills are evidenced in her many contributions to the Child Care Project. She designed and implemented a survey of worker child-care needs and helped to create a system for quantifying the results (without the aid of a computer). Gabriela has participated in organizing public meetings at which she has been a key speaker. She has helped to prepare written materials and reports. She has engaged in extensive research into child care options and regulations and participated in meetings with funders. And then, once again, she was forced to make the painful decision of not applying for any of the teaching assistant positions she was essential in creating when the child care center opened in September. Gabriela lacked the necessary proof of employment eligibility and was already financially tied to several more lucrative, though less satisfying, jobs.

Ironically, since the inauguration of the child care center, Gabriela is less involved in the EEC program than ever. While she makes great sacrifices to remain connected to the project, it has proven difficult. Her limited time and contact exclude her from many facets of day-to-day decision-making. While the paid staff assume more responsibilities and bigger roles in shaping the direction of the project, Gabriela is forced to assume a more distant, advisory role to the project. The institutionalization of the child care center, while beneficial to many EEC workers, has led once again to the exclusion of the most marginalized—those workers with undocumented immigration status. While Gabriela and others like her have improved their English language skills to an impressive degree, the fluency they have achieved cannot overcome the barriers of class, self-esteem, and legal status that prevent their entry into the jobs to which they aspire.

## Discussion

The original impetus for the EEC project was to provide alternative work for manufacturing workers in downsizing industries while providing educational workplaces with staff that reflected, culturally and linguistically, the population of children attending schools and day care centers in New York. We envisioned that EEC might be the first step on a career path that ended with a teaching position. While Angelica has followed this trajectory, her story is not typical.

Most of the EEC workers enrolled during the first year were still employed in non-professional jobs in the garment industry and other sectors where, despite low earnings, they had steady jobs and the opportunity to boost their earnings through overtime pay. Many couldn't afford to contemplate a career change that required that they substitute for an indefinite period before being hired. The fact that a significant minority of workers were undocumented presented a further conundrum. The workers in this category were often highly educated in their countries of origin, yet were consigned to non-professional work in the United States due to their immigration status. Precisely what appealed to them about the EEC program was the hope of returning to work in their professions. Yet their undocumented status made the already difficult task of linking people to jobs impossible. Structural factors such as immigration status, class, culture, and local politics intervened in the process by which theoretically, according to workplace literacy discourse, education leads to jobs.

135

Despite the program and individual achievements described here, program participants who are prepared in terms of both English language skills and volunteer experience continue to encounter a host of political, bureaucratic, cultural, language, and economic factors that govern access to jobs. This is particularly true during a time of harsh budget cuts and high unemployment. Even the best case scenarios for New York City predict that by 1997 the city will still be 250,000 jobs short of its employment base in 1989 (New York City Economic Policy and Marketing Group, 1994a, 39; 1994b, 1). Public sector cuts are the stuff of daily headlines; in 1995, outraged parents and workers were protesting Mayor Guiliani's attempt to close ten New York City day care centers and classrooms in the public school are understaffed and overcrowded. For periods during EEC's history, the board of education has not even accepted applications or fingerprinted applicants because there are so few openings and such a long list of laid-off paraprofessionals who must have priority for these.

Not only are jobs scarce in New York City, existing jobs exhibit a pattern characteristic of the current U.S. labor market: bifurcation, or the division of jobs into high-skill, high-wage occupations on the one hand and low-skill, low-wage jobs on the other, with the latter dominant. As a result, there is a sharp increase in inequality; in the United States, the wealthiest 1% has more wealth than the bottom 90% (Miller & Collins, 1995, p. 7), while the ratio of poor to rich in New York City equals that of Guatemala (Roberts, 1994, p. 33). Within this context, education acquires increasing importance; a study of New York City dislocated workers shows that those with some college education had shorter periods of unemployment and were more likely to recover lost wages when reemployed (Menzi & Huang, 1994). Even the acquisition of education, however, is tempered by the racial, gender, and ethnic segmentation of the labor market in New York City. According to the New York City Workforce Development Commission, there has been no visible advancement of African Americans and other minorities into new industries or professional, managerial occupations (1993, p. 12). Only one of the top 15 occupations for African-American and Latino men in the city is classified as profession, and 22% of African-American and 21% of Latina women are concentrated in service occupations (compared to 7% of white women). Moreover, the concentration of African-Americans in public sector jobs and Latinos in manufacturing makes them extremely vulnerable to layoffs in the current climate (Von Wagner & Syman, 1994). Lafer points to the increasing segmentation of African-Americans and Latinos into the secondary labor market, with its low wages and lack of opportunities for advancement, as a "fluid strategy for controlling labor" in the current economic and demographic context of New York City (1992, p. 224).

If the context of high unemployment and a bifurcated and segmented labor market provide both obstacles to finding work and an incentive to acquire educational credentials, how do individuals experience and respond to these factors within a workplace literacy program? An equally interesting aspect of this CWE program lies in the relatively small number of participants who actually feel ready to seek work in paraprofessional jobs. For some, work in manufacturing, despite the precariousness of this sector, is not given up lightly in pursuit of a kind of work which is very different and which presents overwhelming bureaucratic and political barriers to participation. For others, the leap in self-image which working in a school requires is a long process. For many immigrants, work in education is a high-status occupation. Others feel that their English is not yet good enough and many lack documentation as legal resident aliens. For most, the road from low level service or manufacturing work to jobs in education is far longer than the planners anticipated, and is fraught with considerations of culture, language, legal status, job security, and class issues associated with the transition to work which is seen as more professional. The response of the participants in this program has pushed us to reexamine assumptions about the meanings of education and training for workers displaced from industries where they are unlikely to be reemployed, and about the ways in which people perceive and utilize career ladders of courses. One issue illustrated by the case studies presented here is how self-esteem is affected by prior educational experiences and class background in the native country and how this influences immigrant perceptions of and decisions regarding readiness for higher status jobs and/or further education in the United States. Another is the ways in which workers use the opportunities presented by education programs as settings in which they can acquire prestige and influence events in ways not possible at work, or as steppingstones for furthering their careers.

In general, the use of education by workers or disadvantaged populations follows a trajectory very different from the middle class pathway of four years of college immediately following high school. Students at the City University of New York, many of whom are working adults, take an average of approximately 6 years to complete a four year degree. Of regular admissions students, about 50% earn degrees; among degree earners, over 47% take 10 years to finish their undergraduate degrees. For regular admissions students who enter two year degree programs, 28% graduate within 10 years (Audrey Blumberg, director of Institutional Research and Analysis, City University of New York, personal communication). Many enter and exit college several times. A study of participants in welfare to work programs indicated that progress varied among the participants, that the process was longer than anticipated by programs and that more incremental steps, in employment and education were required (Herr & Halpern, 1991). Working-class, immigrant,

137

and poor workers or job seekers who attempt to educate themselves into better jobs are taking on much more than the task of individual advancement or self-improvement; they confront structures of class, race, ethnicity, and gender that increase their difficulty at every turn. For immigrant workers, fleeing conditions of high unemployment and low wages in their own country, a class like EEC is one step in a long and often arduous journey.

## Conclusions and Questions

In their discussion of "making it in America," Portes and Rumbaut describes the major influences on immigrant success as labor market conditions, receptivity of the host society, and the context of the immigrant community. These interact with individual factors, such as class and educational attainment, to structure the immigrant experience (Portes & Rumbaut, 1994, pp. 57–142). Given the high unemployment in the United States in general and in New York City in particular during the late 1980s and continuing to the present, along with increasingly anti-immigrant and anti-minority sentiment and efforts at exclusive legislation, the current climate for EEC workers is anything but receptive.

The dilemma for teachers, counselors, and program administrators lies in crafting a programmatic response that recognizes the uses to which workers put work-related education and the pace at which they enter and complete such programs. Programs can be configured in modules that can be completed at different paces, for example, or additional counselors can be hired who can help workers work through the range of institutional and personal obstacles they face. However, many of the barriers to employment and education for EEC participants lie outside of the parameters of programs; they are subjects for the realm of policy. In the current context, which has brought us Proposition 187, these obstacles are likely to increase. What then, is the appropriate response of educators? Is it to voice our experiences and those of our workers, in an effort to create the political will that can change the conditions in which workers struggle to learn and to seize opportunities? In this vein, four years of EEC chronicles the energy, commitment and ability that immigrant workers bring to their twofold objective: to seek a better life for themselves and their communities. While they exemplify an authentic ethic and practice of social responsibility often lauded by politicians of many persuasions, their potential to contribute to the solution of urgent social problems remains largely unrecognized and untapped.

# Note

1. In February of 1992, D'Amico left to become a program administrator at the CWE, while responsibility for project management remained with the LAC.

# References

Carnevale, A. (1995). Testimony at Senate Labor and Human Resources Committee, 1/12/1995.

Delpit, L. (1995). *Other people's children: Cultural conflict in the classroom.* New York: New Press.

Garvey, J. (1992). Learning in and out of the classroom. *Literacy Harvest 1* (1), 9–13.

Guth, J. A. & Wrigley, H. S. (1992). *Adult ESL literacy: Programs and practices.* San Mateo, CA: Aguirre International (ERIC Document Reproduction Service No. ED 348 895).

Herr, T. & Halpern, R. (1991). *Changing what counts: Re-thinking the journey out of welfare.* Evanston, IL: Center for Urban Affairs and Policy Research, Northwestern University.

Lafer, G. (1992). Minority unemployment: Labor market segmentation, and the failure of job training policy in New York City. *Urban Affairs Quarterly, 28*-(2) 206–235.

Menzi, D. W. & Huang, Q. (1993). *Dislocated workers in New York City: Analysis of data from the January 1992 current population survey.* New York: City University of New York Regional Education Center for Economic Development.

Miller, S. M. & Collins, C. (1995). Putting equality back on the American agenda. *Poverty and Race, 4*-(4), 7–8.

New York City Economic Policy and Marketing Group. (1994a ). Quarterly Economic Report, Fourth Quarter 1993.

New York City Economic Policy and Marketing Group. (1994b). Quarterly Economic Report, First Quarter 1994.

New York City Workforce Development Commission. (1993). *The new workforce: Investing in New York's competitiveness.* New York: Report of the Commission to Mayor Dinkins.

Office of Vocational and Adult Education. (1990). *An overview of adult English as a second language programs for limited English proficient adults.* Washington DC: Division of Adult Education and Literacy.

O'Neill, H. & Moss, M. (1992), *Reinventing New York: Competing in the next century's global economy.* New York: Urban Research Center, Robert Wagner School of Public Service, New York University.

Portes, A. & Rumbaut, R. (1990). *Immigrant America: A portrait.* Berkeley: University of California Press.

Rees, F. (1993). Adult literacy programming: Whose needs are being served? *Adult Education Quarterly 3-*(3), 160–170.

Roberts, S. (1994) Gap between rich and poor in New York City grows wider. *New York Times,* pp. 33–34.

Rodriguez, R. (1982). *Hunger of Memory.* New York: Bantam.

Von Wagner, M. and Syman, S. (1994). *A profile of the New York City labor force.* New York: New York City Economic Policy and Marketing Group, Office of the Deputy Mayor for Finance and Economic Development.

Young, C. D. (1994). *Asking new questions: Assessment for workplace literacy.* Albany, NY: Civil Service Employees Association, Inc. and New York State Governor's Office of Employee Relations.

# FIVE

## "Friends in the Kitchen":
## Lessons from Survivors

*Sheryl Greenwood Gowen and Carol Bartlett*

Ms. Taylor: I tell my girls, when they have a fight, to go into the kitchen, their friends are in the kitchen.
Carol: You mean the knife?
Ms. Taylor: Yes, the knife, the ice pick, the boiling water, the scissors.

This is a story about how two white, middle-class academics learned that their notions about women and literacy were reductive and naive. We learned this from three African-American working-poor women who have been participating in a workplace literacy class that we organized three years ago.[1] These women, through their journal writing, their private conversations with Carol, and their responses to the program have taught us about domestic violence and its direct relationship to their lives, learning, and work. While this is a story that involves only a few women, we believe that it raises significant issues that bear further consideration in the field of worker education. It is a troubling story, and challenges popular wisdom about voice and silence, diversity and empowerment, pedagogy and curriculum. Ultimately, however, it is a story about growth and healing.

In this chapter, we will describe how we came to learn about domestic violence from these women, how that knowledge challenged us to redefine our teaching and pedagogy, and how these women's lives have changed since they began "going to school." We will conclude with a discussion of the emotional, financial, social, and legal complications domestic violence imposes on women's efforts to increase their literacy skills.

## Literacy as Benefit Rather than Need

To set this in a context, let's look first at the program itself, which is a bit of an anomaly. First, unlike most literacy programs, it is not offered in the corporate or industrial world, but in an educational, academic setting at an urban university in a southeastern state. The program provides literacy classes for physical plant, groundskeeping, and maintenance employees, whose pay is quite low. The workers in these departments do, however, have benefits and regular hours, but until recently, there has been very little opportunity for training, and advancement has been difficult.

Those employees who maintain a workplace tend to be invisible to the other, more privileged workers, and it has been true at this institution as well. There are two universes operating within the same physical space. One consisting of faculty, students, and more well-positioned staff, while the other is given over to those who serve and clean up after the first group.

If one observes the cleaning women, for example, one may see, in some instances, a kind of physical shrinking away from others.[2] Walking close to a wall, taking the far corner in an elevator, not wanting to intrude or disturb to empty a trash can, rarely making eye contact with students or faculty. These cleaning women are treated, by many (but certainly not all) as invisible and silent. A story to illustrate the point: When these women are cleaning the men's rest rooms, males will come in to urinate without even acknowledging the women's presence, even though the cleaning women have propped open the door with the large, yellow carts used all over the university for cleaning.

In the university, talk is an underground activity. The physical plant and maintenance departments, like other work areas within the institution, have their own highly evolved, informal methods of oral communication that form an integral part of the labor process. But the formal work design tends to eliminate both talking and collaborative group work. Much of the work has been, until quite recently, assigned to individuals instead of to work teams, and group communication with management has been strongly discouraged.[3]

### The Program

Unlike most workplace programs, this one was initiated in response to a request by a staff member in a year when the state budget had no money for pay raises for staff (although faculty still received merit pay raises that year). In a meeting, the university president explained to the staff, "We can't give you raises. What can we do for you?" A custodian spoke up and said, "This is a school. We want to go to school."

In response to this request, the president decided that offering literacy classes to entry-level staff would be a relatively inexpensive investment and would do much to improve the quality of life for the staff. In a meeting with other administrators, the president explained that it was "inexcusable" that the university offered education courses to everyone in the state but did nothing to offer education to its own employees.

It is important to note that in this decision to offer workplace literacy classes, the articulated goal was to offer literacy as a *benefit* rather than as remediation for some productivity problem. As such, it has been developed from a learner-centered model rather than from a training model. Most importantly, the administration has never required any testing to measure improvement. Rather, the measure of the success of the program has been how many employees attended the classes and whether or not the employees believed that the classes were beneficial. Thus the consumers of these classes were the employees, not the administrators. If the consumers did not like the product, they would not participate and the classes would be discontinued. We suspect, but cannot prove, that if the classes had been designed as a reme-diation effort and had employed traditional testing or even alternative forms of evaluation that the women we are focusing on in this class would not ever have participated.

Many of the program costs have been met by using already existing resources, and thus the actual costs of the program are quite small. For exam-ple, the university's Learning Lab has donated classroom space and the Department of Learning Assistance has donated technical assistance. The classes meet twice a week for a total of three hours. They are open entry/open exit and are offered to both day and evening-shift workers.

### *The Curricula/Pedagogy*

We developed the class on what the literature has described as the pre-ferred learning styles of both women and of African-Americans.[4] Specifically, we chose to emphasize cooperative learning, a humanized, pragmatic curricu-lum, and an emphasis on connection and caring. These characteristics also fit with our own preferred teaching styles, which reflect our own notions of women in terms of "connection, circles or chains of caring" and of teaching as a "moral enterprise" (Kazemek, 1986, p.p. 23–24). That is, we have tried to place caring in the center of teaching and to encourage the group members to care for one another. Our goal has been for students to grow in the acquisition of knowledge and the enhancement of skills within an ethical or moral framework. The donated space, materials, and instructional support from members of other academic units across the university have also modeled this collaboration and caring. In each instance, the space, materials, and instructional expertise have been offered by women who function in a variety of roles (faculty, department chairs, directors of non-academic units). The physical structure in the learning lab (designed by a woman) also allows a collaborative use of space, with large tables, comfortable chairs, carpeting, plants, and artwork.

We also, on a tacit level, planned to work from a critical pedagogical base. Both of us have been concerned with issues of social justice and worker exploitation. Our goals have always included a critique of the power relations in the workplace. While we have not considered ourselves radical critical pedagogues, much of the critical literacy discourse has informed our practice.[5]

## Learning from the Learners

After six months of classes, we learned what we thought would be our most important lesson. The presumptions about the learning styles of women and African Americans described by the literature cited above were not well-received by the women participating in this class. In short, it became clear to both of us that many of our assumptions were wrong. Specifically, we learned that

1. the women in the class were not comfortable working in groups.
2. they were offended with attempts at developing a "critical literacy" that examines the political aspects of their working lives.
3. they came for reasons that often remained secret.
4. they had a difficult time setting learning goals of any kind and then pursuing them to completion.
5. many of them did not initially see print as engaging.

In short, the women in the class did not seem to want or need the kind of collaborative group learning that has been described in the literature as being particularly suitable for women and for African-Americans. In particular, they did not themselves think of literacy as socially constructed, but rather as something one acquires in isolation and in silence.

Several incidents have drawn us to these puzzling conclusions. First, we assumed that, after their initial shyness, talking informally in class would be a relatively comfortable thing. But even though the physical space invites communication through the arrangement of tables and chairs and through the instructional materials, the class participants remained unusually silent. They seemed unwilling to talk in groups and often whispered or simply did not talk at all, but worked intently and quietly on whatever assignment Carol has devised for them. A few of the women were so timid in class that they rarely looked up from their work and did not look at Carol directly. Eyes remained discretely lowered. The group activities that Carol designed were done by individuals. Given the chance, each woman would have preferred to work in a room by herself. For example, the learning lab has four break-out rooms for tutoring. Many of the women in the class like to move off into those small tutoring rooms to work alone or sometimes in pairs. Others stay in the main room, but generally work alone.

While the literature on learning styles of African-Americans suggests a preference for external motivation (Gooden, 1993; Glasgow, 1994), these women did not respond well to Carol's efforts at being directive. This behavior is not surprising, however, because it reflects adult learning theory (e.g. Knox, 1977) which claims that adults in general prefer autonomy and self-direction. If Carol gets "too pushy" (her own description), the women just leave class for a few weeks and come back when they think that she is ready to let them have the space they need to work.

This need for autonomy is complicated, however, by the women's difficulty setting specific learning goals. Many of the women in the class seem, in Carol's words, to "dither and dally." They want one thing one day, and something else quite different the next. If they say they want to work on spelling, for example, and Carol sets up a series of activities followed by some sort of assessment, they will not show up on the day that the assessment is given. There is a need to set goals, but a difficulty in actually accomplishing them. If Carol tries to talk about the need to set goals, they will again disappear for awhile.

The literature also suggests that collaborative literacy work is a political act and that a critical understanding of one's life emerges in a collaborative literacy program. Carol tried gently to move in the direction of a critical literacy, but her attempts were rejected. A case in point: One night a new employee came to class and began a discussion about some unfairness that she believed could be corrected if her co-workers would get together and go as a group to the assistant manager. Carol saw this as a good opportunity to elicit some writing on a subject that would interest all of them and to begin to look at ways to use literacy to improve their working conditions. Looking back, Carol now describes this as "the BIG mistake." Her efforts were seen by the other women in the class as a great breach of trust. They all stopped coming to class for a few meetings, and when they did begin to come back one of the women explained to Carol that she had overstepped her bounds with them. This worker explained that the class members do not want to bring up anything controversial about work and that someone in the class would report to supervision what went on in class. They each have too much to lose. They didn't see it as Carol's place to bring up controversy. Instead, they wanted the class to focus on non-work issues. These women wanted a safe haven for learning and they didn't want that safe haven to become politicized.

In the first few months of class especially, words seemed to be of little interest to the class. They were much more interested in improving math skills, handwriting, and spelling than they were in improving reading or writing ability. During that time, Carol described the class as "not a particularly safe place to be" for the workers.

By the end of the first six months, we had learned a great deal about what seemed to work and what didn't seem to work in the class. But we were puzzled by what we had learned. We knew that our own assumptions about women and literacy were limited, but we weren't sure why. We now know that at least three of the women in the class have been silenced by the secret of sexual abuse or domestic violence. When we made this discovery, we realized that the learning styles and behaviors that we were so puzzled by in the class are similar to the ways abused women's behaviors and epistemologies are described in the literature (described in detail in below). The initial rejection of a collaborative and critical curriculum is perhaps not unusual for abuse survivors. While the literature shows us (Fingeret, 1983; Gowen, 1992) that poor, low-literate women can be strong and smart and competent, there is a place where illiteracy, economic dependence, and abuse intersect. In the following section we will describe briefly three women who have been living in that intersection.[6]

## Three Women, Three Secrets, Three Stories

The stories of abuse all came out as class members wrote in their personal journals, which Carol has used since the beginning of the classes. Carol has read and responded to these journals only when the women in the class have wanted to open a written dialogue. Carol has encouraged but not forced this dialogue, and many of the women in the class did not initially want to share what they had written with anyone. Ms. Colbert is a good example. She began writing in her journal, held it very privately, and said that no one could look at it. Several months went by with Ms. Colbert writing in her journal privately and quietly. Then one day, Ms. Colbert told Carol she wanted to share what she had written with Carol. The story in the journal was about Ms. Colbert's sexual abuse as a child by her stepfather and her mother's refusal to protect her. She finally was rescued by her grandmother. As Carol pointed out, "It was finally a story of love and support." During all the months of private work in her journal, she had been writing the same story over and over, improving it and making it more explicit with each revision. When Carol eventually read the story, she suggested to Mrs. Colbert that her story might have real value to others and asked her if she might want to share it. Finally, she wrote it anonymously for the literary magazine (called a newsletter) Carol publishes for every one in the Physical Plant. Mrs. Colbert also began writing poetry as she continued writing her story. She also began publishing her poetry in the "newsletter" under her own name. Then she became interested in math, and she figured out that she could move out of public housing and into an apartment in a much better school district for only $2.00 more a month in rent. And she kept on writing her story. She began to talk to Carol about all of this, but it took months of writing and establishing trust first. These conversations were always private. No one else in the class knew about the abuse until she published it in the newsletter, but then it was still a secret of sorts because the writing was anonymous. When she and Carol talked about goals, she finally explained, "Before I didn't have any goals. The secret took up all my space for goals. Now I don't have a secret and I have goals."

The second woman's story came out first in journal writing as well. Ms. Lawson wanted to write for the newsletter, and her written stories were, according to Carol, "about Thanksgiving, Martin Luther King, and loving everyone." Then out of the blue came a long essay about living with an alcoholic. Ms. Lawson also decided to publish her story anonymously in the newsletter rather than discuss it in class. She continued to write in her journal about her husband and his personality with and without alcohol. She wrote that it was getting worse. She wrote that throughout the entire time in the class her husband resented her going to school. She made up lies about the class and never studied at home.[7] Then one day she wrote that she was filing for divorce and had a lawyer who was having papers served on her husband. Her husband told her that he would kill her if she ever divorced him. She doesn't think that he will, and she does not want to lose her house by moving out. She is, as this chapter is being written, in the most dangerous time in her relationship with her husband. It is that point at which the woman has something in print—divorce papers, a restraining order, an arrest warrant—that she is in the most danger of being hurt or killed by an enraged partner who sees the piece of paper as the ultimate denial of what he believes is rightfully his.

Ms. James wrote in her journal that she wanted to write her autobiography some day. Carol encouraged her to start and she did. Of the three women we are discussing, Ms. James was the most ready to tell her secrets when she came to class and was most willing to share these secrets with Carol. In her autobiography she has written three stories of abuse: her father abusing her mother, her first marriage to an alcoholic, and her second marriage to an abuser. She would read and write these stories, then read them over again, and then talk with Carol about her husband's anger and her place in life. While doing math in the class, she figured out that she could refinance a house she owned in another part of the state, buy a condominium, and move out. She did all of this secretly and moved without telling her husband anything. She is doing well, taking a computer class, and continuing to work on her autobiography. Recently, one of her essays was published in a nationally distributed magazine for new readers, along with her picture. Ms. James is the most public of the three women about her abuse. Here is what she has written:

> This is a story about a woman who was very lonesome. She was having lots of problems at home. Her husband was very mean. He would beat her and call her names and made her feel like dirt. She stopped caring for herself like she should. She felt as though she wanted to commit suicide. That woman was me. I started to see myself in a different light when I had a certain accident. I fell in the middle of the street. Cars were coming. They missed me by a hair. As I was lying there a young police officer came to my aid and helped me up. He also helped stop the cars to prevent me from being hit. After that day I started to look at life differently. I thought all men were thoughtless and hateful but this young man proved to be a loving, kind human being who always was willing to help in any way he could. I have never told him how much I appreciated him. But some day I will. I see him every day. And he always has a smile. Just seeing his smile is like a sun shiney day to me. When I am unhappy his smile makes me smile. I know one day he will make a wonderful husband. As for me I am gaining confidence in myself and I am not so lonesome because I know life can be just as radiant as his smile.

This story illustrates an important point. Ms. Lawson does not attribute her "conversion" to literacy, but to the kindness of a stranger, ironically, a man. We do believe, however, that the role the literacy class has played in allowing her the opportunity to write her story is significant. As Herman has observed in *Trauma and Recovery*, inventing a language to express the unspeakable is a necessary step in healing from trauma. "The ability to tell your story—to speak your own mind—is the best antidote to powerlessness" (Miller, 1994, p. 11). The literature on narrative as a teaching and research strategy is already substantial (e.g., Bruner, 1986; Britton & Pelligrini, 1990; Carter, 1993; Chafe, 1990; Cooper, 1992; Paley, 1990; Sarbin 1986; Witherell & Noddings, 1991). A more intentional use of it in workplace literacy classes might help move those women who have been silenced by abuse into a stance of self-as-knower and maker of knowledge.

Ms. Lawson has recently told Carol that there is another woman in the class that is in an abusive marriage. This woman is very private, rarely sits with anyone, and will not write at all. If Carol asks her to write a little, she says she has nothing to say. Instead, she reads newspapers and does worksheets that Carol provides for her. She keeps coming to class, but she has not moved in the ways the three other women have. Recently she has started asking Ms. Lawson why she left her husband. We wonder if she, too, will start to write about abuse in her journal.

## Implications for Literacy Providers

The stories described here are anecdotal and we do not claim that they are generalizable. But we do believe that they surface an important issue that has not been formally addressed in any consideration of workplace literacy curricula and pedagogy for women. However, if we look at the statistics of abuse, we realize that in any workplace class for working poor women, there is a strong possibility that some of the participants might be abuse survivors. This is a research question that clearly deserves more attention because if a woman is a victim of domestic violence, then her reasons for enrolling in a literacy class and the changes that occur in her life as a result of becoming more literate are fundamentally different from the those of women who are not abuse victims. On the other hand, the abuse victim's reasons for not participating in literacy classes are also important to consider in designing both policy and delivery of services, especially in the workplace.

## Women and Abuse

In this country, approximately one in three women will experience some sort of domestic violence. Most of these women will survive the abuse physically, but their healing will take time, and the trauma and the healing will shape the quality of these survivors' homes, their families, and their work. Health and Human Services Secretary Donna Shalala claims that, "Domestic violence is an unacknowledged epidemic in our society" (Smolowe, 1994, p. 20).

But the consequences of spousal abuse as well as childhood sexual abuse are rarely considered in the literature on worker education programs. When employees seek help for these very difficult situations, they logically turn to employee assistance programs, where available.

Given the high number of women who have survived/are surviving sexual or domestic abuse and the ways these experiences and the healing process shape and are shaped by education, it is imperative for adult educators to systematically consider how pedagogy and curricula might allow for advocacy for women as they heal from these abuses. Most importantly, adult educators

149

must realize that women abuse survivors are likely to be participants in worker education programs, especially those designed for front-line, hourly-wage earning, low-skill workers. This is specifically because the two factors that put women most at risk of violence are low education and low wages—the very segment of the workforce that is described as most in need of additional training. Moreover, those women who have lower incomes and who have less job and economic security are not only more likely to be victims of domestic violence, but that violence is also likely to be more frequent and more severe (Arias, 1988). Finally, women with few viable economic alternatives and with little access to community resources are also more likely to remain in abusive relationships and to maintain negative images of themselves (Walker, 1991; Belenkey, Clinchy, Goldberger, & Tarule, 1986). And when women gain the education and skills to break out of abusive situations, they are likely to experience escalated forms of abuse, derision, or even death. For these reasons, working with women survivors requires special skill, sensitivity, and an awareness of the sometime fatal consequences of literacy and empowerment.

## Silence, Cognition, and Violence

Until quite recently research on cognitive and moral development has been based on an assumption that male development was the norm and that female development either mimicked that of males or was deviant. Researchers, including Perry and Kohlberg, for example, studied the unfolding of cognition and decision-making in males only, then cast these results in terms of a human cognitive and moral developmental model. This generalization of the male developmental model as the norm effectively silenced women's unique voices and rendered invisible their ethics of care.

Carol Gilligan's *In a Different Voice* (1982) challenged this invalidation of women's lived experiences. Gilligan argued in her work that women's moral development was quite different from men's.

Building on the work of Gilligan, Belenkey, Clinchy, Goldberger, and Tarule (1986), in their study on women's cognitive development, *Women's Ways of Knowing*, argue for a unique developmental model for the cognitive and moral development of girls and women. In this study, the authors draw on in-depth interviews of women in a wide range of settings, from students on college campuses to clients in social service agencies. From these data they have identified five stages of cognitive and moral development that are quite different from those of earlier studies of men.

While there has been a range of opinions about this female epistemology, their data contain some important information. The first stage in the authors' developmental model is called "silence." The women who appear to be functioning at this stage perceive of themselves as voiceless and mindless, symbolically illiterate, unable to immerse themselves in a meaningful symbol system. For the women in the study who exemplified this stage of development, "words were perceived as weapons. Words were used to separate and diminish people, not to connect and empower them" (p. 24).

It is important to note that Belenkey et al. found very few truly "silent" women in their study. However, those who did fall in that category were not found on college campuses, where many of the interviews were conducted, but presented themselves as clients in social service agencies. These less privileged women had little formal schooling or had been passed along from one grade to the next without any real educational advancement.

Of course, not all abused women are "silent," undereducated, and underemployed. On the contrary. Domestic violence occurs with frightening regularity across all levels of education and job status. What appears to differentiate those abuse survivors who are successful in education and the job market from those who are not, is the level of access to substantial support systems in their communities, such as good education and therapeutic facilities, or even significant family material resources. These young women tended to develop cognitively into women who perceive of themselves as knowers and producers of knowledge. Thus the effects of domestic violence appear to be mediated by community and educational resources. Those women who are least likely to have these resources at their disposal are most likely to remain silent selves, unable to tell the secret of their abuse, and isolated from the support systems they need to begin to heal.

## Schooling Girls for Silence

In subtle ways, the current education system also makes it more difficult for women to develop a sense of self that includes voice and independent action. According to the literature, American girls generally receive an education that is inferior to that of their male cohorts. For example, a recent report from the American Association of University Women (1994) paints a troubling picture: In schools across the nation girls systematically and repeatedly receive less encouragement and less attention than their male counterparts. They are often silenced in order to give privilege to the boys in the class. Specifically, teachers tend to call on girls less in class, and yet at the same time hold girls to more stringent requirements for their scholarship and their deportment. Girls are expected to be obedient and quiet, while boys are rewarded for being vocal and assertive. As a result, by secondary school, girls' achievement generally lags behind boys' even though in the primary and middle grades girls tend to out-perform boys. K–12 curricula and pedagogy tend to exclude girls in terms of both their interests and their cognitive styles.

In addition to the structural aspects of education that tend to silence, school-aged girls are subjected to repeated verbal and physical harassment by both teachers and male students, yet the research indicates that school officials generally fail to protect them from these assaults.

But the silencing of women in schools and other institutions is not only about the civil rights of access and safety. It is also about the deep cultural structures that prevent women from being both competent and feminine. Thus when women exhibit both the ambition and the ability to perform competently in school and later in life, they risk a loss of femininity—a loss of gender-role identification (Brownmiller, 1984; Mulqueen, 1992).

We believe that the research on women's cognitive processing, on their special educational challenges, and their particular gender-role expectations suggests a great deal about program design for teaching literacy to women. For example, seeing words as weapons rather than as connections has been described in previous research on workplace literacy programs that deal specifically with work-related literacy tasks and texts. In previous research (Gowen, 1990, 1992), women in entry-level jobs in an urban hospital were described as both silent and silenced. They, too, often saw work-related print materials as weapons for separation and control rather than as tools for communication and empowerment.

In addition, women who had negative experiences in school are less likely to desire to repeat school-like experiences in an adult literacy classes. And women who perceive conflict between competence and femininity have difficult choices to make in becoming more literate for job-related advancement.

But traditional values have driven much of the curricula in adult education and in functional context approaches to workplace literacy. In both approaches, people and skills are defined as individual units of analysis—separated from their social and contextual networks (Fingeret, 1984; Gowen, 1992, 1994; Kazemek, 1988). The traditional model for adult education is designed for a masculine cognitive style and, moreover, reproduces socially constructed values of competence that the culture maps onto male gender identity.

Alternative forms of adult and workplace education have tended to emphasize collaborative learning groups that encourage learners to take control of their literacy learning through developing voice and action. This can be seen most clearly in the "critical literacy" for personal and political transformation espoused by Freire (1973) and his followers (e.g., Giroux, 1984; Lankshear & McLaren, 1993). But this critical model is not without its problems. For one thing, its emphasis on actively engaging the word and the world is at odds with the culture's very narrow prescriptions about femininity (see

152

Kierstead, D'Agostino, & Dill, 1988; Long, 1989), making critical literacy a conflicting path for many women. This is crucial to our understanding of women's (and men's) attitudes and beliefs about literacy acquisition because sex-role identity is closely linked to measures of self-esteem (Robinson-Awana, Kehle, & Jensen, 1986).

Kazemek pointed out in 1988 that up until that point, there has been no ethnographic or case study research to consider the effectiveness of a collaborative approach to literacy education for women. The program described above has given us the opportunity to carry out such research over an extended period of time. What we must conclude from our experiences is that while collaborative and critical approaches to literacy education might be quite appropriate for many women, they might not provide a good starting point for women who have been silenced by violence and abuse and whose goals are circumscribed by secrets that "take up all the space."

## Reflection on Kitchens and on Literacy Classes

About two years ago a young woman with two small boys and a "live-in man" came to a GED program at a local technical school in the metro-Atlanta area. She was very bright and wanted to get her GED, but the closer she got, the more her man beat her. She confided all of this to her teacher, who encouraged her to get her man to come with her to classes, but he refused and the beatings escalated. Finally, she got tired of it all and shot him one night. She is now serving time for murder and her children are in foster care. She does have her GED, but she has 12 more years of prison time to serve as well.

Still another story: During the break in a GED class at a community college in New York, several women got together and started talking about their men beating them. They were all tired of it and frightened, too. To help one another, they started a support group for battered women. One of the women's ex-husbands found out about it and when he later returned and raped her, he told her, while he was raping her, that he was doing it because of her GED class support group. We are sobered by these stories. They force us to reflect upon the particular consequences of literacy for women who are poor and undereducated and who are caught in abusive relationships. We realize how different our assumptions are about literacy's power to change lives. Change is never easy and true power is dangerous as well as liberating.

The advice about kitchens that opened this piece is the advice that Ms. Taylor gives her daughters. We believe that it illustrates the complexity of women's lives and the complications of their shared experiences. In both a literal and a symbolic sense, kitchens—in cultures where they are part of domestic architecture—are central to women's lives. As spaces given over to the storage, preparation, and consumption of food, they are the site of much of women's work. As spaces given over to talking, nurturing, and connecting, kitchens also are the site of much of the community in women's lives.

For both of us, the kitchen is central to family and community. It is where we prepare food for loved ones and friends, sometimes with creativity and joy, sometimes with fatigue and resentment. It is also where we perform the food rituals associated with holidays, birthdays, weddings, child-birth, anniversaries, illnesses, and funerals. It is where we have nurtured and taught our children and where we still share chores with our husbands. It is where we tell our stories at the end of the day, a place to reconnect. It has witnessed some of our families' most spectacular fights. It has also mistakenly been a place for trying to fill the deepest of hungers with mere food. The kitchen has defined our roles as homemakers, mothers, and community members, but it has never once in either of our lives been a place where we thought about how we could use its tools to defend ourselves from the violence of the men we have lived with.

From three courageous women, we have learned in powerful, startling ways that many of those things most common to women's lives—like kitchens, but also like literacy classes—may be constructed differently for different women, not only because of the obvious variables of the woman's desire, need, expectation, time, and resources to cook or to learn to read, but also because of how much or how little safety she has from physical abuse in her own home. We hope this story will lead others to consider the role that violence and abuse play in the silence and lack of literacy for many women and to develop effective means of support for these women when they decide to tell their stories.

## Notes

1. Our roles in this program: Carol has been the teacher/researcher and Sheryl has been the "technical advisor"/researcher.

2. This is not true of all of the women who work in the physical plant. Many of them are friendly, open, and carry themselves with dignity. But there are some women who fit this more troubling description. We are concerned with this silent minority in this paper.

3. Recently, there has been a change in administrators at the university, and his "vision" is to apply the principles of Continuous Improvement, specifically team-work and treating one another as "customers." What we are writing about here applies to the conditions at the university

before this recent change. What we are describing, then, is the historical present, which, in this instance covers the three years between January 1992 and January 1995.

4. See, for example, Gilligan, 1982; Lyons, 1983, 1987; Belenkey, Clinchey, Goldberger, & Tarule, 1986; Miller, 1986; Gilligan, Lyons, & Hanmer, 1990, for a discussion of women's preferred learning styles and moral decision-making. See Ramirez & Casteneda, 1974; Brooks, 1985; Biggs, 1992; and Gooden, 1993, for a discussion of teaching methods for adult African-Americans.

5. See, for example, Lankshear & Lawler, 1989; Bee, 1993; Lankshear & McLaren, 1993; Rockhill, 1993.

6. It is important to remember that women who have been sexually abused as children and women who are currently in violent relationships are treated quite differently in the clinical literature. We combine them in this discussion because they each were silenced by their experiences and unable to move toward more academic work until they had dealt with their secrets.

7. We believe that this is a significant aspect of a workplace literacy program that is delivered on work time at the workplace. It offers those who need it complete confidentiality. They can take the classes and develop their skills without the abusive partner ever finding out the "secret."

# References

American Association of University Women. (1994). *Shortchanging girls, shortchanging America*. Washington, DC: Author.

Arias, I. (1988, August 21–23). *Economic, social, and psychological resources as predictors of victimization*. Paper presented at the Annual Meeting of the Society for the Study of Social Problems, Atlanta, GA.

Bee, B. (1993). Critical literacy and gender. In C. Lankshear & P. McLaren (Eds.), *Critical Literacy: Politics, praxis, and the postmodern*. Albany, NY: State University of New York Press.

Beleneky, M. F., Clinchy, B., Goldberger, N. & Tarule, J. (1986). *Women's ways of knowing*. New York: Basic Books.

Brownmiller, S. (1984). *Femininity*. New York: Linden Press/Simon & Schuster.

Britton, B., & Pelligrini, A. (Eds.). (1990). *Narrative thought and narrative language*. Hillsdale, NJ: Erlbaum.

Bruner, J. (1986). *Actual minds, possible worlds*. Cambridge, MA: Harvard University Press.

Carter, K. (1993). The place of story in the study of teaching and teacher education. *Educational researcher, 22*(1), 5–12, 18.

Chafe, W. (1990). Some things that narrative tells us about the mind. In B. Britton, & A. Pelligrini, (Eds.), *Narrative thought and narrative language*. Hillsdale, NJ: Erlbaum.

Chodorow, N. (1978). *The reproduction of mothering*. Berkeley: University of California Press.

Cooper, P. (1992). *When stories come to school: Telling, writing & performing stories in the early childhood classroom*. New York: Teachers and Writers Collaborative.

Delpit, L. (1995). *Other people's children: Cultural conflict in the classroom*. New York: The New Press.

Fingeret, H. A. (1983). Social network: A new perspective on independence and illiterate adults. *Adult Education Quarterly, 33*, 133–146.

Freire, P. (1973). *Education for critical consciousness*. New York: Seabury Press.

Glasgow, J.N. (1994). Accomodating learning styles in prison writing classes. *Journal of Reading, 38*, 188–195.

Gilligan, C. (1982). *In a different voice*. Cambridge, MA: Harvard University Press.

Gilligan, C., Lyons, N. P., Hanmer, T. J. (1990). *Making connections: The relational worlds of adolescent girls at Emma Willard School*. Cambridge, MA: Harvard University Press.

Gooden, C.R. (1993, summer). Diversity with style—learning style that is! *Kappa Delta Pi Record, 29(4)*, 129.

Gowen, S. G. (1990). Measuring women into silence/hearing women into speech: Beliefs about literacy in a workplace literacy program. *Discourse & Society, 4*(2), 439–50.

Gowen, S. G. (1992). *The politics of workplace literacy: A case study*. New York: Teachers College Press.

Herman, J. L. (1993). *The aftermath of violence: From domestic abuse to political terror*. New York: Basic Books.

Kazemek, F. (1988). Necessary changes: Professional involvement in adult literacy programs. *Harvard Educational Review, 58*, 464–487.

Kierstead, D., D'Agostino, P., & Dill, H. (1988). Sex role stereotyping of college professors: Bias in students' rating of instructors. *Journal of Educational Psychology, 80*(3), 342–344.

Lankshear, C. & Lawler, M. (1989). *Literacy, schooling, and revolution*. London: Falmer Press.

Lankshear, C. & McLaren, P. (1993). *Critical literacy: Politics, praxis, and the postmodern*. Albany, NY: State University of New York Press.

Long, V. O. (1989). Relation of masculinity to self-esteem and self-acceptance in male professions, college students and clients. *Journal of Counseling Psychology, 36*(1), 84–87.

Miller, M. V (1994, November 20): "Surviving Anne Sexton." *New York Times Book Review*, p. 11.

Mulqueen, M. (1992). *On our own terms: Redefining competence and femininity*. Albany, NY: State University of New York Press.

Noddings, N. (1991). Stories in dialogue: Caring and interpersonal reasoning. In C. Witherall & N. Noddings (Eds.), *Stories lives tell: Narrative and dialogue in education* (pp. 157–170). New York: Teachers College Press.

Paley, V. G. (1990). *The boy who would be a helicopter: The uses of storytelling in the classroom*. Cambridge, MA: Harvard University Press.

Robinson-Awana, P., Kehle, T. J., & Jensen, W. R. (1986). But what about smart girls? Adolescent self-esteem and sex-role perceptions as a function of academic achievement. *Journal of Educational Psychology, 78*(3), 179–183.

Rockhill, K. (1993). (Dis)connecting literacy and sexuality: Speaking the unspeakable in the classroom. In C. Lankshear & P. McLaren (Eds.), *Critical literacy: Politics, praxis, and the postmodern*. Albany, NY: State University of New York Press.

Sarbin, T. (1986). The narrative as a root metaphor for psychology. In T. R. Sarbin (Ed.), *Narrative psychology: The storied nature of human conduct* (pp. 3–21). New York: Praeger.

Smolowe, J. (1944, July 4). When violence hits home: The Simpson case awakens America to the epidemic of domestic abuse. *Time*, pp. 18–25.

Walker, L. E. (1991). Post-traumatic stress disorder in women: Diagnosis and treatment of battered woman syndrome. *Psychotherapy*, *28*(1), 21–29.

# SIX

## Dick and Jane at Work: The New Vocationalism and Occupational Literacy Programs

*W. Norton Grubb*

For much of the nineteenth and twentieth centuries, education has been promoted as the solution to economic problems. In Horace Mann's efforts to institute public education in the 1830s, he described education as "not only a moral renovator and multiplier of intellectual power, but also the most prolific parent of material riches" (Mann, 1842/1971, p. 147). The movement for an explicitly vocational education during the period from 1890 to 1920 similarly justified education as a mechanism for "learning to earn" and a solution to problems of international competitiveness, poverty, and the integration of immigrants into the mainstream of society (Lazerson & Grubb, 1974). Since then, as formal schooling has become necessary for access to most good jobs, the vocational purposes of schooling have become well understood by students. Most high school students will admit that they are there to get a job; others think they are there to get to college—but this too is largely a vocational activity since college is a prerequisite for the best-paid, highest-status occupations.[1]

More recently, a barrage of commission reports—starting with *A Nation at Risk*, which called for educational renewal as a way to restore "our unchallenged preeminence in commerce, industry, science, and technical innovation" (p. 5)—has promoted educational reform as the principal solution to declining productivity, international competitiveness, and domestic problems like poverty and inequality. Federal legislation has followed surging interest in the occupational uses of schooling—what I describe below as the "new vocationalism"—with different programs to support various forms of occupationally oriented education.

There's been an equally long concern in this country with literacy—or, more precisely, with *illiteracy*—and the harm it can cause. The earliest support for public education came in 1647 via the Old Deluder law: "It being the chief purpose of that old deluder, Satan, to keep men from the knowledge of Scriptures," all communities in Massachusetts were required to establish schools so that children could learn to read the Bible (Spring, 1986, p. 3). An address by the commissioner of education in 1886 on "Illiteracy and Its Social, Political, and Industrial Effects" (Eaton, 1882) sounds distinctly modern in the variety of ills ascribed to illiteracy. And the current "discovery" of illiteracy, dating from around 1970, has generated estimates of the number of "illiterates" ranging between twenty and sixty million and has fueled various public and volunteer efforts to do something about the problem.

To be sure, conceptions of why literacy is important have varied. The Old Deluder law was concerned about moral regeneration and social control, while later in the eighteenth and nineteenth century political motives—the need to create a cohesive and law-abiding citizenry from the fragmented communities of the new republic—predominated. During the nineteenth and early twentieth century the rhetoric shifted from moral and political purposes to more economic fears. The current alarms about illiteracy have continued the economic focus—after all, "illiterate" individuals cannot be adequate workers, and they might become public charges—though others concerned with the individual's well-being rather than society's welfare have stressed the liberating role of literacy when an individual can read critically and write persuasively. But whatever the purpose, literacy has been a crucial instrument to achieving it.

These two strands have become intertwined in the current concern with what we might call occupational literacy—that is, preparation for the reading and writing requirements of work. One strand of the new vocationalism is the fear that the literacy skills of workers are inadequate to demands of the workplace. But now, more than in the past, we tend to turn to public policy (and especially federal policy) to resolve problems considered to be widespread—and so the last few years have seen the expansion of support for public programs related to occupational literacy. These include efforts to incorporate more academic content (including more sophisticated reading and writing) in vocational programs, expanded remedial programs linked to vocational education and job training programs, and workplace literacy programs.

Still a third issue has cycled through the history of American education: concern with the reform of curriculum and pedagogy. Although innovation in teaching is often associated with John Dewey and "progressive" education around the turn of the century, in fact there was little departure then from conventional didactic instruction except for young children. Somewhat later, during the 1930s and 40s, a number of pedagogical experiments developed at various levels of the schooling system, culminating in the innovative schools profiled in the Eight-Year Study (Aiken, 1942). These gave way to attacks on "progressive" education during the 1950s, the demise of the Progressive Education Association (Ravitch, 1983), and the return to conventional subjects (especially science and math) after the Sputnik crisis. At the end of the 1960s, a renewed interest in pedagogical innovation emerged once again, with interest in open classrooms, alternative and community-based schools, open schools like Summerhill in England (Neill, 1960), the introduction of work experience and other forms of education outside the schools, and curricular variations like career education (Marland, 1973). Starting in 1983 with *A Nation at Risk*, attention swung back to its recommendation of the "new basics," higher academic standards for students embedded in graduation requirements and new testing requirements, standards for teachers, and an atmosphere of accountability (Tanner & Tanner, 1992).

Currently, partly in recognition that the reforms of the 1980s have done little to improve most schools, there is increased interest in quite different approaches to teaching, including constructivist learning, whole language and the process approach to writing, "contextualized" instruction and notions of cognitive apprenticeship (Collins, Brown, & Newman, 1989), project-or problem-based learning (Prawat, 1993), and curriculum integration (Jacobs, 1989; Fogarty, 1991) including the integration of academic and vocational education (Grubb, 1995b). These innovations have also been adopted in small ways in a variety of schools—though, consistent with the history of teaching innovation (Cuban, 1993), these changes seem more common in elementary and middle schools than in high schools. Unlike some other reforms of the moment—the efforts to professionalize teachers, for example, or choice mechanisms, or restructuring—these efforts focus directly on teaching and learning.

At the moment, then, there's a confluence of interest in the new vocationalism, in literacy generally and occupational literacy in particular, and in new approaches to teaching and learning. But there's a conundrum: The programs that have been enacted to enhance occupational literacy tend not to embody the new approaches to teaching and learning that have been tried elsewhere in the vast educational "system." Instead, they often follow the conventional approach to teaching that I call "skills and drills":[2] fragmented, didactic, teacher-centered, and often quite different in their content from the higher-order skills associated with the new vocationalism. This is, of course, the approach to teaching associated with Dick and Jane and Spot, with generations of basal readers now conventionally lambasted for putting generations of students to sleep. Ironically, the response to alarms about the deficient skills of the workforce has been to devise new programs (and expand old ones) related to occupational literacy, but to neglect the content and pedagogy of these efforts. Dick and Jane are gone from the elementary grades, but they are still alive and well in work-related literacy efforts.

Unfortunately, the neglect of pedagogy may be a fatal one. Without a concerted attention to changing pedagogy, even the best-conceived programs will tend to follow the well-established, familiar approaches of skills and drills—and there are good reasons to think that for many subjects and many students (especially the adults enrolled in many occupational literacy programs) these are the least effective methods. Therefore, we can expect that continued reliance on conventional pedagogy will only undermine their effectiveness. Finally, I take up the question of why policy, and federal policy in particular, tends to neglect issues of pedagogy. The various reasons, by turn technical, pedagogical, and deeply value-laden, provide some ways to understand the prospects for pedagogical reform, to which I turn in the Conclusion.

## The Strands of the "New Vocationalism"

While there are many voices now clamoring for schools and colleges to serve more occupational purposes, they differ in their analysis of the underlying problem, and above all in their recommendations. Some of these advocates call for new kinds of content and others for new approaches to pedagogy, while others are more distinctly conservative. It's worth, therefore, disentangling the various strands of what I (and others) call the new vocationalism,[3] in order to clarify how they vary, and how their recommendations have been both included and distorted in various occupational literacy programs.

The initiator of the current wave of school reform is generally conceded to be *A Nation at Risk*. This publication epitomizes the first strand of the New Vocationalism, with its insistent economic rhetoric: The great threat to our country's future was "a rising tide of mediocrity" in the schools, causing "unthinking, unilateral education disarmament" (p. 5) and a decline in our international competitiveness. To be sure, the emphasis on economic roles for schooling was leavened with a brief nod to preparing a well-informed citizenry: *A Nation at Risk* approvingly quoted Thomas Jefferson's maxim:

I know of no safe repository of the ultimate powers of the society but the people themselves; and if we think them not enlightened enough to exercise their control with a wholesome discretion, the remedy is not to take it from them but to inform their discretion. (p. 7)

But this was an afterthought; the dominant rational for schooling in this and other reports—indeed, the only rationale, in the more utilitarian of the reports like *Workplace Basics: The Essential Skills Employers Want* (Carnevale, Gainer, & Meltzer, 1990)—is its preparation of future workers.

Of course, there was very little novel about the economic purposes artic-ulated in these reports, since from the time of Horace Mann the academic orthodoxy has had its economic underpinnings. The only difference about the claims of *A Nation at Risk* was that the political, intellectual, and intrinsic arguments for the standard curriculum—knowledge as its own reward, the "beauty, pleasure, surprise, personal enlightenment and enrichment at the heart of the classic liberal-arts ideal" (Kean, 1993)—were displaced by eco-nomic arguments. But the *content* of schooling was not to change. *A Nation at Risk* recommended the "new basics"—English, math, science, social studies, and (the only novelty) a half year of computer science. States followed with higher academic standards for students embedded in graduation require-ments, new testing requirements, and new content standards for teachers (Tanner & Tanner, 1990). As many commentators noted, the dominant response was "more of the same"—the same academic curriculum that has dominated the high school since the nineteenth century, taught in roughly the same ways though with a new sense of urgency. In response, enrollments in conventional academic subjects increased—even those subjects (like his-tory and social studies) associated more with political than economic pur-poses, because of their inclusion in the new basics—at the expense of enrollments in vocational subjects, "general" education, art, music, and some electives (Coley, 1994).

The first round of school reform did change course-taking patterns, but otherwise mediocre performance seemed to drag on. One of many responses, in the current bewildering array of reform movements, has constituted a sec-ond strand of the new vocationalism: the argument that the changing econ-omy requires new skills of its workers, and therefore new approaches to teaching in the schools. In the reports of the Secretary's Commission on Achieving Necessary Skills (SCANS), the requirements of the high-skill workplace now require a range of foundation skills—basic skills including reading, writing, math, listening, and speaking—but also thinking skills (like decision-making, problem-solving, knowing how to learn) as well as personal qualities necessary at work like responsibility, sociability, self-management, integrity, and honesty (SCANS, 1991). But these SCANS skills, or "workplace basics," or "generic" skills (Stasz et al., 1993) are not well taught in conventional didactic instruction, with its emphasis on individualized instruction rather than cooperative learning, on abstract principles and decontextualized learning, on fact acquisition rather than problem-solving abilities. Therefore, this argument has led to calls for changing the nature of instruction by including more experiential learning outside of conventional classrooms and more "contextualized" instruction. For example, the W. T. Grant Foundation Commission on Work, Family, and Citizenship, siding with the "forgotten half" poorly served by the conventional academic curriculum, argued for a mix of "abstract" and experiential learning (Youth and America's Future, 1985):

> These experience-based educational mechanisms offer some of the most exciting opportunities available anywhere in America for sound learning and healthy personal development. For some young people, certainly, they can be vastly more productive than schools or colleges. And that is why we consider "educational institutions" to include not only classrooms, libraries, and laboratories, but also other environments where purposeful and effective learning can take place: the workplace, public and non-profit agencies, museums and cultural institutions, the media, youth agencies and community services, field studies and workshops in the out-of-doors, and community-based organizations in the inner city.

Similarly, SCANS (1991) called for revising the abstract approach to learning:

> SCANS believes that teachers and schools must begin early to help students see the relationship between what they study and its applications in real-world contexts. . . . We believe, after examining the findings of cognitive science, that the most effective way of teaching skills is "in context." Placing learning objectives within real environments is better than insisting that students first learn in the abstract what they will then be expected to apply. . . . Reading and mathematics become less abstract and more concrete when they are embedded in one or more of the competencies; that is, when the learning is "situated" in a system or a technological problem. (p. 19)

By referring to the work of cognitive scientists, the SCANS commission explicitly linked the demand of employers to the claims of certain educational reformers. The metaphor of "cognitive apprenticeship" captures this approach: Just as apprentices learn the tasks of their trade in the context of ongoing work, so too the student-as-apprentice-learner would learn academic competencies in some meaningful context, with the support of the master or teacher providing initial guidance ("scaffolding") at early stages and then allowing the apprentice/student to do more on his own ("fading"), and teaching not only the complete range of technical skills but also the interpersonal skills, the customs, and the culture of the craft (Collins, Brown, & Newman, 1989). As a model of teaching, this is quite different from the standard didactic approach in which learning lacks any context, in which the ultimate goal of instruction is either unclear or (as in the case of college admission) abstract, and in which teachers provide information without the monitoring, demonstration, and support of the idealized master.

However, while the methods of instruction may have to change in the second strand of the new vocationalism, this does not mean that the content of formal education should change. The subjects illustrated by proponents of cognitive apprenticeships are still those of the standard academic curriculum. The SCANS reports have suggested how to teach various SCANS skills (e.g., interpersonal skills, systems thinking, and knowledge of technology) in core curriculum areas like English, math, and science. Similarly, the recommendations for the "forgotten half" continued the conventional curriculum of the high school while adding to it various forms of community-based learning. In particular, it has become clear that the "skills employers want" are not those of conventional vocational education. The Committee on Economic Development (1985) declared that "Business, in general, is not interested in narrow vocationalism. It prefers a curriculum that stresses literacy and mathematical and problem-solving skills" (p. 15). Similarly, the Panel on Secondary School Education for the Changing Workplace (1984) concluded:

> The education needed for the workplace does not differ in its essentials from that needed for college or advanced technical training. The central recommendation of this study is that all young Americans, regardless of their career goals, achieve mastery of this core of competencies up to their abilities. (p. 13)

The second strand of the "new vocationalism" has therefore continued the economic and utilitarian emphasis of *A Nation at Risk*, placing employers and skills they profess to need in the driver's seat, and has continued the emphasis on a conventional set of academic subjects though with transformations in the nature of instruction.

The third strand of the "new vocationalism" has more directly addressed the deficiencies of the "old vocationalism"—conventional vocational education in high school dating from the turn of the century, focusing on specific skill training for entry-level jobs. To be sure, pressures for a more general form of vocational education, better connected to academic instruction, have a long history behind them, linked to the deficiencies of specific vocational training on the one hand and problems with the "irrelevance" of academic instruction on the other (Grubb, 1985b, vol. I., ch. 1). These improvements in vocational education have been given a substantial boost by the 1990 Amendments to the Carl Perkins Act funding vocational education. Without clarifying the meaning of integration, the amendments required that every program supported by federal funds "integrate academic and vocational education in such programs through coherent sequences of courses so that students achieve both academic and occupational competencies." Other sections supported tech-prep programs combining high school and postsecondary education (usually community colleges)—an innovation which provides opportunities for linking and integrating both the high school and the postsecondary curricula—and allowed resources for teaching students about "all aspects of the industry" they might enter, another effort to broaden the content of vocational education.

In response, a large number of secondary schools have experimented with various forms of curriculum integration, and tech prep programs—often interpreted simply as vehicles for curriculum integration—have proliferated. Several networks of schools involved in curriculum integration and tech prep have developed. In many cases, the kinds of skills advocated by SCANS and other champions of the high-skill workplace—problem-solving, analytic thinking, and other higher-order thinking skills—are also supposed to be included, though such practices (as distinct from rhetoric about their desirability) vary extensively because they require changes in teaching that are quite difficult to achieve. This form of the new vocationalism therefore represents a reform of vocational education by broadening its content and incorporating more academic skills and SCANS skills (or generic skills), all consistent with other proponents of the new vocationalism. Some forms of integrating academic and vocational education—including the applied academics courses and the Applied Communication course I review in the next section—focus on reforming vocational education itself, concentrating on a group of students who are clearly "vocational" rather than "academic" students bound for four-year colleges; by grafting academic content onto existing vocational programs they typically continue the emphasis on preparation for relatively low-level entry-level jobs right after high school. Other forms of curriculum integration are much more thorough, however: The efforts to develop academies (or schools-within-schools), schools based on several occupational "clusters" or majors, and occupationally oriented magnet schools have the potential for completely restructuring high schools for large numbers of students.

A fourth strand of the new vocationalism has emerged from the new interest in, and legislation for, school-to-work programs. Initially, such programs looked more like the German apprenticeship programs on which they were modeled—that is, work-based programs lasting relatively long periods of time (e.g., two years), capped by a "certificate of mastery" or other portable credential. As this conception became incorporated into federal legislation, it has become a tripartite program incorporating school-based learning, in which academic and vocational education would be combined within "career majors" and linked to at least one year of postsecondary education; a work-based component, hopefully with educational content rather than repetitive drudgery; and "connecting activities" to make the two consistent with each other. The School-to-Work Opportunities Act of 1994 also contains hints of pedagogical reform since it calls for "the use of applied teaching methods and team-teaching strategies," and perhaps (by implication, at least) pedagogies that are more contextualized, student-centered, active (or constructivist), and project-or activity-based. In many ways, then, school-to-work programs extend the reforms of the third strand of the new vocationalism, extending the emphasis on the integration of academic and vocational education and on tech prep and adding a work component to provide a form of learning that formal schooling cannot.

In looking across these four stands of the new vocationalism, the differences are striking. The first has been conservative in every sense of the term, while the other three are reformist in different ways. The first two emphasize academic subjects without any incorporation of occupational content, while the third and fourth incorporate vocational content as well. The four vary in their emphasis on reforming pedagogy, with the second most insistent on changing teaching methods in order to impart the new skills required at work. And the fourth is most emphatic about moving into activities outside the school boundaries, emphasizing the learning potential of employment, though the second and third incorporate this expansiveness as well. The strands of the new vocationalism are quite varied, therefore, and it should not be surprising to find those calling for a more vocational emphasis differing in their purposes and methods. But all the elements of the new vocationalism agree in making the needs of employers and the skills required in employment first among the goals of formal schooling.

## Programs to Enhance Occupational Literacy: Dick and Jane Revived

As part of the new vocationalism, several specific efforts to enhance work-related literacy have been enacted with the past few years. I will concentrate on three in particular: the integration of academic and vocational education; the expansion of remedial programs attached to vocational education and job training programs; and workplace literacy programs. All three have distinct possibilities for enhancing work-related reading and writing, as well as enhancing the higher-order skills associated with some strands of the new vocationalism; but—initially at least—each has tended to be implemented in relatively narrow ways, with pedagogies and content that come largely from the tradition of "skills and drills."

## Integrating Academic and Vocational Education: The Approach of Applied Academics

While efforts to integrate academic and vocational education have a long history, they were given renewed emphasis and specific funding by the 1990 Amendments to the Carl Perkins Act. Even more recently, as mentioned above, the School-to-Work Opportunities Act passed in May 1994 has required school-based components including both academic and vocational content; and the reauthorization of the Elementary and Secondary Education Act (ESEA) funding compensatory education has expanded the funding available at the secondary level, repeating in several places an emphasis on integrating academic and vocational education. Partly as a result of the Perkins Act, a large number of secondary schools, and a small but increasing number of community colleges, have begun to develop various approaches to integrating academic and vocational education (Grubb & Stasz, 1993).

However, there are several drawbacks to the early efforts. One is that the dominant effort has been one of the simplest (perhaps not surprisingly)—the adoption of curriculum materials "off the shelf" that are known as applied academics. These include a course in Applied Communication, using work-related applications to teach reading and writing; a parallel Applied Mathematics course; Principles of Technology, an applied physics sources; and an applied biology/chemistry course. These courses can be used in several ways. Sometimes teachers use them as starting points, and add their own materials and exercises until the results look only slightly like the original curriculum materials. Sometimes they replace the courses of the general track, with Applied Communication instead of general-track English, for example, and Applied Math instead of general math—a change that is probably beneficial because of the low level of general courses. Often, however, applied academics courses are used simply as remedial courses, in place of conventional English and math courses—a reflection of the century-old notion that vocational education, and subjects allied with it, would be more appropriate to the "manually-minded" students who did poorly in academic subjects.

Whatever the variation in its use, Applied Communication has several limitations as an approach to literacy. (See also Mark Jury's more extended critique of Applied Communication in this volume.) It uses examples from work to teach various forms of reading, writing , and oral communication; for example, students write memos and business letters instead of essays about literature, read instruction manuals and business directives, and practice oral interchanges with bosses and co-workers. The first problem, then, is that rather than expanding the repertoire of literacies that students learn, Applied Communication replaces one form of literacy ("school literacy," usually concerned with the simple decoding of standard literature) with another kind of "work literacy," addressing the simplest literacy tasks required at work.[4] A broader alternative would be to present a broader array of literacy-related practices, including those associated with literature and with citizenship, along with work-related practices (e.g., Koziol & Grubb, 1995, and Koziol, 1992). A second drawback is that—partly because the work settings in Applied Communication must be comprehensible for students across a range of occupations—the occupational examples are all contrived; very often they seem artificial and elementary, and therefore lack the motivating power that work settings are supposed to bring to teaching.[5] Third, while Applied Communication suggests a number of more active approaches to teaching— for example, role-playing with the roles observed in work, or possibilities for interviewing community members about their work roles and the skills required in work—there are also many more conventional exercises (e.g., fill-in-the-blank worksheets, grammatical exercises, and extraction of facts from simple text). As a set of *curriculum* materials, Applied Communication is relatively inert in its approach to pedagogy, with little material associated with it that might help teachers make the transition from standard didactic practices to more active and student-centered methods.

The drawbacks of Applied Communication are essentially those of the more general approach of applied academics, and of the integration of academic and vocational education overall. While this kind of curriculum has the power to reshape both the entire high school curriculum and pedagogy (see Grubb, 1995, especially vol. I, chapters 4 and 10, and the conclusion), most current applications are much more modest. In many cases, allowing work to determine the academic curriculum—in settings where educators are primarily thinking of "non-college-bound" students, likely to go into entry-level occupations—leads to academic content of relatively low level and power; for example, English classes for would-be secretaries stress only the mechanics of rewriting, while those for future auto mechanics emphasize the simplest forms of oral communications, interactions with supervisors, and simple workbook entries. Using work to drive content and examples also makes it difficult to develop student-centered practices—since work is typically viewed as a series of externally-imposed tasks over which workers have little discretion. Except in those schools where students are grouped into "academies" (schools within schools), or "clusters" or "majors," or are in occupationally oriented magnet schools—all of which prepare students for a *broad* range of related occupations, from entry-level to the most sophisticated professional positions—occupational examples are likely to come from narrowly defined entry-level occupations, and are therefore likely to seem contrived and distant to many students uninterested in that occupation.

Above all, as Berryman (1995) has argued, the movement to integrate academic and vocational education is principally a curriculum effort, not necessarily a pedagogical reform. Even though curriculum integration and its occupational orientation are conducive to the approach I call "meaning making," and can be interpreted as the heir to Deweyan approaches to "education through occupations" by using occupations as the context or lens to motivate all academic instruction (Dewey, 1916, ch. 23; Grubb, 1995b, vol. I, ch. 1), it is certainly possible to teach an integrated curriculum with the methods of "skills and drills." Until teachers are retrained in distinctly different approaches to pedagogy, any new curriculum materials are likely to be taught in the same old familiar ways. (See especially the article by Judy Kalman and Kay Losey in this volume for evidence of "backsliding" in a workplace literacy program.)

### Remedial Education for Vocational Education and Job Training

A second large area in which public policy has, often inadvertently, established work-related literacy programs is that of remedial education (Grubb, Kalman, Castellano, Brown, & Bradby, 1991; Grubb & Kalman, 1994). The problems of inadequate basic academic skills are widespread both in the dominant vocational education programs, which now exist in community colleges and postsecondary technical institutes, and in the kinds of shorter-term job training programs funded by the Job Training Partnership Act (JTPA), welfare-to-work programs supported by the welfare system, and other federal job training programs. In response, a large and chaotic network of remedial programs has sprung up—in community colleges, adult education programs sponsored by a bewildering variety of institutions (and often funded by federal adult education funds), and in job training programs themselves. Many of these are designed explicitly to allow their students to enter particular vocational education or job training programs; others allow students to enter the "regular" programs of community colleges, or prepare them for the GED exam. The dominant subjects are reading, writing, and math; often, within any community, there are two or three levels of such courses offered, in theory allowing individuals to start at any level of preparation and proceed to college-level English and math. In practice, however, information about and referrals among programs are poor, attendance is episodic, and progress is generally slow. There is, with the exception of some community college programs, very little evidence about effectiveness; but there is a pervasive sense of a large unwieldy set of programs, lacking any systematic information about completion or progress, with virtually no evidence of success. (See also the chapters in this volume by Marisa Castellano and by Juliet Merrifield.)

One reason for the dreary state of remedial education is that innovative teaching practices are rare. The vast majority of remedial programs follow the most conventional didactic pedagogy . There are, to be sure, some more innovative practices in community colleges, and some efforts to develop approaches more consistent with the tradition of meaning making.[6] But these are few and far between: The low status of remediation, the unfamiliarity with pedagogical issues in the job training community, the dominance of the GED exam with its reliance on conventional multiple-choice questions, and the inattention to pedagogy in much of the adult education "system"—with its large numbers of poorly trained part-time teachers and its shifting population of students—are all to blame.

While evidence about the effectiveness of different approaches to teaching is generally lacking, there are powerful reasons to be skeptical about the effectiveness of "skills and drills" in remedial programs. Most obviously, this approach violates many maxims of effective practice in adult education, especially the common assertion that curriculum materials should be adult-centered, should involve tasks meaningful to adults, and should use varied approaches. A very different challenge is that, by construction, most individuals enrolled in remedial programs have not learned basic reading, writing, and math despite eight to twelve years of instruction in skills and drills in their elementary and secondary schooling. Why another try with the same approach—particularly in the very short programs typical in JTPA and welfare—should succeed when it has previously failed over longer periods of time is unclear. Despite the general lack of evidence about the potential effects of alternative pedagogical strategies, then, there are strong *a priori* reasons for thinking that greater experimentation with different teaching methods are necessary to improve this approach to work-oriented education.

### Workplace Literacy Programs

The most direct efforts to develop occupational literacy have been the workplace literacy programs established by Congress in the late 1980s, administered by the Department of Education. This legislation has provided grants for various local organizations to develop programs that enhance the reading and writing capacities of workers in various occupational settings. The programs are operated by employers themselves as well as unions, community-based organizations, and educational institutions including adult schools and community colleges; they typically take the form of a short series of classes—sometimes located at the workplace, sometimes at an educational institution—to teach the reading and writing skills necessary for a particular occupation or a closely related group of occupations. Because the concerns about the basic skills of the workplace have concentrated on the failures of workers who are relatively low in the occupational hierarchy, most workplace literacy programs concentrate on entry-level workers, rather than the professional-level workers who typically benefit from the training sponsored by firms themselves.

Very quickly, workplace literacy programs have developed an orthodox approach to their teaching: the method known as functional context training. (See also the more extensive analysis of workplace literacy programs in Kathy Schultz's chapter in this volume, or in Schultz, 1992, and the chapters by Sheryl Gowen and by Judy Kalman and Kay Losey.) Functional context training seeks to "integrate literacy training into technical training" on the grounds that learning basic skills is easier in the context of vocational training where such skills have obvious application (Sticht et al., 1987, p. 107). Functional context training also recognizes that the knowledge and skills needed for the workplace are different from those required in school-like exercises (Resnick 1987; Sticht, 1988; Venezky, Wagner, & Ciliberti, 1990). Its proponents argue that there are motivational advantages because trainees can see the purpose of learning basic skills related to their future occupations.

Typically, functional context training replaces decontextualized materials with reading materials and writing exercises drawn from a particular occupation—for example, instructional manuals, resumes, business letters, and other work-oriented memos. (These are often similar to the materials in Applied Communication courses.) However, this approach does not consciously change the other assumptions underlying its teaching methods. As a result, some functional context programs represent substantial departures from skills and drills, while others preserve many elements of conventional teaching. For example, Sticht and Mikulecky (1984, p. 13) describe a functional context program to train word processors:

> Assignments were planned to integrate language and machine skills. Much of the classroom simulated actual job demands. Students would compose business communication that other students would edit and later produce in final form on word processing equipment. A good deal of the work involved using actual business communication that was handwritten in rough draft form with editing notations. The job simulation training that integrated language and machine experience ranged from about 5 percent of assignments the first week to nearly 100 percent in the final weeks. Class assignments attempted to replicate the time constraints present in business performance. Though much of the work was done on an individual level, some work made use of worker teams, which again replicated workplace conditions.

Based on this description, the program incorporated several elements not normally associated with skills and drills: the use of materials drawn from work settings; interaction among students in editing and in the use of work groups; and job simulation, which introduces modeling as a form of learning as well as the behavioral and interpersonal dimensions of work.

However, in other cases functional context programs seem more like skills and drills. In one example, Sticht identified two reading tasks: reading to do, composed of 186 subtasks; and reading to learn, composed of 143 subtasks (Sticht, 1979); then the program provides extensive drill and practice in locating and extracting information from job-reading materials. Each module includes a pre-and a post-test. Each module consists of materials and numerous worksheets requiring that the person performs the tasks indicated by the module name.

In one strand of the Army's "Functional Literacy" or FLIT program, described as a "modular, self-paced, mastery-based program of job reading task training" (Sticht et al., 1987, p. 114), individuals were given materials drawn from one of six specific occupations. They were also given drill and practice in using a table of contents, an index, tables and graphs, and a manual to look up facts, and drills in following instructions and filling out forms—all practices familiar from skills and drills.

While the functional context approach does overturn a fundamental practice of skills and drills—its tendency to divorce instruction from any possible context in which competencies might be used—in other respects functional context training is compatible with either skills and drills, with meaning making, or with eclectic approaches drawing from both pedagogical traditions. It has been particularly susceptible to developing long lists of necessary skills, based on job task analysis and literacy audits (as Schultz demonstrates in her chapter in this volume)—a practice that tends to lead to "skills and drills." And the partisans of functional context training have paid scant attention to teacher training, without which no change in pedagogy will take place. It is a mistake, therefore, to interpret functional context training as a complete replacement for conventional remediation since it replaces only some of the assumptions underlying skills and drills, and it can too easily lead to programs that look like conventional teaching. And, like many of the efforts to integrate academic and vocational education, functional context programs usually concentrate on the simplest and most utilitarian literacy competencies—replacing "school literacy" with "work literacy" rather than expanding the repertoire of competencies or consulting the worker-as-student about what he or she needs most.

The occupational literacy programs that have been established and expanded within the last decade vary, of course: They concentrate on different levels of the education system, ranging from high school students to adults; the settings vary, from high schools to community colleges to job training programs to work sites; and their purposes vary, from reconstructing the high school to providing the prerequisites necessary for vocational skills training to remedying the deficiencies of particular groups of workers. But they share distinct similarities, especially at this early stage in their implementation: a tendency to let entry-level jobs and low-level skills, rather than the higher-order skills associated with high-skill work, dictate the content; the practice of replacing one narrow form of literacy ("school literacy") with another ("work literacy"); and a general neglect of innovative pedagogy. Each of them has promise, but realizing this promise will require greater attention to the vision and details of these programs.

## The Poverty of Policy: The Inattention to Pedagogy

The conclusion that the most common occupational literacy programs have tended to replicate conventional approaches to teaching—even in situations (like remedial education) where there are good reasons to think that such approaches are ineffective—raises a larger question: Why has public policy—and federal policy in particular, since federal policy has tended to play a leading role in these changes—been so unconcerned about pedagogical issues and teaching innovations?[7] The efforts to enact occupational literacy programs have typically provided funding, but little of the technical assistance, evidence of exemplary programs, or staff development that might improve teaching. Understanding the reasons for this imbalance might help educational innovators and reform-minded policymakers change this aspect of policy—so that a new generation of programs might have more appropriate approaches to teaching embedded within them.

Based on the occupational literacy programs described in the previous section, there seem to be at least nine reasons for the shape policy has taken:

1. The conventional politics that underlies policymaking is—in a political system dominated by interest group liberalism—largely concerned with the division of the spoils, not with the fine details of program structure. The dominant debates are those about the allocation of money, not with what recipients do with the money; the dominant issues are those raised by powerful interest groups, not those principles generated by conceptions of good practice.[8] There is no interest group for innovative pedagogy—and therefore no voice for it in the political process. To be sure, there is now a constituency for "effective education," generated by the alarms about the breakdown of public education—but with a vast array of ideas about what more effective

education might be, policymaking returns to interest-group politics once again, without the ability to discern the value of pedagogical innovations.

2. The instruments of federal (and state) policy are not especially effective in encouraging pedagogical innovation. The dominant methods by which policymakers work their will include funding and regulatory mandates to constrain how funds are spent and public institutions operate—but these are awkward mechanisms to change the practices of teaching, which requires an elaborate process of understanding the philosophical and pedagogical routes of alternative practice, of practice, feedback, and revision over considerable periods of time.[9] The other instruments of policy—capacity-building and system-changing efforts (McDonald & Elmore, 1987; McDonald & Grubb, 1991)—are better-suited to the kinds of staff development and professional development centers that could foster pedagogical innovation; but the use of these instruments has been comparatively rare, and most staff development has been both unsystematic and unconcerned with pedagogical innovation.

3. There has been a long-standing division between the perspectives and preferences of policymakers and administrators—who tend to think in terms of institutions, programs, and large numbers of individuals— and teachers, whose concerns are those of the classroom and individual students. The kinds of competencies required of each group are different; each moves in different worlds, and neither group has a good understanding of the concerns of the other. Each relies on different disciplines, with policymakers coming from backgrounds in law, economics, policy analysis, political theory, organizational behavior, and management, while teachers rely on the person-centered discipline of psychology. The result is that policymakers often have little idea of how the policies they enact affect the classroom, or about the numerous implementation problems these policies encounter. For their part teachers are often unaware of the origins and intentions behind the policies that come down to them, often in distorted ways. This division means that issue of pedagogy—the responsibilities of teachers—are not central to the concerns of policymakers.

4. In an era when substantial changes require evidence on their behalf in order to counter the *status quo*, there has been almost no evidence that innovative teaching methods work better. Of course, there are different kinds of "evidence" that different people find persuasive; but the evidence that most policymakers have in mind is statistical evidence, which would demonstrate superior outcomes for an experimental group taught with innovative techniques compared to a control group

with standard techniques. However, there is relatively little of this direct evidence available,[10] partly because the efforts to evaluate different instructional methods have used inconsistent conceptions of instruction, and therefore inconsistent observations of classrooms (see Romberg & Carpenter, 1986, for math, and Hillocks, 1986, for writing). In addition, different approaches to teaching generally emphasize different goals, as the testy interchange between McKenna, Miller, and Robinson (1990) and Edelsky (1990) about the evaluation of whole-language programs illustrates: Advocates of teaching in the meaning-making tradition usually stress "authentic" tasks and higher-order competencies, notoriously difficult to assess reliably, while those following skills and drills are more likely to be content with standardized tests. But without firmer evidence, it becomes difficult to persuade policymakers that a change should be supported by public funds—and pedagogical innovation is one of the casualties.

5. In a period of time when accountability has become crucial, student-centered approaches are difficult to enact. By their nature, student-centered approaches lead in directions that *students* specify; these directions are likely to be relatively less controlled, more heterogeneous, less amenable to standardized testing and other mechanisms of accountability. The forms of accountability favored within the tradition of "meaning making"—now being developed under the banner of "authentic assessment" and other alternatives to conventional standardized testing—have not yet been well-codified, and pose problems of reliability and comparability that make them poorly suited for accountability in conventional policymaking.

6. The dominant interests in many strands of the new vocationalism are the interests of employers, not the interest of students. Student-centered approaches may be incompatible with employer-centered approaches; for example, the interests of students might be to develop the skills that would allow them to escape entry-level or routinized work, rather than to be able to perform that work with greater facility. This conflict often takes the form of debates over how narrow or general occupationally focused programs should be, with some individuals (including protectors of conventional vocational education) arguing for relatively narrow, job-specific education while others argue for more general forms of education that can prepare individuals for a range of occupations.

7. As part of the new vocationalism, an infatuation with work-based education and training has developed, partly based on a veneration of German apprenticeship systems with their supposedly contextualized, "relevant," and "hands-on" instruction and partly based on a denunci-

ation of conventional school practices in the United States, which provide decontextualized instruction in academic subjects stripped of any applications to the world outside the schools. From the viewpoint of such infatuation, any form of work-based education (as in workplace literacy programs) or any effort to use work as a context for instruction must be superior to standard practice, and issues of pedagogical methods are usually ignored. However, as Berryman (1995) has pointed out, the setting for instruction does not change the nature of the pedagogical challenges: Routinized work settings and hierarchical authority relations will generate "skills and drills" instruction at work, just as easily as in schools—as has happened in numerous work-based literacy programs.

8. The excesses of advocates within the tradition of meaning making have often given pedagogical innovation a bad name, and neither policymakers nor the public is likely to embrace practices that are associated with such extremism.[11] For example, the arguments one sometimes hears that children need not learn how to spell, or that knowledge of grammar is irrelevant, or that drills are never appropriate, or (in the realm of math) that the ability to carry out conventional arithmetic or to use algebraic notation is relatively unimportant, or more generally that knowledge of subject-specific content is less important than certain "thinking skills" or process skills or self-esteem or multiculturalism—these and other excesses strike many parents and policymakers as ridiculous, and they taint any pedagogical reforms associated with them as silly. While these positions are often (but not always) distortions of the positions that pedagogical reformers take, the appropriate discussions about pedagogy usually involve relatively subtle discussions of the sort that are difficult to carry out in either policy debates or in the media—with the result that discussions about teaching are often truncated.

9. Above all, different traditions in teaching are linked to different values and traditions in interpreting the world more generally (Bruner, 1990). The opposition of the right, including the religious right, to various educational innovations is linked to their view of the world (and religion) as a set of fixed practices (including sacred texts) passed on by the authorities of one generation to another, with little room for individual interpretation or innovation. In a society in which such beliefs are closely held among a broad spectrum of individuals, not all of whom would consider themselves conservatives, pedagogical practices that embody individual interpretation and the search for personalized meaning will always be anathema—and will be fiercely fought in public policy at all levels.

The different reasons for resistance to pedagogical innovation in policy-making are by turns technical, in the sense that they are rooted in limitations of the policymaking process as it has developed in this country (as are reasons 1 through 5), and political, in the sense that they reflect deeply-held differences of value (as are reasons 6 and 9), and pedagogical (as are reasons 7 and 8). Their confluence is powerful, however—particularly given the difficulty of changing long-established practices.

## Conclusions: What Prospects for Reform?

At any moment both "traditional" and innovative or "progressive" elements are present within education—and the strengthening of one and weakening of the other, in response to larger social and economic currents as well as the exhaustion of particular reforms, generates the sense of cycling among different changes, of "reforming again and again and again" (Cuban, 1990). At the present moment, when there are many curricular and pedagogical reform movements, there are also contrary tendencies that are conservative, homogenizing, and centralizing:[12] the efforts to establish a national curriculum, with national standards, national tests and national skills standards; the efforts to establish competency-based instruction and to define long lists of decontextualized skills including "the skills employers want" (Carnevale, Gain, & Meltzer, 1990); the curricular movements to reinstate the classics (e.g., Adler, 1989; Hirsch, 1987; the CIVITAS curriculum by Quigley & Bahnmueller, 1991), or to return to the "essentials" of education (Sizer, 1992); and the various projects to develop curriculum standards for specific subjects, all of which threaten to reemphasize the standard subjects of the nineteenth century and to eliminate interdisciplinary and integrated teaching. And of course the elections of November 1994, with their substantial shift to the right, could also usher in a new round of educational conservatism.

The present confluence of educational "movements" includes at least two—the strands of the new vocationalism that emphasize occupational content in addition to the standard academic curriculum, and the various efforts to incorporate innovative pedagogies associated with meaning making—that directly challenge the academic orthodoxy of the nineteenth century, and its modern manifestations in the conventional college-prep curriculum and the new basics. But these two elements are not well knit in current occupational literacy programs, which emphasize occupational purposes and unconventional groups of students but without modifying traditional pedagogy. What is the hope that current efforts to develop occupational literacy programs can also incorporate innovative pedagogies? Why should we think that the current interest in innovative pedagogy will be more effective than the movements of the 1930s and 1960s?

One reason is that the demands from outside the schools have changed. The current trends in employment are to develop more integrated production and flatter hierarchies in which there are fewer levels of supervision and more responsibilities for production-level workers (Bailey, 1989; Berryman & Bailey, 1992; Grubb et al., 1992), reducing the separation of management and execution, of academic and vocational. As a result, the business community has spent the past decade decrying "narrow vocationalism" and calling for workers with higher-order thinking skills, communications skills, problem-solving abilities, greater independence, and initiative. These are not the kinds of capacities which conventional instruction can convey, and the new basics of the 1980s have failed to substantially improve the quality of education. The reports of the SCANS commission and their call for contextualized and integrated instruction are clear examples at the national level of demands for new approaches to teaching, with other legislation including the Carl Perkins amendments of 1990 and the School-to-Work Opportunities Act reinforcing integrated instruction.

But demands from outside education, and top-down reforms, have never been especially effective. So a second reason for optimism is that external pressures for reform are consistent with internal motivation—with the desires of teachers themselves to be professionalized in the sense of retaining (or gaining) greater control over the "stuff" of teaching, over curriculum and pedagogy. Unlike other reforms—for example, the accountability movements of the 1980s that passed greater power to state and federal officials, via tests, graduation requirements, and other mechanisms of external control—many current efforts to reconfigure curriculum and instruction return power to teachers (Andrew & Grubb, 1995). Reforms which lead by giving more responsibility to teachers must grapple with their uneven acceptance of greater responsibilities, of course, but they are likely to have more effect than are changes imposed upon unwilling teachers, who can thwart anything they want to within the classroom.

Yet another reason for optimism about innovative instruction is that it presents a way of addressing another urgent problem which educators themselves, as well as those external to the schools, want to resolve: improving the quality of education for low income and other "at-risk" students, including many minority students and many adult students who show up in adult and remedial programs. Critics of conventional education have long pointed out its inequities, and these criticisms have been louder in the current period because of increases in the numbers of low-income, minority, and non-English-speaking students—the kinds of students who have in the past been shunted into vocational programs, who end up in remedial education in community colleges and job training programs.

In my interpretation, standard decontextualized approaches to teaching present motivational problems for all students, but some of them—the children of well-educated parents who can provide them the context for learning that schools themselves lack, or middle-class children whose teachers are more likely to depart from the boring rituals of skills and drills in favor of discussion and independence—are better able to cope with these deficiencies (Grubb, 1995a). Those left behind are students without their own sources of motivation, without the models among family or community members to enable them to see the distant "relevance" of school to future life, and students whose parents are poorly educated or who have jobs for which formal schooling is irrelevant (or who lack jobs at all). These are precisely the students whom we end up labeling "at risk" of school failure. The educational failure is due to a complex interaction: Conventional teaching following the methods of skills and drills assumes a motivation that many lower-class children (and a substantial number of middle-class children too) lack.

In searching for ways to improve the education of low-income and "at risk" students, the various solutions that operate on parents—parent education, parent involvement, family literacy campaigns—and those efforts that compensate for the deficiencies of parents (including compensatory education and early childhood programs like Head Start) have had limited success. The alternative—changing teaching so that intrinsic motivation is improved, by providing contexts meaningful to students themselves—has been less rarely proposed, perhaps since such approaches to teaching have been so uncommon for any groups of students at any level of the schooling system. However, recent reviews of teaching and learning for disadvantaged children have concluded that more active, student-centered approaches in which student have greater initiative are the most promising ways of teaching such individuals (Knapp & Turnbull, 1990; Knapp, & Shields, 1990; Knapp, Shields, & Turnbull, 1992)—methods which are consistent with the innovative pedagogies in the tradition of meaning making.

A final reason for optimism is simply associated with time: The efforts to integrate academic and vocational education, the expansion of remedial education, and workplace literacy programs are all less than a decade old. It is not surprising, given the long history behind conventional approaches to teaching and the institutional and policy constraints that persist, that initial efforts follow well-established patterns, replicating the narrow forms of the old vocationalism and the instructional methods of "skills and drills." This argument from the weight of history implies that several tasks will be important in the years ahead: The effort to maintain these kinds of programs in place, so that innovation can continue to take place; and the insistence that continued evolution is necessary, rather than allowing educators to think that a workplace literacy program once established, or an Applied Communication course added to the curriculum, is sufficient. With such persistence, we can hope that occupational literacy programs can become more innovative in their pedagogy and content—leaving behind Dick and Jane for older students and workers just as they have become outmoded for younger children.

## Notes

1. High school students rank vocational goals higher than intellectual, personal, or social goals. However, both parents and teachers rate intellectual goals the highest, and rank vocational goals third and fourth, respectively—creating a potential conflict in how they all view high schools. See Goodlad, 1984, ch. 2. A record number of college freshmen in fall 1993 cited vocational reasons for attending college: 75.1% cited being able to make more money, up from 49.9% in 1971, and 82.1% cited its value in getting a better job, up from 71% in 1976. See Higher Education Research Institute, 1994.

2. The approach I call "skills and drills" has been variously described as teacher-centered, "skills development", the "conventional wisdom," and passive learning; the alternative approach, which I label "meaning making" because of its parallels to interpretive traditions outside education (Bruner, 1990), is also referred to as student-centered, active learning, "holistic" instruction, and teaching for meaning. I emphasize that there are many distinct strands to each approach, and each is internally consistent—whereas hybrid or eclectic forms of instruction that draw on both traditions are likely to be internally contradictory. See Grubb & Kalman, 1994 or Grubb, Kalman, Castellano, Brown, & Bradby, 1992. While "skills and drills" is an approach to pedagogy, it is also linked with certain kinds of content because the tendency to fragment complex competencies into subskills and to stress part-to-whole instruction winds up emphasizing certain component skills (like grammar and spelling) rather than competencies (like critical reading) that are presumably the goal.

3. This is my own attempt to disentangle various strands of thinking that are related to the occupational roles of school. For other discussions of the "New Vocationalism," each of which argues for one strand, see Benson, 1992, Spence, 1986, Gray, 1991, Claus, 1989, Lewis, 1991, and Simon, 1983.

4. The critique that innovative practices often *replace* a standard practice with another, rather than *adding* to the repertoire of the school curriculum, is similar to Ravitch's (1983, ch. 2) critique of the excesses of "progressive" education.

5. My favorite example is the case of an Applied Math class using the "home economics" application of a mother with triplets, calculating the amounts of formula necessary; the appeal of the example to the class I was observing, of junior and senior boys, was nil.

6. The "system" of remedial education (including that of adult education) is large enough, and free enough from regulation, so that innovative practices exist in various nooks and crannies; many community-based and experimental programs, including the innovative practices that come to the attention of the literacy community, have been funded partly with public money.

7. This question is part of a larger agenda understanding how a set of macro-social forces—including historical influence, economic influences, social values and norms, institutional structures, and public policy—influence teaching. This question has rarely been even raised, let alone answered; however, see Cuban's (1993) historical work, and several of the essays in Cohen, McLaughlin, & Talbert, 1993. Current efforts to understand the effects of some state-level innovations, including curriculum frameworks and standards, will provide other information relevant to this point.

8. An excellent recent example outside the arena of occupational literacy programs has involved compensatory education, funded by the Elementary and Secondary Education Act (ESEA). As part of the process of reconsidering this act, a series of excellent studies of effective teaching of low-income children was sponsored by the Department of Education—a series arguing for some pedagogical alternatives to conventional teaching (Knapp & Turnbull, 1990; Knapp & Shields, 1990; Knapp, Shields, & Turnbull, 1992). However, the public discussion of reauthorization was completely devoid of any mention to these pedagogical issues, with the exception of a general distrust of pull-out programs; the allocation of funding and the revision of the formula for allocating funds among school districts received the majority of attention.

9. For an excellent case study of one teacher trying to change her practices, see chapter 10 of Tharp and Gallimore, 1988.

10. Some direct evidence based on learning outcomes of the superiority of alternatives to conventional teaching is available for elementary students

(Knapp, Shields, 7 Turnbull, 1992); a meta-analysis of writing has shown that the presentational (or didactic) mode and the conventional teaching of grammar are the least effective approaches (Hillocks, 1986); and some specific practices have been confirmed superior, like cooperative learning (Slavin, 1987).

11. The more general form of this argument is that each approach to teaching has its own special forms of extremism and its own special pitfalls. The extreme forms of skills and drills, for example, have been the subjects of ridicule for their rigidity and stupefying boredom at least since the 1890s, of which the attacks on the Dick and Jane series are one example. On some of the extremes of "progressive" education, see again Ravitch, 1983, ch. 2.

12. See especially Clune, 1993 on the centralizing versus decentralizing impulse in school reform.

# References

Adler, M. (1982). *The Paideia proposal: An educational manifesto*. New York: Macmillan.

Aikin, W. M. (1942). *The story of the eight-year study*. New York: Harper & Row.

Andrew, E. N., & Grubb, W. N. (1995). The power of curricular integration: Its relationship to other school reforms. In W. N. Grubb (Ed.), *Education through occupations in American high schools*. Vol. I: *Approaches to integrating academic and vocational education*. New York: Teachers College Press.

Bailey, T. (1989, May). *Changes in the nature and structure of work: Implications for skill requirements and skill formation*. Berkeley, CA: National Center for Research in Vocational Education.

Benson, C. (1992, December). *The new vocationalism in the United States: Potential problems and outlook*. Unpublished paper, School of Education, University of California, Berkeley.

Berryman, S. (1995). Apprenticeship as a paradigm of learning. In W. N. Grubb (Ed.), *Education through occupations in American high schools. Vol. I: Approaches to integrating academic and vocational education*. New York: Teachers College Press.

Berryman, S. E., & Bailey, T. R. (1992). *The double helix of education and the economy*. New York: The Institute on Education and the Economy, Teachers College, Columbia University.

Bruner, J. *Acts of Meaning*. (1990). Cambridge, MA: Harvard University Press.

Carnevale, A., Gainer, L., & Meltzer, A. (1990). *Workplace basics: The essential skills employers want*. San Francisco: Jossey-Bass.

Claus, J. (1989, December). Renegotiating vocational instruction. *The Urban Review, 21*(4), 193–206.

Coley, R. (1994). *What Americans study revisited*. Princeton: Educational Testing Service.

Collins, A., Brown, J., & Newman, S. (1989). Cognitive apprenticeship: Teaching the craft of reading, writing, and mathematics. In L. Resnick (Ed.), *Knowing, learning, and instruction: Essays in honor of Robert Glaser* (pp. 453–494). Hillsdale, NJ: Erlbaum.

Cuban, L. (1990, January). Reforming again, again, and again. *Educational Researcher, 19*(1), 3-13.

Cuban, L. (1993). *How teachers taught: Constancy and change in American class-rooms 1890–1990* (2nd ed.). New York: Teachers College, Columbia University.

Dewey, J. (1916). *Democracy and education: An introduction to the philosophy of education*. New York: Macmillan.

Eaton, J. (1882, December. *Illiteracy and its social, political, and industrial effects*. New York: Union League Club.

Edelsky, C. (November 1990). Whose agenda is this anyway ? A response to McKenna. *Educational Researcher, 9*(8), 7–11.

Fogarty, R. (1991). *The mindful school: How to integrate the curricula*. Palatine, IL: Skylight Publishing.

Goodlad, J. (1984). *A place called school: Prospects for the future*. New York: McGraw-Hill.

Gray, K. (1993, January). Why we will lose: Taylorism in America's high schools. *Phi Delta Kappan, 74* (5), 370-374.

Grubb, W. N. (1995a). The old problem of "new students": Purpose, content, and pedagogy. In E. Flaxman and H. Passow (Eds.), *Changing populations/Changing schools.* 94th Yearbook of the National Society for the Study of Education. Chicago: University of Chicago Press.

Grubb, W. N. (1995b). *Education through occupations in American high schools* (2 Vols.). New York: Teachers College Press.

Grubb, W. N., Dickinson, T., Giordano, L., & Kaplan, G. (1992, December). *Betwixt and between: Education, skills, and employment in the sub-baccalaureate labor market.* Berkeley: National Center for Research in Vocational Education, University of California at Berkeley.

Grubb, W.N. , Kalman, J., Castellano, M., Brown, C., & Bradby, D. (1991). *Readin', writin', and 'rithmetic one more time: The role of remediation in vocational education and job training programs.* Berkeley: National Center for Research in Vocational Education, University of California at Berkeley.

Grubb, W. N., & Kalman, J. (1994, November). Relearning to Earn: The role of remediation in vocational education and job training. *American Journal of Education, 103*(1), 54–93.

Grubb, W. N., & Stasz, C. (1993). *Integrating academic and vocational education: Progress under the Carl Perkins Amendments of 1990.* Berkeley: National Center for Research in Vocational Education, for the National Assessment of Vocational Education., U.S. Department of Education.

Higher Education Research Institute. (1994). *The American freshman: Twenty-five year trends.* Los Angeles: Higher Education Research Institute, University of California at Los Angeles.

Hillocks, G. (1986). *Research on written composition: New directions for teaching.* Urbana, IL: ERIC Clearinghouse on Reading and Communications Skills and National Conference on Research in English.

Hirsch, E. D. (1987). *Cultural literacy: What every American needs to know.* Boston: Houghton Mifflin.

Jacobs, H. H. (Ed.). (1989). *Interdisciplinary curriculum: Design and implementation.* Alexandria, VA: Association for Supervision and Curriculum Development.

Kean, P. (1993, May/June). Building a better Beowulf: The new assault on the liberal arts. *Lingua Franca, 3* (4), 22–28.

Knapp, M. S., & Turnbull, B. J. (1990). *Better schooling for the children of poverty: alternatives to conventional wisdom.* Vol. 1: *Summary.* Washington, DC: U. S. Department of Education.

Knapp, M., & Shields, P. (January, 1990). *Better schooling for the children of poverty: Alternatives to conventional wisdom. Vol. 2: Commissioned Papers and Literature Review.* Washington DC.: U. S. Department of Education.

Knapp, M., Shields, P., & Turnbull, B. (1992). *Academic challenge for the children of poverty.* Vol. 1: *Findings and conclusions.* Washington, DC.: U. S. Department of Education.

Koziol, K. (1992). *Novels and short stories about work: An annotated bibliography.* Berkeley, CA: National Center for Research in Vocational Education.

Koziol, K, & Grubb, W. N. (1995). Paths not taken: Curriculum integration and the political and moral purposes of education. In W.N. Grubb (Ed.), *Education through occupations: in American high schools.* Vol. II: *The challenges of implementing curriculum integration.* New York: Teachers College Press.

Lazerson, M., & Grubb, W. N. (1974). *American education and vocationalism: A documentary history, 1970–1970.* New York: Teachers College Press.

Lewis, T. (1991). Difficulties attending the new vocationalism in the USA. *Journal of Philosophy of Education, 25*(1), 95–108.

Mann, H. (1971). Fifth annual report of the secretary of the board. Reprinted in M. Katz (Ed.), *School reform: Past and present* (pp. 140–149). Boston: Little, Brown. (Original work published in 1842.)

Marland, Jr., S. P. (1974). *Career education: A proposal for reform.* New York: McGraw-Hill.

McDonnell, L., & Elmore, R. (1987). Getting the job done: Alternative policy instruments. *Education evaluation and policy analysis, 9*(2), 133–152.

McDonnell, L., & Grubb, W. N. (1991). *Education and training for work: The policy instruments and the institutions.* Santa Monica, CA: The RAND Corporation, R-4026-NCRVE/UCB.

McKenna, M. C., Miller, J. W., & Robinson, R. D. (1990, November). Whole language: A research agenda for the nineties. *Educational Researcher, 19*(8), 3–6.

Neil, A. S. (1960). *Summerhill: A radical approach to child rearing.* New York: Holt Publishing Co.

Prawat, R. S. (1993). The value of ideas: Problems versus possibilities in learning. *Educational Researcher, 22*(6), 5–16.

Quigley, C., & Bahnmueller, C. (1991). *Civitas: A framework for civic education.* Calabasas, CA: Center for Civic Education.

Ravitch, D. (1983). *The troubled crusade: American education 1945–1980.* New York: Basic Books.

Romberg, T., & Carpenter, T. (1986). "Research on Teaching and Learning Mathematics: Two disciplines of scientific inquiry." In M. C. Wittrock (Ed.), *Handbook of research on teaching* (3rd ed.). New York: Mcmillan.

Schultz, K. (1992). Training for basic skills or educating workers? *Changing conceptions of workplace education programs.* Berkeley: National Center for Research in Vocational Education.

Secretary's Commission on Achieving Necessary Skills (SCANS). (1991). *What work requires of schools.* Washington, DC: U.S. Department of Labor.

Simon, R. (1983, Summer). But who will let you do it? Counter-hegemonic possibilities for work education. *Journal of Education, 165*(3), 235–256.

Sizer, T. R. (1992). *Horace's school: Redesigning the American high school.* Boston: Houghton Mifflin.

Slavin, R. (November, 1987). Cooperative learning and the cooperative school. *Educational Leadership, 45*(3), 7–13.

Spence, D. (1986, Fall). Rethinking the role of vocational education. *Educational Horizon, 65*(1), 20–23.

Spring, J. (1986). *The American school, 1642–1985.* New York: Longman.

Stasz, C., Ramsey, K., Eden, R., DaVanzo, J., Farris, H., & Lewis M. (1993). *Classrooms that work: Teaching generic skills in academic and vocational settings.* Santa Monica, CA: RAND.

Sticht, T. (1988). Adult literacy education. In E. Rothkopf (Ed.), *Review of research in education* (Vol. 15, pp. 59–96). Washington, DC: American Educational Research Association.

Sticht, T., Armstrong, W. B., Caylor, J. S., & Hickey, D. T. (1987). *Cast-off youth: Policy and training methods from the military experience.* New York: Praeger Publishers.

Sticht., T., & Mikulecky, L. (1984). *Job-related basic skills.* Columbus, OH: National Center for Research in Vocational Education, Ohio State University.

Tanner, D., & Tanner, L. (1990). *History of the school curriculum.* New York: Macmillan.

Tharp, R., & Gallimore, R. (1988). *Rousing minds to life: Teaching, learning, and schooling in social context.* New York: Cambridge University Press.

Venezky, R. L., Wagner, D. A., & Ciliberti, B. S. (1990). *Toward defining literacy.* Newark, DE: International Reading Association.

Youth and America's future. (1988). *The forgotten half: Pathways to success for America's youth and young families.* Washington, DC: The William T. Grant Foundation Commission on Work, Family and Citizenship.

# SEVEN

## "It's Not Your Skills, It's the Test": Gatekeepers for Women in the Skilled Trades

*Marisa Castellano*

## Introduction: Women, Work, and "Skills"

Since the 1970s, women have entered occupations in the skilled trades, which include construction workers like plumbers and carpenters, as well as craft workers like machinists. There was a steady increase in women's participation in the trades, from 4.1% of tradesworkers in 1973 to 8.1% in 1983. However, during the 1980s, the number of women in the trades stayed relatively stable, and by 1991 was only 8.6% of the total (Women's Bureau, U.S. Dept. of Labor, 1993). Over much of this same 25-year period, American employers began to enumerate ever more requirements for entry into all occupations, and increasingly, to assess applicants' ability to meet these by administering tests.

In this paper[1] I discuss the relationship between these two trends: how women's access to high-paying jobs in the skilled trades has been limited by an ideology of skills and testing, which often obscures people's competence rather than allowing it to be displayed. I argue that human ability develops through social processes and is thus best displayed as such. It is not reducible to a series of test scores. We must complicate such monolithic accounts of ability, particularly as we seek to understand trends in female and minority employment in sectors from which they have historically been excluded. This is the case because the school subjects which are often assessed—math and science—are those for which women and minorities traditionally receive less preparation.

Using data from an ethnographic study of a job training program for women interested in skilled trades occupations, I explore the ways in which test-taking literacy—the habits of mind necessary for negotiating written tests about "sentient" knowledge (cf. Zuboff, 1988)—acted as a roadblock to these women's attempts to work in the skilled trades, and I suggest future directions for increasing women's participation in such occupations.

## Women and Work

Scholarly attention to working women is a relatively recent phenomenon, although the fact of women working outside the home for wages is not. In the United States, working class women and women of color have always worked (Amott & Matthaei, 1991). Research increased as women began to enter the labor force in large numbers (Seidman, 1978; Stromberg & Harkess, 1978).

Currently, women are pursuing a wider range of careers than ever before (Women's Bureau, U.S. Dept. of Labor, 1993). However, most working women are still concentrated in clerical and service sector jobs, which rarely offer career advancement opportunities (Bureau of Labor Statistics, U.S. Dept. of Labor, 1991). Such jobs do not pay a living wage to support a family, nor do they provide health insurance or other benefits. Often, women in poverty are forced to choose between taking such jobs or going on public assistance, which includes health benefits for their families. Many of these women would prefer to provide for themselves and their families, but they were not educated at a time or in a place that encouraged women to excel in math or science (Horsman, 1990). These subjects lay the groundwork for many careers that provide financial security, but with this alternative closed, they opt for the security of public assistance (Gittell & Moore, 1989).

Given this background, it is no surprise that where offered, programs which train women for higher-paying, non-traditional jobs such as those in the skilled trades are popular, and they are increasing in number (Coleman, 1993). Such jobs are an attractive alternative to clerical or retail work, for reasons of intrinsic and extrinsic satisfaction: the product of the work is concrete, the pay is high, and the sense of independence from authority is strong. Nevertheless, barriers exist for women who attempt to enter the trades. Below I discuss the ways in which entrance requirements kept many of the women studied from joining the more prestigious and high-paying of the skilled trades.[2]

## Perspective on Skills, Testing, and Literacies

The theoretical perspective I adopt in this paper developed out of research on cognition and learning, which recently shifted from studying individual cognition to a focus on the situated, social nature of learning (Lave & Wenger, 1991; Vygotsky, 1978). Learning, knowledge, and skill exist in a context, and they develop as people become increasingly responsible members of the community engaged in the relevant practice. A process of enculturation occurs as newcomers try to enter the community (Brown, Collins, & Duguid, 1988). I have chosen this analytical framework because, beyond being theories developed by researchers, these ideas also describe the socialization process that is said to occur as apprentices move toward full membership, or journey-level status, in the skilled trades (Haas, 1989; Riemer, 1979).

The concept of "skills," as defined in government and industry reports (*The bottom line*, 1988; Day & Rossman, 1991) has little currency within the perspective of situated learning and knowledge. These reports, decrying workers' "lack of skills," assume that skills are constant, quantifiable traits and abilities that reside inside a person. Applicants can be assessed and sorted into those who are and are not "skilled enough" for the job. Such assumptions constitute what has been called the "dispositional" model of human behavior, because of the presumed stable and static nature of traits and abilities (Haney, 1982). The instrument most often used to measure "skills" is the pencil-and-paper test, including standardized tests designed to assess or predict achievement.

The growth in the use of standardized testing for employment selection purposes is analogous to its growth in educational institutions (Business Council for Effective Literacy, 1990; Haney, Madaus, & Lyons, 1993). While testing as a means of ranking and selecting people is not new (Webber, 1989), psychometricians and the modern testing industry claim to have developed an objective way to sort achievers from non-achievers (Gifford, 1993; McDermott & Hood, 1982). Given American society's propensity to appeal to science as the ultimate and objective authority (Goldstein & Wolf, 1994; Lewontin, Rose, & Kamin, 1984), standardized tests came to be the accepted means of sorting people for various purposes. The problem, as Gifford has noted, is that "those abilities that lend themselves to precise measurement" (1993, p. 6) are assumed to have greater predictive value for education and employment than those that do not, while the qualities perceived to be important in a situated perspective on learning, such as the ability to create personal networks, think creatively, or learn from ongoing activity, do not lend themselves to such measurement.

191

Another source of concern about standardized testing is the existence of certain kinds of bias. There is a fairly unanimous consensus that standardized tests are not neutral measures of intelligence or achievement (Gifford, 1993; Johnson, 1987; Nobles, 1987); in fact, Butler (1989) claims that these "'scientific' measures" were designed precisely "to show the biological inequality of groups" (p. 269). It is no surprise, then, that different groups score differently on such socially constructed, culturally bound artifacts as standardized tests, and that the factors along which they consistently differ are gender, race/ethnicity, and income level—precisely those factors which produce other inequities in our society (Gifford, 1993).

Jones (1993) has shown that the bias in question is not so much test item or psychometric bias, in which specific question items are more difficult for one group than for another, even when the "distributions of ability" (p. 23) for the two groups are the same, but rather that minorities have differential opportunities to master the test content because they are far more likely to live in poverty and attend less well-funded schools. As Lewontin (et al., 1984) noted, we must look to social and economic rather than "innate" factors for answers to A. R. Jensen's famous query in the *Harvard Educational Review* (1969), "How much can we boost I.Q. and scholastic achievement?"

Beyond bias, the validity of standardized tests, that is, the degree to which they measure what they purport to measure, has also come into question (Business Council for Effective Literacy, 1990; Synk & Swarthout, 1987). A low score on a standardized test can mean that the applicant has not been exposed to the concepts being tested—hardly predictive of future performance. It can also signal test anxiety. Such multiple possible conclusions from test scores make them poor indicators of ability or future performance.

In employment uses of standardized tests, validity refers to the ability to predict worker performance through test scores. While test designers have been careful not to generalize claims, researchers of standardized testing for employment purposes have generalized the result of validity studies across various settings, ignoring situationally specific factors such as organizational norms and values, centralization of decision-making, and the physical environment of work (James, Demaree, & Mulaik, 1994). According to the situated learning perspective adopted here, such factors will surely affect worker performance, making generalization of the usefulness of these tests across job types highly questionable.

Two conclusions can be drawn from this brief discussion of standardized testing in schools and the workplace.[3] First, the effect of these bias and validity problems has been "to close off rather than open up future opportunities" for disadvantaged and minority students and job applicants (Oakes, 1991, p. 17). Second, standardized tests do not predict future performance so much as they assess applicants' exposure to a certain set of experiences and their ability to display it in a testing situation. This measure of "skills" happens in a context which is unlike most job contexts. For example, job duties rarely include taking tests and will often only include the test topics in oblique ways, if at all. In addition, in real job situations, coworkers may be sought for help and answers, leading to workplace learning; yet on tests, people must work alone.

Standardized tests demand competence in a kind of literacy which is school-based. Like all literacies, test-taking literacy is a situated social practice that acquires its value in the functions it accomplishes for participants (Street, 1984). There is no singular "skill" called literacy, for literacies always reflect the many social groups which use them (Gee, 1991). Literacies are comprised of social practices that are developed and displayed in situated ways (Darrah, this volume; Hull, this volume; Street, 1984); any assessments outside of those situations will necessarily yield only a partial account.

Assessing students' or job applicants' test-taking literacy accomplishes a sorting function. The fallacy of using it as a gauge of future job performance arises because the results may disqualify people who can do the work but may not be competent at taking tests.

In this paper I explore the ways in which test-taking and other literacies acted as roadblocks for a group of women trying to join the skilled trades. First, I cite the requirements outlined by the trades community and the measures they use to assess applicants. Then I describe how a job training program for women responded to these requirements in their curriculum, and how women participants in the program fared in their attempts to find jobs in the skilled trades. Using ethnographic research techniques, including participant observation and follow-up interviews, I conclude that we can no longer attribute women's continued low numbers in the skilled trades to a supposed lack of job-related skills. Instead, we must look elsewhere for the major barriers to women's success: to the proliferation of skills requirements, which are operationalized in measures of literacies indexing school rather than workplace achievement, and to the disquiet that results in many women applicants as they face these assessment measures.

## The Study

Skilled Trades for Women (STW) is sponsored by the federal Job Training Partnership Act (JTPA), a joint effort between government and local private industry to develop training programs for the unemployed. STW is housed at Frederick Douglass Community College, an urban institution in a large city in northern California. The student body at Douglass is comprised predominantly of people of color, reflecting the population of the metropolitan area.

STW is a pre-apprenticeship program; it was developed to provide women with knowledge of shop safety, tools and their uses, and the fundamentals of certain trades. It precedes rather than replaces trades apprenticeships. The training lasts 19 weeks, and includes classes in industrial maintenance (an introduction to carpentry, plumbing, and electricity), welding, and sheet metal. STW also requires that women take self-paced math and English, in order to prepare for apprenticeship entrance exams and for their value on the job. As one shop instructor put it, "You use math and English every day on the job. If you don't have good English skills, you'll never run jobs [i.e., be in charge of them]." Finally, STW requires that women take a weight-training class, primarily to develop upper body strength.

I became a participant observer of the STW program in the spring of 1992. Of the 16 women who completed the program, 15 were African American, one was Latina. They ranged in age from 22 to 46, and all but one of them had children. Twelve of the women received Aid to Families with Dependent Children (AFDC), two were on disability, one was collecting unemployment benefits, and the final two had other income sources to support them through the training period. The goal of the ethnographic study, of which this paper is a part, was to discover the range of knowledge and abilities women needed to succeed in the skilled trades, and how it was taught and learned in the job training program.

In order to flesh out this description of the program and participants that semester, let us learn more about one of them, whom I call Dolores. Dolores immigrated from Colombia in the early 1970s, married and started a family, and then was divorced. She was in her forties and had three children whom she supported with AFDC and child support from their father. Her work experience included warehouse stocker, order checker, and cashier. She had not exuded much confidence at the beginning of the STW program: She repeatedly got lost on the somewhat labyrinthine campus of Douglass Community College, and she was sure that her weakness in math would prevent her from achieving her goal of becoming an electrician.

After the program ended, she went to the electricians' union but the line of applicants was so long, she became discouraged and left. Instead, she joined the laborers' union. After a few short-term jobs she landed a permanent job with a contractor, through a connection she had made. Dolores was the sole Latina in STW, and she and I had a bilingual relationship. When I asked her how she had gotten her permanent job, she explained, "*Esto es solamente palanca, si tienes quien te acomode*" ("This is all just a matter of leverage, of having someone who can get you in").

Dolores flagged traffic near construction sites and helped on remodeling jobs. In order to get more training, she went to work for a different company, digging trenches for electrical crews. While at first she lacked experience, she

194

learned to use various types of equipment, and earned a reputation for competence. Equally importantly, she learned to use tenacity to pursue the jobs she wanted and get experience. She developed relationships with others, building the necessary networks to ensure that she worked steadily. Her contact with electricians reawakened her interest in that trade, and she will likely apply to work in it in the future.

## Requirements of the Practicing Community

### Division of Apprenticeship Standards

Trade union and employer representatives in each trade work with federal and state agencies to develop the entrance requirements and curriculum for apprenticeship programs, thus they are highly variable. Written exams became part of the inscription or application process for many trades in the early 1970s, according to a local apprenticeship community outreach program director. Prior to that time, entrance into many of these trades was based on informal connections, usually a family member, who could "get you in" when the inscription period came around.

In an undated apprenticeship information guide written for "high school counselors and others who come in contact with young people," California's Division of Apprenticeship Standards (DAS) lists "the prerequisites for careers as skilled craft workers," which may be grouped as follows: basic literacy, specialized academic knowledge, technical literacies, and physical abilities. The DAS description of each follows.

Prospective tradesworkers must be able to read, write, speak English well, and have a "more than fundamental" knowledge of arithmetic. They must certify their mastery of basic literacy with a high school diploma or equivalent. Implicit in this requirement, of course, is test-taking literacy, since most schools require some demonstration of achievement through written, often standardized, tests.

Applicants will be at an advantage if they are familiar with specialized academic subjects as well: higher math, physics or chemistry. As for technical literacies, these vary from trade to trade, so the DAS guide lists only general topics which one might find in a high school industrial arts program: drafting, blueprint reading, and welding. The guide also claims that those with "mechanical aptitude" are likely to succeed in the skilled trades, yet they do not define this or give any examples. Finally, applicants should also meet such physical qualifications as fitness, agility, strength, good hand-eye coordination, and the ability to work at heights.

## Unions and Employers

Work in the skilled trades differs from other sectors in several ways, perhaps the most striking of which is that a worker's employer is the union, regardless of the company for which one is presently working. Sometimes workers are permanently hired by private companies or public districts, but even then they remain union members. "Permanent hires," as they are known, have protection against the ups and downs of the construction market, where workers expect occasional or seasonal unemployment.

Union members are dispatched to work by the union. There are two ways of getting dispatched, and the trades can be classified in this way. The resulting distinction also reflects a status differential within the trades (Riemer, 1979), along the lines of wage ceilings, and perceived skill and exertion levels. First, there are the "hunting license" or support trades, which tend to have open inscription (application) periods without entrance examination requirements. Applicants are given a "letter of subscription," which means they have filed the necessary paperwork and are eligible to seek work—on their own. The letter is their license to hunt for work. Examples of these trades are carpenter and cement mason.

"List" trades, also known as the elite trades, are only open a short time for inscription, such as two hours per day for a two-week period every two years. Applicants take an exam, those who score well are interviewed, and these results are combined to rank order the applicants. Those above the cutoff point form the work list, with the highest scorers on the top of the list and thus the first to be dispatched to work. Workers may not look for their own jobs. Examples of elite or list trades are plumber and electrician.

Employers and trade unions specify the skills they seek and the exams they administer on announcements for job or apprenticeship openings. I examined such documents from three private companies, four government agencies or districts, and 14 trade union locals, and found the requirements similar to those in the DAS guide, although they tended to be more specific and operationalized. I will limit my discussion to those which appeared on more than one announcement.

*Basic Literacy.* Proficiency in reading, writing and arithmetic is to be documented through high school transcripts and, in the elite trades, through batteries of standardized tests. These multiple choice exams, often several decades old, test reading comprehension, sentence completion, and arithmetic computation, including decimals and fractions. I found no trade which tested written expression. Figure 7.1 shows question items typical of the exams.

Figure 7.1: Typical Standardized Test Items

1a) The adoption of labor-saving devices in the farming regions ( ) the need for large families.

(A) hastened          (B) emphasized
(C) determined       (D) decreased
(E) characterized

1b) What is the area (in square feet) of a rectangular parking lot which is twice as long as it is wide, if the fence around it is 300 feet long?

(A)   1,500
(B)   3,000
(C)   5,000
(D)   6,000
(E) 10,000

*Specialized Academic Knowledge.* High school transcripts rather than tests are used to certify the algebra requirement for apprenticeships in elite trades. Indeed, many unions do not include exam items on algebra beyond the fundamentals of algebraic expression. With respect to science, there were no high school course prerequisites in any trade or job announcement I saw. However, many elite trades include a "mechanical reasoning" multiple-choice exam, which tests one's grasp of paper representations of mechanical concepts (i.e., projectile motion), objects (pulleys, gears) and their operation. Therefore, while high school physics is not required, such a course broadens an applicant's exposure to the test material. As one study guide put it, if mechanical concepts are difficult, "you may do well to review basic physics" (ARCO, 1986, p. 3). Figure 7.2 shows a typical mechanical reasoning test item.

Figure 7.2: Mechanical Reasoning Test Item

Which man can lift the
53. load more easily?
(If equal, mark C)

A     B     C        A        B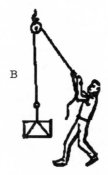

*Technical Literacies.* Elite trades requiring entrance exams often assess the ability to utilize in job-related contexts literacies which applicants have acquired elsewhere. For instance, the Industrial Training Classification Test (Lawshe & Moutoux, 1942), designed for pre-employment selection of adult trainees, consists of arithmetic items in a shop math context. Figure 7.3 shows the type of problems encountered on this test. As is seen, a work context is provided, thus making them a slightly more meaningful measure than the other exams. In addition, there are no choices among predetermined answers, which is also more reflective of real job situations.

Figure 7.3: Shop Math Test Item

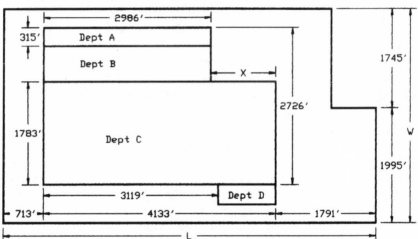

1. **What is the length of the lot?**

2. **What is the width of the lot?**

3. **How much longer is Dept. C than Dept. B?**

A different type of technical literacy is assessed by another common test in the elite trades apprenticeship battery: spatial relations. Literacy in spatial relations involves one's ability to "read" and mentally manipulate two-dimensional drawings of three-dimensional objects. Figure 7.4 shows a typical multiple-choice test item on spatial relations, in which one must mentally "fold" the given geometric figure and match the outcome to one of the choices. Visual and conceptual literacies such as these, which are thought to predict job performance, are thus assessed in the same way as the academic literacies above: through written multiple-choice tests rather than observing ability in action.

Figure 7.4: Spatial Relations Test Item

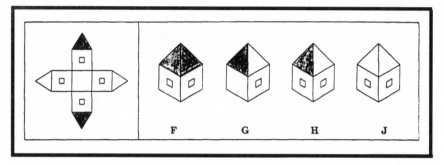

*Physical Abilities*. Many job and apprenticeship opportunities require certain physical abilities, and applicants are tested accordingly. They may have to lift 90 pounds and carry it 50 feet. The county public works department gave a timed performance exam in which applicants were assigned physical tasks and assessed on whether they knew the proper shovel to use or how to push a wheelbarrow correctly. A final example is the Bennett Hand-Tool Dexterity test, given to applicants of trades such as electrician and sheet metal worker, as "a measure of proficiency in using ordinary mechanics' tools" (Bennett, 1965, p. 2). Applicants are timed as they loosen nuts and remove bolts from one side of a test block and fasten them to the other side, first using two tools and then spinning the nuts off with their fingers.

## The Response of the STW Program and Its Participants

Those in charge of the STW program are aware of the requirements set out by the skilled trades community, and have developed the curriculum to help women meet them. As is the case every semester, the women in this study came to STW with a broad range of experience, interests and abilities. In addition to this foundation, STW provided an introduction to and practice in the kinds of literacies which have been described above.

### Basic Literacy

All of the women possessed a high school diploma or equivalent. This was a prerequisite for the STW program, to ensure that once the women finished, they could go on to apprenticeships, which often only accept applicants with such credentials. STW includes self-paced academic classes for instruction or review in basic math and English. Depending on a woman's pace through the math workbook, she could practice solving problems with fractions, decimals, percents, geometric measures, and introductory algebra. The women in this study had little trouble with the content, but there was no motivation to work hard or at all, so many women did not get a significant amount of practice. The STW English class focused on clear written expression, producing résumés, and reading creative writing by and about working women. It was not a challenging class, and some women resented having to take it at all. The instructor graded them more on quantity than quality (i.e., the number of pages written in a journal and attendance rather than journal content or class participation).

## Specialized Academic Knowledge

Women rarely enter the STW program with a strong command of specialized academic subjects. Of the 16 women enrolled in STW during the semester under study, only four had taken algebra; for two of them, it had been 25 years earlier. One problem with penalizing those without this knowledge is that high school instruction in such subjects is often part of the college preparatory curriculum. People who are not in the "college track" courses have then closed the door on the skilled trades as well, which are among the few lucrative career options for the non-college-educated. Another reason not to penalize people without this knowledge is that it can be taught. Many of these subjects are part of the apprenticeship curriculum for such elite trades as plumbing or electricity.

Further, informal conversations with journey-level tradesworkers reveal that specialized academic knowledge is more necessary in the apprenticeship classes than on the job. In actual work situations, either the context makes calculating options a moot exercise, or often, the numerical values that calculations provide can also be found by measuring or reading a gauge or instrument of some kind. This is not to say that this knowledge is unnecessary, but that there are often alternative ways to accomplish what it accomplishes, and in fact, on the job, the non-calculative means are preferred.

Regardless of this, STW recognizes the gatekeeping functions that such school literacies play, and provides an introduction to the ways in which algebraic and geometric ways of solving problems are used in many trades. They do not call them algebra or geometry, though, in order to keep the program practical and avoid possibly negative or intimidating associations.

## Technical Literacies

In a discussion of women entering the skilled trades, Weston noted that technical know-how is often indexed by written tests ("signs of ability to do the job," 1990, p. 143), rather than by actual performance. Thus, what is

200

being assessed is one's test-taking literacy at least as much as the content. In addition, Darrah exposed the notion of "mechanical aptitude" as a "myth enacted in the workplace" (1991, p. 36). In the factory he studied, job applicants were led near machinery to gauge their comfort level, and they were asked if they had a shop in their garage. Darrah pointed out that the myth of the necessity of mechanical aptitude for certain jobs is perpetuated by only hiring applicants who are "tinkerers," when in fact, "the success of most virtuoso operators may be attributed to their curiosity and problem-solving abilities, and the interpersonal and communicative skills which allow them to build networks of helpers" (p. 36). As Weston also put it, "it is often a symbolically constituted impression of productive capacity that gets a person the job" (1990, p. 143).

Few of the women in STW had taken courses in industrial arts or had prior experience with the technical literacies which are assessed in entrance exams, thus making their ability to constitute such an impression of capacity minimal. STW provided practice in shop math and spatial relations. Most acquired this latter literacy fairly rapidly. Many tests and study guides refer to spatial relations as an aptitude, implying innate ability, although they admit, "Spatial relations tests have been shown to respond positively to increased familiarity with the tests and practice with the kinds of questions asked" (ARCO, 1986, p. 2). And indeed, research on gender and spatial relations has shown that while girls score consistently lower than boys on such tests (Linn & Petersen, 1986), girls' scores can be improved significantly by a few hours' training (Caplan et al., 1985; Tartre, 1990). Given this, one must question the validity and replicability of these spatial relations tests.

While many of the women in this study lacked such school-based experiences, they had practical experience in specific activities undertaken in some trades. Some claimed to have grown up watching or helping their fathers in home shops. Once, they were asked to list all of their "blue-collar" work experience, including non-paid work such as assembling a child's bicycle or fixing a can opener. Figure 7.5 shows the key phrases of many of their replies, grouped by trade when possible. The women's prior experience in projects such as sewing and laying carpet or tile provided experience laying out patterns to achieve a functional product, which is especially helpful in trades such as sheet metal.

Another way that the women displayed technical literacy was in their response to the hands-on projects that were assigned. Some women brought hand and power tools from home when they saw that STW either did not have these tools to lend, or there were not enough of them. These were women who knew which tools were useful for which projects. Others brought in "do-it-yourself" books from home to help them carry out the assigned projects.

| Figure 7.5: The Women's Technical Experience Prior to STW | |
|---|---|
| *Automotive:* | *Home Improvement:* |
| changing oil | wallpapering |
| changing brakelights | laying carpet |
| | painting |
| *Plumbing:* | remodeling kitchen |
| fixing leaky faucet | adding a bathroom |
| | laying tile |
| *Electrical:* | |
| installing light fixtures | *Miscellaneous:* |
| | sewing |
| *Landscaping:* | laminating fiberglass |
| weeding | soldering materials |
| planting | assembling equipment |

In addition to the experience the women brought with them, their certificates of completion of the STW program meant that they had made their own toolboxes, done gas and arc welding, laid out and worked sheet metal into predetermined forms, and worked in crews to construct functional, small-scale water delivery systems and electrical circuits.

## Physical Abilities

The physical education which most women in the United States receive in public school attempts to develop fitness, agility, strength, and endurance. Some women come to STW in good physical condition; others do not. One STW instructor claimed that if a woman could juggle a baby in one arm and a bag of groceries in another while opening the car door, she was strong enough for the trades. This may be true, but it does not take into account the endurance necessary for tradeswork.

STW includes a weight-training course. However, it was not sufficient, in part because one class taken for one semester is not enough, but also because the women were not given individualized instruction and help setting goals. As a result, some of them were not prepared for the level of exertion that was expected of them on the job. But most of the women quickly adapted, and several with steady work noted that they were developing stronger bodies and gaining stamina in response to the hard work.

An initially low degree of physical abilities does not necessarily portend failure on the job. In fact, there is good reason to end our stereotype of the skilled trades as occupations which only muscle-bound men can perform. Contractors and other firms have seen their workers' compensation costs skyrocket in recent years. They can no longer afford to have workers injure their backs lifting things manually. On many jobsites, it is against regulations to lift more than 50 pounds without hoists or other mechanical aids (Deaux & Ullman, 1983).

## Program Follow-up

### *Job Placement*

Job placement is the criterion against which all JTPA programs are judged (cf. Merriefield, this volume). A program can expend resources to help participants find jobs for 90 days after the training ends. In the case of STW, this includes paying the women's union initiation fees. After the 90th day, those people who are not working are considered "negative placements." This is an especially difficult criterion to meet for programs which prepare people for construction work, since a person may work for weeks until a particular job is done, and then be laid off and not working when the follow-up contact is made. This, along with a large number of women who had not worked at all, and a random sampling follow-up technique, resulted in a low official placement rate. However, a closer examination of the women's experiences reveals a much more textured reality.

By the end of the placement period, ten women had joined various trades. Five joined the laborer's union, which is unique among construction trades because there is no apprenticeship. Laborers have no curriculum, no increasing wage scale, and no career ladder.[4] They do the clean-up, hauling, and helping for other construction workers. While STW encouraged and prepared women for the higher prestige trades, the program staff also described the laborer's job as a chance to work with members of all the other trades and, if given the opportunity and they seize it, laborers can master many trades.

Four women joined the carpenters' union, and one joined the piledrivers' union. Like all support trades, these do not require applicants to take entrance exams. It is significant for this cohort, for the STW program, and perhaps for women in general, that no woman in this group was successful at getting a job which had an entrance exam as a requirement.

With respect to the other six women, one of them returned to school for drafting. Another took a clerical job. Two suffered auto accidents and could not work at all for months, and I lost touch with one woman. The sixth joined the laborers' union, although it was too late to be counted as a placement for STW.

Thus ended the "numbers game" for this cohort of STW trainees. But my follow-up telephone conversations with them for another two years provide a more complete picture of their post-STW trajectories, and how other

203

aspects of their lives, such as their health and their children, influenced their work lives. It is valuable to our understanding of job training programs, and of women's work experiences, to follow a cohort for longer than 90 days and get detailed reasons behind the choices they make or are forced to make.

By the time of this writing, I was in contact with ten of the original 16 women. Four women had been permanently hired, two as laborers in private, non-contractor firms; one as a carpenter for a contractor; and the fourth by a property management firm to look after public housing units. A fifth continued to pay her laborers' union dues and worked when she was called, which was not often. The others ranged from having definitely given up on the trades to continuing to consider those occupations as a goal to pursue when circumstances allowed.

Women tend to enter the elite trades in fewer numbers than they do the support trades (Bureau of Labor Statistics, U.S. Dept. of Labor, 1991). Perhaps the experiences of the women in this study can provide some insight into why this is so, since all but one of the 12 women who worked in the trades chose support trades. The women who chose to join the carpenters' union claimed to do so out of an interest in carpentry. A major factor guiding the choice of those who went into the laborers' union was that they could sign up immediately, as opposed to waiting for the elite trades' inscription periods and having to take the exams. Many felt they could acquire experience first as a laborer and later decide if they wanted to specialize. The expediency of the laborer choice may have been made clear to some women as they looked for jobs and took tests at government agencies, utility districts, and the like. One woman, speaking for others as well, said they were being barraged with written tests which they felt unfairly substituted for demonstrations of ability, or assessed abilities which they assumed would be taught as part of the work. She said, "What we don't like is we've been taking all kinds of tests. Teach us once we get on the job."

We should not underestimate the degree to which a desire to avoid tests or other displays of school-based literacies affected these women's choices. The STW instruction and practice in the various requirements listed above may have served to show them the range of literacies they would need to master, and, paradoxically, to dissuade them from attempting to take such exams, at least until they had more experience. We must remember that passing the test was more than a one-time accomplishment; it meant committing to a four- to five-year-long apprenticeship program, often including demanding coursework in math and applied physics, as well as working and raising their families. This may not have been a realistic option for some in the group. Thus, ironically, there may have been as much or more anxiety about *passing* such a test as there was fear of taking or failing it.

Other factors working against women joining the more elite trades have to do with institutional structures: for example, a union's inscription period may not coincide with a woman's decision to join, and she may have to wait up to two years. Also, elite tradesworkers are dispatched to work from a rank-ordered list, meaning that depending on the demand for workers, a woman's position on the list, and the extent of the informal means by which other workers bypass the list, she may not work often. Women who are the sole source of financial support for their families cannot afford lengthy periods without pay. Thus, we see that important reasons for women's choosing support over elite trades have less to do with possessing "the skills" perceived to be necessary as they do with being in the right place and time to display them, and displaying them in certain preferred ways.

Let us look more closely at the one woman who attempted to join an elite trade. Brenda was in her thirties and had two children, whom she had supported with AFDC. She had become pregnant before finishing high school, but graduated from a school for expectant teens. She then worked as a warehouse stocker, an assembler of diving equipment, and an industrial sewing machinist. On the advice and encouragement of her mother, a cosmetologist herself, Brenda left factory work and trained to be a cosmetologist. According to her, she passed the state boards "with flying colors," and worked with her mother for 11 years.[5]

Brenda moved from Los Angeles to northern California after her divorce. She decided to pursue a different career, and signed up for STW. There, her favorite class was sheet metal, and her enthusiasm for it showed in her attendance and her quality work. She decided to join that trade and fortunately, the inscription period coincided with this desire. However, she did not pass the math portion of the entrance exam,[5] and was disqualified. As she put it at the time, "It's not your skills [that matter], it's the test."

Because STW would only pay Brenda's union initiation fees during the placement period, she had to make an expedient choice.[7] She joined the piledrivers' union, which has no inscription period and does not require applicants to take an entrance exam. There she found a low beginner apprentice wage, heavy physical labor, and frequent layoffs as jobs ended. "I want to be getting something permanent," she complained to me after she was laid off for the third time in two months.

Brenda's nascent skill at sheet metal work was rendered invisible by the entrance procedures for the apprenticeship. If "it's not your skills, it's the test," then how can we explain her success on the cosmetology boards? One illuminating factor is that this latter exam is 75% performance demonstration: actually giving facials, manicures, and cutting and styling hair (California Dept. of Consumer Affairs, 1986), so that her work competence was being evaluated, rather than her ability to take a test. As has been shown, the tests given by the sheet metal and other elite trades are not as grounded in job performance.

The next time I talked with Brenda, she had given up piledriving and had started another job training program, this time for forklift operator. She told me the program promised to place trainees in jobs, which was what she needed. A few months later when I tried to contact her again, her phone number had been disconnected. Brenda's experience is indicative of what many women face as they struggle to better their lives: Requirements that signal achievement in the school context are used as barriers to entrance into the workplace context (see Horsman, 1990). It is crucial that women's opportunities to join the skilled trades not be curtailed by test-taking literacy requirements. Women must be given the chance to perform on the job and to succeed or fail based on their ability to do the work.

## Discussion

We have examined standardized testing, its role in employment selection in the skilled trades, and how it played out in the lives of some of the women in this study. We have seen that looking "skilled" enough to join many elite apprenticeships is a different type of activity than displaying competence on a construction site: The former takes place in school-based literacies while the latter is situated in the work itself.

Trying to locate skill exclusively inside applicants and trying to predict learning through written tests shifts responsibility away from the master/apprentice relationship, where learning has traditionally been located in apprenticeship. It is the master's task to legitimize new members (Wenger, 1990), meaning that the onus for teaching and accepting newcomers, and a share of the responsibility for their success or failure, lies with the community. These responsibilities have been transferred to entrance exams, and this dependence on them is unreliable and undesirable. There is widespread recognition within the trades community that rather than testing for necessary work abilities, these tests are just "to scare people away," "to limit access," and "a weeding out process," as three apprenticeship coordinators told me. We need to rethink the relationship of these tests to the apprentice selection process.

The debate over race and gender bias in standardized testing has not been completely resolved, nor is it so simple a relationship as the fact that historically excluded groups score lower on these tests. For some, it is also anxiety over taking the test, which measures a set of practices they might not have mastered or had to work with in decades, and which may not reflect their ability to do the job (cf. National Commission on Testing and Public Policy,

1990). Many of those who fear these tests will be dissuaded from even attempting to join the higher-paying and more prestigious trades. In other cases, a woman may have decided to enter a given trade only to find that the inscription period (and entrance exam) was months away. Such scheduling simply does not coincide with the way women who support families must lead their lives.

There needs to be a fairer way to pare down the number of applicants so that women and minorities are not so disproportionately affected. The mechanical reasoning and spatial relations tests also assess exposure to certain experiences and school courses, not any innate capability. Thus, these tests also appeal to the "dispositional" model of human behavior and ability described above. The only defensible tests, from the perspective of situated learning, are the physical performance tests and, to some extent, the shop math tests. The former simulate typical job duties in some trades,[8] and the latter offer the opportunity to use math in ways quite similar to the ways it is used in the jobs being applied for. In any case, merely picking and choosing among these tests will not make the process fairer. More fundamental changes are needed, to which I now turn.

The conclusions I draw arise from the suggestion that perhaps the use of standardized tests is a convenient excuse for both parties involved. For employers and trade unions, tests function as a "scientific" means of justifying a lack of diversity in the trades, in that they can claim they attempted to hire women and minorities, but their test scores were not up to par. An apprenticeship outreach program director has validated this hypothesis as a plausible account within some elite trades. On the other hand, for many of the women and minorities who are interested in skilled trades occupations, tests can function as a convenient excuse not to take on the challenge of the higher-paying trades. This hypothesis is validated by some of the women in STW, as well as STW shop instructors and apprenticeship coordinators with whom I spoke, who have worked with women and minorities for years. I would argue that if these hypotheses are accurate, the actions of both groups reveal that standardized tests have outlived their usefulness as predictors of job performance and have become instead a justification for maintaining the status quo.

I propose several ways to move beyond this impasse. First, in order to avoid the appearance of using entrance exams as gatekeepers, trade union apprenticeship programs should instead place increased weight on alternative means of selection. Many schools and businesses have in fact done so, with workplaces leading the way (Business Council for Effective Literacy, 1990). Reilly and Warech (1994) discuss alternative employment selection measures, including work samples, interviews, and job simulations. They note that trainability tests, which present applicants with job-related training materials and then assess their acquisition of them, are perceived as fairer by applicants.

207

A disadvantage of trainability as an alternative selection method is that the cost can be prohibitive.

Another proposal, which has already been made in the school context, is to teach test-taking literacy (Jones, 1993; Wilson, 1986). Rosser (1989), in a study of African American and European women and men's performance on math question items from the Scholastic Aptitude Test (SAT), examined each group's solution methods. She found that the women tended to rely more on mathematical knowledge than on test-taking literacy, and concluded that it is crucial for women to learn how to take tests. While it seems ironic that a program training women for careers in the skilled trades should have to teach test-taking literacy, this is the extent to which psychometry has pervaded work life. Until more refined ways of assessing worker potential become common, women must learn the specific practices which will help them meet entrance requirements.

The STW program already provides practice in the content areas of these exams, but women and minority trainees need explicit instruction in test-taking strategies, such as reading beyond the question item to see what is being asked. Learning how to recognize the traps which standardized test designers set and how to get beyond unfamiliar or intimidating subject matter would also go a long way toward alleviating test-taking anxiety.

In the STW English class, there should be a focus on how to pass the reading comprehension and vocabulary portions of entrance exams, as well as perhaps work on mathematical word problems and how to set them up as equations. The STW math class already presents its subject matter in the same decontextualized way as it is found on the exams. However, this is not an intentional pedagogy, and test strategies are not explicitly given. In addition, the problems of those who never benefited from completing exercises in workbooks are only exacerbated by this method. The math class needs to prepare women for the practical ways in which mathematical concepts and operations are used in skilled trades workplaces. In addition to the workbook, math should be presented and practiced within a shop or trades context. This type of presentation might help women perform better on the standardized tests as well as on the job.

Assessing candidates for school and work inevitably means allocating a finite number of opportunities among people who are competing against each other (Gifford, 1989). In the case of the skilled trades occupations, standardized tests do not provide definitive enough information to be the principal tool with which to do this. This study suggests that if employers and apprenticeship gatekeepers used alternative measures of assessment instead of or in addition to standardized tests, women and minorities would have a better chance of joining the more elite trades. Until this time, however, STW and other skilled trades training programs for historically excluded groups would do well to include test-taking literacy in their curricula.

## Notes

1. I would like to gratefully acknowledge the support of the Soroptimist International Founder Region and the American Association of University Women fellowships.

2. For a discussion of other hurdles besides test-taking literacy which women must scale in order to succeed in the skilled trades, see Castellano, 1995.

3. For a multifaceted treatment of testing and the issues surrounding it, see the National Commission on Testing and Public Policy's series, Evaluation in Education and Human Services.

4. This situation has since changed, as the U.S. Department of Labor recognized construction laborer as an apprenticeable occupation (Bradford & Krizan, 1994).

5. This description of Brenda's rather extensive job history runs counter to stereotypical images of welfare mothers as lazy and content to remain on AFDC.

6. Brenda also took spatial relations and mechanical reasoning tests, which she said she passed.

7. This is an example of the conflict between JTPA regulations, trade union apprenticeship inscription periods, and a woman's goals.

8. Although the timed nature of these physical performance exams is problematic.

## References

Amott, T. L. & Matthaei, J. A. (1991). *Race, gender and work: A multicultural economic history of women in the U.S.* Boston: South End Press.

ARCO Editorial Board (1986). *ARCO study guide: Mechanical aptitude and spatial relations tests.* New York: Prentice Hall.

Bennett, G. K. (1965). *Hand-tool dexterity test: Manual of directions.* New York: The Psychological Corporation.

*The bottom line: Basic skills in the workplace* (1988). Washington, DC: U.S. Dept. of Education and U.S. Dept. of Labor.

Bradford, H., & Krizan, W. (1994). Laborer declared an occupation. *Engineering News-Record, 232*(21), 12.

Brown, J. S., Collins, A., & Duguid, P. (1988). *Situated cognition and the culture of learning*. Palo Alto, CA: Institute for Research on Learning Technical Report 88-008 (Shorter version appears in *Educational Researcher, 18*(1), 1989, 32–42).

Business Council for Effective Literacy (BCEL). (1990). Standardized tests: Their use and misuse. *BCEL: A newsletter for the business and literacy community, 22* (Available from BCEL, 1221 Avenue of the Americas, 35th Floor, New York, NY 10020).

Butler, J.S. (1989). Test scores and evaluation: The military as data. In B. R. Gifford (Ed.), *Test policy and the politics of opportunity allocation: The workplace and the law* (pp. 266–291). Boston: Kluwer Academic Publishers.

California Department of Consumer Affairs, Board of Cosmetology (1986). *Scope for cosmetology examination*. Sacramento, CA: State of California Consumer Services Agency.

Caplan, P. J., MacPherson, G., & Tobin, P. (1985). Do sex-related differences in spatial abilities exist? A multilevel critique with new data. *American Psychologist, 40*(7), 786–799.

Castellano, M. (1995). *The tools of the trade: Women acquiring the discourse of the skilled trades*. Unpublished dissertation, University of California, Berkeley.

Coleman, E. (1993, Spring). *Breaking out of the pink-collar ghetto: Nontraditional jobs provide wider opportunities for women* (pp. 28–31). Ford Foundation Report.

Darrah, C. (1991). *Workplace skills in context*. Unpublished manuscript. (Shorter version appears in *Human Organization, 51*(3), 1992, 264–273).

Day, F. & Rossman, E. (1991). *An analysis of America's construction industry workforce and occupational projections, 1990–1996*. Washington, DC: Home Builders Institute of the National Association of Home Builders.

Deaux, K. & Ullman, J. C. (1983). *Women of steel: Female blue collar workers in the basic steel industry*. New York: Praeger Publishers.

Gee, J. P. (1991). *Social linguistics and literacies: Ideology in discourses*. Bristol, PA: The Falmer Press.

Gifford, B.R. (1989). The allocation of opportunities and the politics of testing: A policy analytic perspective. In B. R. Gifford (Ed.), *Test policy and the politics of opportunity allocation: The workplace and the law* (pp. 3–32). Boston: Kluwer Academic Publishers.

Gifford, B. R. (1993). Introduction. In B. R. Gifford (Ed.), *Policy perspectives on educational testing* (pp. 3–18). Boston: Kluwer Academic Publishers.

Gittell, M. & Moore, J. (1989). Denying independence: Barriers to the education of women on AFDC. In S. Harlan & R. J. Steinberg (Eds.), *Job training for women: The promises and limitations of public policies* (pp. 445–479). Philadelphia: Temple University Press.

Goldstein, H. & Wolf, A. (1994). Recent trends in assessment: England and Wales. In L. C. Wing & B. R. Gifford (Eds.), *Policy issues in employment testing* (pp. 225–268). Boston: Kluwer Academic Publishers.

Haas, J. (1989). The process of apprenticeship: Ritual ordeal and the adoption of a cloak of competence. In M. Coy (Ed.), *Apprenticeship: From theory to method and back again* (pp. 87–105). Albany, NY: SUNY Press.

Haney, W.M. (1982). Employment tests and employment discrimination: A dissenting psychological opinion. *Industrial Relations Law Journal, 5*, 1–86.

Haney, W. M., Madaus, G. F., & Lyons, R. (1993). *The fractured marketplace for standardized testing*. Boston: Kluwer Academic Publishers.

Horsman, J. (1990). *Something in my mind besides the everyday: Women and literacy*. Toronto, Ontario: Women's Press.

Hull, G. (1993). Hearing other voices: A critical assessment of popular views on literacy and work. *Harvard Educational Review, 63*(1), 20–49.

James, L. R., Demaree, R. G., & Mulaik, S. A. (1994). A critique of validity generalization. In L. C. Wing & B. R. Gifford (Eds.), *Policy issues in employment testing* (pp. 13–76). Boston: Kluwer Academic Publishers.

Jensen, A. R. (1969). How much can we boost I.Q. and scholastic achievement? *Harvard Educational Review, 39*, 1–129.

Johnson, S. T. (1987). Test fairness and bias: Measuring academic achievement among black youth. *The Urban League Review, 11*(1–2), 76–92.

Jones, L. (1993). School achievement trends for black students. In B. R. Gifford (Ed.), *Policy perspectives on educational testing* (pp. 19–74). Boston: Kluwer Academic Publishers.

Lave, J. & Wenger, E. (1991). *Situated learning: Legitimate peripheral participation.* Cambridge, MA: Cambridge University Press.

Lawshe, C. H. & Moutoux, A. C. (1942). *Industrial training classification test.* Chicago: Science Research Associates.

Lewontin, R. C., Rose, S., & Kamin, L. J. (1984). *Not in our genes: Biology, ideology and human nature.* New York: Pantheon Books.

Linn, M. C. & Petersen, A. C. (1986). A meta-analysis of gender differences in spatial ability. In J. S. Hyde & M. C. Linn (Eds.), *The psychology of gender: Advances through meta-analysis* (pp. 67–101). Baltimore, MD: Johns Hopkins University Press.

McDermott, R. P. & Hood, L. (1982). Institutionalized psychology and the ethnography of schooling. In P. Gilmore & A. A. Glatthorn (Eds.), *Children in and out of school: Ethnography and education* (pp. 232–249). Washington, DC: Center for Applied Linguistics.

National Commission on Testing and Public Policy (1990). *From gatekeeper to gateway: Transforming testing in America.* Chestnut Hill, MA: Author.

Nobles, W. (1987). Psychometrics and African-American reality: A question of cultural antimony. *The Negro Educational Review, 38* (2–3), 45–55.

Oakes, J. (1991). The many-sided dilemmas of testing. In the William T. Grant Foundation's Commission on Work, Family and Citizenship and the Institute for Educational Leadership (Eds.), *Voices from the field: Thirty expert opinions on America 2000, the Bush Administration strategy to "reinvent" America's schools* (pp. 17–18). Washington, DC: Editors.

Reilly, R. R. & Warech, M. A. (1994). The validity and fairness of alternatives to cognitive tests. In L. C. Wing & B. R. Gifford (Eds.), *Policy issues in employment testing* (pp. 131–224). Boston: Kluwer Academic Publishers.

Riemer, J. (1979). *Hard hats: The work world of construction workers.* Beverly Hills, CA: Sage Publications.

Rosser, P. (1989). *Gender and testing.* (ERIC ED 336 457)

Seidman, A. (1978). *Working women: A study of women in paid jobs.* Boulder, CO: Westview Press.

Street, B. (1984). *Literacy in theory and practice.* Cambridge, England: Cambridge University Press.

Stromberg, A.H. & Harkess, S. (1978). *Women working: Theories and facts in perspective.* Palo Alto, CA: Mayfield Publishing.

Synk, D. & Swarthout, D. (1987). *A comparison of black and non-minority validities for the General Aptitude Test Battery.* (ERIC ED 310 172)

Tartre, L. A. (1990). Spatial skills, gender, and mathematics. In E. Fennema & G. C. Leder (Eds.), *Mathematics and gender* (pp. 27–59). New York: Teachers College Press.

U.S. Dept. of Labor, Bureau of Labor Statistics. (1991). *Working women: A chartbook.* Bulletin No. 2385. Washington, DC: Author.

U.S. Dept. of Labor, Women's Bureau. (1993). *Handbook on women workers: Trends and issues.* Washington, DC: Author.

Vygotsky, L. (1978). *Mind in society.* Cambridge, MA: Harvard University Press.

Webber, C. (1989). The mandarin mentality: Civil service and university admissions testing in Europe and Asia. In B. R. Gifford (Ed.), *Test policy and the politics of opportunity allocation: The workplace and the law* (pp. 33–59). Boston: Kluwer Academic Publishers.

Wenger, E. (1990). *Toward a theory of cultural transparency: Elements of a social discourse of the visible and the invisible.* Irvine, CA: University of California, Information and Computer Science Dept. Technical Report 90-41.

Weston, K. (1990). Production as means, production as metaphor: Women's struggle to enter the trades. In F. Ginsburg & A. L. Tsing (Eds.), *Uncertain terms: Negotiating gender in American culture* (pp. 137–151). Boston: Beacon Press.

Wilson, R. (1986). *Black education in the world workforce: A demographic analysis.* (ERIC ED 279 753)

Zuboff, S. (1988). *In the age of the smart machine: The future of work and power.* New York: Basic Books.

# EIGHT

## Widening the Narrowed Paths of Applied Communication: Thinking a Curriculum Big Enough for Students

### *Mark Jury*

> *I think most of us are looking for a calling, not a job. Most of us, like the assembly line worker, have jobs that are too small for our spirit. Jobs are not big enough for people.*
>
> —Nora Watson *in* Studs Terkel, *Working*

"Education's in the pits right now," my former principal told me shortly after I'd left teaching for graduate school. "We're taking old subjects that aren't applicable, and teaching them in an age-old fashion. It's just not working. Our kids can't compete out in the job market. What we need is the applied concept to bring the curriculum up to the '90s."

His perceptions of students' inability to compete on the job market were not uncommon then and are even less so now. Reports linking education and the economy have been a growth industry at least since the appearance of *A Nation at Risk* in 1983. One of those reports, *Investing in People: A Strategy to Address America's Workforce Crisis* (Commission on Workforce Quality, 1989), offered a response to workplace challenges detailed in *Workforce 2000* (Johnson & Packer, 1987). Among the commission's specific recommendations was a call for schools to "offer applied instruction, such as vocational technical education, that emphasizes transferable academic skills including reading, mathematics, science, communication, and problem-solving" (Commission on Workforce Quality, p. 10). With increasing frequency, applied academics programs have been held up as a remedy for education's ills and, in turn, the economy's woes.

The Northwest Regional Educational Laboratory (NWREL) reported in the spring of 1991 that 58 high schools in Washington and Oregon were offering applied communication classes (1991b, p. 1). The NWREL survey results show that by December of that same year, the number had risen to 141 high schools in Washington alone, 197 for the entire five-state region (Owens, 1991, p. B-1). More recently, the applied academics concept received endorsement in federal legislation. The School-to-Work Opportunity Act of 1994 authorizes the "use of Federal funds . . . as venture capital to underwrite the initial cost of planning and establishing statewide School-to-Work Opportunities systems" (Section 3 (a) (4) ), including school-based learning programs which, among other things, "integrate academic and vocational learning (including applied methodologies and team-teaching strategies), and incorporates instruction, to the extent practicable, in all aspects of an industry, appropriately tied to the career major of a participant" (Section 102 (4)).

I began this analysis with some familiarity of the applied academics concept, the concept of integrating those aspects of vocational and academic curricula seen as relevant to the modern workplace, a concept intent on providing students with a "meaningful context" for learning, by which is meant a work-related (or work-as-imagined-in-the-classroom) context for learning.[1] I was familiar with the concept, but I wanted to know more about the embodiment of that concept: What do applied communications curricula look like? What do they offer that is new or reforming, and on what theoretical ground do they base these reformed offerings? What, according to such curricula, is "applicable" and what, by virtue of its being left out, is deemed "inapplicable"?

Tharp and Gallimore (1988) have referred to America's periodic calls for school reform as an "irregular series of national spasms that, from time to time, grip the nation" (p. 1). Any reform effort able to hang on from spasm to spasm deserves attention. When that effort not only hangs on but is said to be "gaining momentum throughout the country" (Northwest Regional Educational Laboratory, 1991b, p. 1) and then is convulsed into the language of federal legislation, the need for critical examination increases. This chapter begins to respond to that need by examining the applied communications branch of the applied academics movement. Specifically, I examine a popular, packaged version of applied communications published by the Agency for

215

Institutional Technology (AIT).[2] Because this packaged program bears the name Applied Communication, I'll refer to it hereafter as AIT/AC to avoid confusing it with the general notion of applied communication. I focus on the AIT/AC curriculum for a variety of reasons. First, it's widely available through a consortium of states, and it's often supported by state and local school system-sponsored staff development programs. AIT/AC has also received significant corporate support. In Washington state, for instance, the Boeing Company provided grants and seed money to school districts for implementation of AIT/AC's curriculum (Northwest Regional Educational Laboratory, 1991b, p. 1; 1991a, p. 3). Also, AIT/AC has received enthusiastic endorsements from highly regarded educational reform advocates. In a report to the Council of Chief State School Officers, for instance, Willard Daggett, director of the International Center for Leadership in Education, not only recommends applied methodology but names AIT/AC in particular (see Daggett, 1991, 1992).

AIT/AC is significant also for its similarity to curricula used in courses some companies offer (or require of) their employees as the companies begin to implement self-directed work teams or in other ways attempt to restructure themselves as "high performance" workplaces. The curricular similarities range from workbook exercises and videotaped scenarios of problem-solving and communication in the workplace to a break-it-down-into-tiny-steps pedagogy.[3] Consistent with this pedagogy, and key among the curricular similarities, is the view of communications as a thing to be taught, a set of discrete skills, packaged and ready to be delivered to students—tidy sequences for writing memos, using the phone, listening effectively, getting along with supervisors and co-workers, analyzing problems and proposing solutions. Each assignment is cast in a work-related context ("As a manager of a plumbing supply warehouse, write a memo to . . . "), and in this sense the assigned behavior is applied communication—communication applied to a (contrived) work-related context.

Typically, applied communication curricula designers, and their corporate cousins, portray communication as a relatively unproblematic, neutral package of skills, a set of specific steps to be followed in a prescribed order—that is, problems can certainly arise which render communication "ineffective," but these problems are for the most part predictable and can be remedied, if not avoided altogether, when those involved in the communication follow "The Six (or Five or Seven) Steps For Effective Speaking" and "Effective Listening." In this analysis I suggest that we view communication not as a neutral package of skills, but as engaged linguistic activity, as critical and conscious use of language, as a complex process of negotiated understandings influenced by context and ideology, by social relations, by access to information, by culturally influenced interpretations (cf. Bourdieu, 1991;

216

Fairclough, 1989; Gumperz *et al.*, 1979; Hull et al., 1994b; Volosinov, 1973). I argue that this perspective should become an explicit part of any curriculum intent on expanding students' literacy, and that literature—typically ignored in applied curricula—can help foster this critical consciousness of language and at the same time offer critical perspectives on "all aspects of an industry."

My former principal would be right if he were to argue that portions of the following critique of applied communications could just as easily be leveled at traditional subjects as they are traditionally taught, at those "old subjects" taught in an "age-old fashion." In typical Advanced Placement English courses, students apprentice as literary critics. In lower-track English classes, they apprentice as bureaucrats, filling in blanks and writing by templates. An alternative certainly seems in order. Unfortunately, in narrowly conceived applied communications classes, students apprentice as reformed Bartlebys: Bartlebys, the Team Players; Bartlebys, the Obsequious, who prefer—nay, who are delighted—to copy and verify and run errands, who quickly, easily and unquestioningly adapt to a rapidly changing society. Better alternatives exist.

## Talk in a Box: A Modular Approach to Communication

AIT/AC describes itself as "a comprehensive set of learning materials designed to help high school students develop and refine job-related communication skills." The entire program is currently divided into seventeen instructional "modules," with each module divided into ten lessons. An instructor's guide, student worktext, and video are provided for each module. Though numbered, there is no prescribed sequence to the modules. Teachers are encouraged to pick and choose which of the seventeen modules—and within each, which of the lessons—seems appropriate for their particular goals, their particular course, their particular students. If a teacher were so inclined, the modules could be used as the curriculum for a stand-alone course, though teachers as well as state and district curriculum coordinators I talked with noted that it's more common to find portions of the curriculum integrated into existing courses.

The ten lessons in each module are divided into two sections. The first seven lessons introduce the students to a particular workplace skill, which is framed in terms of a problem (e.g., how to participate effectively in groups or how to present a point of view). This section also introduces the student to specific strategies for approaching the problem. Typically, these strategies include: charts and checklists to help students identify components of the problem; lists of steps to follow for analyzing the components identified in the first set of charts and checklists; lists of steps to follow in order to act on

217

the problem, including a checklist to determine whether that action should be in oral or written form; a checklist for evaluating the student's performance of the previous steps.

These first seven lessons also present the problem in brief scenarios and ask the students to practice the strategies as they've been outlined. The examples, the scenarios, are drawn from a wide range of job settings and cover a wide range of issues. A lesson in one module, for instance, asks students to watch and respond to a video in which a hair designer has to locate information about the new look his client wants; another lesson in a different module asks students to write a departmental memo about a company's policy on sexist language. Some of these exercises ask students to write memos or brief letters (most of the writing tasks call for a page or less), while other exercises ask students to manipulate the details in a prewritten memo. For instance, an exercise asks students to look at a memo written to food service workers, outlining tasks to be completed by the end of the evening shift. The students are to decide whether table cloths should be changed before salt and pepper shakers are filled and returned to the tables, or vice versa. They are then to rewrite the memo reflecting the most efficient order. Other exercises call for the student to check off items on a chart, to fill in some blanks, to match vocabulary terms with definitions, or to supply short answers to questions.

The second section, lessons eight through ten, offers more opportunities for practice in particular (though broadly conceived) occupational areas: home economics; agriculture; business and marketing; health occupations; and technical, trade, and industrial occupations. In this second set of lessons, the exercises are more "context specific" than in the first set. For instance, Module 2, Lesson 7 is a general summary of locating and using information in the workplace and so the vocabulary review focuses on such generic terms as enclosure, descriptor, index, table, flowchart, sales representative, and database. By contrast, the vocabulary list in Module 3, Lesson 8's health occupations section is made up of terms more specific to a health occupations context—mucus, nausea, secretions, vomit.

AIT/AC's attention to processes and to planning might be seen as one of its strengths. This process orientation is an improvement over an assign-it-and-sit-down pedagogy, which assumes that if the student knows what the final product should look like and when it is due, then that's enough "teaching" for one unit. AIT/AC's approach is to give students a clue of what's expected of them and some direction for carrying out the tasks. But AIT/AC has a tendency to overdirect, and in doing so it turns a potential strength into a weakness. Consider Module 6, Participating in Groups. The worktext spells out how to recognize an effective work group, how to be an effective member of a group, how to act as a new member of a group, and how and when to observe a group. It spells out what to notice to find out how work gets done in a group, what to notice to find out who are the influential members of the group, what to notice to find out about communication patterns. In a program as carefully scripted as this, when do students begin to frame their own questions, arrive at their own conclusions? At what point do students begin to build their own processes for questioning, inferring, testing, defining, and concluding? We'll consider this issue more in a moment when we look at the module on using problem-solving strategies.

This same rigid, prescriptive approach defines the program's writing pedagogy. Rather than provide a process which students shall follow, we would do better to design lessons in such a way that students reflect on their processes, and on how they as writers adjust their approaches to different tasks. But that's part of the danger of asking students to write nothing but memos: Students risk believing that *all* writing might be approached from the same direction, through the same series of steps along the same well-trimmed path. Consider the following assignment, taken from Module 6, Lesson 10, Reporting on Group Interaction (pp. 73–75). This assignment is the culminating activity of the module and is listed as suitable for all occupations. Students have been asked to describe and analyze a group and then to report (in writing) their observations and recommendations. See Figure 7.1 for the module's instructions.

Figure 8.1: Module Instructions

**Prewriting or Planning the Report**
Remember to plan your writing.

- Analyze the information from your observations.
- Organize the information in a way the audience will recognize (chronologically, most important to least important, comparison and contrast, cause and effect).
- Use word cues to make the most important points clear to the reader ("next," "most important," "because").
- Use examples to clarify and illustrate your message.
- Use visual aids to clarify and illustrate your message when appropriate.

**Drafting**
Once you have decided what to write and the best order in which to present the information, begin drafting your description of group interaction.
Describe the group.

- how many members are there
- the purpose of the work group
- do not refer to individuals by name

Describe the communication pattern.

- who talks to whom and how often
- who listens and asks for clarification
- who proposes new ideas, coordinates ideas, encourages trust and cooperation, and evaluates group progress

Compare what you observed with the ideal pattern of interaction.
State your recommendations for improving participation and communication.

- communication skills that are important for effective participation
- participation skills that are important for successful interaction
- leadership and team-building skills that will enable the group to meet its goals

**Reviewing and Sharing**

Remember that a first draft is rarely a final written product. One way to discover what changes you need to make is to share your description with someone else. Don't worry about them "messing up" what you have written.

The suggestions you receive when you share your draft should lead to better written communication.

When revising

- reread the draft with the audience in mind
- be sure the purpose is clear so that the audience will understand what you mean
- adjust the writing to fit the knowledge and language of the audience
- if necessary, reorganize sentences to show how one idea related to another

**Revising, Editing, and Proofreading**

Look for better ways of expressing your ideas. That includes everything from reorganizing the entire description to changing paragraphs, sentences, words, or ideas. Next, edit the entire description to refine and polish it. Correct any spelling, punctuation, and grammar. This polishing will give your writing a clean, correct, final appearance. Remember to use a format that is familiar to your readers.[4]

Several aspects of this assignment run counter to what researchers have long suggested about writing and writing processes. This AIT/AC assignment presents writing as a brisk march toward product along a clean, well-lighted, linear path: No mud, no switchbacks, no detours, no dense undergrowth, no surprises. The path is already laid out. The "Prewriting or Planning the Report" section assumes that organization is a particular step separate from and determined in advance of the writing; once a decision about organization is made, the writer can move right along, can attend to other more important details, not bothering to look back. The theoretical basis for this approach to writing is unclear. A number of researchers (e.g., Emig, 1971; Perl, 1979; Sommers, 1980; Flower & Hayes, 1981) have taken care to describe writing as a recursive process, not as a series of steps and stages, as this AIT/AC assignment would seem to suggest. Not even cognitive theorists, who stress the importance of planning in the composing process, would embrace AIT/AC's approach to writing. Flower and Hayes (1981), for instance, see writing as problem-solving, with planning the single most important aspect in writing, perhaps *the* thing which separates the competent, practiced writer from the not-so-competent, unpracticed writer. Yet Flower and Hayes would take exception to AIT/AC's prescriptive approach, saying that "there is no single 'correct' way to write. There are only alternative approaches to the endless series of problems and decisions writers must confront as they work through the process of composing." They acknowledge that while some alternatives might be more effective than others, the goal of a writing program is "not to prescribe a proper process, but instead, to give writers increased awareness of alternatives" as they confront the multiple constraints of writing (p. 56).

Other theoretical camps would distance themselves even farther from the AIT/AC approach. Freedman (1987), for instance, argues from a Vygotskian perspective that a student's development as a writer and thinker is determined less by the student's awareness of cognitive processes than by "the substance of social interactions" during the process of writing. Freedman refers to these interactions—the informal and formal, oral and written, teacher and peer responses to writing—as "collaborative problem-solving" or "jointly accomplished teaching and learning. Both the teacher and learner negotiate the parts they play" (p. 9).

It's significant, then, that AIT/AC's writing plan is not laid out by the student or by the student in collaboration with peers or teachers—it's not the student's plan, not the student's process, not part of a negotiated activity. Many of the writing decisions have already been made for the student. The worktext determines for the student the topic and the information to be included, it suggests the order for that information, and it imposes a final form. The "Drafting" instructions give the illusion of student involvement, student decision-making, but it's a fleeting illusion. The final step in the drafting stage, where the student is to make recommendations, is little more than a multiple-choice test masquerading as writing, since the student has already completed nine lessons driving home the worktext's image of the ideal group. Consequently, the students learn less about writing than about completing an assignment. And that's consistent with the AIT/AC approach:

Here's your task. Here's your system. Now go about your job efficiently. If we're to take seriously the chorus of reform—"Changes in the economy imply the need to know how to learn. . . . Literacy requirements have . . . shot up. . . . Previously supervised workers [must] self-regulate or self-direct" (Berryman, 1990, pp. 7, 8, 9)—then the AIT/AC approach, with its prescriptive processes channeled through a worktext, leaves us to struggle with two important questions: First, at what point in AIT/AC do students step back from their work and reflect on their own processes, on what worked for them or what didn't work and on what they might do the next time around? And, second, at what point and in what ways do students enter the negotiations and become more active players in the problem-solving process of writing?

Consider these questions as we look at one more example from the AIT/AC curriculum, an example which offers a good sense of AIT/AC pedagogy—Module 3: Using Problem-solving Strategies. AIT/AC defines a problem as "anything that causes difficulty, uncertainty, or doubt." The assumption: A problem is a thing that presents itself. We will know we are in the presence of a problem when we feel troubled or uncertain. Combine this idea with the goals spelled out in the student worktext. Under the heading "What Will You Learn from Module 3?" students are told that "today's business leaders are looking for employees who can adapt to a workplace that is becoming more and more complex" (Module 3, p. i). The curriculum views the workplace as a thing that "is becoming," its change inevitable and apart from human agency. AIT/AC asks students to adapt to change, not to carve out an active role in that change, not to challenge or work to shape that change. Nowhere in AIT/AC is change viewed as socially determined. It follows then that AIT/AC's curriculum would place emphasis on students as employees using prescribed strategies to solve contrived problems. In the worktext, the student is presented with a problem, is given a specific process of analysis to follow, is directed to list and evaluate possible solutions, and is provided with a format for presenting recommendations. The student is so carefully directed every step of the way that the emphasis truly is on *using* problem-solving strategies, not on *posing* problems and proceeding from there through analysis toward solutions.

AIT/AC's approach presumes clean solutions, presumes "right" and "wrong" approaches to problems of some pure or natural variety, problems untainted, for instance, by the ways that access to information is unevenly distributed in actual work settings and thus precludes particular solutions. Lave (1988), on the other hand, suggests that in practice we find "dilemmas to be resolved, not problems to be solved"—a perspective that takes more fully into account students and workers as actors in complex social settings, which in turn is consistent with descriptions of "high performance" workplaces (for descriptions of such workplaces, see Applebaum & Batt, 1993, and

Commission on the Skills of the American Workforce, 1990). A perspective that accounts for students and workers as actors, not as passive beings in a changing world, requires that communications teachers help students develop the language of action, help students understand language *as* action. As Harris (1991) has noted:

> We need to talk about language not simply as a form of expression but also as a form of action—to study how it gets used to advance causes, to argue competing definitions of the self and world, to form groups and alliances, and to resist the claims of opposing views and factions. We need, that is, to show how personal and social uses of language are rarely discrete but are rather almost always intertwined. (p. 643)

## The Language of Group Participation: A Question of Culture

Perhaps the most often cited rationale for an applied communications curriculum (whether AIT/AC or a homegrown version) is its emphasis on developing interpersonal skills through group participation. Some teachers credit AIT/AC with helping them reshape their classes around more student interaction and small-group work. As a former colleague of mine put it, describing the influence an applied communications approach had on her teaching: "I think I was like most business teachers. I ran a machine-oriented, technical program. I focused on a piece of equipment. But I spend a lot more time on group work now, trying to cultivate those social skills."

Her new-found interest in and attention to people's interactions with people is consistent not only with business and industry's purported shift toward a "team" concept in the workplace, but also with theory highlighting the sociocultural aspects of learning, and literacy development as social dialogue (e.g., Bakhtin, 1981, 1986; Volosinov, 1986; Vygotsky, 1978). And it's consistent with research claiming cooperative learning groups to be effective participant structures for many students (Slavin, 1988, 1989; Slavin & Oickle, 1981; Swisher, 1990; Tharp & Gallimore, 1988).

We might be thankful for any attempt to move teaching beyond what Hillocks politely calls the "presentational mode" of instruction, the "most common and widespread [yet] least effective mode examined" (Hillocks, 1986, pp. 246–247). Such classrooms are marked by students slogging through the ubiquitous workbooks, assuming a listening posture while teachers talk, or perhaps participating in "discussions" characterized by a teacher-dominated IRE pattern: teacher *I*nitiates the question, student *R*esponds, teacher *E*valuates the student response (see Mehan, 1982; see also Sinclair &

Coulthard, 1975). In a world where typically "Teachers out-talked the entire class of students by a ratio of about three to one" (Goodlad, 1984, p. 229), any program that seems to nudge teachers a bit to the side and draw students closer to the center of the action seems worth a closer look.

AIT/AC's module on group participation has the potential to awaken students' awareness to some of the social and cultural complexities of verbal and nonverbal communication, some of the "subtle, but systematic and context-specific rules governing verbal interaction" (McCarty et al., 1991, p. 42; see also, Hymes, 1972, 1986; Philips, 1972; Heath, 1982). The module prompts students to think in terms of a group's "rules" and "norms" of interaction—about rules for turn taking, topic selection and topic switching, and about norms for directness and indirectness, for politeness, for eye-contact, for pacing. In one activity, AIT/AC asks students to observe group talk and "describe the flow of communication. Look for patterns. Who talks to whom and how often? Who listens? Who uses nonverbal signals to indicate interest, boredom, frustration?" (Module 6, p. 59). I'd feel more comfortable, however, if that last question were changed to, "Which nonverbal signals do you interpret as showing interest, boredom, or frustration?" Perhaps even better would be, "How do you interpret each group member's nonverbal behavior in this instance, in this context?" Reframing the question in ways that invite interpretation and that highlight context might lead to a richer discussion of the complexities of communicative styles (emphasis on plural), a discussion which begins to get at the processes behind the behaviors we call a style (see McCarty et al., 1991, for a caution against simplistic notions of cultural "styles"). As it is, the question suggests that nonverbal behavior seen in particular instances by particular people from particular sociocultural backgrounds as a sign of boredom, for instance, or of politeness, will be seen as such in either those same or different instances by anyone from any other sociocultural background. The danger is that a particular style of interaction will come to be regarded as *the style*, others as somehow inefficient, deficient, or corrupt. And sure enough, in Lesson 10, directions for writing up an observation of group interactions tell the student to "Compare what you observed with the ideal pattern of interaction" (p. 74). The assumption: If communication isn't working, it's because not all members of the group have achieved a level of competence in *the ideal style*. This ignores the possibility that some people in the group might be operating off different norms or might be interpreting in different ways than others in the group the very context they're in the process of constructing.

The worktext tells students that when they join a group they have a responsibility to identify the group norms. It also tells them that "successful membership in a work group begins with an understanding of the group and how it makes decisions as well as with effective communication skills" (Module 6, p. 6). A section headed "receiving information in a group" (p. 8) speaks of the student's need to "understand and interpret . . . ideas and opinions." It encourages students to withhold judgment, and when judgment is called for, to base that judgment on "issues, not personalities." But at the same time, it advises that people who make groups work are those who "look interested. Face the speaker and give nonverbal signals of interest. Lean forward and react positively by smiling or nodding." That is certainly a norm for some members of some groups in some settings. But politeness and interest and deference and frustration and so on are inscribed and enacted differently in different social systems, are interpreted differently by different players in different social contexts, are influenced by relationships intertwined within and across contexts. For a curriculum to suggest otherwise is not simply naive but troublesome—it can reinforce misunderstanding, exacerbate the very problems it hopes to address.

Applied communication is, in part, about learning the language of new social settings—the language of a new workplace, for instance. Or within a familiar setting, it is about learning the language of change—the language of "self-directed work teams" or of "total quality management," for instance. It's important to remember, then, that "because learning a language is learning to exercise both a social and a personal voice, it is both a process of socialization into a given speech community and the acquisition of literacy as a means of expressing personal meanings that may put in question those of the speech community" (Kramsch, 1993, p. 233). Unfortunately, AIT/AC doesn't seem to recognize the last part of that equation, the possibility of this "third place" or "third culture," as Kramsch calls it. Instead, AIT/AC emphasizes the process of socialization, proposing that the essence of a group is, or should be, "issues, not personalities," and that a group is a fairly static thing, an entity to be understood, entered into, adapted to. Kramsch reminds us that "culture is difference, variability, and always a potential source of conflict when one culture enters into contact with another" (1993, p. 1). We would do well to embrace that difference, that variability, that conflict. Kramsch argues convincingly that:

> a critical language pedagogy that values dissent, dialogue, and double-voiced discourse . . . shows how learners can use the system for their own purposes, to create a culture of a third kind in which they can express their own meanings without being hostage to the meanings of either their own or the target speech communities. (pp. 13–14)[5]

# Applied to What? A Question of Context

Applied communication boosters note that AIT/AC encourages connections with the world beyond the school, and the importance of these "real-world" connections, they claim, is detailed in research in the cognitive sciences: "At the heart of this research is the presumption that intelligence and expertise are built out of interaction with the environment, not in isolation from it" (Berryman, 1990, pp. 10–11).[6] But while Berryman (1988, 1990, 1993), along with much of the research she cites, speaks of interactions with or in isolation from the environment and of contextualized or decontextualized learning, Lave and others (see especially the contributors to Chaiklin & Lave, 1993) reject such dichotomies. Lave (1993) argues that there is always "context"—"a social world constituted in relation with persons acting" (p. 5)—and therefore always learning: "Learning is an integral aspect of activity in and with the world at all times. That learning occurs is not problematic. . . . What gets learned . . . depends on the subjective and intersubjective interpretation of the how and why of ongoing activity" (pp. 8, 10).

Curricula, then, should invite students into the world in enabling ways, in ways that open the students up to new possibilities, to new roles. Unfortunately, the AIT/AC worktexts do not invite students to participate in the world in substantially different ways than do the tasks of many traditional classrooms. And even if the AIT/AC worktexts were closed and put away, the problem would remain that the program defines The Environment it would have students "interact with" as The Workplace. Granted, schools help broaden or extend the range of students' meaning-making processes when they help students negotiate tasks which the students themselves regard as "necessary and relevant for life" (Vygotsky, 1978, p. 118). But while certain work within certain workplaces will be of certain interest to certain people, a shift in focus from academic tasks to imagined work tasks within a classroom certainly cannot guarantee engaged students who "participate in changing ways in a changing world" (Lave, 1993, p. 5). It seems fair to assume that students, as with the rest of us, define work more broadly than those tasks assigned by employers, that if asked what work they find "necessary and relevant for life" they would look not just within but beyond the workplace, to their work in athletics, in academics (even, in some cases, to their work in traditional classrooms), in councils, clubs or gangs, in neighborhoods, families, or churches. A student might find she has a greater need to present her point of view to other members of her basketball team than to her supervisor at work. She might find herself more engaged in new ways, taking on new roles, in the activities of her tribal youth council than in her after-school job.

Applied communication advocates argue that their curricula meet students' "needs," but the assumptions these advocates make about particular students and their particular needs leave their curricula focused on limited and limiting work settings at the expense of other social settings, other contexts, other interests, other demands. Bourdieu would describe these assumptions as a kind of symbolic violence—the curriculum, "instead of telling the child what he must do, tells him what he is, and thus leads him to become durably what he has to be" (1991, p. 52). We would do better not to assume students' "needs" but instead to help students expand their social—and therefore their communicative—repertoire. We would do better, that is, to develop coursework which engages students in a wealth of activities across a range of settings, settings and activities which call on the students to write, draw, talk, compute, create, troubleshoot, and problem-solve not simply because these are tasks which in someone's mind model work-activities, but because the tasks are made necessary for a variety of reasons within the various settings, much in the ways that working on a student newspaper, for instance, makes necessary the students' involvement in their communities as alert citizens, as business people, as investigators, as artists, writers, editors, marketers. Or they are tasks made necessary in the ways that serving on an effective student government makes necessary the students' involvement in the school community, actually calls on them to present proposals before the school administration, organize events, deal with (and at times create) crises, chair and attend meetings, assume airs of importance, inhabit offices, work the phones, work the system, run into and try to work around administrative stonewalling, and so on.

## What to Write, What to Read: A Question of Genres

It might be argued that AIT/AC broadens students' literacy practice by swinging the doors of the classroom open to the world outside, introducing them to a genre they might not have worked with otherwise: the memo. After all, when students are asked to write in school, they are too often asked to stick within a carefully scripted expository mode—a five-paragraph essay, for instance. This irrepressible form is to composition what chickweed or quacgrass is to gardening: No matter how hard we might try to weed it out, it keeps cropping up. (For commentary on the limited nature of literacy practice in classrooms, see Applebee, 1981, 1984; Goodlad, 1984; Hillocks, 1986; Applebee, et al, 1990; for commentary on eradication of chickweed or quackgrass, see your local extension agent.) But AIT/AC doesn't *add* to the students' genre options, it *replaces* one genre with another. Is the program, then, really swinging doors open for students, or is it opening one door as it closes others? And does this new door really lead to the outside world or into a closet (a dead-end, even if that closet is janitorial or otherwise work-related)?

Reform advocates cite such studies as New York's Career Preparation Validation Study to justify a curricular emphasis of applied communications: "Although *Reading for Personal Response* is a valuable adult skill, it is considered unimportant in the work world," and "Findings indicate that *Writing for Personal Expression* and *Writing for Social Interaction* are seldom used on the job" (Daggett, 1991, p. 13). However, in order to improve current practice, a literacy curriculum must do more than simply introduce students to and provide guided practice in a selected new genre, or in a limited set of genres, each following a standard form—the request letter, the response letter, the memo, the bar graph and pie chart, the cover letter and resumé, the job interview. It must do more than provide guided practice in traditional school genres—the persuasive essay, the personal experience paper, the research paper, the literary analysis paper.

While familiarity with particular genres may help students negotiate particular written demands at work and school, recent research on community and workplace literacy suggests that successful communication in work and community more often depends on an ability to negotiate "hybrid discourses" than on facility with a particular genre (Flower, 1995). According to Flower, hybrid discourses "arise in multicultural settings, in interdisciplinary projects, and in emergent communities (and) are marked by the often productive, often uneasy alliance of multiple ways of talking and writing, multiple representations, and/or multiple sign systems."[7] This can be seen in the research of Hull, Jury, Ziv, and Schultz (1994b), where on the manufacturing floor of an electronics manufacturing plant, workers from varied cultural, educational, technical, and professional backgrounds interact in ways that challenge, set aside, or circumvent the company's official language, as represented by certified documents—by sanctioned corporate genres, if you will. Hull *et al.* note how work activities in the factory are often mediated by multiple forms of representation—talk, writing, drawings, demonstrations, models—within inter-ethnic or inter-status exchanges. Not only is work facilitated through these exchanges, these sometimes contentious, sometimes messy, yet often productive attempts at merging multiple perspectives, but in these exchanges workers also negotiate and renegotiate their authority within the plant. Such research suggests that the multiple demands of high-tech, multi-ethnic workplaces in rapidly shifting markets do not call for a static set of skills or facility with particular genres, but rather for ways of negotiating, of finding common ground. More important than any static set of skills are schools and workplaces which honor this negotiating, which nurture multiple perspectives and accommodate multiple forms of representation—schools and workplaces which grant students and workers the authority to draw on their own experience, to add their perspectives to decision-making processes, even as they (or in order that they might) expand those perspectives and that experience.

Similar arguments have been raised by other researchers working from a Bakhtinian perspective. Dyson (1992, 1993), for instance, noting that students are provided a limited range of "social stages" as they move through school, calls for "child-permeable literacy curricula [which] may allow children to experience the artistically rich and diverse culture in our society" (1992, pp. 41, 42). Such curricula, she says, should encourage students to develop even further the genres they bring with them to school—jokes, cartoons, stories, and songs, for instance—even as it asks them to explore new genres, or to combine genres they had previously seen as separate, serving separate functions. Such curricula, I can imagine her suggesting, might encourage students to explore the poetic possibilities of the memo, as poet Marianne Moore did in letters to the Ford Motor Company in response to their request that she help them name a new model. (Ford, it should be noted, did not select any of Moore's suggestions. They settled instead for the name *Edsel*. See Weathers, 1980, pp. 89–91, for samples of these letters.)

If such "child-permeable" curricula exist, they apparently become clogged as students move through middle school and high school, channeling students into purely academic or narrowly vocational tracks. With researchers claiming that "literacy requirements have shot up," it would seem our curricula should try to meet literacy demands by expanding, not limiting, the range of literacy activities students engage in, even—or perhaps especially—as the students get older. Such expanded curricula should include not only the standard business genres, which are virtually the sole focus of AIT/AC, but the literary-artistic genres as well. And these genres should both be woven in with and allowed to grow out of student projects, student activities, in ways that encourage hybridity—in ways that encourage exploration and combination and invite poetic memos and creative negotiations of meaning, negotiations which draw on multiple representations and encourage multiple perspectives.

I should note that AIT/AC doesn't ignore literature altogether, although perhaps it would be better if it did, considering how it reduces that literature. For instance, in the brief annotated bibliography in the back of the instructor's guide for Module 2, Gathering and Using Information in the Workplace, we find: "Thoreau, Henry David. *Walden*. In much of this work the author devotes his time to gathering information around Walden pond." Yes, well, that's one way to read *Walden*. But are we to ask students to focus only on *where* Thoreau lived and to ignore what he lived *for*? What, then, are we to make of his claim that "as for *work*, we haven't any of any consequence. We have the Saint Vitus' dance, and cannot possibly keep our heads still" (p. 347)? What are we to make of his "wont to think that men are not so much the keepers of herds as herds are the keepers of men, the former are so much the freer" (p. 310)? Maybe we should just ignore this stuff because we are folks who:

> have learned to read to serve a paltry convenience, as [we] have learned to cipher in order to keep accounts and not be cheated in trade; but of reading as a noble intellectual exercise [we] know little or nothing; yet this only is reading, in a high sense, not that which lulls us as a luxury and suffers the nobler faculties to sleep the while, but what we have to stand on tiptoe to read and devote our most alert and wakeful hours to. (p. 357)

If success in the modern workplace truly depends on a worker's capacity for "increased" literacy—for interpretation, for critical judgment and divergent thinking, for not simply solving problems but for sensing them in the first place—then we have to ask if AIT/AC's emphasis on reading-for-information will meet these needs. That is, to what extent do we challenge students' interpretive skills, to what extent do we demand critical judgment, when as a culminating exercise in Module 2, Gathering and Using Information, we ask students in the technical, trade, and industrial section (p. 129) to read a refrigerator repair and maintenance troubleshooting chart, plug in their problem-solving strategies, and answer these questions:

1. What would cause a refrigerator to make a lot of noise?
2. What should you bring with you in case the refrigerator smells bad?
3. The refrigerator is running continuously. What should you do?
4. What action would you take if the freezer door lock were broken?
5. Can a defective compressor motor cause the refrigerator to make a noise?

Restricting the curriculum to these reading-for-information activities does a disservice to students. Such traditional and grossly reductive "culminating" activities, in their devotion to the "applied concept," point students down narrow (and perhaps dead-ended) career paths. We'd do better to offer a broadly integrated curriculum, one that takes seriously the School-to-Work Opportunities Act's language about students exploring "all aspects of the industry." Even if we wanted to stay within the "technical, trade, and industrial" focus of the example above, we'd do better to engage the students in broader practice, practice which offers students a more global view of the industry, including its social and political spheres. Why limit their practice to repair? Why not engage them in some kind of activities that not only require them to crawl behind the system (refrigeration *and* political-economic), trou-

bleshooting noise and stench, but which also require them to join poet
Stephen Dobyns as he stands:

> . . . staring into the refrigerator
> as if into the place where the answers are kept—
> the ones telling why you get up in the morning
> and how it is possible to sleep at night,
> answers to what comes next and how to like it.

## Alternatives that Move beyond the World of Work

> *The great question that hovers over this issue,
> one that we have dealt with mainly by indiffer-
> ence, is the question of what people are for. Is
> their greatest dignity in unemployment? Is the
> obsolescence of human beings now our social
> goal? One would conclude so from our attitude
> toward work, especially the manual work nec-
> essary to the long-term preservation of the
> land, and from our rush toward mechaniza-
> tion, automation, and computerization. In a
> country that puts an absolute premium on
> labor-saving measures, short workdays, and
> retirement, why should there be any surprise at
> permanence of unemployment and welfare
> dependency? Those are only different names for
> our national ambitions.*

> Wendell Berry, from *What Are People For?*

I'll admit it: I'm an old guy raised on the old subjects. And I'll even admit that
my former principal was on to something, that I have taught those old subjects in ways that rendered the subjects irrelevant to many students. I will
argue, however, not only that those old subjects can be made relevant, but
that they must, and that they must remain in the curriculum for all students
for a variety of reasons, not the least of which is to prod students (and teachers) toward answers to Dobyns' questions. It seems right to demand that any
curriculum purporting to be work-based or work-centered should, at the very
least, encourage speculation about and visions of "What comes next and how
to like it." This is especially critical at a time when *Fortune* declares "The End
of the Job" (September 19, 1994) and *Business Week* heralds "The New World

of Work" (October 17, 1994). It's for this reason as much as any other that I'll take issue with my former principal's claims that literature is "not applicable."

Poet, teacher, and critic Robert Hass would say the answers to Dobyns' questions lie in the images we carry with us:

> It seems to me we all live our lives in the light of primary acts of imagination, images or sets of images that get us up in the morning and move us about our days. I do not think anybody can live without one, for very long, without suffering intensely from deadness or futility. And I think that, for most of us, those images are not only essential but dangerous because no one of them feels like the whole truth and they do not last. Either they die of themselves, dry up, are shed; or, if we are lucky, they are invisibly transformed into the next needful thing; or we act on them in a way that exposes both them and us. (1984, p. 303)

Similarly, Maxine Greene recognizes as essential danger, as necessary exposure, those images given particular shape in or conjured up by the arts:

> It is not uncommon for the arts to leave us somehow ill at ease, nor for them to prod us beyond acquiescence. They may, now and then, move us into spaces where we can create visions of other ways of being and ponder what it might signify to realize them. (1991, p. 27)

I'm left to worry, then, what images—of work, of self, family, community—AIT/AC's multiple modules inspire and what images they suppress. I'm left to wonder what alternate visions other curricula might suggest or help construct, and to speculate on how we as teachers might help students make sense of, challenge or shed particular images. Applied communications is typically offered as a class for seniors. It seems to me that of all the school years, this senior year, the year of wandering out, is the very time when students should be most challenged to create new visions, should be most encouraged to construct and reconstruct their guiding images, their brief and partial truths about the possible worlds of work and their possible places in those worlds. Unfortunately, applied communications tends not to be about moving *beyond* acquiescence, but about acquiescing. Not about creating visions, but fitting into one. Not about other ways of being or of becoming, but about *a way* of being.

The literary-artistic genres in general, and that old subject poetry in particular, can be incorporated into the curriculum, can be presented, explored, taught, in ways that encourage student writers and readers to move beyond AIT/AC's simple problem-solving strategies, to become more critically conscious of the world—including the world of work—and become conscious of the language of that consciousness.[8] We might help move students toward this critical awareness by asking them to reflect on their notions of the language of power, the language of rage, the language of the sacred, the private, the public, the familial. We might ask where their notions of language come from, and how those notions, how that language, shapes their world and their images of themselves in that world? Will they see that language or its familiar images in their reading, or will their reading challenge familiar images?

The literary genres have importance beyond the images they both offer and challenge. Equally important are the interpretive and critical perspectives textual study can bring to the modern, text-saturated workplace, to workplaces in which activity is dictated by documents mandated by international standards organizations, including documents documenting how documents are to be documented and who has what authority to do the documenting, who has the responsibility to read the documents, and what corrective action must be taken in the event of undocumented activity (see Hull *et al.*, 1994a, 1994b; Hull, this volume). These documents are just part of the larger text of the organization itself, a text which includes market demands, scheduling and production pressures, customer and labor relations, the company's history within the industry and within the community, employees' work and education histories, workers' relations with fellow workers and bosses, and so on. Communicating in the workplace, then, means reading, interpreting, and critiquing this corporate text. Consider, then, how Scholes' (1985) definitions of "textual knowledge and textual skills" (reading, interpretation, criticism) make sense in terms of "reading" the workplace-as-text:

> Reading: "Knowledge of the codes that were operative in the composition of any given text and the historical situation in which it was composed" (p. 21).
> Interpretation: "A matter of making connections between a particular verbal text and a larger cultural text" (p. 33). On the one hand, interpretation is a matter of "listening and obedience"; on the other, of "suspicion and rigor" (p. 48).
> Criticism: "A critique of the codes . . . out of which a given text has been constructed" (p. 23). The "need to confront both the naturalistic attitude—this is the way things are, people can't help themselves—and the objective detachment of the narration—this is the way things happen, I am just recording" (p. 37).

We can build from Scholes' textual activities with the "communication skills" Witte finds meaningful in naturally occurring situations:

- Reading (and interpreting) a given situation.
- Reading signs of deception in a given situation.
- Reading signs of honesty and goodwill in a given situation.

- Identifying and opening windows of constructive opportunity in a given situation.
- Adapting or developing strategies for action predicated on one's knowledge of a given situation.
- Making informed and appropriate decisions in a given situation about what can or cannot be said, about what needs or need not to be said, about how or how not to say it, and about when or when not to say it.
- Collaborating with others during reading and writing in a give situation.
- Accessing and applying metacognitive knowledge of communication (1993, pp. 26-27).

Similar to Witte's communications skills is Blau's "personal literacy," which he describes as a:

- Capacity for sustained focused attention.
- Willingness to suspend closure—to entertain problems rather than avoid them.
- Willingness to take risks—to predict and be wrong, to respond honestly, to offer variant readings.
- Tolerance for failure—willingness to reread and reread again.
- Tolerance for ambiguity, paradox, and uncertainty.
- Intellectual generosity and ego-permeability—willingness to change mind, to appreciate alternative visions, and to engage in methodological believing as well as doubting.

Blau admits that the dimensions of personal literacy read more like character traits than literacy skills, but nevertheless he sees them as an integral component of a "humane literacy." And they seem to fit nicely in the workplace, seem to lend themselves to the sort of divergent thinking the business world says it wants. In fact, don't these traits characterize, to some degree, a good worker, a good citizen, a good partner?

Some of the more interesting and promising alternative approaches to narrowly defined applied communications programs build on this combination of textual and personal literacy by emphasizing what Witte terms "the necessary relationship between communication and community" (1993, p. 31). One such program is "CityWorks," described as "the centerpiece of the ninth grade program" at the Rindge School of Technical Arts in Cambridge, Massachusetts. The project-based curriculum is designed "to help students understand their community and its needs, and ultimately to see themselves as people who can affect that community and create new opportunities for themselves and others who live or work there" (Rosenstock & Steinberg, n.d.,

p. 8). Working closely with a variety of community members—with "real clients" and in "apprentice-master relationships"—students become immersed in activities which require "observation, rumination, documentation, and exhibition" (Rosenstock, 1995).

Waterford Mott High School in Michigan has tried a similar approach, developing a team-taught, interdisciplinary program, combining language arts, social studies, mathematics, science, and computer technology. A general theme for the year is proposed ("Rights and Responsibilities" was the theme the first year), and the teachers then help students identify and confront problems in their community related to that theme. The students develop and strengthen over the course of the year those procedures parceled out in AIT/AC: They investigate, gather information, analyze data, propose a problem for intensive study, gather more information, write, interview, submit proposals, work in study teams—all with the goal of "presenting and defending their solutions to a relevant community audience" (Monetta, 1992, pp. 7–8).

At University Heights High School, an alternative public high school located on the campus of Bronx Community College, students engage in "integrated problem-solving projects," assembling their work in portfolios and reflecting on the ways in which that work demonstrates their proficiency in seven broadly defined "domains and habits of learning" (including, for instance, "communicating, crafting and reflecting," "connecting the past, present and future," and "taking responsibility for myself and my community"). Students present and defend their portfolios before a "Roundtable"—a gathering of people from the school and the larger community. It's through such Roundtable assessments, not grades or credits, that students move from level to level through to graduation (Cushman, 1994; Allen, 1995)

Within a more traditional classroom setting, for a "communications arts" curriculum (to borrow Witte's term) which is more explicitly tied to specific workplaces, we might consider the approach Walter Masuda has taken in the first-year composition course he teaches at Contra Costa College, a community college located in the San Francisco Bay area. He asks his students to conduct a microethnography of literacy in:

> the immediate environment of your workplace, a workplace in which you would like to seek occupation, or a classroom here on campus. The guiding research questions you will be asking as you observe your research settings will be, "What kinds of literacies are valued here?" and, more broadly, "What kinds of tools would I need to determine the modes of communication valued in any given social situation?" These questions involve many sub-questions (e.g., "Who determines what literacies are valued?" "What are the power implications involved?")

that we'll be discussing in class—questions that will help you to focus your observations down to a "do-able" project. (from a course handout; for further details,
see Masuda, 1995)

Continuing from these examples, then, another work-related alternative
to applied communications might be a hybrid curriculum which aims to take
students through a look at home and work, work and home, a curriculum
which asks students to look at what happens when people uproot home to
look for work, and what happens when, once home is firmly established, people find their work uprooted. Such a curriculum should ask students to wonder about the nature of work, and about the rewards, the trials, the
tribulations, the power and the politics of work. It should ask them to develop
some sense of the history of work in their communities. It should encourage
them to ask questions about the necessity of work, of being of use, and of
being used, encourage them to wonder about the impact of certain work on
the land and on the spirit. It should ask them to ask questions of their community, of their teachers, of their parents, and of themselves. In short, it should
prompt them to use language to look at the world—including the world of
work—critically.

One of the chief ironies of having to argue for a project-based applied
communications program is that vocational education has always prided itself
as being more active, more inquiry-based, more student-centered than traditional academic programs. Yet these characteristics have been abandoned in
programs such as AIT/AC. Applied communications has not distanced itself
far enough from the standard teaching—that is, from the narrowly contextualized academics—it repudiates. In an important sense, then, a project-based
course is a call to reclaim Dewey's vision of vocational education, a vision of
education as engagement in purposeful activity, as work integrated with a play
attitude. It is also a call to reclaim Dewey's understanding of vocation: "The
dominant vocation of all human beings at all times is living—intellectual and
moral growth," necessarily defined "with some fullness in order to avoid the
impression that an education which centers about it is narrowly practical, if
not merely pecuniary" (1916/1960, pp. 362, 358). Dewey urges us to remember that:

We naturally name [a person's] vocation from that one of the callings which distinguishes him, rather than from those which he has in common with all others.
But we should not allow ourselves to be so subject to words as to ignore and virtually deny his other callings when it comes to a consideration of the vocational
phases of education. (1916/1960, p. 359)

236

# To the Real Work

> To the real work, to
> "What is to be done."
>
> Gary Snyder, from "I Went into the Maverick Bar"

Agreed: Rapid change seems to characterize modern workplaces, and students must be prepared to confront the challenges such workplaces present. But work doesn't exist apart from the rest of our lives. It's because our lives, our families, our communities, are so tightly interwoven with our work that we must offer students more thorough, more critical, more challenging curricula than we find in either the current incarnations of applied communications or the traditional language arts classrooms they propose to replace. We can't pretend that students-as-workers exist apart from the politics that shapes global markets and influences global migration, or the politics that reacts to shifting markets and migration. We can't separate a work-related curriculum from the issues surrounding California's Proposition 187, for instance, or other such attempts to ban particular children from public schools and other social services. A high school language arts curriculum which presumes to make connections to the worlds of work should not simply acknowledge the linguistic changes a community undergoes as patterns of immigration and migration change; it should confront the resentment which old-timers (even teenaged old-timers) harbor toward those they label "alien," those they hold responsible for the rapid changes in their work, their neighborhoods, their schools, their lives. It will have to ask students to consider what's happening in their own communities, their communities' workplaces and in communities and workplaces around the world that has prompted people to pull up roots and become "aliens." It will have to prepare students for the politics of change, that tangle of issues around economics, environment, gender, religion, race, and class. The curriculum will have to recognize students not as helpless in the face of change, but instead as a legitimate part of the processes which influence change. Students need to decide what's right for their own lives and for their communities, and need to find ways to make "right" things happen. Some will say this is the stuff of a civics class. Others will say this is a call for community service. I suppose both claims are right. But it also seems like a language class, a literacy class, a class where students make sense of the world through language.

# Notes

1. Part of that familiarity grew out of my own teaching experience, including two years of team-teaching a composition course with Judy Sato, a business teacher at Sedro-Woolley High School in northwest Washington. As part of the preparation for the course, and at the urging of our principal and her vocational director, we attended state-sponsored workshops introducing the applied communications curriculum I critique here. We opted not to use that curriculum and instead developed our own. Judy and Jim Johnson, her current team-teaching partner, have since improved that curriculum, reworking it in ways more consistent with programs I'll describe later in the chapter.

2. To provide a point of contrast as I analyzed the AIT/AC curriculum, I visited two comprehensive high schools and one vocational technical center which had been recommended by school officials in the Midwest and Pacific Northwest as exemplary sites for the development of applied communications programs. I looked at their home-grown curriculum materials (as opposed to off-the-shelf materials such as AIT/AC), observed classes, and interviewed students and teachers as well as building, district, and state administrators. I've tried to make sense of those observations both in terms of literacy research and theory, and in terms of two years of ethnographic fieldwork in electronics manufacturing plants, a study of the role literacy plays in how work gets done in high-tech workplaces undergoing organizational change.

3. This pedagogy was stated explicitly in a course I observed in an electronics manufacturing plant in California's Silicon Valley. The course was designed to teach line workers in the plant the communication and problem-solving skills the company had decided were necessary for workers' successful participation in self-directed work teams. The focus of the particular class session was "Teaching Job Skills to Co-Workers." Taped to an easel at the front of the room was the purpose of the day's lesson: "To help you teach someone a new skill by breaking down into small steps what the person needs to know" (field notes, 1/9/95). Many organizations concerned with training and industry standards work from a similar notion of teaching and learning as the dis-aggregating and re-aggregating of "bundles" of skills. For instance, the American Training Standards Institute (ATSI), which identifies itself as "a not-for-profit research corporation . . . formed to support and enhance the emerging national skills infrastructure," imagines "the unbundling and rebundling of existing training courses into a library of 'skill-objects' [which] will have an identi-

cal match to [an] individual skill-assessment and IDP [individual development plan] data base." ATSI further imagines the "unbundling" of courses "into individual skill-units" which are then "transposed into numerous 'skill learning events'" (ATSI, http://steps.atsi.edu/atsi/atsibp).

4. Here the worktext provides a sample of a memo.

5. Though the focus of Kramsch's work is on foreign language teaching, any teacher, especially one interested in language, literacy, and culture, is likely to find her book helpful for rethinking pedagogy, text, context, and culture.

6. For an example of applied academics boosterism, see Daggett, 1991, 1992. For an overview of cognitive science perspectives on learning for the workplace, see Berryman, 1993. For a critical perspective on notions of context and learning, see Lave, 1988, 1993, in press. For a little entertainment, read the work of all three in one afternoon: Daggett cites Berryman extensively, but Berryman makes clear that "learning in context" as she understands it "does not refer to a vocational or applied curriculum" (1993, p. 385). Meanwhile, although Berryman draws extensively on the work of Lave and others, she overlooks the challenges Lave makes of those others' theories of learning and their definitions of "context."

7. See also Kramsch, 1993, especially her discussion of notions of "interculturality" in chapters 7 and 8, "Teaching Language along the Cultural Faultline" and "Looking for Third Places."

8 This is not to suggest that students are without critical consciousness. In fact, I've argued elsewhere (cf. Hull & Jury, 1994) that the opposite is true. The point here is that one goal of any curriculum should be to draw on and further develop this consciousness.

# References

Agency for Instructional Technology (AIT). *Applied communication*. (1988). Bloomington, IN:

Allen, D. (1995, April). *Keeping student work central*: The New York Assessment Collection. Seminar conducted at A Symposium of California's Restructuring Schools, Burlingame, CA.

American Training Standards Institute (ATSI). (1995, August 1). *ATSI Home Page*. World Wide Web: http://steps.atsi.edu.

Applebaum, E, & Batt, R. (1993). *Transforming the production system in U.S. firms*. A report to the Sloan Foundation. Washington, DC: Economic Policy Institute.

Applebee, A. N. (1981). *Writing in the secondary school: English and the content areas*. Urbana, IL: National Council of Teachers of English.

Applebee, A. N. (1984). Contexts for learning to write: Studies of secondary school instruction. Norwood, NJ: Ablex.

Applebee, A. N., Langer, J., Jenkins, L. B., Mullis, I. V. S., & Foertsch, M. A. (1990). *Learning to write in our nation's schools: Instruction and achievement in 1988 at grades 4, 8, and 12*. Princeton, NJ: Educational Testing Service.

Bakhtin, M. M. (1981). *The dialogic imagination*. (M. Holquist, Ed.; C. Emerson & M. Holquist, Trans.). Austin: University of Texas Press.

Bakhtin, M. M. (1986). *Speech genres and other late essays*. (C. Emerson & M. Holquist, Eds.; V. W. McGee, Trans.). Austin: University of Texas Press.

Berry, W. (1990). *What are people for: Essays*. San Francisco: North Point Press.

Berryman, S. E. (1988). *Education and the economy: What should we teach? When? How? To whom?* Occasional paper no. 4. Institute on Education and the Economy, Teachers College, Columbia University. New York: IEE Publications.

Berryman, S. E. (1990). *Skills, schools, and signals*. Occasional paper no. 2. Institute on Education and the Economy, Teachers College, Columbia University. New York: IEE Publications.

Berryman, S. E. (1993). Learning for the workplace. *Review of Research in Education, 19*, 343–401.

Blau, S. (1988, March). Humane literacy. In S. Blau (chair), *Creating a literate environment*. Workshop conducted at the Conference on College Composition and Communication, Seattle, WA.

Bourdieu, P. (1991). *Language and symbolic power*. (G. Raymond & M. Adamson, Trans.). Cambridge, MA: Harvard University Press.

Chaiklin, S. & Lave, J. (Eds.). (1994). *Understanding practice: Perspectives on activity and context*. New York: Cambridge University Press.

240

Commission on Workforce Quality and Labor Market Efficiency. (1989). *Investing in people: A strategy to address America's workforce crisis.* Washington, DC: Department of Labor.

Cushman, K. (Ed.). (1994). A community sets standards around the table. *Performance: Progress Reports from the Coalition of Essential Schools, No. 7.* Providence, RI: Coalition of Essential Schools.

Daggett, W. R. (1990). Keynote address. Maine symposium on education [Video]. The Maine Development Foundation.

Daggett, W. R. (1991). *Identifying the skills students need for success in the workplace: Implications for curriculum and assessment.* Prepared for Council of Chief State School Officers. Schenectady, NY: International Center for Leadership in Education.

Daggett, W. R. (1992). Job skills of 90's requires new educational model for *all* students. *Liaison Bulletin, 18*(5), 1–19.

Dewey, J. (1960). *Democracy and education.* New York: Macmillan. (Original work published in 1916).

Dewey, J. (1963). *Experience and education.* New York: Collier Books. (Original work published in 1938).

Dobyns, S. (1987). How to like it. In *Cemetery Nights.* New York: Penguin Books.

Dyson, A. H.(1992). The case of the singing scientist: A performance perspective on the stages of school literacy. *Written Communication, 9,* 3–47.

Dyson, A. H. (1993). *Social worlds of children learning to write in an urban primary school.* New York: Teachers College Press.

Emig, J. (1971). *The composing processes of twelfth graders* (NCTE Research Report No. 13). Urbana, IL: National Council of Teachers of English (NCTE).

Fairclough, N. (1989). *Language and power.* London: Longman.

Flower, L. (1995, April). *Intercultural hybrid discourse in community literacy.* Paper presented at the Annual Meeting of the American Educational Research Association, San Francisco, CA.

Flower, L. & Hayes, J. R. (1981) Plans that guide the composing process. In C. H. Frederiksen & J. F. Dominic (Eds.), *Writing: The nature, devel-*

*opment and teaching of written communication*, vol. 2 (pp. 39–58). Hillsdale, NJ: Lawrence Erlbaum Associates.

Goodlad, J. I. (1984). *A place called school: Prospects for the future.* San Francisco: McGraw-Hill.

Greene, M. (1991). Texts in the margin. *Harvard Educational Review, 61*(1), 27–39.

Gumperz, J. J., Jupp, T. C., and Roberts, C. (1979). *Cross-talk: A study of cross-cultural communication.* Havelock Centre, UK: National Centre for Industrial Language Training.

Harris, J. (1991). After Dartmouth: Growth and conflict in English. *College English, 53,* 631–646.

Hass, R. (1984). Twentieth-century pleasures: Prose on poetry. New York: Ecco.

Heath, S. B. (1982). Questioning at home and at school: A comparative study. In G. Spindler (Ed.) *Doing the ethnography of schooling.* New York: Holt, Rinehart, and Winston.

Hillocks, G. Jr. (1986). Research on written composition: New directions for teaching. Urbana, IL: NCTE/ERIC.

Hull, G., & Jury, M. (1994, April). *"Everything I do is a skill": Vocational students and workers construct lives and careers.* Paper presented at the Annual Meeting of the American Educational Research Association, New Orleans, LA.

Hull, G., Schultz, K., Jury, M., & Ziv, O. (1994a). *Changing work, changing literacy? A study of skills requirements and development in a traditional and restructured workplace.* Interim report. Berkeley, CA: National Center for the study of Writing and Literacy.

Hull, G., Jury, M., Ziv, O., & Schultz, K. (1994b). *Changing work, changing literacy? A study of skills requirements and development in a traditional and restructured workplace.* Interim report 2. Berkeley, CA: National Center for the Study of Writing and Literacy.

Hymes, D. (1972). Introduction. In C. B. Cazden, V. P. John, and D. Hymes (Eds.), *Functions of language in the classroom* (pp. xi–lvii). New York: Teachers College Press.

Hymes, D. (1986). Models of the interaction of language and social life. In J. J. Gumperz & D. Hymes, *Directions in sociolinguistics* (pp. 35–71). New York: Holt, Rinehart and Winston.

Johnston, W. B., and Packer, A. E. (1987). *Workforce 2000: Work and workers for the 21st century*. Indiana: Hudson Institute.

Jury, M. (1994, February). *Mistaken identities: Employing working-life histories to reinterpret workers and work events*. Paper presented at the Ethnography in Education Research Forum, Philadelphia, PA.

Kramsch, C. (1993). *Context and culture in language teaching*. New York: Oxford University Press.

Lave, J. (1988). *Cognition in practice: Mind, mathematics and culture in everyday life*. New York: Cambridge University Press.

Lave, J. (1993). The practice of learning. In S. Chaiklin & J. Lave (Eds.), *Understanding practice: Perspectives on activity and context* (pp. 3–32). New York: Cambridge University Press.

Lave, J. (in press). *On changing practice: Three moments in the anthropology of apprenticeship*. New York: Cambridge University Press.

Lave, J., & Wenger, E. (1991). *Situated learning: Legitimate peripheral participation*. Cambridge: Cambridge University Press.

Masuda, W. (1995, March). *Doing an ethnography of ethnographies: Bridging the academic-vocational divide in a community college writing program*. Paper presented at the Ethnography in Education Research Forum, Philadelphia, PA.

McCarty, T. L. (1991). Classroom inquiry and Navajo learning styles: A call for reassessment. *Anthropology and Education Quarterly, 22*, 42–59.

Mehan, H. (1982). The structure of classroom events and their consequences for student performance. In P. Gilmore & A. A. Glatthorn (Eds.), *Children in and out of school* (pp. 59–87). Washington, DC: Center for Applied Linguistics.

Monetta, A. (1992, August). High school interdisciplinary team creates powerful outcomes. *The High Success Connection, 1*(2), 7–8.

National Commission on Excellence in Education. (1983). *A Nation at Risk*. Washington, DC: U.S. Government Printing Office.

National Governors' Association, Gov. Bill Clinton, Chairman. (1987). *Making America work: Productive people, productive policies*. Washington, DC: Center for Policy Research, NGA.

Northwest Regional Educational Laboratory. (1991a, Winter). *Northwest Connections*. Portland, OR:

Northwest Regional Educational Laboratory. (1991b, Spring). *Northwest Connections.* Portland, OR:

Owens, T. R. (1991). *Northwest applied academics regional survey.* Portland, OR: Northwest Regional Educational Laboratory.

Perl, S. (1979). The composing processes of unskilled college writers. *Research in the Teaching of English, 13,* 317–336.

Resnick, L. (1987). Presidential address: Learning in school and out. *Educational Researcher, 16* (9), 13–20.

Resnick, L. (1990). Literacy in school and out. *Daedalus, 119*(2), 169–185.

Rindge School of Technical Arts. *CityWorks.* (1991). Modules One–Five. Cambridge, MA:

Rosenstock, L. (1995, February). Integrated teaching and learning: Onward through the fog. Keynote address at the California Partnership Academies Statewide Conference, Santa Clara, CA.

Rosenstock, L., & Steinberg, A. (n.d.). *Beyond the shop: Reinventing vocational education.* Available from Rindge School of Technical Arts, Cambridge Public Schools, Cambridge MA.

SCANS (The Secretary's Commission on Achieving Necessary Skills). (1992). *Learning a living: A blueprint for high performance.* Washington, DC: U.S. Department of Labor.

Scholes, R. (1985). *Textual power: Literary theory and the teaching of English.* New Haven: Yale University Press.

School-to-Work Opportunity Act of 1994. Public Law 103-239. (May 4, 1994).

Sinclair, J., and Coulthard, M. (1975). *Towards an analysis of discourse.* London: Oxford University Press.

Slavin, R. E. (1988). Cooperative learning and student achievement. *Educational Leadership, 46*(2), 31–33.

Slavin, R. E. (1989). Research on cooperative learning: Consensus and controversy. *Educational Leadership, 47,* 52–54.

Slavin, R. E., and Oickle, E. (1981). Effects of learning teams on student achievement and race relations: Treatment by race interactions. *Sociology of Education, 54,* 174–180.

Snyder, G. (1974). I went into the Maverick Bar. *Turtle Island*. New York: New Directions Books.

Sommers, N. (1980). Revision strategies of student writers and experienced adult writers. *College Composition and Communication, 1*, 378–388.

Swisher, K. (1990). Cooperative learning and the education of American Indian/Alaskan Native students: A review of the literature and suggestions for implementation. *Journal of American Indian Education, 29*(2), 36–43.

Terkel, S. (1974). *Working: People talk about what they do all day and how they feel about what they do*. New York: Pantheon.

Tharp, R. G. & Gallimore, R. (1988). *Rousing minds to life: Teaching, learning, and schooling in social context*. Cambridge, England: Cambridge University Press.

Thoreau, H. D. (1975). Walden. In C. Bode (Ed.), *The portable Thoreau* (pp. 258–572). New York: Penguin Books. (Original work published in 1854).

Volosinov, V. N. (1986). *Marxism and the Philosophy of Language*. (L. Matejka & I. R. Titunik, Trans.). Cambridge, MA: Harvard University Press. (Original work published 1929).

Vygotsky, L. (1978). *Mind in society: The development of higher psychological processes*. (M. Cole, V. John-Steiner, S. Scribner, & E. Souberman, Eds.). Cambridge, MA: Harvard University Press.

Weathers, W. (1980). *An alternate style: Options in composition*. Rochelle Park, NJ: Hayden.

Witte, S. P. (1993). *No guru, no method, no teacher*: The communication domain and the NACSL. Madison: Wisconsin Center for Education Research.

# II

*Perspectives from
the Factory Floor*

# NINE

## Complicating the Concept of Skill Requirements: Scenes from a Workplace

### *Charles Darrah*

How people work effectively at their jobs is a question of enduring importance to employers and educators. Answering it is especially difficult today due to the proliferation of job titles, the introduction of new technology into the workplace, and indeed, the creation of entire new industries during recent decades. In fact, jobs may appear to be so diverse as to obviate generalizations about how people perform them. This empirical challenge is, however, greatly simplified by the availability of concepts which allow researchers to analyze and compare workers and jobs. I refer here to the concept of skill requirements, which is widely used to describe both the attributes of jobs and the characteristics of people that allow them to perform those jobs. The student of work and workplaces thus confronts a formidable empirical task, but one for which he or she is seemingly well equipped with a concept—skill requirements—that is sufficient to the challenge.[1]

Understanding how people work is especially timely since educators, business and industry leaders, and public policymakers have conducted an unrelenting debate concerning whether American workers are adequately prepared for a world of work that is being profoundly transformed. This debate has been conducted through public and private reports[2] and a scholarly literature that collectively paint a distressing picture in which too many

American workers are unqualified for present and future jobs due to the changing skill requirements of work and the deficiencies of schools (Johnston & Packer, 1987; Whitman, Shapiro, Taylor, Saltzman, & Auster, 1989). The need for increased worker literacy figures prominently in these reports (Holmes & Green, 1988; U.S. Department of Labor, 1989; Business Council for Effective Literacy, 1987; U.S. Department of Education, 1992).

The presumed gap between the abilities of workers and the requirements of jobs is only exacerbated by calls for "high performance" workplaces intended to redress the nation's competitive woes (Brown, Reich, & Stern, 1992; Commission on the Skills of the American Workforce, 1990; Lawler, 1992; Marshall & Tucker, 1992). Such workplaces are vaguely and inconsistently defined, but they are broadly characterized by self-managing work teams responsible for continuous process and quality improvement, a flat organizational hierarchy with increased communication and training, and improvements to the quality of working life.

Despite the various positions held in this debate, the concept of skill requirements is widely used to analyze both the characteristics of jobs (e.g., task demands and role requirements) and the qualities of the people (e.g., abilities, talents, and capacities) who perform them (Spenner, 1990). In fact, the concept of skill requirements is the seemingly obvious, natural way to describe work, one which requires little justification or attention. Again, while the empirical challenge appears daunting, we may take comfort in the concept of skill requirements.

In this chapter I argue, to the contrary, that the concept of skill requirements is far from a "natural" category for analyzing work, for it constitutes a particular way of looking at workplaces, the people in them, and the activities they perform. The purpose of this chapter is to assess the consequences of this concept as a way of seeing work. I will do so by reviewing the tenets that underlie the concept of skill requirements, and by delineating the resulting picture of work they provide. Next, we explore the production floor of Kramden Computers, a manufacturer of computer workstations. This company was the subject of a ten-month ethnographic study conducted to assess how people performed a sample of jobs that required a high school diploma or two-year technical certificate. Finally, we will revisit the concept of skill requirements in order to assess its adequacy as the primary or exclusive mode of analyzing work.

## The Concept of Skill Requirements

The concept of skill is ubiquitous in discussions of work, but it is inconsistently defined and applied (Spenner, 1990). Skill levels are sometimes inferred by reference to broad occupational groupings, while other researchers measure them indirectly by reference to wage rates or educational levels. Other studies measure skills directly by various survey, archival, or historical methods.

The concept of skill requirements is used in this chapter to refer to analyses of work which decompose people or jobs into components that are presumed to be necessary in order to perform the work (Darrah, 1994). This approach proceeds by analyzing jobs in order to establish the abilities workers must possess so they may effectively perform tasks and fulfill role requirements. The content of jobs is typically treated as if it varies independently of the characteristics of workers, thereby creating the constraints to which new workers must adapt. The function of education thus becomes narrowly defined as one of providing people with the skills required by the jobs.

This concept of skill requirements varies in details, but in its broadest outline it characterizes scholarly studies of work (Braverman, 1974; Hirschhorn, 1984; Spenner, 1983, 1985), job analysis (Fleishman & Quaintance, 1984; Hackman & Oldham, 1980), performance appraisal (Gruenfeld, 1981), public policy reports (U.S. Department of Labor, 1991), discussions in professional journals and books (Carnevale, Gainer, & Meltzer, 1988; Gordon, 1991) and articles in the popular press. In fact, the concept is so commonplace that its adequacy is rarely questioned; it is the natural, obvious way to describe work.

Clearly, work can be analyzed using the concept of skill requirements, but at question are the pictures of work which result from such an endeavor. How we understand work is especially germane to developing educational reforms that are responsive to changes in the nature of work. For example, efforts to facilitate the school-to-work transition by young people necessarily rest upon assumptions about the nature of work that may be unexamined and even spurious (Barton & Kirsch, 1990; Drucker, 1993; Reich, 1992).

Despite the diverse approaches to skill requirements, the concept is based on several tenets which are seldom examined, but which are salient to our understanding of work (Darrah, 1994). First, skill requirements decompose workers or jobs into bundles of discrete characteristics or "skills" that measure what is important about work. The influential SCANS Report, "What Work Requires of Schools," is illustrative. The report identifies categories of skills which are deemed necessary for success in the workplace ("competencies") and the skills presumed to underlie them ("foundations") (U.S. Department of Labor, 1991). These skills were defined and classified by a panel of experts prior to the analysis of specific jobs. The importance of each skill to a sample of fifty jobs was then assessed by interviewing three to five individuals who either performed or supervised each job.

The preceding analytical exercise effectively describes work in terms of the relative importance of a list of skills defined a priori. These skills are mutually exclusive, and collectively they provide a comprehensive, exhaustive description of the job, although the question of how discrete skills are articulated into a skilled worker is left unexplored. The result is a composite worker who is presumed to utilize a specific profile of skills, although no actual worker may in fact do so. Our attention is thus directed to whether incumbents possess particular skills, rather than to how their jobs shape their learning or the incentives they have to perform at work.

Second, the concept of skill requirements implies that the skills identified are required in some direct, obvious way. Logically, if the skills were absent, the work would not get done. This suggests that workers holding the same jobs or performing the same work must be in command of the same repertoire of skills, and that there are necessarily single ways to perform nominally identical tasks. Formulated in this way, the concept of skill requirements is inherently individualistic. The individual worker is decomposed into a bundle of requisite skills that he or she presumably possesses; the worker as a member of a community of co-workers who may have diverse skills is ignored. The resulting picture of work is clear and certain, and supports unambiguous claims as to the proper, even necessary, preparation of workers.

Third, the concept of skill requirements abstracts people from the specific, concrete contexts in which they work by treating the workplace as a mere backdrop to their actions. The workplace as a context for skilled performance becomes a given: It is simply there as a constraint upon the human actions that are performed within it. The specific contours of context appear inevitable, shaped by exogenous and inexorable factors such as technological innovation or market competition. The idea that workplaces are the product of human choice by those who work in them is absent (Child, 1973; Thomas, 1994). Ideally, the skilled worker appears to be one who can move freely between such settings, carrying his or her skills like so much luggage, and transferring those skills effortlessly into new contexts.

The exclusion of actual workplaces from analyses of skills has important consequences for understanding work. It explains outcomes in the workplace by analyzing the skills workers do or do not possess, thereby excluding from analysis how the workplace structures the learning and action that occurs there. Workplaces are thus treated as fundamentally sound, and the main challenge for employers is to attract properly skilled individuals. It also views jobs as having objective characteristics that provide a basis for specifying the worker: The person as an active, co-producer of the workplace is missing.

The concept of skill requirements accordingly fails to provide a neutral discourse for analyzing work since it rests upon tacit assumptions that mold how we see work, workers, and workplaces. The resulting picture of work may be clear and drawn with strong brush strokes, but it is the consequences of this way of seeing which most concern us here. In order to explore this issue we must abandon the tidy world of skill requirements and plunge into the exigencies of daily life in an actual workplace. The assembly area ("production floor") of Kramden Computers, a northern California manufacturer of computer workstations, is one such workplace. I suggest that by lingering on the production floor while observing and talking with workers and their supervisors, a deeper and richer picture of work emerges, one that challenges the adequacy of skill requirements as a way of seeing work.

# A Case Study: Kramden Computers

Kramden Computer's[3] production floor was one of the sites studied for ten months during 1987-88 as part of the Educational Requirements for New Technology and Work Organization Project conducted at Stanford University.[4] Fieldwork consisted of participant observation, semi-structured interviewing, review of written materials such as product and manufacturing documentation, and structured observations of workers as they performed their tasks. Workers in several supporting departments, such as Quality Assurance, Manufacturing Supporting Engineering, Stocking, and Production Control were also interviewed. I was granted free access to all meetings attended by production management, as well as production worker team meetings.

Kramden Computers designed and manufactured half a dozen model lines of computer systems for various business applications. Each unit weighed between 30 and 70 pounds, exclusive of the keyboards and display screens. The company was founded in 1976 by an enterprising engineer and it held no patents, but instead responded quickly to technological advances in the industry. This resulted in a rapid product cycle, with at least one new product introduced annually.

Kramden Computer's management was organized into four levels (president, vice presidents, managers or directors, and supervisors) which administered departments clustered into functional areas. Fieldwork was conducted in one such area, Manufacturing, specifically the production floor constituted by the Board Test, Mechanical Assembly, and System Test departments. A production manager had overall responsibility for these departments, while the Quality Assurance ("QA") inspectors, who work alongside the production workers, reported to another manager. Below the production manager were two Board Test supervisors (one per shift), two day-shift supervisors (one each for Mechanical Assembly and System Test), and one swing-shift supervisor responsible for the entire production floor during his shift.

The production floor was located in a single story, concrete building typical of light manufacturing in the area. Workers entered through a small lobby where they signed an employee roster, showed their badges to a security guard, and then passed through an office door into the assembly area. Five parallel assembly lines topped with small metal rollers extended across the area. Work benches laden with tools, test equipment, binders of documentation, and parts abutted each assembly line every six or eight feet. Some computers would sit on tables humming softly as they cycled through a series of automatic tests, while others rested on small wooden pallets placed on the rollers as they awaited further processing.

The linoleum floor sparkled, and the entire room was brightly lit. Music played softly over a loudspeaker system, and large windows along one wall framed a view of an artificial stream outside. The aisle along the windows led to an employee cafeteria, other Manufacturing offices, and to the Board Test room.

Production floor work consisted of assembling parts into a "system," or colloquially, a computer. Such a system passed several electronic tests and then had to accept the UNIX software that controlled its operation. The system had to contain the correct number and combination of modules, such as hard disk, streaming tape, or floppy diskette drives, and printed circuit boards ("PCBs"), each updated with the latest revisions in circuitry and components. Each module had to be properly "pinned" with small electrical connectors in order to make it compatible with the others in the system. The unit was examined by Quality Assurance inspectors, and a record of its history on the production floor was created by production workers and QA inspectors who entered data onto the paperwork that accompanied it on its journey.

Production work was performed by several categories of workers, each assigned to a separate department. Board Test technicians ("techs"), who held electronics technician certificates from community colleges or trade schools, tested individual PCBs, diagnosed ("troubleshot") PCBs that failed tests, repaired them by removing and installing components (e.g., EPROMS, capacitors, microprocessors, etc.), and "reworked" boards requiring changes in wiring or components. Mechanical Assembly workers ("assemblers") took the parts comprising a unit from delivery carts, installed them in a metal chassis, and made the required mechanical and electrical connections between parts. The test operators of System Test performed two functions. Some ran the diagnostic tests on each system, while others (informally, "system repair techs") diagnosed and repaired system failures by searching for loose connections, running diagnostic tests manually to isolate the cause of failure, and if required, installing replacement parts.

Production workers were hired directly by the production manager and his supervisors, and were paid hourly. Company management followed a strategy of minimal staffing and seldom hired new workers until a production crisis was reached. Mandatory overtime typically occurred toward the end of each month as pressure to meet quotas mounted. Annual layoffs were typical, if seldom severe, and perceived productivity determined who was laid off. Because of the wide availability of qualified workers and the presence of other employers, attachment to firms in the area was low.

Supervisors completed biannual employee assessments of performance and recommended corrective actions to improve work skills, but workers failing to act upon such recommendations were not penalized. Some board techs, for example, had been warned for years that they needed to complete specific electronics courses at a community college, but they had failed to do so. In fact, worker reviews were based on attendance and tardiness, both of which, supervisors reported, were easier to monitor than performance. Although satisfactory reviews supported pay raises, promotions or lateral moves were based upon the worker's reputation among engineers, supervisors, and others positioned to observe work habits.

Kramden Computers invested little in automated production technology: Its products were manually assembled using torque drivers, pliers, sidecutters, and screwdrivers. More prominent were the computer terminals controlling various electronic technologies. These included the diagnostic tests loaded into the newly built computers from floppy diskettes, and Autotest, the computerized system that controlled the cycle of tests. Repair techs entered data into a database at several dedicated terminals, and they used the computerized Debugger System to aid their diagnoses. These technologies gave the production floor a "high-tech" appearance, but they were subject to numerous operational variances.

Training for production workers was minimal at best, and employees were expected to bring with them the requisite experience or certification. Little training of any sort was offered by the company, despite ubiquitous requests from workers. When a training course was ultimately developed, it fulfilled few needs, was deemed a failure, and was soon abandoned.

Kramden Computer's organizational heroes were the engineers who quickly designed new applications for technological breakthroughs made elsewhere in the industry, and production work was deemed to be unskilled and to contribute little to the company's profits. However, neither production management nor production workers acquiesced in these assessments of their work. Production management campaigned constantly for resources, and production workers fought complementary battles for recognition of the difficulty of their work.

# Scenes from the Production Floor

We will now take a closer look at some scenes of life on the production floor. These scenes do not provide an exhaustive, systematic picture of production work; they are best viewed as vignettes which reveal the complexity and ambiguity of everyday life there. They also introduce the perspectives of the workers whose voices are so often omitted from discussions of skill requirements and education.

## Tasks and Skills

Management, engineers, and production workers concurred that the tasks of computer assembly and testing were relatively simple, and that the assembly line presented a predictable, lineal flow of products between work areas. This assessment remained constant during the months of interviews with managers, supervisors, and engineers, but interviews with the production workers and observations of them at work revealed a more complex reality. Workers initially said that their jobs and assembly work were simple, and that there was very little to say about them.[5] However, observations revealed that shortages of parts were ubiquitous and products were frequently removed from storage in order to be modified to meet specific customer needs. As a result, workers often returned to work on units as needed parts arrived over hours or days: Interruptions were the rule, not the exception. One assembler remarked that remembering "where you are" in assembling the computers was overwhelming: "We're always starting to build one thing and then we move to something else." Other workers admitted that they sometimes forgot to complete some assembly steps due to the repeated interruptions. One commented, "I've been pulled away in the middle of putting some screws in and mean to get back to it [the computer], but sometimes I can't." Many such units were subsequently rejected by Quality Assurance inspectors, a condition the workers attributed to the interruptions, and management attributed to "poor workmanship" by the assemblers.

System repair techs, too, worked simultaneously on several defective units. Their work entailed using computerized tests to locate faulty parts, exchanging ("swapping") those parts for new ones, and then retesting each unit. Engineers and managers claimed the work was uncomplicated because diagnosing the cause of failure within a modularized component was unnecessary, and in fact, prohibited. The repair techs agreed with that assessment, but they explained that it missed the point: The challenge was to systematically and simultaneously juggle swapping in several units while the automated tests cycled through their sequences. Over one eight-hour shift, for example, I observed a veteran repair tech simultaneously diagnosing and repairing three to six defective units. Because some diagnostic tests took thirty minutes or more to cycle, he swapped modules between the units in order to rapidly localize the fault. He and other repair techs claimed this strategy of swapping was necessary because it minimized time consuming trips to "the cage" where formally documented exchanges of defective parts occurred.

Although many production floor tasks were standard for the industry, workers often performed them in slightly different ways. The work of PCB technicians, for example, involved the application of electrical and electronic principles to PCBs that were similar to those used by other manufacturers. Yet discussions with the workers indicated that some attempted to apply textbook knowledge of electronics to the defective PCBs, while some others barely understood schematic diagrams of them. Technicians utilized differing combinations of reasoning, memory, playfulness, cooperativeness, and communication in order to perform their jobs. While mastery of the principles of digital electronics was prized, supervisors and engineers concurred that it did not automatically translate into greater productivity. In fact, supervisors claimed that greater knowledge was risky, since it could tempt its possessor to perform unauthorized repairs.

### The Quandary of Requirements

The fieldwork suggests that the sense in which skills are required can be unclear. On the one hand, workers often failed to do things that were in some sense required of the job, although they remained valued employees. Sometimes this reflected deficiencies in job descriptions which were not even based on analyses of work in the firm. For example, management routinely borrowed standard job descriptions from other local firms, reportedly a widespread industry practice. Accordingly, system repair techs were required to understand specific electronic principles such as Ohm's Law, although they and the production manager concurred that these were irrelevant to the job.

In other cases, workers lacked skills required by the job, but remained productive employees. The ability to write was needed in order to compose unambiguous notes, but few such notes were composed. Miscommunication was endemic since English was a second (or third or fourth) language for many of the production workers. Interpreting subtleties in usage often proved difficult, especially in the "shift passdown notes" which were simultaneously descriptive and prescriptive. For example, in one note a swing-shift worker wrote, "We have about 31 boards on hold because the bar code labels and ser-

257

ial numbers put wrong locations. Make sure you check it when you work with that boards."[6] The admonishment to "check it" drew the ire of the day shift counterpart who responded angrily responded in his note, concluding with, "I suggest you next time make sure to check it with [supervisor] before you give us some advice." Even seemingly neutral, descriptive comments ("24 computers were rejected last night") were often interpreted as accusations of wrong doing, and feuds between shifts could suddenly erupt, slowing down production and requiring mediation by supervisors. Thus, written communication can be viewed as a required skill, albeit one that few if any workers possessed. Nevertheless, we must question the sense in which a skill is required if it is not routinely exhibited in the workplace.

## The Team Concept

The organizational basis of work on the production floor became more complex when, during the second month of fieldwork, management reorganized the production floor into work teams: The "team concept" had arrived. PCB technicians, assemblers, test operators, and repair techs were placed on teams, each of which was assigned responsibility at the start of a month for one or more model lines. Team members were told that each team was like a separate company with each team member a "vice president," but workers soon noted that management retained all its prerogatives. Team members were encouraged to cooperate with each other while competing vigorously with other teams. Indeed, the production manager hoped that a team's increased "ownership" of its products and the competition with the other teams would result in increased productivity.

Despite management's expectations, knowing just when cooperation or competition was appropriate proved confusing. In one dramatic incident that occurred only days after the new regime was inaugurated, a supervisor asked a team to "loan" its board test technician to another team since she had been specially trained to work on that team's products. The team members carefully considered the request and ultimately denied it, claiming that they needed her labor in order to meet their production quota. The supervisor, who privately acknowledged that he was furious with this affront to his authority, permanently removed the woman from the team. Team members interviewed about the incident claimed they were merely trying to act according to the new rules in which they were vice presidents responsible for meeting production quotas, and in which they competed with other teams. The supervisor's solution remained permanent, word spread quickly among the teams, and other teams immediately retreated from opportunities to make decisions.

## Seeing the Big Picture

Supervisors encouraged teams to "see the big picture" in order to better plan their work. "Seeing the big picture" took the form of calculating the number of units to be built each day in order to reach a monthly production target assigned by management. The task was complicated by the fact that the computers passed through diagnostic tests that took several days: More computers had to be assembled early in the month in order to have sufficient "product in the pipeline" as the end of the month drew near. The teams resisted both taking the daily inventory of their computers, as well as performing the calculations needed to determine subsequent "build totals."

The supervisors lamented the teams' inability to regulate their daily production of computers, but the workers saw it quite differently. From their perspective, learning to understand the entire manufacturing process and to perform the calculations to determine a daily production target were irrelevant since factors beyond their control constrained their actions. For example, the company built its products for independent distributors who delayed purchases while they shopped for lowest prices. Only a quarter of the monthly production total was known at the start of a month, making it difficult to plan more than five days ahead. The delays in orders were exacerbated by distributors who used the calendar month, rather than the fiscal month used by Kramden Computers. Since the latter ended about the twentieth day of each month, the distributors had another ten days before the end of their month to place orders. Thus, they attempted to delay ordering just when Kramden Computer's salesmen were pressuring them to do so. The Production Control department anticipated product demand, but workers were constantly removing completed units from the warehouse and "reconfiguring" them for last-minute orders.

The Design Engineering department's decision to build computers from modules that were placed in a chassis, secured with a few screws, and connected by cables also shaped tasks and skills. These modules were fabricated by external vendors and shipped to Kramden Computers, thereby limiting the variety of tasks performed by its workers. Internally, such modules were technological wonders, but workers were prohibited from penetrating their workings.

Production of PCBs was subcontracted to several vendors, and shortages of needed parts was a daily occurrence beyond a team's control. Workers claimed that it was a waste of their time to perform calculations that were routinely rendered superfluous when a vendor failed to deliver PCBs as scheduled. And, they argued, if they met production targets, management brought out more "kits" of parts to assemble: There was no incentive to meet production targets. One team spokesperson remarked:

Don [a supervisor] is mad 'cause no one wants to spend time taking the inventory or learning to figure how much to build. He said he'd teach us how to do it, but no one cares. Why does it matter? There's nothing to do at the start of the month and no parts. Then we get orders and work for a while, but then we run out of parts. Then we work like crazy—lots of overtime—the last week to get everything out. There's no reason to plan. Just work hard then take it easy the start of the month.

Workers also complained that management had adopted a narrow and self-serving definition of the "big picture." One group of system repair techs, for example, had previously toured the firm's Customer Service department in order to obtain ideas about performing their work more efficiently and to see first hand the products that customers had returned. Although this visit was reportedly useful to members of both departments, the production manager banned further visits because he feared his workers might use them to transfer to another department. One system repair tech who had unsuccessfully requested another excursion concluded, "It's all bullshit learning about everything. They don't want that. They just use it to blame us when something goes wrong, but they don't even want us talking to engineers."

In addition, Kramden's supervisors had long maintained control over the production floor by restricting the information available to workers. System repair techs were barred from having schematic drawings of the computers they repaired because management deemed them to be unnecessary. Supervisors remarked that any technician requesting such documentation must be contemplating "board level" repairs (i.e., replacing parts on a specific PCB) that were beyond their competence. Workers remarked that supervisors allowed them only the information they believed was needed in order to perform their tasks, and they prohibited any documentation that would allow them to learn more and possibly advance their careers. Supervisors even joked that they controlled the workers "through ignorance."

### Managing Relationships

Managing relationships of authority on the newly formed teams proved difficult for team members, as well as for supervisors. Each team was comprised of members from both shifts, so that traditional shift rivalries now became played out within each team. Each "half" of the team elected a monthly spokesperson, but there was no overall team leader. Team members were to rotate as spokespersons, but the position remained ill-defined and spokespersons received no guidance as to their duties or how to perform them. They were frequently placed in situations where they attempted to coordinate tasks with which they were unfamiliar, a special problem when the spokesperson was a low-status, newly hired worker.

The dilemmas of being a conscientious spokesperson were dramatically illustrated in the case of Sally, a newly hired assembler, who had been involved in numerous arguments with her teammates. In particular, she argued with Michelle, one of the team's two other assemblers, over the daily allocation of tasks. She soon developed a reputation as a troublemaker who was best avoided. John, the team's other assembler, was serving as the team spokesperson when Sally intensified her attacks on Michelle, and simultaneously began missing work or leaving early for various reasons. Although Michelle tried to avoid confrontation, Sally was relentless, and finally one day both women began screaming at each other over their work bench. John tried to calm both women and pleaded with them to resolve their dispute quietly so as not to attract the attention of management, but Sally turned on him and yelled, "I really don't like the kind of person you are." John screamed at Sally and finally a supervisor trotted out to physically separate the two workers. Soon thereafter Sally was terminated for repeatedly wearing high heel shoes to work, a violation of safety rules. John quietly completed his term as spokesperson.

In discussing the case, John said he felt betrayed by Sally because he, as spokesperson, had "protected" her on several occasions by telling the supervisors that the team had no objections to her leaving work early. Although the team had repeatedly asked the supervisor to assign Sally to another team, they had been told to resolve the issue internally. In fact, a supervisor had privately commented to me that one benefit of the team concept was that he and his colleagues could avoid becoming involved in nasty interpersonal disputes since the teams were after all "companies" with vice presidents.

The team was well aware of the dilemma. When asked if her dispute with Sally was a matter for the team to resolve, Michelle replied, "The team concept is just a front for them [i.e. management]. They still do whatever they want." Other team members had come to John and asked him to solve the problem of Sally, but his power was limited. The supervisors had been advised about Sally but had done nothing, so John concluded that they offered no solution. He had no formal power to discipline a co-worker, and feared that if he did so Sally would retaliate when she assumed the role of spokesperson. Still, he felt compelled to act. Sally was abusing the team concept that had to this point improved the working life of lower-status workers by reducing the intrusions of supervisors. John also believed that because he was the spokesperson, his own reputation and that of the team would suffer if team members fought. He concluded, "All I could do was try to get them to 'cool it' and talk about pride in the team."

Cultural differences in conflict resolution also affected this case. John, Sally, and Michelle were all born in the United States, while the remainder of the team members were immigrants from Southeast Asia. The latter said that while they were annoyed by the fighting they did not wish to confront Sally and Michelle about it since it "made people feel bad." One repair tech commented, "It just isn't our way to confront someone about that." All the team members agreed, too, that they were not sufficiently compensated to tackle difficult interpersonal problems. A Latina worker on another team commented, "We just want to come here, do our jobs and go home. Not fight, not argue. It's their [i.e., the supervisors'] job to handle that."

In considering this case we can clearly see that it can be analyzed in terms of the skills various workers (and supervisors) lacked. However, the team concept, which ultimately was terminated by management, impinged not merely on skills but on the very definition of the self in the workplace. The team concept required workers to participate in tacitly defined ways, such as correcting the behavior of co-workers, or more generally, communicating with diverse teammates, and making decisions for which few felt adequately prepared. One supervisor remarked that the team concept even changed the qualities he sought when hiring people. Previously, he looked for workers with technical expertise and who could methodically follow instructions without "talking back." "Now we want them to communicate, and a lot of the old-style workers who you could give anything to and they'd just do it, can't adapt. We're asking them to communicate, and that's not why they got hired in the first place."

The team concept also transformed the worker's relationship to the corporation by requiring that they demonstrate their pride and willingness to participate even if they felt the entire endeavor was an ill-conceived managerial experiment. Because the team concept was so ambiguously defined, workers constantly searched for evidence of it in the comments of supervisors. For the latter, the team concept organized only part of their work day since their duties extended beyond the production floor. For the workers, however, the team concept transformed all facets of the working day. A few weeks after the reorganization one worker remarked, "Who knows what they want? It'll fail, like everything else they try. But it's our job and we have to try to make it work. What else can we do?"

### Giving Feedback

Workers were formally encouraged to contribute ideas, but they had little capacity to effect change or improvement in their situation. When one team identified a problem caused by lengthy cables and reported it to their supervisor they were told to "forget it," since the company had already purchased all the cables it would ever need for the product.

Even officially sanctioned attempts to involve the teams in problem-solving failed, most spectacularly when the Quality Assurance department initiated a "closed loop problem-solving" system in which teams identified faulty material encountered when assembling computers. Responsibility for the faults was then assigned by engineers to a department which was directed to correct the problem and report to the team that first identified it. The program was greeted with skepticism, but it proved highly successful in identifying problems. However, it overwhelmed the capacity of various engineering departments to respond, thereby annoying several high-ranking managers. Accordingly, it was discontinued after several weeks.

### Living in a World of Contradictions

The team members frequently commented on the contradictions between the behavior expected of them and of that exhibited by management. They pointed out that they were being asked to communicate openly, while management operated in secrecy. They argued that the cooperation they were asked to exhibit was unrewarded in the company, for they frequently saw uncooperative people promoted. They heard supervisors and engineers boast of "getting" or "beating up" people in other departments through various stratagems, and concluded that cooperation was not valued by the firm. Still, they performed as if they were committed team members who communicated openly and cooperated with others. "What can we do?," one test operator asked rhetorically. "We need the jobs and they [i.e., management] won't listen to us. This team concept isn't working and soon it will go away. They will end it."

## Skill Requirements Revisited

We now turn to the question of what our glimpses of life on Kramden Computer's production floor have to tell us about the tenets of skill requirements. We begin with the belief that decomposing work and workers into bundles of skills provides an adequate picture of work. Our excursion suggests that while work can surely be decomposed into skills, the temporal connection between tasks and their overlapping nature may be left out. On the production floor, the worker's practices in managing this complex flow of tasks were essential, but difficult to conceptualize as an atemporal set of skills.

Understanding work practices may reveal inconsistencies in the demands placed upon workers. For example, the current discussion of workplace skills includes supposedly higher-order skills such as initiative and planning, skills clearly desired by Kramden's management. However, the production workers simultaneously performed multiple tasks, which management described as flexibility, also a desired skill. The workers indicated that this minimized the value of planning and reduced the opportunities to demonstrate initiative, since their work load was largely imposed upon them. Thus, planning, initiative, and flexibility existed in a sort of uneasy tension, and workers were hard pressed to demonstrate each.

Another challenge to the adequacy of the concept of skill requirements comes from the team concept introduced by management. Although it clearly changed tasks, roles, and, by implication, job skills, it also encroached on previously private areas of the workers' selves, as they were suddenly required to act like different people than they had been. Hochschild (1983) and Kunda (1992) note that strategies intended to internalize corporate values and norms in workers are associated with "deep acting" by workers who are compelled to present convincing performances that they are indeed particular kinds of people. What the worker feels is no longer private, and workers may eventually become the people that they initially only pretended to be. Working in such workplaces may well require the ability to interpret subtle cues, and the ability to manage self-impressions, but it requires much more as well: the engagement of the whole person, and not just their selected characteristics.

The idea that some skills are required is intuitively plausible, but our journey suggests that the concept of requirements must be carefully examined in each workplace. Workers often failed to do things that were in some sense required, although they remained valued employees. Sometimes this reflected inadequate job descriptions, but often workers did lack competencies required by the work, but remained productive employees.

The notion of skill requirements assumes that workers of the same job confront a common set of tasks and employ largely identical ways of completing them. Our journey indicates alternative ways of performing tasks that entail different skills, suggesting that a set of objective task characteristics need not require a single set of skills. For example, troubleshooting was described as one skill, but it was performed somewhat differently by the various PCB and system repair techs.

Workers also identified as important skills that were unrecognized by management. Workers reported that they constantly strained to find signs of the ill-defined team concept in the pronouncements and actions of supervisors, but this constant effort at interpretation went unrecognized by supervisors who defined the team concept. Although virtually all workers were suspicious of the team concept, they also felt compelled to act as loyal supporters who were trying their best to adapt to new expectations. They discussed strategies to protect themselves by withdrawing from opportunities to participate while simultaneously appearing to be staunch supporters of the new regime. Workers had learned to avoid seeing problems in order to control their own agendas, while also appearing to be willing to tackle any problem that threatened production. This was a complex theater that was unacknowledged by the production floor management.

The social nature of work also challenges the concept of required skills. Discussion of workplace skills focuses on what is required of individuals, and how the latter relate to each other at work is addressed via the social skills needed by a prototypical worker. This picture is incomplete. Workers do much more than accommodate each other, for they typically participate in interpersonal networks that generate, retain and transmit crucial work-related knowledge. Working within such networks requires more than simply getting along with co-workers, with its individualistic focus. Instead, they become part of a community of practice (Lave & Wenger, 1991), and abilities lacking in individuals may well emerge from the entire community.

Workers also performed many activities at work which were necessitated by organizational inefficiencies. The formally illicit practice of "robbing" new kits in order to finish building partially completed computers reflected the firm's poor planning and production control. Likewise, the time consuming procedure of turning in defective parts for new ones led the repair techs to maintain illicit "stashes" of parts under the assembly lines for emergency repairs. The policy of minimizing written documentation on the production floor made developing a network of helpers essential, and it placed a premium upon the oral transmission of production-floor knowledge. In effect, considerable effort was expended to compensate for organizational and technological inefficiencies. The skills to do so are required in order to meet production quotas, but removing the inefficiencies is an alternative strategy, one that Kramden Computers seldom explored.

The fieldwork also demonstrated that competencies could be important in different ways. Sometimes workers and supervisors spoke of skills as important if they had to be exercised in order for the work to be completed. For example, mechanical assemblers needed considerable manual dexterity in order to attach components with screws and thread cables between them, and they pointed out that many people with large hands were unable to perform the intricate work. On other occasions, importance referred to an assessment of the level of a competency required by a worker. Competence in troubleshooting often fit this pattern: It might be infrequently required and peripheral to daily work, but when it was needed it was perceived to be needed at a higher level than those skills used routinely. Skills were also important if they were used constantly, even if at a low level. For example, workers and supervisors concurred that under the team concept, the ability to communicate was suddenly important.

The lesson to be drawn from these examples is that skill requirements are not derived in any simple way from asking people about their jobs (or the jobs of others), or observing them at work. Skill requirements are constructed through a social process, and we may legitimately ask how that construction proceeds.

Larger workplace systems, too, played an important role in structuring the individual performances we witnessed on the production floor. We saw that "seeing the big picture" was required by management, but to do so was to delve into the historical relationships between management and the workers. There were tacit limits to exploration that the teams struggled to discover, for clearly they were not encouraged to inquire about everything, regardless of management's statements. Again, we see the importance of being able to interpret the ambiguous and tacit constraints that confronted the curious workers as they explored farther and farther away from their familiar tasks. The systems that they were to understand were not simply there awaiting discovery, but they were formally defined and even concealed by the same supervisors and managers who criticized the teams' inability to detect them.

This case suggests that how the workplace structures the learning that occurs there must be incorporated into our analysis of work and skills (Darrah, 1992). Clearly, workplaces differ in the extent to which their workings are revealed to workers. This sort of workplace visibility is critical to the models guiding action that workers can construct.

Incentives also influenced skills, as strikingly demonstrated during the company's flirtation with the team concept. Supervisors were convinced that the experiment failed because workers lacked the cognitive skills to regulate their team's daily production, but as noted, the workers simply viewed this task as irrelevant. Management, too, was convinced that the teams lacked the social skills needed to conduct meetings, an assessment with which many workers concurred. But discussions with the teams indicated a more fundamental problem: The teams were deeply suspicious of managerial intentions since they had not previously solicited the workers' advice.

As we saw, patterns of feedback also influenced the skills observed. Workers were formally encouraged to contribute ideas, but they had little capacity to effect change, and they were repeatedly given reasons why their ideas were irrelevant and could not be acted upon. Ultimately, they simply withdrew from opportunities to "participate."

The availability of information, the incentives and disincentives to take action, opportunities to do so, and the accuracy of feedback regarding actions taken thus are crucial facets of skill requirements in any workplace, but are all too frequently omitted from discussion. It would be a mistake, however, to assume that context comprises an integrated, functional whole that molds skills in consistent directions, since workers may encounter contradictory

266

expectations that are difficult to assess. Yet much of the educational policy literature represents work as changing in ways that require new or higher levels of skills, and accordingly, the worker simply needs to learn the requisite skills and apply them.

For Kramden's production workers, inconsistent and even contradictory messages were typical, and were recognized as such by the workers. Supervisors used the team concept to attack each other by helping teams compose shift passdown reports that obliquely challenged the other shift's judgment or effort. The workers' ability to cooperate was assessed by a management which refused to cooperate with adjacent departments. And they were told to act autonomously, but they were barred from possessing the information that would allow them to do so.

Our journey through the production floor suggests three other warnings for those who would describe skill requirements. The first is methodological in nature: Accounts of skill requirements are constrained in complex and often tacit ways that shape what we as observers think is important. For example, technology and the direct labor of assembling, testing, and repairing computers proved to be easier to describe than work organization. In effect, a subtle technological bias was built into the very act of describing the production floor, since material objects provided convenient reference points for the stories told by workers, engineers, and supervisors.

More generally, the production floor reminds us that our understanding of work is based upon our capacity to describe what people do in workplaces, and this capacity is constrained in significant ways. Kramden's workers and supervisors typically simplified and clarified the complexity of work. Accordingly, job analyses based on verbal accounts by workers or supervisors must be approached with caution. Yet observing work in situ brings its own constraints. Some tasks were rumored, but were performed rarely, if ever, and I was unable to observe how workers performed them.[7]

The second caution is political in nature: Identifying skill requirements is an act of power with enormous organizational consequences. The whole edifice of skill requirements situates blame or responsibility in people and their (lack of) skills, instead of in organizational context. Again, the team concept is illustrative. Management accounted for its failure by pointing out the deficiencies of individual workers, many of whom did lack important skills. The oft-told tale of a non-English-speaking woman elected as team spokesperson exemplified the skill-deficient worker: She taperecorded team meetings for her daughter to translate nightly. Such striking practices served to direct management's attention away from the numerous structural disincentives to participation, and they instead focused on hiring "better skilled" workers who would make the team concept function smoothly.

Third, our excursion suggests the need to pay careful attention to the concept of literacy in the workplace. Arguments in favor of increased literacy requirements assume either the presence of information upon which workers must act, or the workers' involvement in generating information. Yet the saga of Kramden Computers reminds us that we cannot take for granted these conditions, but we must empirically demonstrate them in each workplace. Kramden's management desired greater literacy by its production workers, but "control through ignorance" made it a peculiar literacy, indeed. The production floor also reminds us of the continued importance of an oral tradition at work through which most information was transmitted. Improved literacy may be desirable for many reasons, but it may not translate directly into productivity gains in all cases. In Kramden Computers, the barriers to improvement were fundamentally organizational, and not solely the deficiencies of individual production workers.

Kramden Computers is only one workplace among many, and generalizations from it must, of course, be made with caution. Nonetheless, our journey through it suggests that the concept of skill requirements must also be handled with caution. It is not a concept that is wrong, but it simplified and even distorted our understanding of the work that occurred on the production floor. Any conceptual framework necessarily simplifies, yet we must be concerned about the characteristics of that simplification. In the present case, the concept of skill requirements represents workers as bundles of discrete characteristics who are seemingly engineered to meet the specifications of the workplace. The workplace itself is presumed to be external to the analysis of work, and thus, while workers may need improvement, workplaces do not. The analysis presented here challenges this view and suggests that the very real problems encountered in workplaces will only be addressed when an understanding of workplaces as socially constructed arenas which structure the learning that goes on within them is incorporated into the discussion of future workplace skills.

## Notes

1. Portions of this chapter are based on Darrah, 1990, 1992, 1994, and 1995.

2. Examples of this discourse include National Research Council, 1983 Committee on Science, Engineering, and Public Policy, 1984 Carnevale, Gainer, & Meltzer, 1988 U.S. Departments of Education and Labor, 1988 U.S. Department of Labor, 1989 National Center on Education and the Economy, 1990 and U.S. Department of Labor, 1991, 1992a, 1992b.

3. Kramden Computers and all individual names are pseudonyms.

4. The Educational Requirements for New Technology and Work Organization was conducted at the School Education, Stanford University, and was directed by Henry Levin (Stanford) and Russell Rumberger (University of California, Santa Barbara). The project was supported by a grant from the Spencer Foundation. Mimi Beretz, Michelle Deatrick, Chistine Finnan, Greg Pribyl, and Allison Work were members of the project team.

5. Other researchers (Kusterer, 1978) have found similar simplifications when workers describe their jobs.

6. Transcriptions of oral and written text are presented verbatim.

7. The characteristic distortions resulting from thin descriptions based on brief visits to a workplace are discussed in Darrah, 1992.

# References

Barton, P.E. & Kirsch, I. S. (1990). *Workplace competencies: The need to improve literacy and employment readiness.* Washington, DC: Office of Educational Research and Improvement.

Braverman, H. (1974). *Labor and monopoly capital: The degradation of work in the twentieth century.* New York: Monthly Review Press.

Brown, C., Reich, M., & Stern, D. (1992). Becoming a high performance work organization: The role of security, employee involvement, and training. (Working Paper No. 45). Berkeley: Institute of Industrial Relations, University of California.

Business Council for Effective Literacy. (1987). *Job-related basic skills.* New York: author.

Carnevale, A., Gainer, L., & Meltzer, A. (1988). *Workplace basics: The basic skills employers want.* Alexandria, VA: American Society for Training and Development.

Child, J. (1973). *Man and organization.* New York: John Wiley and Sons.

Commission on the Skills of the American Workforce. (1990). *America's choice: High skills or low wages!* Rochester, NY: National Center on Education and the Economy.

Committee on Science, Engineering, and Public Policy (1984). *High schools and the changing workplace: The employer's view.* Report of the Panel on Secondary School Education for the Changing Workplace. Washington, DC: National Academy Press.

Darrah, C. N. (1990). *Skills in context: An exploration in industrial ethnography.* Unpublished doctoral dissertation, Stanford University.

Darrah, C. N. (1992). Workplace skills in context. *Human Organization, 51,* 264–273.

Darrah, C. N. (1994). Skill requirements at work: Rhetoric versus reality. *Work and Occupations, 21,* 64–84.

Darrah, C. N. (1995). Workplace training, workplace learning: A case study. *Human Organization, 54,* 31–41.

Deal, T., & Kennedy, A. (1982). *Corporate cultures: The rites and rituals of corporate life.* Menlo Park, CA: Addison-Wesley.

Drucker, P. F. (1993). *Post-capitalist society.* New York: Harper Collins.

Fleishman, E., & Quaintance, M. (1984). *Taxonomies of human performance.* San Francisco: Academic Press.

Gordon, J. (1991, March). Skilling of America. *Training,* pp. 27–35.

Gruenfeld, E. (1981). *Performance appraisal: Promise and peril.* Ithaca, NY: New York State School of Industrial and Labor Relations, Cornell University.

Hackman, R. & Oldham, G. (1980). *Work redesign.* Menlo Park, CA: Addison-Wesley.

Hirschhorn, L. (1984). *Beyond mechanization: Work and technology in a post-industrial age.* Cambridge, MA: MIT Press.

Hochschild, A. (1983). *The managed heart: Commercialization of human feeling.* Berkeley: University of California Press.

Holmes, B. J. & Green, J. (1988). *A quality work force: America's key to the next century.* Denver, CO: Education Commission of the States.

Johnston, W. B. & Packer, A. B. (1987). *Workforce 2000: Work and workers for the 21st century.* Indianapolis, IN: Hudson Institute.

Kunda, G. (1992). *Engineering culture: Control and commitment in a high-tech corporation.* Philadelphia: Temple University Press.

Kusterer, K. (1978). *Know-how on the job: The important working knowledge of "unskilled" workers.* Boulder, CO: Westview Press.

Lave, J. & Wenger, E. (1991). *Situated learning: Legitimate peripheral participation.* New York: Cambridge University Press.

Lawler, E. E. (1992). *The ultimate advantage: Creating the high involvement organization.* San Francisco: Jossey-Bass.

Marshall, R. & Tucker, M. (1992). *Thinking for a living: Education and the wealth of nations.* New York: Basic Books.

National Research Council. (1983). *Education for tomorrow's jobs.* Committee on Vocational Education and Economic Development in Depressed Areas. Washington, DC: National Academy Press.

Peters, T., & Waterman, R. (1982). *In search of excellence.* New York: Harper & Row.

Reich, R. B. (1992). *The work of nations: Preparing ourselves for 21st-century capitalism.* New York: Vintage Books.

Spenner, K. (1983). Deciphering Prometheus: Temporal change in the skill level of work. *American Sociological Review, 48,* 824–837.

Spenner, K. (1985). The upgrading and downgrading of occupations: Issues, evidence, and implications for education. *Review of Educational Research, 55,* 125–154.

Spenner, K. (1990). Skill: Meanings, methods, and measures. *Work and Occupations, 17,* 399–421.

Thomas, R. J. (1994). *What machines can't do: Politics and technology in the industrial enterprise.* Berkeley: University of California Press.

U.S. Department of Education. (1992). *Workplace literacy: Reshaping the American work force.* Washington, DC: Office of Vocational and Adult Education, Division of Adult Education and Literacy.

U.S. Departments of Education and Labor. (1988). *The bottom line: Basic skills in the workplace.* Washington, DC: U.S. Government Printing Office.

U.S. Department of Labor. (1977). *Dictionary of occupational titles (4th ed.).* Washington, DC: U.S. Government Printing Office.

U.S. Department of Labor. (1989). *Investing in people: A strategy to address America's workforce crisis.* Commission on Workforce Quality and

Labor Market Efficiency. Washington, DC: U.S. Government Printing Office.

U.S. Department of Labor. (1991). *What work requires of schools.* Secretary's Commission on Achieving Necessary Skills report for America 2000. Washington, DC: U.S. Government Printing Office.

U.S. Department of Labor. (1992a). *Learning a living: A blueprint for high performance.* Secretary's Commission on Achieving Necessary Skills report for America 2000. Washington, DC: U.S. Government Printing Office.

U.S. Department of Labor. (1992b). *Skills and tasks for jobs.* Secretary's Commission on Achieving Necessary Skills report for America 2000. Washington, DC: U.S. Government Printing Office.

Whitman, D., Shapiro, J. P., Taylor, R., Saltzman, A., & Auster, B. B. (1989, June 26). The forgotten half. *U.S. News and World Report,* pp. 45–53.

# TEN

## If Job Training is the Answer, What is the Question? Research with Displaced Women Textile Workers

*Juliet Merrifield*

Tracy is a thirty-year-old mother of two, who sewed pants for 12 years at the Company's factory in Blount County, Tennessee, until the plant closed. The announcement that the plant was closing came the day that the workers returned from their Labor Day, 1988 holiday. Some of the workers had heard about the closing the night before on the 11 o'clock news. About 50 to 60 "well-dressed higher-ups" from company headquarters were up on the stage, and the news was announced to the entire plant over the public address system. The reasons given for the shutdown were the high cost of worker's compensation in that plant and the ready availability of other jobs in the area.[1]

Tracy's story, and that of the other women who worked with her, is as important in the 1990s as it was in the 1980s. The Company, founded in the mid-nineteenth century and run on paternalistic lines for many years, engaged in a pattern familiar to other U.S. manufacturing corporations: closing U.S. plants, consolidating operations, reducing its U.S. workforce, at the same time opening new plants overseas. Like the rest of the U.S. apparel industry, the Company went looking for cheaper labor and found it in the Third World.

The pattern continues—indeed the North American Free Trade Agreement (NAFTA) is suspected by many of exacerbating the problem of manufacturing flight. This plant closing was different from many that had gone before because the Company had learned much from its earlier plant closings in other states. It offered a substantial package to workers, including severance pay based on years of service, and three months "notification pay" (not required by law at that time, although now required under the Economic Dislocation and Worker Adjustment Assistance Act [EDWAA]). The Company and the responsible government agency, the Job Training Partnership Act (JTPA), made a major commitment to retraining. Retraining was to be the answer for the Company to exit gracefully with its public relations image intact and for JTPA to show what could be done when enough notice is given and employers cooperate. Retraining would put the women back to work, many of them in non-manufacturing jobs.

Because that expectation continues to undergird much of the discussion about education and training for adults in this country, it is an important candidate for close and critical examination. The research project reported here followed a group of women from the plant almost two years after it had closed and asked what difference job training had made in their ability to get a good job. In the 1990s, as adult education and job training are coming under increasingly tight scrutiny by Congress, and policymakers are demanding "results," our findings are relevant. We found the expectation that retraining will enable workers to find good jobs comes up short. We found that *how* you structure job training and basic skills education makes a difference, and that some legislative changes are needed. Our study ends with recommendations for how retraining could live up to its promises. But we also suggest that job training alone cannot be the answer to structural economic change. To focus on retraining without paying attention to job creation is one-sided, and probably ultimately disappointing.

Behind global economic trends lie human stories. At the time the Company closed its Blount County jeans and corduroy plant, the average age of its 835 workers was 45 years (*Knoxville News Sentinel*, October 9, 1988). Ninety-two percent were women, and their average length of employment with the Company was 14 to 16 years. For these workers, age, gender and limited formal education exacerbated the normal difficulties of displaced workers in finding comparable jobs.

Tracy and many others broke down and cried when the news was announced—boxes of tissues had thoughtfully been provided throughout the plant. Like most of the workers, Tracy's first reaction was shock. The weeks during which the workers had to sew the plant out were very rough for all of them.

A week after completing her sewing, Tracy went to work at McGiven's, another sewing plant in the nearby city of Knoxville. Every day at lunchtime she would cry for the sense of family at the Company, the sense of stability she had lost. She says never again will she feel that a job is forever.

In the first weeks after the plant closed, Tracy told us, the local Job Training Partnership Act program (JTPA) held classes on how to cope with the closing. Workers were given a booklet on social services in Blount County. An "outplacement counselor" talked to them about how to interview. They were given a list of training available under the Job Training Partnership Act, but no information was available about jobs. Representatives from the local community college and other training institutions set up tables in the crowded and confusing conditions of the cafeteria.

Although Tracy had started working at McGiven's and although she had a young family, she wanted to train. She took classes for ten weeks, four nights a week, funded by JTPA. During the first five weeks she took a pharmacy technician course, a microcomputer course, and a typing course. During the second five weeks she took courses in *Lotus* 1 2 3 and word processing. At the end of ten weeks she was earning the equivalent of her average wage at the Company and no longer qualified to take the classes free, and she discontinued.

Tracy had not graduated from high school, but she did not take the GED classes that were offered because she didn't want people to know. The meeting where people signed up for GED classes was public, and Tracy felt that they should have talked to people individually. Instead of taking the classes she went to the public library and got a book to study for the GED. After studying the book for a week or so she took the GED test and passed.

A Licensed Practical Nurse (LPN) program was offered, and Tracy wanted to enroll, but the class lasted for one year and trainees were discouraged from working during that time. At the time of the closing, unemployment payments were only scheduled to last for six months, and because her family needed her income she did not go into the LPN training. In the spring, a six-month extension was granted to those people who were in school, so she would have been able to finish the course after all.

In many ways, Tracy was one of the lucky ones in this plant closing. She was young, healthy, a good, fast worker, and was able to get another job at once. Although sewing jobs these days are insecure, and she often does not work full weeks, she does at least have a job, health insurance, and union representation. But none of that relates to the job training she took.

## Economic Change and Education

We all live in a time of economic change and uncertainty. No one can feel that they have their job for a lifetime. Manufacturing workers in particular have watched many of their jobs go overseas. In the 1970s and 1980s, close to

200,000 textile jobs were lost in the South alone. As a result, the regional economy has shifted away from a manufacturing base. In 1970, almost one third of Southern workers were employed in manufacturing, with textile, apparel, and furniture as key industries; by 1990 fewer than one in five Southern workers held production jobs (*In These Times*, 12/26/90, pp. 12–13). The "new" jobs being created to replace the old are mainly in trade and services, and generally offer lower pay and fewer benefits.

Job training is often seen as the answer to the changing demands of the global economy. These new demands have changed the metaphors with which we speak about literacy. In the literacy crises of the 1980s, military or medical metaphors abounded—we spoke about "waging war" on illiteracy, and "eradicating" illiteracy as if it were a deadly disease. In the 1990s we tend to use the metaphors of industrial machinery—we speak of "retooling" the American workforce, of "upgrading" skills like we upgrade our computers. We don't speak so much of literacy, as of "basic skills," the foundation on which job specific skills are to be built. The focus has shifted from literacy as an end in itself, a "good thing" to have, to literacy primarily as a means to a particular end—a job.

In the high-performance work organizations which are projected as the basis for our future prosperity, all workers are supposed to make decisions about their work, to think critically to solve problems and work in teams rather than competing on piece rates. Part of the rationale for increasing literacy skills is that they enable workers to take this newly active role in their workplaces. Hart-Landsberg and Reder (1993), for example, document the increased demands for literacy skills in a high performance workplace. They note that teamwork substantially increases the demand for communication as well as literacy skills, and that the "skills-poor" are at a substantial disadvantage in such a work setting.

The sophisticated skill demands of high performance workplaces contrast markedly with the limited demands of traditional "Taylorist" manufacturing processes. This contrast leads to the questions posed by reports like *America's choice: High skills or low wages?* (National Center on Education and the Economy, 1990), which focus on adjusting to changing economic structures and how American industry can compete better on global terms. Job training is suggested as the answer to these issues: to increase the skills of the individual American worker, produce a skilled workforce, and enable more people to obtain higher-paying high-skill jobs. People who see job training as the answer tend to assume that "if we build it, they will come" applies not just to baseball fields but also to a high-skill workforce. Good jobs will follow good skills.

Workers themselves are often suspicious about whether the reality will match the promises. They are very aware of power differences within their workplaces, of the potential for exploitation wearing a different face. Gowen's (1992) ethnographic study in a workplace literacy program alerts us to power relationships impacting on education programs. Workers in declining manufacturing jobs, watching their old jobs move to parts of the world where workers are less literate but also willing to work for much lower pay, may question whether "good" jobs will really be there. They question whether or not the growing service sector really offers good alternatives to traditional manufacturing jobs in terms of wages, benefits, and working conditions. Hull's (1993) case study of a vocational banking and finance program shows that little conventional literacy was needed for the actual jobs being offered, which were entry-level proof operators. Job training may have little to do with the answer to these kinds of questions: Job creation is the issue, and that has to do with economic policy and corporate controls.

## Government Support for Job Training

The Job Training Partnership Act (JTPA) was established by Congress before the recent emphasis on retooling the American workforce, but has become a principal component in government efforts to do so. The 1982 act was passed to provide job training, job placement, and remedial education for low income people, older workers, youth, and displaced workers. Title III of JTPA, which provided services for displaced workers, was replaced in 1989 by the Economic Dislocation and Worker Adjustment Assistance Act (EDWAA), responding to a stampede of plant closings. The new act requires advance notice of plant closings, and it expands responses by providing more training and other services for dislocated workers. This new program was not in place at the time of the plant closing in our study.

JTPA was designed to have strong "performance standards" in which the agencies administering its programs are assessed on their success in placing clients in jobs. Such performance standards have a built-in tendency to encourage "creaming," providing services to applicants most likely to be "successes" by being placed in jobs quickly, while avoiding applicants who, because of age, gender, education level, or other factors, will be harder to place. The General Accounting Office (GAO, 1986, 1987, 1989) concluded in a series of reports that JTPA programs generally invest fewer resources in the less job-ready—high school dropouts in particular are underserved. In response to such studies, JTPA has amended the way it sets performance standards to allow more time for job placement of people with more limited literacy and job skills. Again, these changes were not in place at the time of our study.

# Research on Retraining

When we reviewed existing research, we found only a few other studies focusing on women displaced workers. Gaventa (1988) had studied a group of mainly women textile workers in Knoxville, Tennessee, whose company shifted operations to Mexico. He found that these women had great difficulty finding full-time jobs. Ninety-two percent of the women he surveyed had actively sought jobs since the plant closing, but only 56% had been able to find a job at all. Less than half of these were full-time jobs. All but one woman had lost wages. However, unlike the women in our study, only a handful of the women in Gaventa's study had been offered JTPA training: Most did not know that the program existed.

Smith and Price (1988) studied the training decisions of a group of displaced women textile workers in rural Georgia. They found that younger women were much more likely to participate in job training than older ones. They also found that the women's perceptions of job opportunities open to them with retraining were heavily influenced by their family and community contexts. Family responsibilities often meant that women in these rural areas had to take less desirable jobs.

Leigh (1990) surveyed existing evidence about outcomes of job training for displaced workers. Most programs he reviewed served primarily skilled male workers. He found overall evidence that job search assistance services did impact on labor market outcomes, including earnings, placement, and employment rates. However, he did not find conclusive evidence of the impacts of job training: "There is not clear evidence that either classroom or on-the-job training has a significant net impact on employment or earnings" (Leigh, 1990, p. v).

Outcomes of job training for women in particular were surveyed by Maxfield (1990) in his synthesis of research on employment and training programs for low-income adults. This population is different from ours, in that it is primarily recipients of Aid to Families with Dependent Children (AFDC) or low-income minority female single parents. His findings suggest that the effectiveness of programs varies greatly, not only with internal program factors but also with the health of the local economy and the characteristics of the population being served. He found that on the whole, the women who had the least education and work experience benefited the most from these programs, while those who already had substantial work experience benefit less. Overall, he concludes, "the benefits in terms of increased earnings have tended to be modest, and generally not sufficient to lift low-income families out of poverty" (Maxfield, 1990, p. 12). His study is paralleled by more recent evaluations of welfare reform programs, including GAIN in California (MDRC, 1994).

## The Research Collaboration

The Center for Literacy Studies has an ongoing interest in education and the economy in Tennessee. Part of the University of Tennessee's College of Education, the center's mission is to build the capacity of communities in our region to meet the needs of adult learners. Since its founding in 1988, the center's work has included research, program development, staff development, and technical assistance to literacy programs in southern Appalachia.

Living and working close to Blount County and knowing some of the laid off women workers, we were curious about whether retraining could enable manufacturing workers with limited job skills—and often limited literacy skills—to move into comparable employment in another sector of the economy. As women ourselves, we were especially interested in the experiences of women workers. The Southeast Women's Employment Coalition (SWEC) shared many of these interests, and they provided funding for the research.

As we talked informally with women who had worked at the plant about their experiences, their feelings, their hopes, and fears, we found a group of women who were feisty, smart, thoughtful, and angry about what had happened to them. They had their own questions about the plant closing and the training program. We asked these women to meet with us to help us plan a study. Short of time between family obligations, work, and school, they agreed to come for one meeting. But at that one meeting they took an initiative and interest in the study which they never lost. They became an advisory committee which met many times, and worked closely with Center for Literacy Studies staff in designing and carrying out the study, analyzing data, and drafting recommendations.

This collaborative approach, conducting research "with" rather than simply "on" a group of subjects is important to understand. Mainstream social science research methodologies have commonly attempted to apply to human research the standards of "objectivity" as well as the methods of natural sciences. They value the separation of researcher from subject and "expert" knowledge over experience-based knowledge. For years, criticism of this positivist tradition has come from Marxists, feminists, critical theorists, and others. Like these critics, we value experience-based knowledge, and believe that participants in the research are as capable as we are of critical, rigorous, and open-minded inquiry.

Our study is in the tradition of participatory research and action research, both of which place importance on collaborative forms of inquiry. In participatory research, for example, "the researchers and the researched cooperate in a joint process of critically understanding and changing the social situation, so as to improve people's daily lives, empower them, and demystify research" (Cancian & Armistead, 1990, p. 1). Action research has also often used collaborative methods, although its focus has been more on impacting particular problems or situations rather than empowerment (Brown & Tandon, 1983).

Participatory research allows for a range in the degree of participation and control over the research process by the community or group taking part. However, several years experience with participatory research in other settings (see Merrifield, 1993) lead me to think that this particular project was not strictly participatory research. The women of our advisory committee had considerable influence over the research design (in fact they changed it significantly). They also influenced how it was conducted, and took an active role in the process of the data gathering and data analysis. However, they did not initiate the research and, in an academic setting, control and accountability for research rest ultimately with the university.

Budd Hall (1993) has pointed out the inherent tensions and contradictions when academic researchers engage in participatory research. We call our study "collaborative research" rather than participatory, and feel that similar approaches are very feasible for other university-based researchers. The women in our advisory committee had their own reasons for taking part in the study, which included their hope that it would help other women like themselves have a better training experience than they had had. The study was also a way for them to close an important part of their lives, by finding out what had happened to fellow workers, by reflecting on the strengths and difficulties of the plant closing, and by making recommendations for how it could have been done differently. For us, the collaboration produced richer and more useful research than if the researchers alone had been involved. At the same time it met our standards for rigorous and critical inquiry.

Our original questions about the role of education in reemployment were broadened by the Advisory Committee, and eventually became three broad research questions:

1. How do women perceive the options available to them when their plant closes, including retraining and education?
2. How do women make choices about participating or not participating in training and education opportunities?
3. What differences do their participation in training or education make in their subsequent employment experiences?

These questions were explored through a survey of a random sample of 100 women who had been employed at the plant. Interviews were carried out in 1990, some twenty months after the plant closed. Many of these interviews were conducted by trained members of our advisory committee, which we believe helped increase our response rate (to 77%). Based on the only two pieces of published data for the entire workforce—age and length of employment—our sample was representative of the larger workforce. In addition, the rate of participation in JTPA programs was the same for our sample as for the total workforce—around 50 percent.

## What Difference Did Training Make?

The short answer is, not much. We compared employment experiences of the women who had taken part in a training program or GED class with those who had not participated at all. We looked at their employment status at the time of the interview, the kind of jobs they obtained, wage and benefit level, and job satisfaction. Seventy-six women had held a job since the plant closed (although only 61 were employed at the time of interview).

At the time of the interview there was no significant difference in employment status between those who did train and those who did not participate at all. Just over half of the women we interviewed had a full-time job 20 months after the plant closed. Another 8 percent had a part-time job, and 19 percent were unemployed. Others were still in school, had taken early retirement, or were disabled. About half of those who did not train, like those who did train, had a full-time job (see Table 10.1).

Table 10.1: Employment Status at Time of Interview

| Employment status | Job-specific training | GED preparation | Did not train | Total |
|---|---|---|---|---|
| Full-time job | 21 (51%) | 8 (38%) | 24 (50%) | 53 |
| Part-time job | 3 ( 7%) | 2 (10%) | 3 ( 6%) | 8 |
| Unemployed | 6 (15%) | 4 ( 9%) | 9 (19%) | 19 |
| Still in school | 9 (22%) | 6 (29%) | 2 ( 4%) | 17 |
| Retired | 1 ( 2%) | 0 | 5 (10%) | 6 |
| Disabled | 1 ( 2%) | 1 ( 5%) | 5 (10%) | 7 |
| TOTAL | 41 (100%) | 21 (100%) | 48 (100%) | 110 |

*Note:* Adds to more than 100 respondents because some women took both job training and GED preparation.

However, the longer women stayed in a training program, the more likely they were to have a job. Those who enrolled in training for more than three months (either in a 12-month LPN class or in a year-long office skills program) were most likely to be employed—86 percent of them had a full-time job and the rest were still in school. Those who started but did not complete even a short training program were least likely to have a full-time

281

job—only 22 percent of them had a full-time job and 44 percent were unemployed (see Table 10.2).

Table 10.2: Employment Status by Length of Training

| Employment status | Non-completers | Trained less than 3 mo. | Trained more than 3 mo. | Total |
|---|---|---|---|---|
| Full-time job | (22%) | (54%) | (86%) | 29 |
| Part-time job | (11%) | (4%) | (14%) | 5 |
| Unemployed | (44%) | (12%) | 0 | 10 |
| Still in school | (11%) | (25%) | 0 | 15 |
| Retired/ Disabled | (11%) | (4%) | 0 | 3 |
| TOTAL | (100%) | (100%) | (100%) | 62 |

*Note:* Table sample includes only women who took job training and/or GED preparation.

Job training did make a difference in the kinds of jobs the women obtained. Those who did not train at all, and those who only enrolled in GED classes, were most likely to have a job in manufacturing (63%), usually another sewing factory (see Table 10.3). More of the women who entered job training had been able to move into another economic sector: 41% were in service jobs, 15% in retail trade, and only 37% were in manufacturing. For the most part, however, there was not a close correlation between the jobs women trained for and those they actually got. Thirteen women enrolled in an office skills program, and seven of them were working in office jobs at the time of interview. However, 7 of the 36 women who did not train at all were also working in office jobs at the time of the interview.

Table 10.3: Industry of First Job

| Industry | Job training | GED preparation | Did not train | Total |
|---|---|---|---|---|
| Manuf. | 10 (37%) | 9 (69%) | 22 (63%) | 41 (55%) |
| Transport/ communic | 1 (4%) | 0 | 1 (3%) | 2 (3%) |
| Trade | 4 (15%) | 0 | 2 (6%) | 6 (8%) |
| Services | 11 (41%) | 4 (31%) | 9 (26%) | 24 (32%) |
| Construction | 1 (4%) | 0 | 1 (3%) | 2 (3%) |
| TOTAL | 27 (100%) | 13 (100%) | 35 (100%) | 75 (100%) |

*Note:* Table sample includes only women who had been employed at all since the plant closing.

The women we interviewed consistently lost wages, as other studies have found for displaced workers. When we compared their last wage before the plant closed to the wages of their first job after the closing, we found that average wages dropped by 24%, from $7.08/hr to $5.36/hr. Less than a quarter of the women who had a job maintained the same wage level or increased it. Half took wage losses of 25 to 59 percent, and a quarter experienced wage losses of 60 percent or more (see Table 10.4). There is no statistically significant difference between those who took job training or GED preparation and those who did not.

Table 10.4: Wage Changes

|  | Job training | GED preparation | Did not train | Total |
|---|---|---|---|---|
| Increase | 2 (7%) | 1 (8%) | 3 (8%) | 6 (8%) |
| Same | 5 (19%) | 4 (31%) | 2 (6%) | 11 (15%) |
| Decrease < 25% | 10 (37%) | 3 (23%) | 7 (19%) | 20 (26%) |
| Decr. 26-59% | 5 (19%) | 0 | 12 (33%) | 17 (22%) |
| Decrease > 60% | 5 (19%) | 4 (31%) | 11 (31%) | 20 (26%) |
| Insufficient data | 0 | 1 (8%) | 1 (3%) | 2 (3%) |
| TOTAL | 27 (100%) | 13 (100%) | 36 (100%) | 76 (100%) |

*Note:* Table sample includes only women who had been employed at all since the plant closing.

The women also lost the benefits attached to a job with the Company. All had had employer-paid health insurance which covered dependents, and were represented by a union. In their new jobs most did not have a union and half got jobs without employer-paid health insurance. Those who had moved out of manufacturing jobs were most likely to lose: None of the women in office jobs had union representation and 72% lacked health benefits. Some who were offered health insurance with their new jobs could not afford to pay for it:

My employer offers insurance but I can't afford to take it out . . . just can't afford it. It's $40 a week and I just can't. . . . [I have been without health insurance] ever since the plant closed, two years in September.

In October our insurance will cost us $200 a month because of his [husband's] disability. . . . My husband's test was $800, the insurance paid half. The room was $500, the insurance paid $300. It wouldn't take long to lose everything. He goes to the doctor once a month and will get worse—never get better.

283

Longer term training, a year or more in length, seems to have paid off in terms of employment, wages, and job satisfaction. However, few women in our survey had taken part in this longer-term training. Most of those who trained took part in short-term, 10-week classes on a variety of subjects, and did not stay in training for more than three months. These were as scattered in content as those Tracy described, and seem to have done little to equip the women for major career moves. One woman told us her experience with a computer course:

> They should have started with basic computer, instead of starting us out as if we knew about it already. The class moved too fast. I don't feel I learned anything in that class to help me. . . . I thought that if all the classes they were offering were like the one at Pellissippi State I took, which did not do me any good, why should I waste my time trying to take any other classes that would not do me any good? I don't feel I should put on an application that I had computer training when I don't know anything at all about it. I didn't learn anything about the computer that I can remember to do.

That experience contrasts with that of a woman who had taken LPN training: "It made me realize I had potential. . . . I feel it was a wonderful opportunity to express myself as an individual. I feel it is a spiritual calling as well as a good trade."

If job training is to be an answer, then, these experiences suggest that the kind of job training makes a difference. Short courses on disjointed topics, like those Tracy took, for the most part did not translate into good new jobs for these women. More of the longer and intensive courses did prepare women for better jobs. Given this, we need to understand how women came to make the choices they made about entering into training.

## Making Choices

Women have many constraints on the choices they can make at any one time. At the time the plant closed, these constraints included what training was offered by JTPA and the women's own family and attitudinal factors.

The training options on offer were restricted in several ways. First, only those women who had a high school diploma or a GED could enter a job training class at all—others had to pass their GED first. Since many of the women at the plant (37% of the women in our survey) did not have a high school diploma or GED when the plant closed, this became a significant barrier. Twenty-one women enrolled in GED classes, but only 13 of these had passed the GED test by the time of our survey. Eleven of these had passed it soon enough to enroll in additional job training. In all, a quarter of the women in our survey were prevented from engaging in job training because of their limited education.

Time was another restriction on the training offered by JTPA, and especially on the longer term training. At the time the plant closed workers were given three months "notification pay" by the Company, followed by 26 weeks of unemployment pay. Beyond that nine-month period, they were told there would be no money to continue schooling. Those who needed to keep a steady income coming in for their families did not enroll in long-term training, such as in nursing, because they did not believe they would have ongoing financial support. As it turned out, the Trade Readjustment Act (TRA) subsequently provided an extension of training funds for workers displaced because of foreign competition, but this extra funding was not announced until mid-1989.

A further restriction on job training options was a function of the JTPA funding formula itself. A JTPA staff member explained to us their dilemma: "Ideally there would be uncommitted money to determine the connection between the workers' jobs skills and the job market. But if we don't spend all of our budget in a year, we lose that the next year. And plant closings are unpredictable. We've had a lot this year and money is tight. We have to take a contractual approach and plan programs a year ahead, guessing at the numbers we will have in reality."

So JTPA was only able to offer training places in classes it had already contracted for with local community college and vocational schools, and these were not planned with this particular group of women textile workers in mind. By coincidence or design, the courses led to traditionally women's jobs in offices and health care. Training for higher-paid traditionally male jobs as mechanics, metal workers, electricians, carpenters, and so on, was not on offer.

Choices are also constrained by family circumstances. Prime among these constraints on choices is income. For women who are earning a vital part of the family's income, and especially for those who are the sole income earner, taking time to train, while living on unemployment pay, is not a viable option. Time and again, the women who had taken training told us, "You have to adjust your lifestyle, financially and time-wise." "You have to be willing to sacrifice to go to school—you can't have everything you want." Many of those who did not take training needed to get another job immediately to maintain family income:

We had just bought our home, signed the papers the week before the plant closed. I was torn apart, I didn't know how we would make the payments. But my sister helped me get this job and I went right to work. It's hard, and I hate to drive to Knoxville every day, but I have to.

> I wanted to get into the medical field, to have something stable. I signed up for LPN classes but didn't go because I needed a job, and didn't know how long it would be funded or if I could draw unemployment. . . . I guess I would be better off now [if I had taken LPN training] but then I didn't think I could afford to go.

Another constraint for many women was health insurance. For those who had a disabled spouse or child, getting a new job with health insurance as quickly as possible was top priority: "I had to go back to work to get insurance. My husband's medicine is very high-priced."

Attitudes were more important than demographics in limiting women's choices. For example, age in itself was not a significant factor affecting whether the women tried job training or not. But perception of age was significant: Women who said they were "too old to go to school" were less likely to participate in any of the classes offered by JTPA. Having friends who enrolled in classes affected a woman's decision—she was much less likely to enroll on her own. The idea of job training was scary for many women who had been out of school a long time.

As they reflected on their decision to enroll in job training, a group of former Company workers talked to us during their lunch break at the vocational school. Ranging in age from late 20s to late 40s, these women had almost all been sewers and had put in from 12 to 21 years of work at the Company. Several had never worked anywhere else. They talked about the stress of being "in school" and the differences between school and work.

> Betty: I was still doubting the first day I walked up those steps [of the vocational school].
> Jean: The first day of class I about fainted.
> Anna: I cried a lot at first.
> Freda: I thought I was too old, maybe my brain was stale.
> Linda: I had to develop study habits again. You have to think here and I wasn't used to that.
> Betty: We were conditioned not to think at [the Company].
> Jean: I really think that part of the process of building up speed is *not* to think.
> Anna: [the Company] preferred workers not to think—not to speak up for themselves.

These women knew that going for job training is not just like going for another job: It involves skills and abilities that are not demanded in most of the jobs the women had experienced before, and a courage and commitment that not everyone was able to make. the Company workers who enrolled in training were consistently praised by their teachers for their commitment, hard work, and determination. One woman told us: "A lot of the problem was me. I didn't think I had enough education to take some of the classes. I thought I might be embarrassed." Yet this woman completed two courses and attributes her current job to her computer course. Asked if she had ever considered dropping out of the training program, she answered: "I'm not a quitter!"

## What are the Options?

Women make choices within the bounds of what they believe is possible, so it is important to ask about how they perceive their options. The knowledge and expectations women have of the local job market may be important aspects of the options they perceive, as are their feelings at the time the plant closed.

We first asked the women to think back to the time of the plant closing, and tell us what kind of jobs they thought they could get without job training, and then the jobs they had thought were open to them with job training. *Without* job training, about half the women said they believed they could only get an apparel or other manufacturing job; about a quarter said they could work in food services or a restaurant. Few other options were seen as possible without additional job training (see Table 10.5).

Table 10.5: Jobs Believed Available without Job Training

| | Took job training or GED prep. | Did not train | Total |
|---|---|---|---|
| Apparel/other mfg. | 31 (46%) | 34 (50%) | 65 |
| Services/trade | 19 (28%) | 18 (26%) | 37 |
| Clerical/office | 4 ( 6%) | 3 ( 4%) | 7 |
| Minimum wage job | 4 ( 6%) | 3 ( 4%) | 7 |
| Nothing available | 9 (13%) | 10 (15%) | 19 |
| TOTAL | 67 (100%) | 68 (100%) | 135 |

*Note*: The total is more than the 100 respondents because the latter could choose more than one.

The women's expectations of what was possible *with* job training were wider: they split almost evenly between more skilled jobs in manufacturing (30%), clerical or office jobs (30%), and health service jobs (28%). (See Table 10.6.) Office work and health services are both traditional "women's work."

Whether by coincidence or design, they are also the kinds of jobs for which JTPA offered training.

Table 10.6: Jobs Believed Available with Job Training

| | Took job training or GED prep. | Did not train | Total |
|---|---|---|---|
| Apparel | 2 ( 4%) | 5 (12%) | 7 |
| More skilled mfg. job | 11 (20%) | 12 (29%) | 23 |
| Services/retail | 19 (35%) | 12 (29%) | 31 |
| Clerical/office | 21 (39%) | 9 (22%) | 30 |
| Minimum wage job | 0 | 0 | 0 |
| Nothing available | 1 ( 2%) | 3 ( 7%) | 4 |
| TOTAL | 54 (100%) | 41 (100%) | 95 |

Given that most of the women in the plant had worked there for many years, we might expect them to have fairly limited knowledge of the local job market. An important component of making decisions about training would be an analysis of what jobs are out there and what training they require. Stella told us about how the JTPA transition classes prepared the women to adjust to the plant closing and to reenter the job market:

On September 8, they shut the doors. On September 16 to 18, the transition classes started. We met four hours every morning in the cutting room. . . . We talked about how to deal with our self image after losing our jobs, the stages of the grief process. Each day there was a different subject. The teacher let us talk about what we wanted to talk about. One day we just let loose on the hateful supervisors. Then we began to remember the good times. He said that talking about it was part of dealing with it.

Then we looked at options. There was the medical field—there was literature that told us how long the training would be, what it involved, options later, and the job market. There was office skills, and the third option was OJT (on the job training). He said they wouldn't do cosmetology because the job market was saturated.

So the training opportunities offered, and the jobs women themselves perceived as options, were limited: either continue in manufacturing or move into traditionally women's work in offices and health services. We did talk with one woman who had ventured on her own into a non-traditional field, metal working, had taken training and obtained a well-paid job. She said she did not have support or encouragement from JTPA to do so.

Time and the pressure of the plant closing itself affected women's perceptions of the options open to them. Many of the women felt anger toward the Company to which they had devoted so many years, disbelief that this was really happening to them, and shock. Some older women who could take retirement felt a sense of relief: "It was so hard and tiring, and I had been there so long that I just needed out." But many women felt, as one told us, "I had always had an identity and independence because of the security of my job. Now that had been stripped from me without a decision of my own." Others felt hurt and depressed: "Hit rock bottom because of 25 years down the drain. I was 54, no retirement, no insurance, nothing." Some contemplated suicide.

These feelings are an important factor in the decisions women made at the time. A majority (63%) of the women we interviewed said that they did not fully understand the options being offered them by JTPA at the time, in part because they felt rushed, in part because of the stress of the moment of the plant closing. One woman summarized what many told us: "Too much was going on at one time. New information, you don't absorb it all. JTPA was very supportive to me—but there's just so much you can't absorb. Just wasn't getting through to you."

Many women felt they were given too little time in which to make decisions: "We were rushed into signing up for classes because we were told they didn't know how much money was available, and if we didn't get started we may not have funds for what was left."

The structure of JTPA itself constrains staff, who know well what is really needed for displaced workers. One JTPA staff person who had worked with the Company's closing, told us: "It's a dilemma: there is not staffing to do individual counseling, and yet there is no excuse for not straining to do it. . . . JTPA needs a sizable personnel capability to move into a [plant closing] situation with enough presence to do this."

## Is Job Training the Answer?

Job training did not make a lot of difference to the subsequent employment experiences of this group of women, at least in the time frame of the study (20 months). It did not get those who trained more jobs, better-paying jobs, jobs with benefits, or even for the most part, jobs they had trained for. Our study does not argue that job training cannot be "the answer," but it does make us look more closely at what "the question" is.

If the question is whether job training could potentially impact workers' ability to gain skills and knowledge needed for jobs in other occupations, our advisory committee of women who had worked at the plant believe that it could. The group studied the research data, discussed their own experiences and those of their co-workers, and identified a number of recommendations which they felt could enable retraining to make a difference:

1. The retraining has to be oriented to real jobs that exist in the community, and needs to be much more closely tied to job opportunities.
2. The retraining needs to be more thorough, and probably longer, to enable women to change sectors.
3. To enable longer retraining to be accessible to displaced workers, income support and medical support needs to be provided. The 26 weeks of unemployment pay are not enough to retrain for a radically different occupation, especially for the better-paying growth jobs of the service sector (technical, health services, and similar jobs).
4. To make the transition from many years in a production job to another industrial sector is a big leap for workers, perhaps especially for women, and necessitates counseling. The women spoke of their confusion, their lack of knowledge about the job market, their fears about something new, their sense of loss at losing the "community" of their familiar worksite. All these factors indicate that they need individual counseling to enable them to plan, make good decisions, and enter training.
5. Some women found their limited educational backgrounds to be a hurdle on the retraining course that was hard to overcome. In the time frame available for retraining, some women did not make it to job training because they were upgrading basic skills and working toward a GED. It was not an option for them to pursue GEDs and job training together, and as a result they may have increased their literacy skills but did not retrain for new jobs. These women were especially likely to reenter manufacturing jobs.

If the question is not so much about enabling individual workers to gain skills, but rather about creating a high-wage, high-skill economy, the answers have a different twist. When we focus not so much on the workers as on the kinds of jobs we are creating in our economy, job training looks a lot less relevant.

Tracy's story started this chapter, and Stella's story will end it. Stella is middle-aged, with grown sons. At the plant she had been a union activist. She had not graduated from high school, but long before the plant closed she had taken and passed the GED test. When the plant closed, she was one of the group which enrolled in a year-long office skills program at the vocational school. Once she got over being "petrified," she loved being in school—the chance to think, to learn, the possibility to try something new. Because of her self-confidence and speaking abilities, she was asked by JTPA to speak to displaced workers at other plants about her experiences.

When she completed the office skills training program, however, the only jobs she was offered were temporary ones. Because of her union background she would not take these. She had worked at a local laundromat on Saturdays to increase her wages while with the Company, and continued working there while looking for office jobs after the training ended. Wages are low, there are no benefits, no job security, no union. Two years after the plant closed, she still worked at the laundromat and had given up hope of finding an office job.

The plant closing had given her two things that were valuable to her: the experience of being in school and the opportunity to use her severance money to pay off the loan on her mobile home: "Workers at the Company used to say to each other, 'we need to get away from this place.' But we would never leave on our own. We had decent wages and benefits." Despite the apparent failure of her retraining program to achieve the desired goal of a good job, Stella had no regrets. She valued the experience of learning and growing.

Stella's story is not unique among this group of women for whom job training often did not live up to its promises. Many of the women for whom retraining did not lead to good jobs nevertheless told us that they valued the experience. Stella's story suggests that job training can only ever be *part* of the answer to economic restructuring, and that creating good jobs is another crucial part of the answer. When job training enables people to move into temporary jobs, it is not contributing to the creation of a high-skill, high-wage economy. When women engage in training and end up in production jobs no different than the ones they had before, they and the economy gain little. We have to pay attention both to workers' skills and to job creation.

We also have to pay attention to what people want, to opportunities for learning that are not restricted to getting a job, to personal growth and literacy that meets people's needs, not just employers' needs. If job training is to be even a part of the answer, if it is to facilitate the kinds of occupational changes that global economic restructuring makes necessary, it must be tailored to the *context* of particular communities and to the *needs* of individual clients—one size does not fit all. The training program must take into account the particular needs of women—for peer support, for family support, for education about the labor market, and for learning and personal development. Good job training programs should also assume that customers are intelligent people who can be part of planning their own programs. Many of the women we talked to had ideas about how the training program could have been more helpful and more effective, but participants are seldom asked for their opinions by the Congress that designs their programs.

Without a commitment to the resources required by this kind of job training, we have to ask what the question really is. Is the question about creating high skills and high wages, or is the question about facilitating a downward movement from semi-skilled production jobs into lower-paid and lower-skilled service jobs? Tracy moved horizontally, and is as vulnerable to economic change as ever. Stella moved downwards in skills and income, despite her energy, activism, and intelligence. Neither is unusual among this group of women: The unusual women in the group were the few who were able to move into well-paid jobs.

# Note

1. The study on which this chapter is based is described in more detail in Merrifield, Norris, & White, Loetta, *"I'm Not a Quitter!" Job Training and Basic Education for Women Textile Workers*, Center for Literacy Studies, 1991.

# References

Brown, D., & Tandon, R. (1983). Ideology and political economy in inquiry: Action research and participatory research. *The Journal of Applied Behavioral Research. 19*(3), 285–292.

Cancian, F. M. and Armistead, C. (1990). *Participatory research: An introduction*. Unpublished manuscript, Irvine, CA: University of California, Irvine, Department of Sociology.

Gaventa, J. (1988). *From the mountains to the maquiladoras: A case study of capital flight and its impact on workers*. New Market, TN: Highlander Research and Education Center.

General Accounting Office, U.S. (1986). *Dislocated workers: Extent of business closures, layoffs, and the public and private response*. Report No. GAO/HRD-86-116BR. Gaithersburg, MD: U.S. General Accounting Office.

General Accounting Office, U.S. (1987). *Local programs and outcomes under the Job Training Partnership Act*. Report No. GAO/HRD-87-41. Gaithersburg, MD: U.S. General Accounting Office.

General Accounting Office, U.S. (1989). *Job Training Partnership Act: Services and outcomes for participants with differing needs*. Report No.

GAO/HRD-89-52. Gaithersburg, MD: U.S. General Accounting Office.

Gowen, S. (1992). *The politics of workplace literacy: A case study.* New York: Teachers College Press.

Hall, B. (1993). Introduction. In P. Park, M. Brydon-Miller, B. Hall, & T. Jackson (Eds.), *Voices of change: Participatory research in the United States and Canada.* Westport, CT: Bergin and Garvey.

Hart-Landsberg, S. & Reder, S. (1993). *Teamwork and literacy: Learning from a skills-poor position.* Technical report TR93-6. Philadelphia, PA: National Center on Adult Literacy, University of Pennsylvania.

Hull, G. (1993). *"Their chances? Slim and none": An ethnographic account of the experience of low-income people of color in a vocational program and at work.* Berkeley, CA: National Center for Research in Vocational Education. Report No. MDS-155.

Leigh, D. E. (1990). *Does training work for displaced workers? A survey of existing evidence.* Kalamazoo, MI: Upjohn Institute.

Manpower Demonstration Research Corporation (1994). *GAIN: Benefits, costs and three-year impacts of a welfare-to-work program.* New York: Manpower Demonstration Research Corporation.

Maxfield, M. Jr. (1990). *Planning employment services for the disadvantaged.* New York: Rockefeller Foundation.

Merrifield, J. (1993). Putting scientists in their place: Participatory research in environmental and occupational health. In P. Park, M. Brydon-Miller, B. Hall, & T. Jackson (Eds.), *Voices of change: Participatory research in the United States and Canada.* Westport, CT: Bergin and Garvey.

Merrifield, J., Norris, L., & White, L. (1991). *"I'm not a quitter!": Job training and basic education for women textile workers.* Knoxville, TN: Center for Literacy Studies, The University of Tennessee.

National Center on Education and the Economy (1990). *America's choice: High skills or low wages?* The report of the commission on the skills of the American workforce. Rochester, NY: National Center on Education and the Economy.

Smith, S. D. & Price, S. J. (1988). *Women and plant closings: Unemployment, re-employment and job training enrollment following dislocation.* Paper presented at Annual Meeting of the National Council on Family Relations, Philadelphia.

# ELEVEN

## High Performance Work Talk: A Pragmatic Analysis of the Language of Worker Participation

*Oren Ziv*

From practically the minute one examines discourse in a workplace setting, one sees clear evidence of what the philosopher John Dewey described as "power in action" (1930). While power in modern workplaces is often made explicit through titles and organizational charts, other sources of power, such as ethnicity or gender, can remain hidden beneath the surface. And a person's ability to participate and advance in such discourse environments depends on an ability to extract and interpret the more subtle meanings found within language interactions.

This chapter reports a pragmatic analysis of the language used by participants in a training session held in a crowded conference room just off the factory floor at an electronics manufacturer in California's Silicon Valley.[1] When I first looked at this particular training session, I was specifically interested in what could be observed about the relationship between the workers' English proficiency and their ability to participate in formal team-like meetings within the workplace. In particular, I wanted to understand if the leader of the session was making special accommodations within his speech to communicate with the non-native speakers within the room. Clearly, he was speaking differently then he had previously talked in informal conversations or in meetings with his peers or managers. But, as my colleague Glynda Hull observed, his talk seemed quite typical of a manager talking to a room of blue-collar workers. This struck a chord. What was it about the manager's talk that made it seem as if he was talking to workers at a lower-position within the organization? Was he specifically accommodating his audience's language ability? Or was he speaking in a way that asserted his higher status within the workplace?

To explore the beliefs, attitudes, and intentions of the manager and workers within this training session, I use the tools of linguistic pragmatics—including speech act theory, conversational logic, indirect speech-acts, anaphoric deixis, as well as restricted and elaborated codes. My goal in examining this single, transitory discourse event is to reveal values enduring in this workplace. As Paul Ricouer (1981) says, "It is in the linguistics of discourse that event and meaning are articulated." Ricouer argues that such discourse instances are "self-referential," reflecting back on the meanings of its speaker "by means of a complex set of indicators, such as personal pronouns" (p. 133). Therefore, by examining the discourse of particular speakers in a workplace event I will gain access to intentions and beliefs of those speakers.

In the business world, talk is often viewed as diametrically opposed to action: "There are talkers and there are doers." Yet it is just such attitudes that have led to the undervaluing of the importance of talk within the workplace. My aim in this paper is to demonstrate that talk does not distract from work or merely surround work, but is integral to the performance of work itself. Discourse, according to Martin Heidegger, is more than a conduit for thoughts, it is "the 'meaningful' articulation of the understandable structure of being-in-the-world" (*Being and Time*, 1978, pp. 203, cited in Ricouer, 1981). Therefore, I attempt to uncover what it means for workers to *be* in this particular multicultural workplace world, by peeling back the text of a what appears to be a rather simple communications situation. In doing so, I hope to reveal what Robin Lakoff (1990) describes as the more complex subtext and some of the troublesome assumptions which underlie it. Through examining the discourse in this particular workplace event, I argue that the demands for collaboration and communication within high performance workplaces involve more than basic language and literacy skills, but a reconsideration of workers' potential within the social context of work.

# Background

## *Language as Action-Speech Act Theory*

The philosopher J. L. Austin (1962) made the important point that language is action. He argued that by saying something a person is actually performing an act. Further, Austin insisted that it is not merely the content or "proposition" of a speaker's utterance that communicates meaning, but "the total speech act," "the total situation in which the utterance is issued" (p. 52). Austin dichotomized the total speech act into what he called its *locutionary act* and its *illocutionary force*. The *locutionary act* is roughly the propositional content or superficial structure of a message. The *illocutionary force* is the intended force of the speech act, such as informing, ordering, questioning, or promising. Dividing a speech act into its force and propositional content helps unravel the intertwined meanings communicated in an utterance. Unleashing Austin's speech act theory on work talk can show the very important role that talk plays in giving voice to the human intentionality that drives work.

Austin's student, John Searle (1979) makes clear that there are "a limited number of basic things we do with language, we tell people how things are, we try to get them to do things, we commit ourselves to doing things, we express our feeling and attitudes and we bring about changes through our utterances. Often we do more than one of these at once in the same utterance" (p. 29). Searle shows that the total speech act is a social act, intended, at least, "to produce understanding in the hearer" (p. 31). By considering work talk in light of speech act theory, we are able to better understand how speakers of diverse language and cultural backgrounds communicate with each other.

### Grice's Conversational Logic

Some of the most fruitful examples of speech acts to examine are when what the speaker says, the propositional content, are different from what she means, the illocutionary force. Conversational logic, a branch of pragmatic theory pioneered by the philosopher H. P. Grice (1975) gives us an approach for understanding how hearers' understand a speaker's indirect utterances. Grice proposed that a *cooperative principle* governs conversations, namely, "Make your conversational contribution such as is required, at the stage at which it occurs, by the accepted purpose or direction of the talk exchange in which you are engaged" (p. 45). Such a principle underlies the hearer's willingness to do the interpretive work necessary to understand what otherwise could be a series of disjointed utterances. Grice has us recognize that discourse is a cooperative effort in which each participant recognizes "to some extent, a common purpose or set of purposes, or at least a mutually accepted direction" (p. 45). He suggested that the most direct forms of conversations would satisfy the following four maxims: quantity, quality, relation (relevance), and manner. These maxims can be roughly understood to mean:

> Quantity—Provide enough information, but not more than is required for you utterance to be understood.

Quality—Say only what you believe to be true and are in the position to judge its truthfulness.

Relation—Be relevant to the discourse in which your are participating.

Manner—Make your utterance clear, direct, and succinct.

Since conversations rarely uphold all of these maxims, Grice proposed the mechanism of *conversational implicature*, in which hearer's use the discourse context to interpret the speaker's meaning. Such interpretation depends on the participants assuming the cooperative principle, where all parties are confident that the other is trying to communicate in an agreed upon direction. According to Robin Lakoff, when one of the maxims is violated, participants "take inventory of all the other business going on around the speech act itself: the context, social and psychological, in which they are talking, the interactive framework into which the linguistic utterance fits" (1990, p. 168).

Examining those instances in discourse where maxims are violated, yet people still understand each other, we are able to reveal the importance of the social and psychological framework for supporting communication. In workplace discourse, such conversational implicature can uncover knowledge that is relied upon within the confines of the work environment, but often is not acknowledged as skill. For example, when speaking to a group of other workers, the speaker must decide what needs to be spelled out to avoid ambiguities, to make his language understandable to his audience.

### Indirect Speech Acts

One of the most noticeable uses of such implicature occurs when speakers use what Searle has defined as *indirect speech acts*, "in which one illocutionary act is performed indirectly by way of performing another" (1979, p. 31). Indirect speech acts are extreme cases of conversational implicature, where the hearer understands the speaker's meaning, in spite of the utterance meaning something very different if considered outside the discourse context in which it was spoken. The use of indirect speech acts also communicates a message regarding the relationships between the participants. According to Robin Lakoff, "Indirect communication can be understood as a compliment implying that the hearer is intelligent enough to figure it out, as well as a suggestion that the participants share a cultural background, a powerful unifying influence and a good way to achieve cooperation" (Lakoff, 1990, p. 170).

One form of indirect speech acts I've observed as particularly prevalent in informal workplace discourse is irony. Irony violates Grice's maxim of quality in that the speaker is saying something that is either known not to be true or that the speaker has not the ability to assert as true. And, according to Lakoff, "it can be recognized as a playful gambit, not a lie or a bizarre statement, only when participants are sure that they share basic beliefs." Using irony, the speaker assumes that the hearer has a background knowledge that not only includes understanding the literal meaning of the speech act, but its ironic opposite. It places emphasis on the cooperative nature of the indirect speech act, suggesting a psychological unity of understanding between the speaker and hearer. Yet since irony can also be used as a "put down" (such as saying "nice haircut" in an ironic tone, while simultaneously raising your eyebrows), it doesn't always reflect social unity. Irony used in workplaces, even between workers at very different stations within the organization, can communicate subtle and important meanings.

### Elaborated and Restricted Codes

One area of analysis which fits the analytical goals of this paper is examining the form of speech or code chosen by a speaker. Basil Bernstein says such codes "symbolize the form of the social relationship, regulate the nature of the speech encounters, and create for the speakers different orders of relevance and relation" (1972, p. 161). Recognizing speakers' code choices helps define the particular social context in which speakers and hearers negotiate the necessary conversational implicature. Bernstein defines two major types of codes: restricted and elaborated. *Restricted codes* depend on particularistic and context bound understanding, and are often tied to a local relationship or social structure. *Elaborated codes*, on the other hand, are more "universalistic," where meanings are made explicit and less tied to a local social structure, but are played out against a more general backdrop of common knowledge (Bernstein, 1972).

In workplaces, as in most discourse environments, speakers generally use varying degrees of restricted codes. People rely on common background knowledge to perform much of the communicative work for each other. So when speakers do use elaborated codes in business settings, much like Lakoff's (1990) examples of the hyperexplicit language of the courtroom, it is "marked for us; we expect it to have special meaning" (p. 101). Restricted codes suggest some level of intimacy, whereas elaborated codes often signal official discourse (Lakoff, 1990). Within a business setting, the use of restricted codes suggests a commonality among discourse participants: "Hey, we're all in this together." Whereas elaborated codes allow the speaker to take an official stance. The speaker is able to impart what he thinks his audience must know. In doing this, the speaker can also prove his or her own knowledge to others in the room. So examining when a speaker chooses either an elaborated or restricted code can help explicate the stance the speaker is taking towards a group during a particular discourse interaction.

### Anaphoric Pronouns

Pronouns are generally supposed to be "co-referential" in that they refer to some person or object already mentioned in discourse (Green, 1989). However, in business discourse, especially that used by skilled managers, there is often a great deal of ambiguity as to whom is being referred to, especially when using the first-person plural pronoun, *we*.

Robin Lakoff (1990) defines these ambiguous uses of *we* as the inclusive and the exclusive *we*. The inclusive *we* includes the hearers, meaning "you and I." The exclusive *we* means me and some others, but not you. Lakoff describes how skilled politicians manipulate the inclusive and exclusive *we* to get an audience to accept their authority as a function of the common good. While inclusive and exclusive *we* carry the very different emotional forces of closeness or authority, "when they are skillfully woven together, the audience experiences both of these effects together, rather than feeling forced to choose" (pp. 190–191). Used together effectively, the inclusive and exclusive *we* can have a subliminal effect of communicating "unity, comfort, and authority" simultaneously.

Lakoff shows how the choice of pronouns can be used as an effective form of manipulation. "The symbolic functions of the personal pronouns are not accessible to a hearer's conscious analysis, do not arouse suspicion as nouns and verbs might. They get their power through presupposition and suggestion" (p. 194). Pronouns, unlike other parts of speech, are often felt to be determined by the grammar and not through conscious choice; therefore, hearers are less likely to scrutinize their usage as a source of manipulation.

In many ways, an effective business manager is like an accomplished politician. He or she must persuade certain constituencies, while having the power to compel others. Often, managers have authority over some area or function of the business, yet no direct control over the people who work within that area. Therefore, they must harness all of their discourse skills to get workers to perform actions to their liking. Using pronouns effectively can be a strong way to emotionally control a given discourse event.

## Method

### Site and Participants

*EMCO.* The manufacturing plant in which the event examined takes place we call "EMCO"[2] (for electronics manufacturing company). EMCO is a Fortune 500 company with worldwide employment of over 10,000 and approximately 350 employees in its Silicon Valley plant. EMCO carries out design, assembly, quality checks, testing and packaging of circuit boards for diverse products, from helicopters to elevators to computers. The plant represented, in theory, a "high-performance" workplace, having adopted innovative practices such as "work teams" and "continuous improvement"; yet, in practice, EMCO is quite traditional in its adherence to a hierarchical organizational structure.

This workplace is quite multicultural—Koreans, Filipinos, Vietnamese, and European-Americans are the dominant groups, although many other groups are present—providing interesting opportunities for studying literacy practices and language use. The plant accepts entry-level employees, although most workers have experience in other Silicon Valley companies; there are some opportunities for advancement within the firm.

The managers at EMCO have allowed us to study work processes in the entire plant, including the work of designers, engineers, and managers, as well as technicians, materials planners, machine operators, and assemblers.

*Movement Log Training.* The particular training session examined took place at 1:30 p.m. in a crowded conference room just off the factory floor at EMCO. There were approximately 15 factory floor workers, both men and women, in the room. The workers sat around a large conference table. All had pens or pencils; some had clipboards.

The purpose of this meeting was to conduct a training session for a revised procedure for completing the Movement Log form. This form is used to track the movement of products as they progress through the manufacturing process. For example, a log must be completed every time a batch of circuit boards is moved from the Surface Mount Operations area, where machines automatically attach components to the board, to the Second Operations area, where more manual processes take place. Lead or materials handlers in each area must complete the form, counting and listing each different part by number. Throughout the day, these forms are inputted into an electronic spreadsheet. And at the beginning of each work day, the Work in Progress (or WIP) report is revised from the movement log data.

The WIP report is very important to honing the plant's efficiency; it is used by managers throughout the factory to schedule production, juggle priorities, and negotiate commitments to the company's customers. However, throughout the plant, the WIP has been recognized as inaccurate and, therefore, only a very rough estimate of where products actually are in the manufacturing process. For instance, Vivian, a lead worker within the plant stated, "The WIP, it's a big laugh, but you have to have some something." Various workers and managers have different opinions on why the inaccuracies exist. Such reasons include: illegible writing, lack of discipline, unlogged movements, and lack of automation. This particular training class is the result of a team-generated initiative to improve the accuracy of the WIP report.

EMCO's long-term solution to the WIP report inaccuracies is to auto-mate the process of accounting for production movements using a bar-code system similar to those found at many grocery store check-out counters. Until that time, the goal is to improve the accuracy of the current manual sys-tem by instilling in workers the importance of completing logs for each movement. Therefore, at the time of the training session, the only procedural change in how workers are already working is that they will now conduct the transfer of products from one area to another at several designated locations, marked by red tape on the factory floor.

In many ways this training session is an unusual event in that factory floor workers do not have many opportunities to participate in group or team meetings at EMCO. It offers an opportunity to examine the talk used by the manager conducting the training session and his interactions with a culturally diverse group of front-line workers.

*Major Participants.* The leader of the session was Mark H., the factory's production control manager. He is the only European-American participant and stood at the front of the room. He is in his mid-thirties and has a bache-lor's degree from a local university. Mark came to EMCO several years ago when another electronics manufacturer he worked for was acquired by EMCO. In a short interview after this training session, he stated that he "loves training people." The reason: "Just to see their faces lighten up with the, you know, 'Hey yeah, that's right, yeah.' Plus, I get the interface back from them. And I learn from them while I'm training, I learn things."

It's important to note that Mark H.'s authority over the workers in the room was tangential and not direct. He is clearly one of the factory's man-agers, but not the front-line workers' supervisor. As he said in an interview after the meeting: "I'm going to talk to the supervisors and ask each supervi-sor to get with them individually and make sure they feel empowered. Because, again, I'm not their boss. I can just tell them what I told them. But I'm not their boss." Mark H. explained his own responsibilities as, "to get product to the floor and get it built in time to meet schedule. Which encom-passes shortage tracking, machine scheduling, all kinds of stuff."

Rudy is a lead worker in the test area of the factory. He is a Filipino-American, who appears to be in his early thirties. He has a high school diploma from the Philippines. Rudy had been observed once prior to this training session in a product team meeting, where he did not speak.

Chin is a lead worker in the hardware area of the factory. Chin is a Korean immigrant in his mid-forties. He has a B.S. in electrical engineering from Korea. He also worked for another company that was acquired by EMCO. He wasn't observed in any other meetings.

## Data Collection

I have used qualitative research methods to guide my data collection. For this particular work event (defined below) analysis, I attended and audiotaped the training session. Afterwards, I informally interviewed the leader of the training session. In addition, I am influenced by the many hours I and other members of our research team have spent on the factory floor, in and out of offices and meeting rooms, engaged in (participant) observation and "shadowing" workers, including two workers participating in the session. We have interviewed several employees at all levels of the plant about their work and education histories, and the work that they were doing at the moment. Most interviews were conducted informally and audiotaped. We have observed a few different types of team meetings and training sessions, audiotaping and transcribing these sessions. In addition, we have collected all relevant documentation.

## Data Analysis

*Work Events.* Because we focus our research on literacy and language within work, our unit of analysis is what we are calling a "work event," or those moments when the flow of work is interrupted and all the interactions and activities (including reading, writing, talk and problem-solving) which contribute to setting routine work processes in motion again (Hull et al., 1994). We are adapting previous work on reading and writing where the unit of analysis has been the "literacy event," or all the interactions and activities surrounding the use of print for a particular purpose in a particular situation (cf. Heath, 1983). To analyze these work events, we identify the rules and strategies that people use to accomplish tasks and goals in this particular social setting and also trace the sources of the rules and strategies, as far as is possible, to workers' previous education, training and experience on the job (cf. Hull & Rose, 1989; Scribner & Sachs, 1991). This particular training session is only one activity in a much larger work event that encompasses all the activities involved in improving the accuracy of the WIP report, described above.

*Pragmatic Analysis.* In order to more precisely determine speakers' intentions during the training session presented, I have systematically reviewed the transcript—seeking patterns of thought and behavior (Bogdan & Biklen, 1982). In particular, I noted utterances where any of Grice's maxims were violated or where the propositional content of an utterance was very different from its illocutionary force. As patterns emerged, I sought confirming and disconfirming evidence from my interviews with the leader of the

303

training session. I then analyzed these patterns, using the tools of linguistic pragmatics—including deixis, speech act theory, and conversational logic—to examine the beliefs, attitudes, and intentions of speakers. In doing so, I drew upon knowledge of the factory's manufacturing processes and organizational workings, based upon my own and other research team members' observational data.

# Findings

Typical of the several training sessions we have observed at EMCO, Mark H., the leader of the session, held the floor for the vast majority of the time. The session itself began with Mark H. making sure every work area of the manufacturing floor had sent at least two representatives. Next, he read aloud the written procedure for completing movement log forms. He explained the justification for the procedure and how to complete the form accurately. This lead to a discussion of why the current procedure was not being consistently followed; reasons for the inaccuracies discussed included: moving assemblies at the end of a shift, legibility, people who shouldn't be moving assemblies, and people on the third shift moving boards. Problems raised and solved during the session included: how to assert authority over people who are not authorized to move assemblies; accounting for assemblies only, not component parts; how to account for assemblies being worked on by engineers; who to ask about questions when completing the movement log forms; and making sure that everyone necessary is trained in the new procedure.

Throughout the session, Mark H. maintained strict control over participation in the session. He validated or invalidated workers' contributions of topics or suggestions of solutions. For example, he judged Rudy's concerns about moving boards at the end of a shift as a "valid problem." On the other hand, another worker's suggestion that material planners are moving parts in an unaccounted-for way was dismissed: "Different subject. Different subject. We can talk about that outside of this." In both his statements and the way he conducts the training, Mark H. drove home a theme that our research team has observed consistently at EMCO: While attempting to implement team-like practices, established management hierarchies and realms of authority continue to be honored.

## *We, You, I*

One of Mark H.'s more subtle but effective uses of language involves social deixis through his choice of pronouns. Like an accomplished politician (cf. Lakoff, 1990), he blurred the distinctions between the inclusive and exclusive *we* to both assert his authority as a member of the factory's management team, yet also to persuade workers over whom he has no direct power. At first, Mark H. started the session by establishing his own authority, making the distinction clear between *we*, the management whose offices are upstairs, and *you*, the factory floor workers who occupy the ground floor:[3]

> H: Okay, we'll go ahead and get started. Chin you can go ahead and grab the door there, and we'll get started. Okay, first of all, everybody know why they're here? Is there anybody that doesn't know why they're here? Or you all want me to tell you why you're here. We're all here, basically, to rehash or go over how to do movement logs. (??) track of one assembly from one work area center to the other work area center. Um, very important job. In fact, it's one of the most important jobs you guys do down here, besides actually building the product is keeping track of where the product is. Because everybody upstairs, all the programs people, and the different managers, and Sam, um, all use what we call the WIP report. I think everybody's seen this. It has all the different boards we build, and all the different work area centers, prep, (?), it's got all these areas here. And it tells us where all the boards are at, in the process, each day, we put this report out every morning.

But soon, Mark H. started varying between his use of the exclusive and inclusive *we*. Clearly, the *we* who make decisions about the factory and need the information collected in the movement log forms are not the same *we* who move boards. He used the second-person *you*, whenever he wanted to directly or indirectly get the workers to do something, communicating that it's their responsibility to do it. And he used *I* when he asserted his own beliefs or desires, especially over areas in which he has control, such as the movement logs themselves or the management of the training session. For example, when explaining that workers should write the actual time of board movements on the log forms and not just check one of three times printed on the form, Mark H. uses *I*, *you*, and *we* within the same utterance:

> H: We're always moving boards, because we're so fast. So, I want you to write in that time. Actually just write it in. But I think everybody's been doing it. The ones I've seen everybody's been writing it in. Now if it happens to be 10:30 in the morning, go ahead, circle it. You know, save you some writing. But make sure you put in the time of day there, and a.m. or p.m. Because we do have other shifts, as well. That'll help us if we have a problem later, we can track down. So you fill that in. After you've got that all filled in, on the top, then you want to put in

the [copics] assembly number, the QAP-9, da-da-da-da-da, or QMI-9, so on and so forth. And you want it to be the exact same part number.

Throughout the session, Mark H. deftly used social deixis and nondeixis (Lakoff, 1990) to subtlety emphasize his own authority and the workers' responsibilities. At certain times the exclusive *we* allowed him to claim authority through his membership with the factory's management. But when his authority was not certain, requiring his skills of persuasion, he shifted to the inclusive non-deixis *we*. And for those instances where he had the power to tell the workers what to do, he used the direct *you* and *I*.

## Irony

From the start to the finish, Mark H. used irony during his talk to suggest a commonality between himself and the workers. Early in the meeting irony was initiated by Chin, one of the workers, in response to a serious question by Mark H. Mark H. then played off the worker's joke to carry forward this style to establish his own position of authority in the meeting.

H: What if you're sick? Who takes over when you're sick?
C: Ohh. Well, you see, I'm not gonna be sick.
[Everyone laughs]
H: Oh, you're not gonna be sick? Oh. Okay. Give me the secret. Actually, I was thinking it would be Mohammed or Choi that would take over, if I know Cabrillo, that's who he would make do it.
C: Okay
H: Right? If I know Tom, he'd make you do that, wouldn't he?
C: Yeah, he would
H: He'd go Chin, and Chin wouldn't answer, and he'd go Chin-Chin
[Laughter]

By responding in this manner, Chin, a factory-floor worker, challenged Mark's H.'s authority to demand this information; yet he presented his challenge within the safety of humor. He signaled his humorous intent by prefacing it with the hedge, "Ohh. Well, you see." The speaker then violated Grice's maxim of quality by asserting information he is not in the position to know. Humans are not in complete control of their own health; therefore, no one knows for certain that they will never be sick in the future. This is clearly an ironic statement; the illocutionary force is very different from the propositional content. I seriously doubt that Chin would have responded similarly to his own direct supervisor. But by presenting his challenge humorously, he also pushed Mark H. to subtly define his own position of authority and rapport with the group.

Mark H. signaled that he caught the speaker's ironic intentions by picking up on his ironic tone with a feigned sense of amazement: "Oh, you're not gonna be sick? Oh. Okay. Give me the secret." Mark H. skillfully responded to the challenge by carrying forward the humorous tone. He suggested that he was not offended by the worker's challenge. Yet, in his response he clearly established his own links with the speaker's direct supervisor, Tom Cabrillo, the clearest figure of direct authority over the worker. And he also indicated his own serious intentions with the word "actually." By stating what he believed would be the response of the worker's supervisor, Mark H. asserted that he understands the thinking of the supervisor and that he belongs to the same authority group as the supervisor. Mark H. then drove home the hierarchical nature of the organization by asking the worker to confirm that the supervisor would "make you do that," which the worker confirmed in a direct manner. However, after clearly establishing his own authority position, Mark H. used humor, subtly mocking the supervisor, and thereby establishing rapport with the workers. From the reaction of Chin and the other workers in the room, I don't believe his saying "Chin-Chin" was meant pejoratively.

Mark H. used irony several other times throughout the session to further his rapport with the workers or to assert his authority in an indirect fashion. For instance, when he asked for one of the men in the crowded room to give up his chair to one of the women, he used irony ("Boy, talk about pressure, I tell you") to diminish any pressure associated with the action. Recognizing that most of the workers were already familiar with the movement log form, which they were discussing, Mark H. joked ironically, "There's a sample on the third page there, of the movement log, which you probably all got memorized and dream about at night, I'm sure." As in the beginning sequence, Mark H. also used irony to subtly assert his authority over workers. For example, one of the workers stated that although he suggested that you could file the movement logs on the data entry clerk's desk, rather than an official basket, he didn't actually do this himself. Mark H. responded, "Okay, well you just said that to cause trouble. Okay. Good work." Or when another worker suggested that she doesn't need to know a certain procedure in her area, he replied, "You're right. But when we transfer you—oh, they didn't tell you yet?"

In particular, Mark H. used irony to poke fun at other workers not in the meeting, and in doing so, establish his own camaraderie with the workers present. Usually, the people at the brunt of Mark H.'s jokes were either supervisors or engineers who are above the workers in the factory's hierarchy, but are either at or below Mark H.'s level. For instance, when advising workers not to rush to move products from one area to the next at the end of a shift, he remarked about their supervisor, "So-I mean, I know Cabrillo's already warming up his car by then." He referred to one of the engineers as "Fast

Freddie" and suggested, "He's good at moving boards," something he should not be doing. On the other hand, he lampooned another engineer who does not move boards:

> H:  Does Tom R-ever move boards? Probably not.
> "You move it!" Tom tells you guys what to do. Right?

Mark H. wove irony throughout the session in order to punctuate his remarks. He told the workers to leave assemblies completed at the end of their shift for the next shift to move, because "they'll have time to move them correctly, 'cause they're just getting on, they're still yawning." And he emphasized that the workers themselves might be distracted at the end of their shifts and prone to errors: "We all clean up, (??), trying to think what we need for dinner that night, you know." He even concluded the session, by stating as people were walking out the door, "I know we all had fun."

### Restricted and Elaborated Codes

One of the most glaring differences in Mark H.'s talk from casual conversation is how he switched between restricted and elaborated codes. He built rapport with the workers by using language dependent on their knowledge of the factory's procedures. At other times, as a function of this being a training session, he reiterated and hyperelaborated the same point several times within a single turn. For example, in explaining that workers should not allow engineers or customers to move boards on their own, Mark H. hammered home his point, seemingly violating Grice's maxim of Quantity, by offering much more information than necessary:

> H:  Basically, these guys they get paid to do other things. They don't get paid to move boards. You guys get paid to move boards. You see them moving boards; stop em. "You guys need to move a board? Great. Where's it going to? I'll fill out the movement log and I'll take care of it for you. Because I'm the gatekeeper. I'm the guy that, I'm responsible for this inventory in my area. Not you." They're not responsible. I mean Roger takes a board from Test. Ah, who do we go to when we're looking for that board? We don't go to Roger, we go to Rudy. "Where's that board?"

Throughout the training session, Mark H. elaborated his explanations with examples that draw upon familiar social interactional frames to scaffold his points about the necessity to accurately complete a movement log form each time a product is moved. When explaining the significance of the worker initialing the form, he stated:

H: And then you will initial it, under issuing, where it says signature, you're gonna initial it. So basically, your initial is saying, yes, this is the correct issuing department, this is the correct receiving department, correct date, correct time, it is the correct part number and the correct quantity, and my initial says it's so. Just like writing a check to the bank. You know? I agree that I'm takin' out two hundred and fifty dollars in cash. And then you sign your check. This is the same thing. Actually, these boards are money. When you think about it. This is how we make our money, by building these.

However, Mark H. also freely shifted from such elaborated codes to more restricted styles, drawing upon the workers' inside knowledge of the factory floor. He used technical terms, product names, and the names of specific workers as general examples of which types of workers need to move boards for what type of purposes. For example, here he answers a worker's question on how to respond when an engineer or technician needs to take a board from the production line:

H: Well now, if they gotta take it, if they're taking it from lets say Test and they're going to Final Ops. Great. We'll make up a movement log from Test to Final Ops. Now lets say Roger needs to take a board because he is going to do a fixture. Right. Or Ronney needs a board because he is going to have an ICT fixture resetup. He needs a board for that.

R: He needs the board for research or customer information or something.

H: Right. They're going to take it out, but they're not going to take it to one of our normal work area centers. That's why I created this Engineering Q-A WIP location.

Here, Mark H. seemingly violated Grice's quantity maxim; he assumed that workers have the background knowledge to use implicature and interpret his examples as indicative of any legitimate reason that an engineer or technician might have for moving a board. Demonstrating the success of Mark H.'s strategy, Rudy elaborated Mark H.'s point, showing he had made the necessary inferential leap.

At times, Mark H. combined elaborated and restricted codes through dramatized examples. For instance, here he described why both the issuing and receiving materials handlers must be present when products are moved and the movement log is completed:

H: Okay, now, Jan went to the gate, and then she called over Chin. And, uh, then he'll go through this new [promo] stuff. Now, it says, if any portion of the movement log is incorrect, the issuing department material handler must adjust movement log and initial the correction. In other words, you said there were two hundred on there? But Chin counted it, and said, "No, there's only one ninety-nine." You're gonna go, "No, there's two hundred. I counted them." You know. But Chin's goin', "No, one ninety-nine." So you've got to verify the recount to make sure that there really is only one ninety-nine. Or, there's two hundred, he's still there, and you can go, "Hey, you don't know what you're talkin' about. Come here, you count it again." Okay? But you guys both have to agree on the counts. Who ever's givin' it to you, and who ever's gettin' it, you both gotta agree on the counts. So you gotta both be there when it's being verified. You don't just fill it out, drop it off, and walk away, and get back with ya' later. No. You gotta do it right then and there. Okay?

Here he drew on the workers' restricted knowledge of where and when a movement between Chin and Jan would take place. In the same turn, he elaborated and dramatized how such a movement should be properly conducted. Throughout the session, Mark H. used elaborated and restricted codes to both emphasize his authority in dictating how the procedure should be carried out, and yet develop enough rapport to get the workers to listen to what he had to say.

### Implicature and Limited English Proficiency Workers

During this particular training session, I was struck by my inability to understand the comments of several of the participants. Yet, it appeared as if both Mark H. and the other workers had no problems understanding each other. In transcribing this event, I found myself still having to listen several times to Rudy's utterances, often at different speeds, and yet, I was still unable to make out some of his words. On the other hand, Mark H. was able to clearly understand and easily carry on a discourse with Rudy and the other workers.

In the following example, Mark H. and Rudy drew upon their shared understanding of both the manufacturing process and the pressures that drive production within the factory to support speech that was incomprehensible to me at the time it was uttered:

R: I think the problem (???) is that when the board is very hot, you give a lot (?), and then like, you go home at six o'clock. And then, (??) around 4:55. And there's still a lot of assembly (?) to verify.

H: Uh-huh

R: That's where we have our biggest problem. (?????)

H: So we wait until the, "Oh, oh my God, it's near the end"=

R: =That's right.

H: Get it all together, and let's move it all at once?

R: Yep

H: Okay, we'll-we'll discuss that a little bit later. That's a good point, though. Um, I'll write that down, and we'll come back to how we can go around-at the end of shift, you've got a lot of problems.

R: Yes.

H: Okay. So, we'll come back to discuss that, because that's a valid problem, 'cause I've seen that.

R: It's not just only the people that do their paper work and then=

H: =They do their paper work, they give you the boards, okay, I'm goin' home. And they take off. And you're stuck there with all these boards, and you want to go home too, and then you get in trouble for working over-time.

R: Mmm.

H: But you're not supposed to work over-time, right?

R: Yeah, that's true, but=

H: =Okay, we'll get into that. I'll write it-we'll-we'll get into that. Okay.

Rudy and Mark H. used Grice's cooperative principle to do the necessary implicature to understand each other's utterances. This is different from using a restricted code, where the speakers' language assumed a knowledge of the factory's procedures; here, Rudy's limited English proficiency resulted in his violating the maxim of Quantity by not providing enough information for even me, an informed listener, to explicitly understand his point. Yet Mark H. not only understood Rudy's illocutionary point, he responded with two indirect speech acts: "So we wait until the, 'Oh, oh my God, it's near the end'=" and "Get it all together, and let's move it all at once?" To identify the type of thinking that is causing the problems at the end of the shift, Mark H. used examples, in the dramatic present tense, of what workers might actually think to themselves. In using such indirect speech acts, Mark H. displayed that he was confident that Rudy would understand him. Rudy affirmed that he understood the conversational requirement of this type of interaction by responding interactively with Mark H., "That's right," "Yep."

Next, Mark H. attempted to regain control of the session by validating Rudy's points, then postponing its discussion till later in the meeting. But Rudy would not drop the subject until Mark H. understood the full nature of the problem: "It's not just only the people that do their paper work and then=." So Mark H. quickly elaborated his own knowledge of the pressures involved with moving boards at the end of a shift as a way of getting Rudy to cooperate with his attempt to postpone discussion of this particular issue. When they do return to the discussion much later in the session, Rudy was able to fully describe his real concern: "I think that moving the boards out is not the problem. To receive the boards is the problem."

## Discussion and Implications

### *Power, Authority, and Talk*

Unlike more informal discourse, talk in business dialogues is often about power: who has it, how much of it they have, and who must recognize or conform to it. But the possession of power is often ambiguous—especially in workplaces attempting to stretch formal reporting structures. As we've seen in the event just analyzed, an effective business manager is, in many ways, like an accomplished politician. He or she must persuade certain constituencies, while having the power to compel others. Often, managers have authority over some area or function of the business, yet no direct control over the people who work within that area. Therefore, they must harness all of their discourse skills to get workers to perform actions to their liking. Through talk, Mark H. was able to make the most of his own limited authority. He had no direct power over the workers he was training, since he is neither their supervisor or manager. At the same time, the workers are also asserting their own limited authority through the use of irony.

On at least two occasions, Mark H. emphasized that while taking responsibility for circuit board movements in their area, workers should respect the authority of supervisors or managers. After directing the workers not to move boards during the last fifteen minutes of their shifts, he cautioned, "If your supervisor tells you to do it, they're the boss, do what they say. That's right. But do it right. Take your time to do it right." He also advised the workers that despite the written policy they have just reviewed, they should let Sam, the plant manager, do whatever he wants: "Now, if Sam wants a board, Sam can have a board." But they should ask Sam to sign a movement log at his convenience: "Let Sam walk off with the board. Okay. But fill out that paperwork and get him to sign it later."

The event just analyzed suggests that in restructured workplaces, where hierarchies are supposedly flattened and all workers are asked to take greater responsibility for the factory's overall goals, almost everyone must carefully negotiate the very complex power structures that continue to survive under the surface. With very little power themselves, workers are asked to evoke the authority of written procedures and overall factory goals, such as continuous quality improvement, to perform their responsibilities. Yet, as Mark H.

demonstrated during the training session, such power negotiations often involve very subtle uses of language.

A worker's ability to participate and advance her lot in such complex discourse environments depends on a capability to extract and interpret the more subtle meanings, such as speakers' intentions and beliefs, found within language interactions. She too must be able to interpret and produce what Ricouer (1981) refers to as "the linguistics of discourse" in which "event and meaning are articulated" (p. 133). And yet, such finely-tuned discourse abilities are rarely discussed in association with the greater literacy and language skills required of workers or accounted for in calls to transform the American workplace (see Darrah, this volume). Instead, curricula designed specifically for non-managerial workers often focuses on discrete, "neutral" skills or information processing (see Jury, this volume; Kalman & Losey, this volume).

My analysis here does not suggest that workers lack highly developed discourse abilities. In fact, I believe that workers' discourse skills are, for the most part, still unexamined. Until we fully investigate what workers are capable of doing, we cannot effectively address the educational requirements of changing workplaces.

# Notes

1. This paper is part of a larger study funded by the National Center for the Study of Writing and Literacy and the National Center for Research in Vocational Education. The study is designed to provide information and recommendations about the kinds of literacy instruction that will be most useful in the more technologically complex and redesigned workplaces of the future (Hull & Schultz, 1992). In order to understand literacy and language use in the context of work, the research employs an ethnographic approach, attempting to capture the voices and actions of the participants themselves.

2. All names are pseudonyms.

3. Transcription conventions include: = the point where gaps in turn-taking happens; = between two words means the two sentences are carried on without any stopping; , .. pause, with number of the periods indicating the length of pause; - after a syllable indicates the lengthening of that syllable; - between syllables indicate repeating or stuttering of the same syllable; (?) doubts of the transcriber about the previous word(s); XXXX that the transcriber cannot make out these words or phrases.

# References

Austin, J. L. (1962). *How to do things with words* (2nd ed.). Cambridge, MA: Harvard University Press.

Bernstein, B. (1972). Social class, language and socialization. In P. P. Giglioli (Ed.), *Language and social context* (pp. 157–178). Harmondsworth, England: Penguin Books.

Bogdan, R. C., & Biklen, S. K. (1982). *Qualitative research for education: An introduction to theory and methods.* Boston: Allyn & Bacon.

Dewey, J. (1930). *Individualism old and new.* New York: Minton, Balch & Company.

Green, G. M. (1989). *Pragmatics and natural language understanding.* Hillsdale, NJ: Lawrence Erlbaum Associates.

Grice, H. P. (1975). Logic and conversation. In J. P. Kimball (Ed.), *Syntax and semantics* (pp. 41–58). New York: Academic Press.

Heath, S. B. (1983). *Ways with words.* New York: Cambridge University Press.

Hull, G., & Rose, M. (1989). Rethinking remediation: Toward a social-cognitive understanding of problematic reading and writing. *Written Communication, 6*(2), 139–154.

Hull, G. & Schultz, K. (1992). *Changing work, changing literacy? A study of skill requirements and development in a traditional and restructured workplace.* A proposal to the National Center for the Study of Writing and Literacy and the National Center for Research in Vocational Education.

Hull, G., Jury, M., Ziv, O. & Schultz, K. (1994). *Changing work, changing literacy? A study of skill requirements and development in a traditional and restructured workplace.* Interim Report 2 to the National Center for the Study of Writing and Literacy.

Lakoff, R. T. (1990). *Talking power: The politics of language.* New York: Basic Books.

Lave, J. &. Wenger., E. (1991). *Situated learning.* Cambridge, England: Cambridge University Press.

Reich, R. B. (1992). *The work of nations: Preparing ourselves for 21st-century capitalism.* New York: Vintage Books.

Ricoeur, P. (1981). *Hermeneutics & the human sciences* (John. B. Thompson, Trans.). Paris: Cambridge University Press.

Scribner, S. & Sachs, P. with DiBello, L. & Kindred, J. (1991). *Knowledge acquisition at work*. Technical Paper No. 22. The Graduate School and University Center of the City University of New York: Laboratory for Cognitive Studies of Work.

Searle, J. R. (1979). *Expressions and meaning: Studies in the theory of speech acts*. Cambridge, England: Cambridge University Press.

# TWELVE

## Nurses' Work, Women's Work: Some Recent Issues of Professional Literacy and Practice

*Jenny Cook-Gumperz and Karolyn Hanna*

> *The world turns to women for mothering, and this fact silently attaches itself to many a job description.*
> Arlie Hochschild, *The Managed Heart* (1983)

> *In dwelling upon sound observation, it must never be lost sight of what observation is for. It is not for the sake of piling up miscellaneous or curious facts, but for the sake of saving life and increasing health and comfort.*
> Florence Nightingale, *Notes on Nursing* (1859)

This chapter explores the impact of introducing new technology into hospital nursing practice on both the definition of the knowledge base specific to nursing and on the professional identity that this has helped to shape. The development of an exclusive knowledge base for professional nursing practice over the past 40 years places nursing as a profession in a role that goes beyond that of supporting the doctor, as "a handmaiden," to one of independent, autonomous decision-making (Melosh, 1982). Through examination of textbook accounts of clinical observation and documentation as well as interviews with hospital nurses and nursing educators, we discovered that critical changes in the technological practice of nursing, even in the professional identity of nursing itself, can be seen in the response to the impact of introducing beside computers in hospital nursing. Given the central importance of bedside care for nurses' professional identity, bedside computers in the hospital and the literacy issues embedded in this new practice represent more than just a new technological aid to information processing (Meyer, 1992); rather they bring about a shift in the definition of nursing care and provide a challenge to the established knowledge base of nursing practices. What we want to explore is the significance of this shift and the way that it alters the representation and use of nursing knowledge.[1]

We begin by constructing the gendered history of the development of nursing, an essential part of any account of the influences on what has always been considered women's work. We then turn to an account of the role of documentation in nursing, including our study of the effect of computer technology on bedside care. Our argument will be that such new technologies, and the literacy activities which are a part of their use, exert a considerable influence on nurses' professional identities and the way in which the profession is viewed.

## Women's Work: Caring, Care-Taking, and Nursing

Historically in Western society, nursing the sick, teaching and caring for young children and looking after the elderly have been essentially women's tasks, taking place within a domestic environment. When any of these activities becomes more specialized in its focus and separate from family or home base, the job domain becomes transformed into men's work. Women continue to be recruited for activities where generally the care taking aspects of the task are paramount. These activities include childcare, caring for the old and sick, and more recently the basic literacy tasks of the teaching and processing of text and documents, both within and outside of the home. Together with clerical work, nursing has recently been designated by labor economists as most typical of all women's work (Beechy, 1988; Jenson, Hagen, & Ready, 1988). In any study of women's employment, nursing is one of the largest employment categories where women make up 90% to 95% of the work force (Bakker, 1988). Data from the U.S. Department of Commerce indicate that in 1989 of the employed RNs, 94.2% were female (Davis, 1993).

A key to the continued gender bias in nursing may be found if we look at opinions held by those outside of the profession. The "lay view" of nursing is fundamentally tied to the skills of caring that women exercise in their daily lives. More than any other job in the woman's work world, nursing essentially

317

has a dual character as an occupation. It is desired by women because, while it offers pathway into a professional job, it already seems to bridge into skills which women have developed outside of any professional training (Graham, 1983, 1985).

As Arlie Hochschild points out in the quotation above, women's work is associated with mothering, and wherever caring or care-taking is a component of work activities, the idea of a woman's "mothering" care assumes an unspoken, and therefore ordinarily unrecognized, part of the job. When more generalized professional forms of the tasks occur, the job domain has been assumed by men. For example, book-keeping—that is, taking care of daily financial records—is thought of as women's work, while accountancy is usually considered a man's job; teaching young children has, until very recently, primarily been women's work, while older children were more likely to be taught by men. Likewise in health care, the male role of doctor has focused on the diagnosis, cure, and treatment of disease, while the female role has been on caring, comforting, nourishing, cleansing, and promoting health and healthful living (Dolan, 1973; Lindberg, Hunter, & Kruszewski, 1990; Ellis & Hartley, 1995). With an emphasis on the supportive role that subsumes the woman's ability to take care of others in need, the ready assumption is that nursing can be treated as an ancillary care-taking aspect of medical practice. It is against such assumptions that nursing has had to fight, from the beginnings of its professional development.

The success of this struggle can perhaps be gauged from the observation that nursing is one of the few occupations in which the rationalization of work, characteristic of advanced industrial capitalism, has resulted in an improvement of status and a reduction of work alienation for "the workers."In other words, it seems that nursing has been able to avoid the usual de-skilling associated with rationalization (Braverman, 1974). We argue here that, while still remaining essentially a woman's occupation, this has been achieved through creating a professional knowledge base with the potential for greater power in the labor market. However, nursing still continues to be aligned with women's domestic caring roles and skills, as a recent study of workplace literacy for the National Center for Research in Vocational Education demonstrated (Hull & Cook-Gumperz, 1989). In this study the training of licensed vocational (practical) nurses was explored as one of the favored, first steps for women who were attempting to re-enter career education and the paid labor force. In a first ethnographic encounter with the entry class in a San Francisco Bay area LVN program, 48 of the entry class of 50 students were women. Of these, more than a third had some experience in taking care of the sick at home. It became apparent, then, that not only was nursing seen as women's work by labor economists and others outside of the medical profession, but that the ideology of caring remains central to our views of nursing.

## Caring and Nursing: The Emergence of a Professional Identity

Ironically, even in the present, when the professional identity of nursing has become consolidated, there continues to be a risk that nursing as paid professional work may be seen as merging its identity with the unpaid, unacknowledged caring in the home (Finch & Groves, 1983). Increasingly contemporary medical systems, with very high costs, depend on the unpaid work of family, most often of women, to provide continuing care outside of the hospital (Glazer, 1993). Even as hospital nurses, who must deal with very advanced medical problems, have greatly increased their educational levels and areas of expertise, the fact that the more routine aspects of nursing and everyday care is performed in the home means that nursing expertise loses some of its mystery. And it is just such home-centered experiences that alert women in search of a career to the possibility of using the skills of nursing and caring practiced at home, in ways that can take them back into the labor force and into a professional job.

It is more than mere coincidence that the professional identity of nursing has been tied to the role that women have occupied in a society at any given time, and to the forces impacting that society (Ellis & Hartley, 1995). Nursing, historically dominated by physicians, has made major professional advances over the past 40 years, by preserving a focus on caring for the whole person. Glazer (1993) points out that this has occurred by "struggling with the rest of the medical profession' who wanted nurses to remain a "labor force . . . incapable of autonomous caring" (p. 145). How nursing has made significant professional advances while preserving a focus on patient care as its own special contribution to systematized medical treatment, is a critical part of our exploration of nursing and of the education of nurses.

## Nursing Identity and Nursing Education: A Reciprocal Relationship

While nursing education has traditionally been shaped to capture and suit the educational needs of women, the main labor force for nursing, some significant changes have taken place in the past 40 years. Formerly "trained" as apprentices at hospitals, the education of nurses has now moved into formal educational programs most of which are college-based and offer either A.S. or B.S. degrees. Although a few hospital-based programs remain, they too must meet rigorous accreditation standards as educational programs. The changes in the shape of nursing programs have come about in response to the developing historical position of nursing as a profession in which licensed nurses form a segment of an increasingly complex, specialized, and rationalized professional career structure. Nursing has shifted away from the position of nurses as "the physician's helper" who could be relied upon to be available and to use her gender-based skills, to that of a professional capable of independent care (Melosh, 1982). Once nursing became a degree and college-centered profession, it was able to begin to develop a professional role with a distinctive areas of expertise (Brown, 1948). Yet the gains in status for the nursing profession as a whole in the 1950s and 1960s were accompanied by an attenuation of professional categories as divisions between more and less specialized nurses became clearer (Glazer, 1991; Wagner, 1980).

It was during the 1960s that organizational sociologists labeled the predominantly women's professions—social work, nursing, and teaching—as the "semi-professions" (Etzioni, 1969). Organizational sociologists considered that these occupations relied upon the application of principles of practice developed outside of the work domain. Practitioners were seen as being involved directly in client/professional worker activities but controlled neither the content nor the extent of what was the profession's knowledge base. Additionally, as the introductory comment by Hochschild implies, a strong assumption was made that if women could continue to draw upon their own "gendered" ability to give care in their daily professional work, then somehow their professional contribution was of lesser importance. Recent views of nursing have called for a critical reexamination of the unique contributions of nurses to patient care and medical practice. Moreover, the new professional practice of nursing has been built around the notion of applying the problem oriented approach to nursing diagnosis and has lead to the development of what is now referred to by nurses as "the nursing process," which will be described in a later section of this chapter (Iyer, Taptich, & Bernocci-Losey, 1986). These moves toward redefining their own professional practice has placed nursing in a position to be able to lead a reconception of many of the professional social activities associated with the "helping and caring" professions.

In spite of these changes, however, nursing continues to have a specific domain of knowledge which centers around the unique need "to care for the sick" in a manner which makes the nurse a link between the de-personalized activities of professionalized medicine and the nurses' ability to observe and treat the whole person. It is against the backdrop of this history that we can see that, while the nurses' professional identity continues to be tied to the systematic giving of care, hospital nurses from the beginning have had a tension to overcome between their role at the beside as a "patient advocate" and support, and their management of medical care systems (Nightingale, 1859; Benner, 1985).

## Professional Literacy: How Nursing Expectations are Shaped

In addition to gender-based influences, the identity and practice of nursing has also been affected and shaped by changes in the acquisition, content and processing of knowledge. This section will discuss the acquisition and content of that knowledge as well as its processing and representation.

Nurses are expected to be skillful in observing patients, collecting data using sophisticated monitoring equipment and techniques, and analyzing and interpreting these data in light of an extensive knowledge base—a knowledge base that includes information derived from a variety of other disciplines as well as the discipline of nursing. For example, nurses are expected to understand normal anatomy and physiology, recognize signs and symptoms of disease processes, and explain the rationale for medical interventions as a basis for providing elements of nursing care. Background knowledge from the disciplines of psychology, sociology, and communication is essential for interacting with clients (patients) in a manner that reflects an understanding of psychosocial, spiritual, and cultural factors that influence health and illness. Processes for problem-solving and decision-making, managing personnel and resources, and for planning and coordinating a broad range of activities are all essential to the practice of nursing.

Nurses are also expected to develop skills that enable them to perform a wide variety of nursing tasks and skills, ranging from taking a patient's temperature and blood pressure to monitoring electrocardiograms and determining cardiac output. All this is to be done in a manner that reflects sensitivity and concern for the individual and his or her unique needs.

Examination of these expectations reveals a complex interplay of cognitive, psychomotor, and affective skills in the practice of nursing in the current day. Accompanying the changes in nursing practice are changes in literacy. To demonstrate the escalation in cognitive and psychomotor requirements and the concomitant shift in literacy requirements, we have traced the development of one aspect of nursing, patient observation, from the mid-19th century to the threshold of the 21st century. By examining discussions on the process of patient observation and the requisite documentation of observations in nursing textbooks during the past forty years (1955–1995), further insight into changing perspectives on the professional role of nurses, as well

321

as increases in the depth and breadth of nursing knowledge and literacy requirements for the profession, became evident.

The significance of data collection by direct observation has long been recognized in nursing. Florence Nightingale (1859) herself emphasized the importance of observing the sick: "The most important practical lesson that can be given to nurses is to teach them what to observe—how to observe—what symptoms indicate improvement—what the reverse-which are of importance—which are of none—which are evidence of neglect—and of what kind of neglect. All of this is what ought to make part, and an essential part of the training of every nurse. At present how few there are, either professional or unprofessional, who really know at all whether any sick person they may be with is better or worse" (p. 59).

In her discussion of what should be observed, Nightingale (1859) focuses on what in today's terms would be described as the patient's physical appearance, activities of daily living (eating, sleeping, elimination, physical mobility), and other basic human needs, both physiological and psychological. She advocates the learning of signs and symptoms of disease processes: "There is unquestionably, a physiognomy of diseases. Let the nurse learn it" (p. 66). Her overall perspective on the purpose of observation is evidenced by the comment at the beginning of the chapter concerning the importance of informed observation. Through the century from Nightingale, the shift toward written forms of documentation occurred. And it is this shift which we identify here as an essential alteration in the representation of the knowledge base and the practices that are consequent upon the knowledge base.

In the 1955 edition of *The Textbook of the Principles and Practice of Nursing*, Harmer and Henderson also discuss the importance of developing observational skills. "The nurse who can most nearly distinguish between normal and abnormal behavior—physical, emotional, and mental—and can describe such behavior, contributes in largest measure to the physician's diagnosis. Obviously, the capacity knows no bounds" (p. 259). At that point in time, observational skills were primarily discoveries made by all the senses (sight, sound, touch, and smell). From a technological perspective, measurement of the cardinal symptoms of disease, also called the vital signs (i.e., temperature, pulse, respiration, and blood pressure), was the extent to which mechanical devices were used.

Documentation of observations and nursing interventions were termed *nurses' notes* and were generally presented as a narrative record in chronological sequence. Vital signs were usually recorded on a graph chart. Consider, for example, the following set of nurse's notes excerpted from a handwritten example found in *The Textbook of the Principles and Practice of Nursing* (Harmer and Henderson, 1955, p. 315):

| Date | Hour | Nurse's Bedside Notes |
|------|------|------------------------|
| 4-23-39 | 7:20 AM | Nauseated; will take water but refuses nourishment. |
| | 9:15 | Respiration seems painful, wants to be quiet, dreads moving, is most comfortable on right side. Occasional cough, producing small amount of blood-tinged sputum. Moderate amount yellow vaginal discharge. Enema given with good results but patient seemed exhausted from exertion. |
| | 10:00 | Drank 200 cc. lemonade and vomited almost immediately 225 cc. |
| | 12:00 | Nauseated, refuses any food by mouth. |
| | 1:00 PM | 500 cc 5% dextrose by intravenous infusion (Dr. Livingston) |
| | 2:30 | Mrs. DeSanto seemed cheered by visit from sister who is helping grandmother to take care of DeSanto infant. Mrs. DeSanto told her sister that she thought she had pneumonia but that the doctors "believed she would get well." |
| | 3:30 | Less nauseated, retained 250 cc of ginger ale. Slept for an hour. |
| | 5:00 | Drank 180 cc of broth without aversion but no relish. Says that pain in chest "isn't as bad as it was." Is chilly, extra coverings used and hot water bottle kept at feet. |
| | 5:30 | Breasts slightly distended; total amount of milk removed 20 cc. |
| | 8:00 | Husband says his wife is worried about the cost of her hospitalization and the length of her illness; he thinks this is one of the things that is making her "feel so bad." He was assured that the Social Service Dept. would help tham to work out their financial difficulties. |

Vital signs were usually recorded on a graph chart. Medications administered were frequently documented within the narrative text, but as the number and variety of pharmaceuticals increased, separate forms for documenting medications were also developed. However, nursing documentation remained secondary to nursing observations that were deemed essential to assisting the work of the physician.

Virginia Henderson (1955) also points to a more active role of the nurse-that being "to assist the individual, whether sick or well in the performance of those activities contributing to health, or its recovery (or to a peaceful death), that he would perform unaided if he had the necessary strength, will or knowledge" (p. 4). This client-centered focus, along with feelings that nurses had long been exploited as the hand servants of doctors, fostered the emergence of the nursing profession as a distinct entity. Medicine was viewed as the profession of curing illness, and nursing's role was becoming more independent with its focus on restoring the patient to a state of wellness and preventing illness.

To accomplish the goals of this role, the collection of data and utilization of knowledge to assist individuals has undergone a series of transformations and has evolved into what is now called *the nursing process*. This nursing process is in essence a problem-solving approach applied to nursing, and as such it depends upon providing documentary evidence of all decisions and outcomes. This process includes: systematic data collection (*assessment*); an identification of the client's problems or deficits, as well as strengths or coping abilities (*nursing diagnosis*); identification of individualized goals or expected outcomes and a plan for achieving those goals (*planning*); actual implementation of the plan through nursing activities (*intervention*); and evaluation of the individual's achievement of the expected outcomes (*evaluation*). The process is cyclical and is documented at every stage. As outcomes are evaluated, reassessment of the patient occurs and existing problems may be modified or resolved or new problems may emerge. The nursing process involves interactive problem solving between the nurse and the client (as well as other members of the health care team) and serves as a basis for nursing action and decisions (Alfaro-LeFevre, 1994).

This shift in nursing roles is evident in nursing documentation. Where previously nurses' notes focused on recording observations of patients' behaviors, signs, and symptoms of disease, and the performance of physician-ordered tasks or activities, there is now a much greater emphasis on the nurse's interpretation of observations, mutual goal-setting with clients and their significant others, and the utilization of independent nursing actions to achieve expected outcomes.

Current nursing textbooks (e.g. Kozier, Erb, Blais, & Wilkinson, 1995) include entire chapters on each step of the nursing process and emphasize both techniques for data collection, utilization of the nursing process, and documentation of the same. There are numerous texts devoted to the nursing process or one aspect of it (Carpenito, 1995a; Carpenito, 1995b; Jarvis, 1993; Morton, 1989). These texts include detailed discussions of patient interviewing and obtaining and using the patient's historical data as well as in-depth physical assessment. Nurses now conduct a level of assessment that 40 years ago was either unheard of or was considered to be within the physician's domain.

The change in nursing documentation has revealed some broader issues of the way in which professional nursing knowledge is represented. Journal-type entries have been replaced by problem-oriented records. Consider, for example, the following set of nurse's notes that we collected at the Santa Barbara Cottage Hospital in Santa Barbara, CA:

| Time | # of Problems | NURSING PROGRESS NOTES A-assessment P-plan I-Intervention E-evaluate |
|------|---------------|----------------------------------------------------------------------|
| 1100 | 2 | A-Reported severe cramplike pain in both lower extremeties while walking in hallway with wife. Pt. observed rubbing calves of both legs. Skin color is pale & cool. Pedal pulses weak but palpable. Pt. states "my legs feel numb." |
| | | P-returned to bed w/legs elevated. Continue to monitor. |
| | | I–Administered pain medication. Instructed Mr. Johnson and his wife on the need for rest periods interspersed with exercise. Also explained potential danger with "rubbing calves" |
| | | E-Pain has subsided since receiving medication Color and temperature of extremities returned to normal. Both patient and wife verbalized an understanding of teaching. K. Henson, RN |

In some agencies, observations and interventions by several members of the health care team are integrated into a single document, with the patient or client being the primary focus. Flow sheets have been expanded to accommodate documentation of specific observations and routine or technical aspects of care. The depth and breadth of knowledge required to practice nursing has far surpassed anything that could have been imagined half a century ago.

How the nursing textbooks have described and delineated professional competence over the past 40 years has shown a shift from the original, Nightingale-inspired, observation which was recorded for the benefit of both the nurse and the physician to one of providing documentary evidence of the complex processes of modern medicine and healing while simultaneously focusing on the patient as a whole person rather than as a manifest example of a particular medical condition.

# Professional Identity Influenced by Computer Technology

Expanding technology has brought computer applications to virtually every field of employment. The health care field is no different. The past decade has witnessed the ushering in of computerized "order entry" for notifying various departments of physician orders (e.g., laboratory tests, diet and specialized services such as physical therapy and respiratory therapy), for on-line reporting of laboratory reports, and for a multitude of business applications. (See Hall, 1994; Lenkman, 1985; Steinberg & Toole, 1985; Wann, 1994.) Similarly, within nursing education there has been a tremendous influx of computerized educational programs that present case studies and promote the development of critical decision-making skills in nursing students and medical students. (See Bersky & Yocum, 1994; Lassen, 1989; Newbern, 1985; Sparks, 1994; and Yoder, 1994.) The need to understand and utilize computerized systems is ubiquitous.

Despite these advances in computer technology, the development of systems that utilize computer applications for what is commonly called "charting" has been much slower. Charting, by nurses, typically includes documentation of all aspects of care provided to patients and requires an ongoing interface between nursing staff and the patient's medical record. Depending on patient status and hospital policy, data may be entered into the patient's chart at a minimum of two or three times per eight-hour shift up to several times in any given hour.

To gain a perspective on the effect of computer technology on nursing, we interviewed nurses from three southern California hospitals, each of which is at a different point of computer implementation. One hospital is using computer applications at the unit level for ordering laboratory tests, diagnostic procedures, diet consultations with other health care providers, and so on. At that facility, chart forms have been recently revised to prepare for eventual data entry via computer. The second facility has implemented the system in the critical care areas but has not yet expanded it to the general medical-surgical areas. The third hospital has implemented a system that includes a complete charting package with "bedside computers" for all areas of the hospital (general medical-surgical as well as critical care).

The next section presents an overview of the particular computer system used at that hospital and describes how it is used by nurses to record admission observations, develop a nursing care plan, to document ongoing or daily care, and to access data on the data base.

## Overview of Computer System

The bedside computer system has portable terminals located in each patient's room. They are slightly larger than an "etch-a-sketch" (approximately 8" x 12" x 2") and when not in use are inserted into a wall mounted battery charger. Data are transmitted to the main computer via radio frequency waves. The computer keyboard may be used while it is mounted on the wall or it may be removed and taken any place in the nursing unit. Nurses are encouraged to sit at the patient's bedside when entering data. If privacy is required, the nurse may take the patient and the terminal to a nearby conference room. The terminal may be out of the battery pack for up to 45 minutes.

The terminal is colored with a soft pink/blue holographic screen which prevents viewing from side angles, thus enhancing security. It is activated by touching the screen. As various menus appear on the screen, specific data can be selected and input by pointing and touching the screen with a fingernail or pen or pencil. Data selected will be marked with an asterisk. When the nurse has finished entering relevant data, s/he is prompted to review selections make and then to touch the "send" key. Information is then entered on the patient's record. The patient's chart (database) may be accessed by more than one individual at a time—an advantage especially at times when the patient has been transported off the nursing unit (e.g., to go to X-ray or to the operating room).

### Developing a Care Plan

To develop a care plan the nurse selects the appropriate nursing diagnosis from a menu. Then a series of relevant options for details of the plan of care appear on the screen from which the nurse selects the most relevant options. The system actually cues the nurse to make specific observations. Some nursing diagnoses have up to three or four screens of options available. If greater specificity than the database provides is desired, the nurse may select the key word "comments" and a keyboard appears on the screen. Appropriate comments are then typed onto the screen.

Joint care planning with patients and/or their family is encouraged. The portable computer console makes that possible. Cited as an advantage to using this system was the reduction in time required to develop nursing care plans, from one hour per patient to approximately five minutes.

### Documentation of Daily Care

The chart is set up in a flow-sheet format organized around the nursing care plan. Each element on the care plan has a menu of relevant options for describing observations made and care delivered. Abbreviations and codes are used as much as possible. If greater detail is desired, the nurse types in additional comments, in a space at the end of the work menu but with infinite scroll capacity. There is also a directory for deciphering the codes.

Vital signs are inserted and graphed automatically by the computer. In intensive care units (ICU), the vital signs are recorded directly from the bedside monitors on an hourly basis. Eight-hour and twenty-four hour totals for intake and output are calculated by the computer.

Documentation of medications is also done automatically. Medications are bar-coded and scanned with an optical scanning pen in the patient's room. In addition to documenting the administration of the medication, the computer verifies the accuracy of the drug, its dosage, and the time of administration and alerts the nurse to possible discrepancies. In the event of emergencies where special drugs are needed, there is a mechanism for overriding the system.

### Accessing Data on the Database

Data can be pulled up from the database for review in a variety of formats, depending on what is desired. For example, one can look at everything charted or just one subsection of the chart. There are special programs that display data according to the individual user's specifications. When the nurse comes on duty, s/he receives a printout that includes key items on the plan of care plus a list of medications and treatments. This printout serves as a work schedule for the shift. Data entered on the computer is printed out every 24 hours and paper copies are filed in the patient's chart at the desk.

For the nursing profession the central role of documentation in professional practice signifies a shift from care-giving as simple care-taking activities and medical support to the role of the nurse as a key link in the chain of command for obtaining and processing complex information that contemporary hospital nursing requires. Since it has been estimated that as much as one-third of a nurse's day is spent on documentation, computerization may provide an important revisioning of the documentation process from chore to an important part of nursing day.

## Professional Vision: Computers at the Beside as Well as the Nurse

> *The discourse of a profession involves not only talk between people but also the operations within and upon the working environment within which the profession is situated.*
> C. Goodwin and M.H. Goodwin,
> *Professional Vision* (1992)

In our study we found a complex situation where the technology was only beginning to be recognized as an essential part of the nurses' role in the health care system. The use of computers has been justified in management terms as providing both more accurate and complete data and in a time efficient manner (Meyer, 1992). It is claimed that providing the creation of legible, accurate, attribution and time-coded documents enhances the position of the nurse's contribution to patients' medical records and helps to substantiate responsibility for decision-making. However, in our conversations with nurses and nurse managers, and in our observations of actual uses in the hospital, we became aware that the introduction of computers is bringing about even greater changes in the knowledge representation of nursing expertise. It is these changes that we discuss in this final section.

Our conversations with nurses showed both positive and negative aspects to the introduction of bedside computers. To begin with the negative views, computers were seen as presenting an unwelcome challenge, in fact for many, the threat of a difficult-to-learn technology that increases both documentary tasks and sensory overload. Nursing practice requires the interpretation of several sources of documentary information in order to present unified care plans and evaluations. Some nurses fear that their competency will be compromised. More significantly the technology carries with it the implication of a mechanization of what has been established, over time, as a very personal area of judgment. Considerable concern centered on the felt loss of personal identity. As one nurse commented: " I cannot even see my own signature on the chart."

However, on the positive side, our observations definitely suggest that computers provide a new dimension for nurses to become key players in the flow of information and decision-making. First, when the responsibility for generating accurate and efficient documentation is taken over by "the machine," nurses become freed of some of the more irksome aspects of daily record-keeping. In a study of nursing literacy in the 1980s, it was found that nurses kept various notes of information and observations to be entered later in the chart (Mikulecky & Winchester, 1983). This freedom better positions the nurse to be an advocate for the patient as a whole person within the medical treatment system. The nurse essentially coordinates information on the patient's condition at the bedside and makes this immediately available to all personnel, thus raising the visibility of the nurses' observation and contribution to the documentation process.

Secondly, patient and nurse collaboration is facilitated through the use of "bedside computerized charting," because the screen can serve as a visible and accessible domain where nurse and patient may enter and exchange information together. This highlights a very significant change in practice from the traditional one where the patient's chart is a secret, closed domain accessible only to qualified personnel. In the computerized system the patient and their family can be considered as able to give their own input and as able to receive information directly, thereby involving patients in their own medical planning and healing process.

Thirdly, the nurses' position "at the bedside" can be confirmed, rather than being replaced as was initially feared by some. It becomes possible to reconfigure the "caring space" by placing the information/documentation center at the bedside, rather than away from the patient in a separate, closed space. This puts the patients and their family into an active zone of engagement where medical technology and interpersonal action converge, rather than in the more traditional passive role of sick person/patient confined in a restricted space, that is, the bed within the ward reserved for the ill from which information is removed in order to be examined, tabulated, and documented elsewhere. Such actions previously separated the self of the sick person from the process of treatment and inspection of bodily products (Wolf, 1988). Traditional hospital wards often have lively, active centers in small rooms away from the patients where nurses and physicians congregate and talk, while patients are left alone in their beds, rooms, and wards in the isolation of sickness. In this way a bedside computer may be instrumental in shifting the focus of activity back to the bedside of the patient. As Benner and Wrubel (1989) have recently pointed out, the problem for nursing practice is not the expression of care as such but the creation of a safe place of "controlled caring" where the risks and vulnerability of illness can be addressed.

In this research we have been able to identify some of the ways in which the stages of documentation viewed both historically and in the present time, reflect the development of a professional vision of nursing. We have identified a progression of spatial organization of records and textual arrangements that represents an increasing depth of diagnostic and observational information in a systematized form which increases the professional accountability of the nurse. As documentation has evolved from descriptive narrative accounts of observations, to problem-oriented accounts, and thence to flow charts that can be formatted for the computer, the application of nursing knowledge has been extended. In order for the full potential of bedside computer documentation to be realized, participatory design of software involving daily users will be important (Greenbaum, 1991). And, as has been pointed out in several recent conferences, this means that more women with access to specific women's work concerns may need to become actively involved in computer software design and implementation than ever before (Suchmann, 1991).

Moreover, our main discovery in this research was that computer technology and the literacy practices that surround its use has the potential to challenge, in a positive sense, the ways in which nursing has been viewed historically as "women's work". For computer technology, which has never been viewed as a woman's domain, is being appropriated by the quintessential women's profession. This appropriation allows nursing to combine its traditional expertise of medical caring with the untraditional use of computer documentation technology and thereby to gain an enhanced respect for its professional expertise. Through these new technological uses, the discourse of nursing is beginning another major shift, and as this account has shown, the documentary literacy of nursing has begun to establish a revisioning of professional practice in ways that many women and nurses will recognize.

## Note

1. The authors want to thank Elizabeth Styffe, RN, MN a clinical specialist in information services, for her conversations on the role of nurses in a changing technological society, and Glynda Hull for her comments on the chapter. Previous fieldwork on the literacy preparation for Licensed Vocational Nurse programs was funded by the National Center for Research in Vocational Education, University of California, Berkeley.

## References

Alfaro-LeFevre, R. (1994). *Applying nursing process: A step-by-step guide.* (3rd ed.) Philadelphia: J.B. Lippincott.

Bakker, I. (1988). Women's employment in comparative perspective. In J. Jenson, E. Hagen, & C. Reddy (Eds.), *Feminization of the labor force.* New York: Oxford University Press.

Beechy, V. (1988). Rethinking the definition of work: Gender and work. In J. Jenson, E. Hagen, & C. Reddy (Eds.), *Feminization of the labor force.* New York: Oxford University Press.

Benner, P. (1985). *From novice to expert: Excellence and power in clinical nursing practice.* Menlo Park, CA: Addison-Wesley.

Benner, P. & Wrubel, J. (1989). *The primacy of caring: Stress and coping in health and illness.* Menlo Park, CA: Addison-Wesley.

Bersky, A. K. & Yocom, C. J. (1994). Computerized clinical simulation testing: Its use for competence assessment in nursing. *Nursing and Health Care, 15,* 120–127.

Braverman, H. (1974). *Labor and monopoly capital: The degradation of work in the twentieth century*. New York: Monthly Review Press.

Brown, E. L. (1948). *Nursing for the future*. New York: The Russell Sage Foundation.

Carpenito, L.J. (1995a). *Nursing diagnosis: Applications to clinical practice* (6th ed.). Philadelphia: J. B. Lippincott Co.

Carpenito, L. J. (1995b). *Handbook of nursing diagnosis, 1989–90*. Philadelphia: J. B. Lippincott Co.

Davis, R. (1993, Winter). Mr. R.N. *Graduating Nurse*.

Dolan, J.A. (1973). *Nursing in Society* (13th ed.). Philadelphia: W. B. Saunders.

Ellis, J. R. & Hartley, C.L. (1995) *Nursing in today's world: Challenges, issues and trends* (5th ed.). Philadelphia: J. B. Lippincott Co.

Etzioni, A. (1969). *The semi-professions and their organization: Teachers, nurses and social workers*. New York: Free Press.

Finch, J. & Groves, D. (1983). Introduction. In J. Finch & D. Groves (Eds.), *A labour of love: Women, work, and caring*. Boston and London: Routledge and Kegan Paul.

Glazer, N. (1991). Between a rock and a hard place: Women's professional organizations in nursing, and class, race and ethnic inequalities. *Gender and Society, 5*, 351–372.

Glazer, N. (1993). *Womens' paid and unpaid labor: The work transfer in health care and retailing*. Philadelphia: Temple University Press.

Goodwin, C. & Goodwin M. H. (1992). Professional vision: Perception as professional practice. In B. L. Gunnarson, P. Linel, & B. Nordberg (Eds.), *The construction of professional discourse*. London: Longmans.

Graham, H. (1983). Caring: A labour of love. In J. Finch & D. Groves (Eds.), *A labour of love: Women, work, and caring*. Boston and London: Routledge and Kegan Paul.

Graham, H. (1985). Providers, negotiators and mediators: Women as the hidden carers. In E. Lewin & V. Olesen (Eds.), *Women, health and healing* (pp. 25–51). London: Tavistock Publications.

Greenbaum, J. (1991). Towards participatory design: The head and the heart revisited. In I. V. Erikson, B. A. Kitchenham & K. G. Tijens (Eds.),

*Women, work and computerization* (pp. 33–40). Amsterdam: Elsevier Science Publishers.

Hall, L. (1994). Nurse managers give thumbs up to CES software. *Health Care Computer Tutor, 3*, 2.

Harmer, B. & Henderson, V. (1955). *The textbook of the principles and practice of nursing.*

Hochshild, A. R. (1983). *The managed heart: The commercialization of feeling.* Berkeley, CA: University of California Press.

Hull, G. & Cook-Gumperz, J. (1989). *Preparing a literate workforce.* Research report to the National Center for Research on Vocational Education.

Iyer, P., Taptich, B. & Bernocci-Losey, D. (1986). *Nursing process and nursing diagnosis.* Philadelphia: W. B. Saunders.

Jarvis, C. (1993). *Physical examination and health assessment.* Philadelphia: W. B. Saunders.

Jenson, J., Hagen, E. & Reddy, C. (1988). Introduction. In J. Jenson, E. Hagen, & C. Reddy (Eds.), *Feminization of the labor force: Paradoxes and promises.* New York: Oxford University Press.

Johnson, L. (1994). Does all this technology make a difference? *Innovation Abstracts, 16*, 18.

Kozier, B., Erb, G., Blais, K. & Wilkinson, J. (1995). *Fundamentals of nursing: Concepts, process, and practice.* Menlo Park, CA: Addison-Wesley.

Lassen, R. (1989). Use of computer-assisted instruction in health services. *Nursing Forum, 24*, 13–17.

Lenkman, S. (1985). Management information systems and the role of the nurse vendor. *Nursing Clinics of North America, 20*, 557–565.

Lindberg, J. B., Hunter, J. L., & Kruzewski, A. S. Z. (1990). *Introduction to nursing: Concepts, issues and opportunities.* Philadelphia: J. B. Lippincott.

Melosh, B. (1982). *The physician's hand: Work culture and conflict in American nursing.* Philadelphia: Temple University Press.

Meyer, C. (1992). Bedside computer charting: Inching toward tomorrow. *American Journal of Nursing, 92*, 38–44.

Mikulecky, L. & Winchester, D. (1983). Job literacy and job performance among nurses at varying employment levels. *Journal of Adult Education, 34*, 1–15.

Morton, P. G. (1989). *Health assessment in nursing.* Springhouse, PA: Springhouse Corporation.

Newbern, V. B. (1985). Computer literacy in nursing education: An overview. *Nursing Clinics of North America, 20*, 549–556.

Nightingale, F. (1946). *Notes on nursing: What it is and what it is not.* Philadelphia: J. B Lippincott. (Original work published 1859).

Olesen, V. & Lewin E. (1985 ). Women health and healing: A theoretical introduction. In V. Olesen & E. Lewin (Eds.) *Women, health and healing* (pp. 1–24). London: Tavistock Publications.

Sparks, S. M. (1994). The educational technology network. *Nursing and Health Care, 15*, 134–137.

Steinberg, L. and Toole, J. (1985). Role of systems consultant during the implementation of a patient care system. *Nursing Clinics of North America, 20*, 567–575.

Suchmann, L., (1991). Closing remarks at the Women and Computerization conference. In I. V. Erikson, B. A. Kitchenham & K.G. Tijens (Eds.), *Women, work and computerization* (pp. 134–141). Amsterdam: Elsevier Science Publishers.

Wagner, D. (1980). The proterialization of nursing in the United States, 1932–1946. *International Journal of Health Services, 10*(2), 271–290.

Wann, M. (1994). Software design with RN's input streamlines care. *Nurseweek, 7*, 1, 18.

Wolf, Z. R. (1988). *Nurses' work: The sacred and the profane.* Philadelphia: University of Pennsylvania Press.

Yoder, M. E. (1994). Preferred learning style and educational technology. *Nursing and Health Care, 15*, 128–132.

# THIRTEEN

## Finding Yourself in the Text: Identity Formation in the Discourse of Workplace Documents

### David Jolliffe

As several chapters in this volume make clear, the new workplace is becoming a more literate workplace. Reading, critical thinking, problem-solving and, to a lesser extent, writing are playing increasingly important roles in industry and business, in manufacturing and service alike. More and more organizations are implementing strategies for continuous monitoring, and concomitant adjusting, of quality. More and more organizations are producing customized, value-added products and services to meet specific demands "just in time" for their customers, rather than producing large quantities of a generic product for inventory; accordingly, production processes may change as often as weekly, rather than remaining stable for months or years. More and more organizations are asking workers to interact with computer technology, reading instructions and data from terminals and reporting both quotas and quality back to the machines. All of these innovations suggest a phasing out of the old workplace, in which workers were rarely asked to read, think critically, and solve problems on the job. Fewer and fewer workers today can expect to learn their job via a physical demonstration, to continue to perform the same task for months or years, or to count on someone else to read and document quality data. More and more workers today must read and understand production and quality-control documents, think critically about what they read and how it applies to production and quality, and react quickly and prudently to changes in all aspects of production and service.

Executives, managers, consultants, and even teams of workers have been busy considering how to train (or retrain) a workforce capable of meeting these new literacy demands. The collective product of these deliberations can be termed the "workforce preparedness" literature (see Hull, this volume, for a critical review of this literature). It consistently cites the workers' needs for "basic skills" instruction in the four traditional language arts—reading, writing, listening, and speaking—plus mathematics and occasionally basic computer operations. But this literature frequently sounds another theme as well: It suggests not only that workers in the future must be more capable intellectually but also that they must display certain personality characteristics that the new, more literate workplace apparently calls for. Consider three examples from this literature: Officials of the National Center on Education and the Economy (1990) call for workers who are attuned to issues of product quality, variety of effort, and responsiveness to change; who are able to shoulder more responsibility; and who demonstrate a good "work ethic" (pp. 2–3). Carnevale, Gainer, and Meltzer (1990) include the following in their explication of "the essential skills employers want": knowing how to learn; listening and oral communication; adaptability, or creative thinking and problem-solving; personal management, or self-esteem, goal-setting, motivation, and personal and career development; group effectiveness, including interpersonal skills, negotiation, and teamwork; and influence, or organizational effectiveness and leadership. Under the rubric of "crucial skills workers lack," the National Alliance of Business (1994) cites not only reading, writing, math, listening, speaking, "information skills," and "technology skills," but also "resource management" and "interpersonal skills" (p. 5).

Fostering the development of this new kind of worker represents a commendable yet challenging and politically thorny goal for the workforce preparedness movement: Commendable because workers demonstrating these characteristics would probably be more productive, but, more importantly, de facto more enfranchised within their organization, more creatively involved with entire scope of the organization's production or service; challenging because, historically, production-and service-line workers have been taught that they are responsible only for their own portion of the overall task, that quality is the concern of the quality-control department, that they are responsible solely for their own assigned duties and no one else's; politically thorny because the workforce preparedness agenda comprises not only the development of basic skills but also the inculcation of new personality characteristics—intrinsic motivation, extroversion, cooperation, and so on—and thereby suggests that the workers' personalities in the past were in some way deficient and perhaps even damaging to productivity and the economy. I shall return to this thorny issue of forging new workers' identities regularly in this chapter.

At the risk of oversimplification, let me suggest that there are ultimately only two ways that workers being trained or retrained can learn that they are expected to develop these new intellectual abilities and personality characteristics: by actions or by words. Concerning the former, of course, executives, management, and workers can *do* things together to foster this new, desirable level of initiative, innovation, and responsibility. Concerning the latter, workers can either be *told* that they must evince both better skills and personalities, or they can *read* documents that are conducive of these desired features. My concern in this chapter lies with the latter, and my thesis embodies both an assertion and a challenge: The workforce preparedness movement maintains that the new workplace needs workers who are more committed, involved, and responsible, but many documents that workers must read on the job do little to nurture these traits. If the leaders of American business, industry, and service want more committed and involved workers, then these leaders should pay careful attention to the ways work-related documents either do, or more frequently do not, help workers to become so.

The chapter proceeds as follows: In the next section, I examine the practice of analyzing the readability of workplace documents and argue that an assessment of their grade-level readability might not be the best measure of their accessibility to workers. As an alternative, or perhaps complement, to assessments of readability, I propose a framework for analyzing what I call the workers' *identity formation* in the documents. After that, I present an analysis of a document that beginning workers in a precision metalworking factory in Chicago are expected to read and comprehend. I suggest that the source of this document's difficulty for workers lies not in its grade-level readability, but in its failure to promote the formation of its readers'—that is, the workers'—identities in a productive fashion. I conclude by suggesting avenues for future research and possibilities that analyses of identity formation in work-related documents hold for trainers and workers alike.

## Assessing Workplace Texts: Readability versus Identity Formation

Even a cursory look into many contemporary workplaces reveals a great deal of reading being done on the job by production-and service-level workers. In many sites, for example, they are asked to read documents about their companies' methods of controlling quality and organizing the workforce into teams. Especially in industries which earn recognition from International Standards Organization (ISO) 9001, an international body that certifies quality control, workers must read documents about all phases of operation—intake and inventory, production, shipping, and distribution. In response to this increasing volume of reading, the workplace preparedness movement has voiced two kinds of concerns: that the documents are readable, and that workers are *capable* of reading them. Generally, the movement has acted on these concerns in relatively predictable ways: by assessing the readability of the documents as a prelude to making them more accessible to workers, by striving both to hire workers who are more capable readers, and by offering various kinds of support to workers who want to improve as readers.

A general and potentially troubling assumption about *grade-level readability* underlies all these efforts. That is, the efforts assume that an abstraction called "readability" can be made concrete and quantified; that texts can be analyzed, and the ease or difficulty with which they can be read can be specified with a grade-level designation; that a person's reading abilities can be assessed and given a grade-level-equivalent ability score; that the grade level of a text can be lowered or raised by manipulating certain of its features, usually the number of syllables per word and the number of words per sentence; and that a person's grade-level reading abilities are improvable.

A typical method of determining the readability of workplace documents is the FORCAST formula, developed originally for analyzing military training manuals and promulgated in the workplace preparedness literature by Philippi (1991). Here's how FORCAST works:

> Count the number of one-syllable words in a 150-word passage.
> Divide that number by 10.
> Subtract the answer from 20.
> Formula: Readability = 20 − (number of one-syllable words ÷ 10)
>
> (p. 216)

For example, if a 150-word passage contains 94 one-syllable words, you would divide 94 by 10 and get 9.4; then you would subtract 9.4 from 20, and get 10.6. Thus, the grade-level readability of the text would be 10.6, about the high school sophomore level. Philippi recommends that planners of workplace preparedness programs use FORCAST to analyze work-related documents. Then planners can convert these documents into cloze tests, constructed from passages with every seventh word deleted, which test-takers are directed to replace. These tests then can be given to potential participants in order to determine which ones—those with limited success replacing the deleted words—might experience difficulty reading the documents on which the tests are based. Philippi notes that FORCAST "has a high statistical correlation to other readability formulas and the advantage of being more accurate for use with workplace materials" (p. 216).

Readability formulas like FORCAST—indeed, the whole notion of grade-level readability—represent a quandary for workplace preparedness planners and students, a quandary that often they seem unaware of. When planning a workplace training program, a planner nearly always conducts a "literacy task analysis" (see, e.g., Philippi, pp. 104–134). As part of this process, the planner collects samples of workplace documents—brochures, manuals, process sheets, and so on—for use in developing a functional, context-sensitive curriculum. A standard practice, as suggested above, is to analyze the grade-level readability of these documents. Later, when planners are assessing the basic skills of workers to identify potential participants in the program, a standard practice is to give the Tests of Adult Basic Education (TABE), standardized, norm-referenced tests that produce grade-level-equivalent scores in reading, writing, and math. The TABE scores are used, in part, to identify workers who might have difficulty reading and understanding the aforementioned workplace texts.

Here's the quandary, then: Planners administer the TABE tests, even though they acknowledge that grade-level-equivalent scores are relatively meaningless for workers who may have been out of school for as long as 30 or 40 years. As a presenter at a recent conference on workforce preparedness put it, planners often admit with an air of resignation, "Oh, we just TABE the workers," all questions of the validity of TABE aside (Askov, 1995). The situation is rife with contradictions: On the one hand, planners gather documents, analyzed for grade-level readability, that they want to teach workers how to read; on the other hand, workers are designated as potential participants in the program on the basis of grade-level-equivalency scores that even many planners concede to be meaningless. The FORCAST formula suggests that if workers are experiencing difficulty reading workplace documents, their authors could lower the grade-level readability of the texts by including more one-syllable words in them. But if the grade-level-equivalent scores of workers are not valid, *should* authors try to make the texts more "readable" just by simplifying their lexicon? If workers can't read and process the workplace documents effectively, might there not be other sources of difficulty besides the grade-level readability of the texts?

Clearly, workplace preparedness specialists need to take two routes out of this quandary. First, they need to develop new methods of assessing the basic skills of workers that do not rely solely on grade-level-equivalency scores. Though this project lies beyond the scope of this chapter, I am pleased to note that some efforts are being made in this direction in the workforce preparedness movement (see, e.g., Bixler & Askov, 1994; *Work Keys*, 1995). Second, they need to develop new ways of analyzing workplace documents to determine what features about them might make them difficult for workers to read and understand. As an outgrowth of this kind of analysis, they need to consider ways to alter the texts so they are more understandable, and they need to generate methods of teaching workers how to process these documents more effectively.

I have found new tools for analyzing the potential accessibility of workplace documents in the work of the British critical linguist Norman Fairclough. Fairclough's work, most recently developed in *Discourse and Social Change* (1992), suggests even more questionable assumptions about the use of grade-level readability analyses and grade-level-equivalency assessments of workers. First, such practices assume that workplace texts are simply another set of tools for the worker to use, in this case, tools composed of words (preferably monosyllabic) and sentences, rather than, say, ratchets and gears. Second, these practices assume that workers process these documents in a value-empty, ideologically neutral fashion, that the workers simply decode the texts and act upon them, without any involvement as real, human beings whose personal identities might affect the interaction.

Fairclough's work makes clear that all documents, including workplace texts, are more than simply tools, more than mere bundles of syntax and lexical choices, and readers are more than simply decoding machines who process texts and act upon them. Workplace texts, Fairclough would argue, are instantiations of *discourse*. To develop new ways of assessing workplace documents for their accessibility to workers, one must analyze these texts as discourse and speculate about the ways writers and readers both construct meaning and are constructed as meaningful by the operation of discourse.

In *Discourse and Social Change*, Fairclough offers a comprehensive definition of discourse that is central to the task of analyzing workplace documents and making them more accessible to workers. According to Fairclough, discourse is "language use as a form of social practice" (p. 63) which exists in a "dialectical relationship" with social structure (p. 64). That is, "[o]n the one hand, discourse is shaped and constrained by social structure in the widest sense and at all levels," especially by social class and institutions such as the law and education. "On the other hand," however, "discourse is socially constitutive . . . of all those dimensions of social structure which directly or indirectly shape and constrain it: its own norms and conventions, as well as the relations, identities, and institutions which lie behind them" (p. 64).

Fairclough distinguishes three dimensions of this socially constitutive, "constructive effect of discourse." First, he maintains, discourse helps to construct the "social identities" and "subject positions" of "social subjects," such as readers and writers. Second, he says, "discourse helps construct social relationships between people." Third, "discourse contributes to the construction of systems of knowledge and belief." In summary, Fairclough notes: "These

340

three effects correspond respectively to three functions of language and dimensions of meaning which coexist and interact in all discourse . . . , the 'identity,' 'relational,' and 'ideational' functions of language" (p. 64). He provides an example to clarify these constitutive categories. In schools, the "speech of the classroom" helps to construct not only the identities of "teachers" and "pupils" but also a social relationship in which the teachers orchestrate the pupils' activities and evaluate their performances. Ideologically, this relationship generally reproduces a society's systems of knowledge and belief about the nature of schooling, but it is also "open to transformations which may partly originate in discourse" (p. 65).

Certainly, one could choose to see these three categories as separate entities. In order to examine workplace documents, however, I think it makes sense to acknowledge the categories' interrelatedness and to treat the constitutive effect of the discourse in the texts as a complicated, but finally singular, phenomenon. After all, when the discourse of a workplace document posits, as we shall see below, the identity of workers as good "company people," it simultaneously proposes a social relationship of planned cooperation among all levels of management and labor, and it constructs, as a presupposition, the belief that everyone in the company is, in fact, interested in quality control and increased productivity. Since the categories are so interrelated, I refer to the constitutive effect of the discourse in workplace documents with the term *identity formation*. I begin my analysis with the simple question, "What features of this document *invite* readers to find themselves in the text and to *construct* social identities, relations, and belief systems that the readers can accept and live within?" Once again, Fairclough's work is helpful: He introduces the concept of a text's *interdiscursivity*, representing the degree to which its discourse resembles any other discourse that the readers might encounter in their lives, either at work or away from it. The more a text is interdiscursive with discourses in which readers can find identities, relations, and belief systems with which they are comfortable, the more they can *find* themselves within it.

According to Fairclough, the features of discourse that constitute identities, relations, and ideologies are organized by "interdiscourse," a cognitive construct which he defines as "the complex interdependent configuration of discursive formations" that serves as "the structural entity (underlying) discursive events" (p. 68). Interdiscourse, in turn, is embodied in two kinds of intertextuality: "manifest intertextuality," in which "other texts are explicitly present in the text under analysis"; and "constitutive intertextuality," or "interdiscursivity," which is "the configuration of . . . conventions" from other discourses "that go into [a text's] production" (p. 104). Suppose, for example, that a news story reports that the emergence of a victorious party in an election amounts to a brave new world for American politics. This sentence is *manifestly intertextual* with both Miranda's exclamation in *The Tempest* and with the title of Aldous Huxley's dystopic novel. Suppose that the same story explains that the victorious politicians "scored a knockout punch" at a particularly successful rally. This sentence is *constitutively intertextual* or, more simply, *interdiscursive* with the discourse of sports reportage.

According to Fairclough, four general text features contribute to a reader's sense that a text is interdiscursive; each of these features capitalizes on an interdiscursive relation to help construct identities, social relations, and ideologies. The first is genre, "a relatively stable set of conventions that is associated with, and partly enacts, a socially ratified type of activity" (p. 126). As Fairclough explains, "A genre implies not only a particular text type, but also particular processes of producing, distributing, and consuming texts" (p. 126). Consider, for example, the genre of the "infomercial," a type of television program one finds on many television stations. The program's purpose is to sell whatever product has bought the air time, and it exploits its interdiscursive similarity to the genre of documentary programs produced by legitimate news organizations. Ideologically, this interdiscursivity invests the infomercial with a sense of importance and credibility, whether warranted or not. Genre, to Fairclough, is a superordinate category that draws together all four features he analyzes under the rubric of interdiscursivity.

The second feature is "activity type," or "the structured sequence of actions" and "the participants involved in the activity—that is, the set of subject positions which are socially constituted and recognized in connection with the activity type" (p. 126). Consider, for example, a kind of advertisement that runs in the sports sections of many newspapers. It looks just like a news story (a generic interdiscursivity) with boldface headlines and small columns of one-sentence-per-paragraph exposition, except it has "ADVERTISEMENT" written in small type at the top. The headlines announce: "Latest Scientific News: Male Pattern Baldness Cured." To create an impression of novelty and importance, this text exploits an interdiscursivity with the "news report" activity type (see Fairclough, p. 129) in which an anonymous reporter gives the news receiver the gist of a story in headlines, then a slightly longer gist in the lead, then a development of details.

The third feature is style, which Fairclough divides into "tenor," or "the sort of relationship that obtains between participants in an interaction"; "mode," or "whether texts are written or spoken or some combination of the two"; and "rhetorical mode," which "can be classified with terms such as 'argumentative,' 'descriptive,' and 'expository'" (p. 127). Fairclough's explanation of the phenomenon he calls "synthetic personalization" provides a useful example of the interdiscursivity of style. Synthetic personalization is "the simulation of private, face-to-face, discourse in public mass-audience discourse" such as "print, radio, television" (p. 98). When, say, a bank's advertisement says, "Trust us—we want to be your friend," it is capitalizing on interdiscursivity with friendly, spoken, generally expressive discourse between people.

The fourth general feature is "discourse" used as a count noun, for example "a discourse" or "these discourses" (p. 128). "Discourses correspond roughly to dimensions of texts which have traditionally been discussed in terms of 'content,' 'ideational meanings,' 'topic,' 'subject matter,' and so forth," Fairclough writes (pp. 127–28). Thus, for example, one can analyze textual examples of "techno-scientific medical discourse" or "feminist discourses of sexuality" (p. 128) and analyze the effects the texts achieve by exploiting this interdiscursivity.

In addition to these four general features that are conducive of interdiscursivity, Fairclough defines a number of more specific textual aspects that may be analyzed under the rubrics of genre, activity type, style, and discourses and that potentially affect identity formation by means of interdiscursivity. For example, he counsels discourse analysts to look for "presuppositions," or "propositions which are taken by the producer of the text as already established or 'given'" (p. 120), and for "ethos," or textual constitutions of the character of both the writer and the readers (p. 166).

Under "transitivity," Fairclough prompts analysts to examine the concepts of "process type" and "nominalization." In general, processes described in texts can be analyzed as "relational" (processes of "being, having, becoming, etc."); "action processes, where an agent acts upon a goal" (p. 178); "event processes," which "involve an event and a goal" and are "generally realized" as "intransitive clauses" (p. 180); or "mental" processes of "cognition, . . . perception, . . . and affection" (p. 180). In action processes, Fairclough notes, it is particularly important to analyze the degree to which readers are cast in the roles of agents or patients—that is, active participants or passive recipients of the action involved. "Nominalization is the conversion of processes into nominals," he explains, "which has the effect of backgrounding the process itself . . . and usually not specifying its participants, so that who is doing what to whom is left implicit" (p. 179).

Fairclough advises analysts to be aware of the way the "modality" of statements signals "the extent to which [text] producers commit themselves to, or conversely distance themselves from, propositions: their degree of 'affinity' with the proposition" (p. 142). Finally, he counsels analysts to look for instances of "wording" and "metaphors," which constitute specific lexical manifestations of different discourses (pp. 191–195).

While they are not as systematic, neat, and quantifiable as the variables in readability formulas, I have found that Fairclough's analytic categories—his concept of interdiscursivity, the general features of genre, activity type, style, and discourse, and the specific aspects of presupposition, ethos, transitivity, modality, wording, and metaphors—do provide valuable windows into workplace documents and the degree to which workers find the texts accessible enough to find themselves within them.

## A Sample Analysis

The precision metalworking industry, which stamps, mills, and fabricates the thousands of small metal objects that surround us daily, offers a textbook example of the changing workplace. With customized, "value-added" production for "just-in-time" delivery, with continuous quality control, and with team-based operations, workers in many shops, especially smaller ones, are regularly placed in situations demanding careful, critical reading, correct documentation, and clear written reporting of operations. With the cooperation of the Tooling and Manufacturing Association, an 800-company consortium of precision metalworking companies in the Chicago area, I have spent a great deal of time during the last 2 years visiting metalworking shops, talking to managers and workers at all levels about their visions of preparing a workforce for the new workplace, and examining the documents that workers must read and that managers tell me they can't.[1] In this section, I analyze identity formation in one such document that entry-level workers in a metalworking shop are expected to read and understand.

The impetus to conduct this analysis came from a conversation I had with Todd Korner, the owner of a relatively small company in the northwest corner of Chicago. Todd's company, which employs about 100 people in the Chicago factory and another 100 or so in a similar shop in rural Tennessee, was founded by his father; his son works at the Chicago site and will take over the company when Todd retires. The company bids for and receives contracts primarily from automobile and electronics companies; during my visits, the plant was producing metal parts that would hold the sound systems in new automobiles and that would become the outer casings of small microwave ovens.

Todd is dedicated to Chicago. "I want to hire Chicago kids," he told me. "I'll even hire dropouts, but they've got to be able to read." When I asked him to show me what kinds of materials he expected them to be able to read, he gave me a copy of a 114-page, spiral-bound book entitled *Leadership Through Quality: Problem Solving Process User's Manual* (1985), produced by the Xerox Corporation. "Leadership Through Quality," as I discovered, is Xerox's team-based management and operations system. Because Todd's companies receives contracts from Xerox Development and Management, his company is encouraged to use the system to develop "employee involvement teams." Todd explained that he gives this book to new workers and asks them to read the introduction before they report for their first day. "A lot them just can't read it," he told me. What follows is the introduction in question. I have numbered the paragraphs for ease of reference.[2]

1. The goal of employee involvement is to give Xerox people increased influence over their work. In the past several years, one of the major routes to achieving that goal has been the creation of problem-solving teams: groups of employees who meet on a regular basis to identify and solve work-related problems.

2. Today thousands of people participate in hundreds of such groups across Xerox operating units; all levels and functions are represented. Their efforts have resulted in millions of dollars in cost savings and unprecedented improvements in the quality of Xerox products and services.

3. Many of the people now in problem-solving groups were skilled individual problem solvers; some had no experience in tackling work problems. Group problem solving has been successful because of a systematic, *common* problem-solving process that has been taught to virtually all participants of employee involvement groups. This process, which was developed several years ago, provides groups with a road map to follow, a common language of problem solving, and a set of tools and techniques.

4. Employee involvement, along with competitive benchmarking and quality improvement, is one of the foundations of Leadership Through Quality. As Leadership Through Quality is implemented throughout Xerox, employee involvement will become the way all of us go about accomplishing our business.

5. To achieve that objective, Xerox people who have not yet experienced group problem-solving training will have the opportunity to do so before receiving the three-day quality improvement training. Insofar as possible, the training will be delivered to family groups: a manager and those who report to him or her. When people who work together learn new skills together, it's usually easier to transfer those skills to their work environment.

6. Problem solving in family groups will be similar to that done by employee involvement groups. Both will focus on work-related problems and use the same problem-solving process and tools. Both groups will have the support and help of either employee involvement facilitators or quality specialists.

7. There will be some differences as well. Problem solving in family groups will probably be more informal, perhaps even integrated into the regular staff meetings or ongoing work routine. With the family group manager as one of the members, it is expected that a higher percentage of a family group's recommended solutions can be implemented without approval of higher levels of management.

8. Training family groups in problem solving does not eliminate the need for employee involvement groups. Many of the latter, for example, are tackling cross-functional problems beyond the scope of a single family group. Those who have participated in employee involvement groups can help others in their family groups become proficient in problem-solving.

9. As Leadership Through Quality problem-solving training cascades, more and more people are likely to be using the process in both environments—their family groups and their employee involvement groups.
10. This manual presents the basic information you need to apply the six-step problem-solving process. It is also intended to serve as a reference after training. (pp. 1–2)

I analyzed two 150-word passages of this text using FORCAST. One yielded a grade-level readability score of 11.8, the other a score of 11.7. While these are above the range of what Philippi refers to as the "intermediate reading level" (p. 216), they should be within the ken of high school seniors. Using Fairclough's tools, I looked for features of the prose that might influence identity formation, or the degree to which a reader might find himself or herself within the text.

Given the Leadership Through Quality's explicit goal "to give Xerox people increased influence over their work," the text begins with a step in the wrong direction with a sentence representing an event process, cast in an intransitive clause. The general intransitivity of the first paragraph is reinforced with the nominalization, "employee involvement" and the passivity of "the creation of problem-solving teams," the latter cast in a sentence that states an action process but does so with this passive nominal phrase. The first paragraph clues the reader that he or she is expected to assume the ethos of "Xerox people," but the reader learns nothing about what exactly he or she is supposed to *do* to assume this character.

The second paragraph begins with another action process, "thousands of people participate," but again the process is stated intransitively. This intransitivity is once again reinforced by the passive verb, "are represented." The paragraph ends with a sentence depicting another event process, "Their efforts have resulted," cast intransitively.

The third paragraph is noteworthy for its invocation of ethos and its reinforcement of the readers' passivity. We learn that being part of a group of "skilled individual problem solvers" is no longer acceptable; we find that the readers must now, in a metaphor from the discourse of contact sports, "tackle" work problems in a group. Notice that this problem-solving method "has been taught" and "was developed." So far, no one is doing anything to anybody else in this text. "This process . . . provides groups with a road map to follow"; no agents seem involved yet, only patients.

The fourth paragraph is dense with nominalizations: "employee involvement, "competitive benchmarking," "quality improvement," "employee involvement" again. The verbs in the paragraph consist of two copulas—"is" and "will become"—and one passive, "is implemented." The paragraph invokes the first-person plural ethos—the only first person reference in the

346

entire text—as we learn that "employee involvement will become the way all of us go about accomplishing our business." We, the readers, have not been asked to *do* anything yet, but we have been urged to become "Xerox people" and to join the group that calls itself "we" and "us."

We learn in the fifth paragraph that we readers are apparently among that number "who have not yet experienced group problem-solving training"—notice, again, that training is something that happens to you, not something you do—and that we "will have the opportunity to do so before receiving the three-day quality improvement training." Depicting one's participation in a training seminar as an "opportunity" might be seen as patronizing, if not euphemistic, wording—one is reminded of the discourse of draft board notices and jury duty letters. Once again, we see that this training is something we readers passively "receive," not do. The text uses a warm, yet clever metaphor in its advising that "the training will be delivered"—note the passivity again—"to family groups." Suddenly "we" are not just "Xerox people"; "we," as Sister Sledge put it in the hip discourse of the 1970s, are "family." The sixth paragraph is noteworthy again for its lack of human agency and for its introduction of two new characters, whose ethos we are expected to comprehend: "employee involvement facilitators" and "quality specialists."

The seventh and eighth paragraphs offer extremely interesting examples of the ways modality can influence affinity, or the apparent degree of "warmth" and commitment to a proposition. Notice that problem-solving work will "probably" be more informal, "perhaps even integrated into the regular staff meetings or ongoing work routine." Will it, or won't it? The long sentence that ends the seventh paragraph is particularly full of potential compromises: "it is expected"—by whom, we might ask?—"that a higher percentage of a family group's recommended solutions can be implemented"—not "will" or "must" or "should"—"without approval of higher levels of management." Does this sentence, notably cool in its affinity, give *carte blanche* to the problem-solving groups to implement solutions they generate? I wouldn't bet on it, but how is the reader supposed to know? At the end of the eighth paragraph, after we have learned that employee involvement groups are, metaphorically, "tackling cross-functional problems," we discover that experienced employee involvement group members "can help others"—again, not "will" or "should"—"become proficient in problem-solving." Once again, the affinity is cooled by an uncertain modality.

The penultimate paragraph, invoking a metaphor from the great outdoors, amplifies the power of problem-solving training: We are warned that it "cascades" throughout the company. The last paragraph offers an action process with a nonhuman actor—"This manual presents the basic information"—and changes the reference to the reader, which has been third person, "Xerox people,' and first person, "we" and "us," to the second-person, "you."

My conjecture is that it's not solely the grade-level readability of this text that makes it difficult for beginning workers at Todd Korner's company to read. I believe that workers find this text, and many others like it that they have to read, difficult to find themselves within, extremely *non-interdiscursive*, to coin an ungainly term. The genre of new employee instructions is probably not alien to them, but within this particular instantiation of that genre, they encounter depictions of activity types—actions without agents specified, events with only goals and no actors—that don't seem to include them. Stylistically, they encounter example after example of intransitivity and passivity, shifting pronoun references to themselves as readers, and extremely mixed messages about affinity, or the degree to which the authors of this document, whoever they are, are actually committed to the content it conveys. The document greets the readers early on with the discourse of worker involvement and influence, but its own discourse makes it hard for readers actually to buy into this ideology.

## Some Possible Courses of Action

The job of preparing a workforce capable of taking up and succeeding with the literacy tasks presented by the new workplace is formidable, and clearly many parties need to get involved. Educational institutions at all levels—schools, colleges, and universities—need to cooperate in developing programs that will help students learn to read more correctly, critically, and efficiently, to write more clearly and effectively, to speak articulately, and to think and solve problems creatively. Business, industries, and service organizations need both to cooperate with schools and to work independently to develop programs to help workers be able to accomplish these same tasks.

Part of the way business, industries, service organizations, and educational institutions can cooperate involves this issue of document readability and workers' identity formation. Certainly, as I hinted above, research and development projects need to take up the task of finding new ways to assess workers' abilities that don't rely on grade-level equivalency scores. To complement this effort, research and development need also to develop new ways of looking at workplace documents besides grade-level readability analyses. This chapter has offered just one such alternative method of analysis, a method that might best be used not to replace readability analyses, but instead to supplement them.

One of the most promising ways, I would conjecture, to determine whether workers find a text readable is not simply to analyze the document but to draft several versions, varying them on principles of, say, activity versus passivity, transitivity versus instransitivity, and affinity achieved through modality, and ask workers to read them and describe which versions they find most accessible. Better yet, why not ask workers themselves to get involved with *writing* the company's documentation of quality control, team-based management and operations, and production processes. If the workplace preparedness movement wants involved workers, why not get workers involved?

## Notes

1. With thanks, I acknowledge the assistance of Jerry Baginski, education director of the Tooling and Manufacturing Association. The names of informants in this chapter are, by agreement, pseudonyms.

2. I gratefully acknowledge the permission of Nick Argona of the Xerox Corporation's Supplier Total Quality Strategy Team to reproduce this material.

## References

Askov, E. N. (1995, February). *Workplace literacy skills assessments: Options and CAI alternatives*. Paper presented at Workforce 2000, The Workforce Landscape: Change and Challenge, San Diego, CA.

Bixler, B., & Askov, E. N. (1994). Assessment courseware for workplace literacy. *Mosaic: Research notes on literacy, 4* (1), 4–5.

Carnevale, A. P., Gainer, L. J., & Meltzer, A. S. (1990). *Workplace basics: The essential skills employers want*. San Francisco: Jossey-Bass.

Fairclough, N. (1992). *Discourse and social change*. Cambridge, England: Plenum.

National Alliance of Business. (1994). Crucial skills workers lack. *Work America, 11* (6), 5.

National Center for Education and the Economy. (1990). *America's choice: High skills or low wages*. Rochester, NY.

Philippi, J. (1991). *Literacy at work: The workbook for program developers*. New York: Simon & Schuster.

*Work keys*. (1995). Iowa City, IA: ACT Publications.

Xerox Corporation. (1985). *Leadership through quality: Problem-solving process user's manual*. Webster, NY: Author.

# FOURTEEN

## Teamwork and Literacy: Teaching and Learning at Hardy Industries

*Sylvia Hart-Landsberg and Stephen Reder*

Fieldnotes from a first visit to Hardy Industries,[1] a factory manufacturing automobile accessories for the international market, described an initial perception that heavy machinery seemed to dominate the manufacturing work:

> The first time I entered the production area, strong signals that this was a heavy industrial environment struck my senses (unaccustomed as they were to the factory setting). My guide (a Hardy employee) made sure I put on the pair of plastic goggles he handed me to protect my eyes from flying metal particles, the waste of machines that grind parts from metal bars. I learned right away to keep glancing through the scratchy plastic in the direction of beeps from forklifts, in order to stay out of their way. When a machine operator explained his or her work to me, the loud drumming of machinery all around made it necessary for me to lean close to the speaker and the machine. Even so, it was hard to hear the words. The noisy environment looked and smelled dirty, too: Fine metal grit covered everything. Kitty litter was scattered on the floor to absorb oil spills. All the factory work seemed to be a matter of handling massive machinery. Workers were constantly observing, interacting with, and conferring over their machines and the parts spewing out of them.

Contrary to first impressions, ensuing field observations and interviews soon revealed that mechanical work was far from the totality of the production and assembly-line workers' jobs. In explaining their tasks, workers spontaneously explicated the continual challenges of both literacy and teamwork skills in their jobs. Literacy included skills like reading parts lists to set up new assembly jobs, applying algebra to operating computer-numerically-controlled machines (CNCs), and collectively writing complex descriptions of production steps and reasons for them. Teamwork challenges that employees brought up included cooperating with "difficult" coworkers, taking others' points of view, holding one's temper, participating in meetings, fitting one's work to others' paces, and interviewing individuals across the plant and in other plants (including some across the country) to understand their expectations for products.

In this chapter we examine the ways workers applied, learned, and taught teamwork and literacy skills at Hardy Industries. Several years before the study the company's management had introduced a "high performance" production model along the lines of Toyota. A fundamental part of this restructuring was a reorganization of the approximately 450 workers into 19 teams. Each production team had a "leader" and a "quality technician" (who oversaw quality-control activities) with desks near the production and assembly lines. Management assigned each team responsibility for making or assembling certain products. In tandem with this work organization, the company adopted management/production approaches widely touted in modern business for improving productivity: total quality control (for monitoring quality), continuous improvement (involving workers in planning work processes), and the just-in-time inventory system (for reducing waste). The overall purpose of these approaches was to increase the diversity of workers' tasks as well as their participation in production decisions and responsibility for quality output.

These changes had profound implications for the skills required of workers. Jobs that previously had been more mechanically oriented now came to encompass more complex cooperation and communication. To structure incentives for learning these skills, the company designed an innovative compensation system known as Pay-for-Knowledge (PFK), which was being implemented at the time of the research. This system based a worker's pay on skills and knowledge which he or she had demonstrated. To upgrade their existing skills and develop new ones, workers had a variety of options, including in-house, company-sponsored classes on teamwork and other subjects; community college courses; education planning sessions with team managers; and individualized instruction in factory tasks. PFK mandated that workers participate in these learning activities and document their skills. Significantly, this system was more than a structure for assigning requirements and rewards

351

for learning; PFK was so complex and important that it constituted an additional set of required work activities in itself.

## Theoretical Framework and Research Questions

### Literacy as Cultural Practice

There has long been an ongoing tension between two broad conceptions of literacy, one centered in a paradigm of *individual skills*, the other in a paradigm of *cultural practice*. Within the individual skills paradigm, literacy skills and activities are assumed to develop and operate through processes that are only marginally influenced by the social contexts in which they occur. From the cultural practice perspective, however, literacy is conceived as a set of social or cultural practices which are intimately bound to context (Goody, 1986; Heath, 1983; Scribner & Cole, 1981). Literacy development is seen as a process of socialization rather than as the result of decontextualized teaching and learning of skills. Individual differences in literacy result from differential access to and engagement in the functional roles associated with those cultural practices (Lave & Wenger, 1991; Reder, 1987, 1992).

Issues of literacy education, assessment, and instruction contrast sharply between these two paradigms. In the individual skills paradigm, literacy is essentially viewed as something which people carry around in their heads from setting to setting and from task to task. As Reder (1994) has described, there is a strong tendency in this paradigm to use the "dipstick model" of literacy: Individuals' (e.g., workers') literacy abilities are assessed by metaphorically opening up their heads and inserting a measuring instrument. If the dipstick shows "enough" literacy, then there are no literacy problems to worry about. But if the dipstick shows an individual to be a "quart down" (or less metaphorically, a grade-level down), it is assumed that formal instruction can add some more literacy to the "tank" and bring the individual's literacy level to the "fill line." The metaphorical fill lines, of course, are constructed as the "literacy requirements" of tasks, jobs, workplaces, or education and training programs. Contemporary "workplace literacy" programs, for example, usually have the objective of raising the literacy skills of individual workers to pre-specified levels which someone has determined are "required" for effective job performance. But critical observers of such efforts have pointed out that the productivity "problems" in such workplaces often have little to do with the basic skills of the workers (Balfanz, 1991; Darrah, 1992; Gowen, 1992; Hull, 1993; Schultz, 1992). Careful empirical observation and analysis indicate that contextually sensitive issues of organizational politics, power, and work design often underlie concerns which managers, policy makers, and, indeed, the public gloss as literacy problems (Darrah, 1992; Gowen, 1992; Hull, this volume).

The present study was conceptualized within the paradigm of literacy as cultural practice. Literacy is conceived as *the use of written materials in cultural practices*. Important practical and theoretical questions about the development and utilization of literacy in this paradigm include: (1) how the use of writing is incorporated into existing activities; (2) how writing is used to innovate new cultural practices; and (3) what processes underlie the socialization of the given practices (Reder, 1994). The recurrent, culturally patterned uses of writing in various activities constitute what Scribner and Cole (1981) termed *literacy practices*. Much ethnographic research has been carried out in recent decades about the nature, development and socialization of literacy practices across an impressive range of settings. Reviews are available elsewhere (e.g., Cook-Gumperz, 1986; Goody, 1968; Ferdman, Weber, & Ramirez, 1994).

Systematic research on literacy practices in workplace settings is far less abundant. Seminal work done by Scribner (1984) and colleagues demonstrated the extent to which workers' apparent abilities to manipulate work-related written materials are closely bound to the contexts of their use. Reder and Green's (1983) study of literacy in an Alaska fishing village and Gowen's (1992) study of literacy among hospital workers illustrated the extent to which literacy practices are situated in and shaped by features of the organizational, political and historical context. There has been considerable research within the past decade on the social and cognitive organization of work under the rubric of activity theory (e.g., Engestrom, 1991; Engestrom & Middleton, in press; Scribner & Sachs, 1990, 1992; Shaiken, in press). This work has tended to focus on the use of tools and technologies as mediators of activity systems. These studies of the fine microstructure of work activities demonstrate how closely coupled the use of written materials is with other communication and coordination techniques at work. Reder and Schwab (1989), for example, studied the ways in which various genres of oral and written communication were situated in the collective work of product engineering teams in a high-technology manufacturer. They found that communicative practices were organized in ways which seamlessly crossed the media boundaries between speech, writing, and electronic texts. This suggests that much of the activity-theoretic research on the incorporation of new and emerging technologies into the workplace may be generalizable to understanding the ways in which literacy (an "older" technology) is incorporated into activity systems in the workplace.

## Teamwork as Distributed Cognition

The functioning of teams in the workplace was analyzed in terms of distributed cognition (e.g., Hutchins & Klausen, in press; Linde, 1988; Suchman, in press). Communication and coordination of activity among members of a work team are seen as being situated in the patterned social interactions of the members as they collaborate to accomplish their collective tasks. Hutchins and Klausen's analysis of the work of a cockpit crew, for example, illustrates closely articulated relationships among the structural roles of team members, the task and contextual knowledge they bring to the endeavor, the ways in which they utilize shared tools and technologies in the work environment, and the strategies of cooperation and communication that underlie their collective accomplishment of work tasks. Suchman's careful studies of airport traffic controllers illustrate the ways in which such finely articulated collaborative arrangements are situated in the physical and cognitive workspace collectively constituted by the team. Linde's analysis of cockpit collaboration in police helicopter missions reveals just how closely such patterns of distributed cognition are fitted to the demand characteristics of the work task and environment.

Although there has been little parallel research on the ways in which team members collaborate when use of written materials is difficult for one or more members (as will be the case in the present study), there has been much research about the fundamentally collaborative nature of literacy practices in other settings. Shuman (1983), for example, has studied collaborative literacy in multiethnic urban neighborhoods. Fingeret (1983) has found that adults who lack literacy skills often collaborate closely with others in their social networks who have better control of written materials. Reder and Green (1983) characterized teamwork (often involving collaboration around literacy) in terms (if not in terminology) of distributed cognition within several domains of village life, including work activities such as fishing. So there is good reason to suppose that the distributed cognition framework will prove useful for understanding the development of teamwork in the present study.

## Literacy and Organizational Restructuring

Manufacturing industries, both across the world and in the United States, are increasingly "restructuring" (or considering it) in response to emerging changes in their industries: heightened global economic competition, the introduction of new manufacturing and information technologies, and the demands of changing market conditions such as shortened product cycles (Best, 1990). The restructuring often involves changing the social organization of production work, as by organizing production workers into self-managing product teams, responsible for many functional aspects of the product (e.g., designing and engineering the production process, maintaining inventory, manufacturing and assembling products, marketing and so forth). Such product-centered teams are widely believed to require more literacy (i.e., use of written materials) than do the traditional work configurations. Literacy is, according to such accounts, needed by team members to create and manipulate shared representations of work processes, to collectively identify and resolve problems as they arise, to monitor and refine the production processes, to maintain inventory, and so on.

Although there have been numerous accounts and even some careful descriptions of the changes undergone by individual companies (e.g., Shaiken, in press), there has been little research on whether such organizational changes require or even generate heightened levels of literacy in the workforce. The present study, by following a company closely as it restructures, attempts to track such changes in literacy and teamwork with ethnographic methods.

The implementation of a new skill-based compensation system as part of Hardy's restructuring is of particular interest in the study because it appears (at least on the surface) to put the company's money where its proverbial "mouth" is. Management is actually creating direct wage incentives for workers to acquire the literacy and teamwork skills which it asserts workers need to function effectively as members of the reorganized production teams. Unlike most "workplace literacy" programs—in which workers have far less if any direct incentive to acquire the skills which the management apparently wants them to have (cf. Gowen, 1992; Hull, this volume)—Hardy's new compensation system actually creates strong incentives for learning by linking pay directly to learning outcomes. Unfortunately, studies of a wide variety of such skill-based pay systems (e.g., Jenkins, Ledford, Gupta, & Doty, 1992) have focused on their features and implementation processes from a management perspective and have not yet addressed their complex impacts on workers and their learning. Broader reviews of the role of incentives in workplace education and training (e.g., Hirsch & Wagner, 1994) have also been more programmatically focused than learning outcome focused. The present study will attempt to look explicitly at the complex impact of pay-for-knowledge compensation on workers and on their development of literacy and teamwork.

### Research Questions

A number of interrelated research questions thus frame the current study:

- (How) do changes in the social organization of production work impact the literacy requirements of workers and the structure of the literacy practices in which they engage?
- Do the organizational innovations of direct incentives and support systems for acquisition of literacy and other work skills bring about desired participation in training, learning, and development of skills and knowledge?
- (How) do changes in the social organization of literacy practices affect workers' opportunities for learning and the educational processes available to them in the workplace?
- What range of impacts do the observed changes in teamwork, literacy, and teaching and learning processes have on workers?

### Research Approach

This study grew out of a long-term research project that used a multi-method approach (cf. Agar, 1986; Geertz, 1973). The aim of the study was to understand ways that variously structured educational incentives affect individuals' learning and career development, on the one hand, and ways that individuals' development and application of skills affect work environments, on the other hand. The Hardy research was one part of this wider set of studies.

Table 14.1 depicts the two phases of research activities carried out at Hardy during the two-and-a-half-year association between the authors and Hardy Industry personnel. Throughout both phases the Hardy Human Resources Department facilitated the research by providing statistical data and explanations of company policy as well as by stepping back to allow the authors autonomy and wide access to company locations and personnel. The two phases actually overlapped in time, but their emphases differed.

# Toward a Conceptualization of Literacy in the Workplace

This section presents the findings which contribute to a reconceptualization of workplace literacy as shared cultural practices that evolve with the social settings of which they are a part. These findings are organized into subsections on "The Pay-for-Knowledge Compensation System," "Teamwork," and "Literacy."

### The Pay-for-Knowledge Compensation System

Literacy was central to the PFK system. In addition to mandating that workers upgrade literacy and other skills to apply to production and meetings, the system used literacy as a means of documenting those skills.

Table 14.1: Research Activities

| Phase | Activities and Settings | Timeline |
|---|---|---|
| **1. Focus on the company context for manufacturing work:** Hardy Industries' evolving mission, organization, atmosphere, and PFK compensation system | **Observations of** production and assembly lines and on-site basic skills instruction | 1990 and 1991 |
| | **Interviews** with personnel at many levels of the company hierarchy | 1990 and 1991 |
| | **Collection and analysis of company databases, training materials, documents and employee surveys** on dates of hire, education and training, skills, team assignments, and attitudes towards restructuring | March 1992- October 1992 |
| **2. Focus on the roles of literacy and teamwork skills** in production, meetings, and the PFK system and the meanings of these skills for workers. | **Participant observation** in class for new employees | March 1992 |
| | **Participant observation** in team problem-solving class with interviews of class members | March and April 1992 |
| | **Participant observation** in meeting on Failure Mode Effects Analysis | May 1992 |
| | **Focus group** of Human Resource Department personnel on team "personalities" | May 1992 |
| | **Participant observation** of production and assembly lines, meetings, and individuals | September and October 1992 |

PFK was founded on the idea that success in the competitive global market for automobile parts demanded extensive changes in work organization. The management believed that the success of these changes in turn depended on workers' prowess in the interrelated areas of machine operation and communication. Since, as mentioned earlier, the company designed PFK to structure means and incentives for workers to develop such skills and knowledge, it is essential to understand this system as the context in which the teamwork and literacy under study took place. In what follows we explain the workings of PFK by examining the main activities comprising Hardy manufacturing jobs, the skills PFK outlined as necessary for these activities, ways that PFK promoted development of these skills, and workers' responses to this learning challenge.

*Production* was defined as making, assembling, or packaging parts or preparing materials and tools for the work that occurred on production or assembly lines. The direct results were products for the company to sell.

*Meetings* focused on work processes or settings. Participants usually left the lines and never made, assembled, or packed products in the meetings. There were two basic types of meetings: *team meetings* (weekly for most teams) to discuss and plan team activities and *work process meetings* to analyze and improve specific work processes or worksite standards. Work process meetings included sessions for writing FMEAs (Failure Mode Effects Analysis procedures), process control instructions, quality improvement processes, and worksite standards.

*Pay-for-Knowledge activities* involved workers in classes, tests, and assessments with peers and managers. Although some skills were assessed at production stations (as when an experienced worker "signed off" the skill of packing and labeling hubs correctly), all PFK activities were considered to be supplemental to, and different from, the task of producing hubs, etc.

*The Five Skill Blocks.* The PFK "Bible" was the notebook listing the skills workers used in their jobs and the associated assessment methods and pay levels. Five sections, or "blocks," arranged the skills from basic to advanced. Literacy was a major aspect of all five blocks. The lowest skill block, for example, included the ability to read parts lists and assemble parts to specification; apply the concepts of blueprint reading to interpret terminology, lines, views, and details; use basic math skills to assist the team in problem-solving or planning work activities; and make requests from, listen to, and deliver information to internal customers and document the interaction. The company increased an employee's pay $.15 an hour for each skill mastered, up to a maximum of 14 skills in this block. The literacy skills that were incorporated in the highest block included the ability to diagnose and solve problems with the complex CNC machines, design tools, and perform advanced product testing. College-level coursework was required to document attainment of many skills in this block: Wages rose by $.75 an hour, up to a maximum of four skills, for attainment of these skills. Teamwork skills, for example, problem-solving classes, meeting leadership, and a variety of cooperative tasks, also dotted the pages of the notebook.

*Skill Development and Documentation.* Each employee had to set and carry out his or her PFK goals, a process encompassing diverse literacy practices. In consultation with the team leader, the worker wrote a plan for acquiring specific skills and knowledge by taking courses (e.g., basic math or a high school equivalency program) or asking another employee for instruction (e.g., in packing a part, performing a statistical procedure, or setting up equipment for a new assemblage). To show that he or she had mastered a given lesson, the learner had to pass a course or test or have a qualified employee "sign it off" on the PFK skills sheet. The company offered some courses (e.g., shop math and team problem-solving) in the plant during work hours. To take other courses, workers enrolled at a community college on their own time, and the company paid tuition. All workers had to take certain classes (e.g., team problem-solving); other requirements depended on individuals' needs and ambitions as outlined in their PFK plans. Since many workers performed operations that others needed to learn, the system led them to become teachers and assessors of skills, as well as learners trying to upgrade their own skills. Literacy learning was incorporated in courses, new tasks for which workers sought to upgrade their skills, assessments (in which they were either assessed or assessors), and management of their personal PFK paperwork (detailing the skills they needed and plans for acquiring them, etc.).

*Workers' Responses to the PFK Education Requirements.* As we have shown, PFK was the company's system for constructing literacy, teamwork, and skill development as interrelated sets of practices. This section describes workers' educational backgrounds as the backdrop against which the PFK activities must be viewed. Workers' responses to the opportunities to participate in events that would upgrade skills levels on the PFK are presented to illustrate the wide range of opinions and attitudes, as well as the important role of literacy in PFK activities.

The educational background of the company's production workforce varied from little or no schooling to college degrees. Although the current policy was to hire only people who had a high school diploma or equivalence certificate, approximately 20% of the production workers had been hired before this policy came into effect and had earned neither of these. Those workers who had graduated from high school tended to have little experience applying their literacy skills to specialized technical tasks and collaboration at work. Management and training personnel saw these graduates not as "paper and pencil types" but as "shop types who barely graduated from high school." Many had worked at the company ever since graduating from local high schools.

359

Many Hardy workers embraced the PFK system as a way to diversify their work activities, increase their wages, and advance their status at work and outside the factory. For some, however, PFK meant that they had to gain PFK skills within the next three years in order to retain the wage level they already had attained. These people tended to be older workers who, by virtue of their long employment at Hardy, were earning more under the old compensation system than they would earn under the PFK system (when it was fully implemented) unless they increased their skills in the three-year "grace period." Employees at various levels of the organization, including those older workers, called this situation a "transitional problem" because they expected it to disappear when the older workers retired. This is an example of the fact that the literacy demands of the workplace changed compensation patterns. In this case, the compensation patterns changed in a different way for those with many years of experience than they did for those with less experience. Daniels (1983, p. 144) suggests that the recent emphasis on testing over experience to determine workers' skills may allow "the test to win," causing experienced, skilled workers to lose their jobs. Many Hardy workers expressed the same concern.

Although workers' PFK activities and the meanings associated with them varied, common patterns existed. The passages below illustrate both the importance of literacy in PFK activities and the diversity of workers' reactions to them. (Literacy in PFK activities is discussed again in a later section.)

*"Does Dave get paid for being meeting facilitator?"* At the conclusion of a Rescue Winch Team meeting, Jeff addressed this question to Todd, his team leader. Todd's answer: "Yes." "Then I want to do it too!" Jeff shot back. Employees were apt to be eager to find or create opportunities for developing new skills which would be compensated.

After designating Jeff as facilitator for the next meeting, Todd commenced an informal lesson on one of the facilitator's tasks, agenda writing: "Not to knock [criticize] the way Teresa did it [in the previous meeting], but you're supposed to put the topics down without the names—the way Dave did. But you both [Teresa and Dave] did a good job."

Jeff's question illustrates the way some workers actively sought the chance to develop the skills which PFK identified and rewarded. Acquisition of facilitation skills, in this instance, went hand-in-glove with using the skill in the context of an actual meeting. Assessment of learning progress occurred at the same time, as Todd's comparison of Teresa and Dave shows.

*"I don't want to drive a Hyster for ten cents an hour!"* Workers didn't always perceive "rewards" the same way managers did. Linda of the Miscellaneous Hub Team resented the pressure to learn many skills. A 36-year-old assembler who came to Hardy six years ago as a recently divorced mother with no high school diploma, she was ambivalent about Hardy's education require-

ments, but not about education in general. She described the importance of her daughter's recent graduation from high school and went on to say that, of course, she wanted to continue her own education too, but on her own schedule. Her reason for resisting what she called the company's "pressure" to learn forklift driving: In a company where she had worked previously a woman was crushed to death under one. (A serious forklift accident had also occurred at Hardy in recent weeks.) She also thought that the company was doing too much cross-training (i.e., teaching workers each other's jobs) for its own good: "Everyone's riding around in a forklift!"

Unlike Jeff in the previous passage, Linda did not welcome the chance to learn the skill under discussion. Taking into account the financial reward for driving a Hyster ("ten cents an hour") and the perceived risk (physical danger), she concluded that neither she nor the company benefit from "everyone" having the skill. Linda helps us see that while an individual may value education in general, the meaning of a particular workplace learning opportunity depends more on the particular circumstances under which it is offered than on some general value of new skills.

*"I never imagined that I could operate this machine!"* Emily, a 40-year-old assembler on the Rescue Winch Team, expressed elation after completing her first week operating the Kaltinger, a machine that, according to experienced operators, took at least five years to "know." Sometimes workers appreciated a new skill even though they had acquired it only because it was mandatory. Before entering the labor market Emily had "stayed at home" with her two sons until they left home. She still considered herself a homemaker; for instance, she was engrossed in settling into a new house. Adamant that her primary aim at Hardy was to do routine work, not to assume extensive responsibility during work hours or take classes after hours, Emily initially resented the fact that, in the new environment, she was expected to extend her aims in both these directions. Her team leader, in the interest of "cross-training," assigned Emily to the Kaltinger, an assignment she dreaded. Surprising herself and her teammates, Emily operated the Kaltinger effectively and felt proud to add this accomplishment to her list of PFK skills.

At first, Emily, like Linda in the earlier illustration, was ambivalent about the pressure to learn a specific skill, but after giving in to the pressure she became enthusiastic about her new capability. Hardy skill assessments (on which pay was based) had a profound effect on Linda's (and many others') participation in formal education and other learning activities. Developing skills that she had "never imagined having" became normal, due to the company's mix of pressure, encouragement, opportunity, and incentives.

*"You need the courses if you really want to understand [the machine]."* Some workers believed that, although they already could operate "their" machinery

adequately, relevant courses would make them experts. On the Rescue Winch Team, Chuck, a gray-haired machine specialist who had been operating a Kaltinger skillfully for many years, took a night course on programming the Kaltinger's high-tech successor, a CNC machine which he was already operating for the plant. Ill health caused him to quit the course once, but he enrolled for a second time. Although he felt that he could have challenged the class by passing a test, he decided to ensure proficiency by passing the class itself. Next he planned to take algebra and trigonometry, because he liked math and believed the knowledge would improve his performance on the CNC.

Highlighting the relationship between academic skills and work performance, Chuck voiced the opinion (shared by some other workers) that certain academic classes were valuable for equipping workers to do certain jobs. In fact, he so believed in the value of his programming course that he passed up the chance to secure the PFK certification by simply passing the test. In contrast, some operators of simpler machines did not find required mathematics courses worthwhile for improving their performance. These individuals considered themselves experts on their machines as a result of their experience and therefore did not think that classes were worthwhile for them. No class, they said, could increase their own effectiveness or, in the case of new workers, substitute for experience.

The data in this section on PFK have shown how the new system caused workers, many of whom had seen themselves primarily as producers, assemblers, and packers of parts, to add participation in several types of meetings to their slates. In addition, a major part of their work became learning and being assessed in (or teaching and assessing others in) the skills that the company identified as essential for production and meetings.

Organizing their own PFK work demanded advanced literacy and other communication skills. As the illustrations of workers' responses to this system suggest, reactions to it were varied. Some employees sought to expand the learn-to-earn opportunities PFK represented. Others found the opportunities hollow. Objectors claimed that skills were insufficiently remunerated, risky (e.g., potentially revealing one's low skill levels), time-consuming, and irrelevant to production. Opinions were diverse, but frequent, fervent discussion of PFK (in whispers, when the speakers perceived their words to be anti-management) indicated that workers commonly believed that PFK strongly affected their chances of success at Hardy. Beyond concern about literacy and other skills, they expressed concern about operating within the system to their own advantage. Thus, literacy and social competence were unified in the new system for establishing one's worth as a worker.

## *Teamwork*

Having described the PFK context and the three main categories of work activities (production, meetings, and the PFK system itself), we now analyze the role of teamwork as an aspect of manufacturing jobs. Although literacy is addressed separately in a later section, the descriptions of teamwork here show that literacy and teamwork are inextricably related. Teams formed the social crucibles in which literacy and all other work practices were formed, and these settings presented dilemmas and resources which could promote or retard skills development.

Hardy manufacturing and assembly employees did not frequently talk about their literacy skills, reading levels, or related concepts, but they did frequently discuss "teamwork." (Darrah [1992, this volume] has pointed out that, although production work is primarily a social process, the workers he studied in a wire and cable factory perceived machinery and production, not communication, as central to their jobs.) Although the firm's explicit emphasis on teamwork probably contributed to workers' awareness of it, they stated frequently throughout the research that the main reasons for this awareness were that: (1) their jobs continually demanded it, and (2) it was extremely challenging.

*Teamwork in Production.* Work to produce automobile parts was highly cooperative. The paragraphs below illustrate the organization and challenge of teamwork: ways individuals tried to "keep their teams going" and teams supported their members, and individual construction of the meaning of teamwork. In coordinating team activities, workers created, transmitted, and interpreted written documents. In addition to helping them carry out their work, literacy was also an ever-present tool for negotiating tasks and their meanings.

When Nate, a 45-year-old machinist who had left high school after tenth grade and had not earned a GED, reflected on teamwork, he emphasized its role in production work:

> [Teamwork takes] a lot of smarts! I never really fell into it too much. If one person's goofing off . . . we get into a group about it . . . go at it at a positive level. In [the team I belonged to previously] everyone had their own benches. [There were] different kinds of kits. . . . Each kind had a row [down which the worker walked to collect all the parts needed to assemble one kit]. You went shopping for your parts and checked off on a pick list when you had them. If someone is off or sick, you do their job and yours *and* keep the flow going.

363

Nate's description encompasses three topics which recur in other workers' analyses of teamwork. First, workers often underscored the *difficulty* of teamwork. Nate, who was not confident about his intellectual skills, phrased the challenge in terms of "smarts." His second topic was group *problem-solving*, a common practice in the restructured plant. In one instance of this practice, Melissa, a W808 Assembly Team member spontaneously "stopped the line" (plant jargon for halting a production or assembly line) for a few minutes to discuss the cause of a recurring defect in a hub. As the team spokesperson, she made decisions on the line when the team leader was absent. Occasionally a team scheduled a formal meeting to solve a recurring problem.

Nate's third topic was the *organization of teamwork* on the assembly line. He saw his main task as an independent one, but, if a coworker was absent, the demands of the team came to the fore. Line work meant collaboration, because, as one worker put it, "there is always someone waiting for your work and you are always waiting for someone else's work."

In analyzing Nate's production work (and all other production work in the factory) it is insufficient to say that teamwork was *applied* to the work. Rather, the entire process *was* teamwork, requiring continual communication about, and observation of, what others were doing. Literacy was one important medium for this communication, as Nate's pick lists illustrate. At the same time that Nate was doing teamwork and literacy, he was developing teamwork and literacy skills that he found extremely difficult. Teamwork socialized people to do literacy at the same time that literacy socialized people to do teamwork.

Individuals nurtured their team to keep the line running smoothly. During one lunch break several 611-C Team members, including spokesperson Melissa, sat around their work area to eat and chat. Melissa "took care of things" while the team leader was away and led the team in a daily exercise session. (One worker facetiously referred to her as the team's "mother.") During lunch Melissa made cracks about her bad mood. "I'm really bratty today," she remarked, and then ribbed two teammates about their own bad moods. Back on the line after lunch, she continued to make loud, cheerful remarks which seemed forced, for workers usually talked little on the line. Apparently Melissa was consciously using a strategy to induce smooth teamwork, as suggested by her query to the observer: "How's our communication today?"

Melissa had a distinctive style for trying to exert control over her team's mood. Similarly, many workers made conscious efforts to "keep their teams going." Literacy was not left out of these attempts, as when two women exchanged written accounts of an incident that had led them to disagree. Not all attempts to smooth over team relations employed writing. Workers on 611-C strategized to keep a "difficult" worker from slowing their line speed, and some pairs took turns at unpleasant clean-up chores. Teamwork was at the forefront of people's minds, and literacy was one tool for supporting it.

A team sometimes worked together at nurturing an individual member to improve the entire line's performance. The Rexford, a machine for grinding metal bars into components for automobile accessories, "crashed." Teresa was just concluding her first week operating it. Team members milled around, trying to figure out the cause of the crash. To anyone who was listening, Teresa expressed her guilty feelings: "It had to have something to do with the operator." Jeff disagreed, "The same thing has happened to all of us." Then he warned her that the tooling experts assigned to troubleshoot this problem probably would tease her as they teased all operators involved in such breakdowns. Immediately an expert arrived and took Teresa aside to talk to her. Later another young machinist on the team, Carrie, told the observing author that the problem on Teresa's machine had *not been* her fault: It was the machine's. "Some of the best machinists come out from a situation where the machine crashes all the time," Carrie maintained.

In the aftermath of the breakdown, an item on the team meeting agenda was: "Update on the Rexford." Chuck, the team's oldest worker, with years of experience operating and fixing the machine, recounted that after the crash he had "rebuilt," "remade," "realigned," and "recentered" all the Rexford parts which had been "wiped out really bad," "burnt up," "shoved back," and "had gullies in them." After participants stopped chuckling at the extent of Chuck's chores, he asserted, "It's not Teresa's fault." But Teresa still seemed worried about her culpability: "It was only the second time I've loaded bars . . . but Emily loaded a similar bar [with no resulting breakdown]."

Participants then launched into a technical analysis of bar size and developed a new recording procedure for tracking undersized bars to prevent future breakdowns. Thus the team's response to the breakdown was to support Teresa and attempt to improve the production process by creating a new type of written record. This incident was not unusual at Hardy in terms of the attempt to avoid blaming an individual. (The issue of individual responsibility did arise at times, however, because management emphasized the *individual* duty to maintain high standards as well as *team* responsibility.)

At first glance, the Rexford breakdown simply suggests that a positive environment encourages literacy learning. With scrutiny, however, the incident reveals a recursive relationship between successful teamwork and skills development. Several participants' knowledge of the machine and bar size, not just their good will, first led to the interpretation that Teresa had not been at fault and then to a diagnosis of the problem. The team harnessed the same knowledge to the task of creating a recording system for preventing a future breakdown. Thus teamwork benefited *from* literacy and other skills as much as it contributed to them.

An interview with Sean, a worker who assembled parts on the Gear 44 Team, afforded a view of an individual constructing his own meanings of Hardy teamwork. As he spoke about his transactions with employees in several roles, he showed how he developed his own concept of teamwork—within the context of company policy and practice, but not blindly accepting the company's concept of how people did or should work together. The interview excerpts show, for example, how he built personal meanings that differed from the company's official meanings for the phrases "employee empowerment," "rights," and "a bankable idea." Sean provided background to his understanding of design/assembly relationships and the factory system for improving production:

> I took two classes on ergonomics and design for assembly. Of course people *have got* to have machine skills, but they also could use some design skills . . . . The company's emphasis on employment empowerment—the education is too fractured to help focus on that. The company really wants to increase empowerment. I have suggested putting into the quality manual required design review by assemblers of the designs. We get pilot runs we've never seen before. I act as a mouthpiece. I hear about problems and go to talk to the engineer. Others could go too, but I'm getting better at knowing how to hassle them because I was on swing shift. There it's hard to feel you can communicate with anybody, so I got to doing end-runs around the bosses, not just bringing [suggestions] to the boss in the meeting. In this company [I found out that] you have the right to write a maintenance work order. . . . Maybe they don't want you to know you can do that [because] it would lead to a flurry of things that don't really need to be done.

Sean's reflections revealed the understandings of company policy that he had formed through interaction with company personnel. In his opinion: Assemblers should take courses on design and review designs before they are piloted; in order to be heard, one had to do "end-runs" through unofficial channels of communication; and management concealed the "right" to submit a work order. Sean's words hint that he thought the company's intentions to empower employees were not manifest in the ways they dealt with them. Asked for an example of an attempt he had made to get engineers to pay attention to a suggestion, Sean recounted what happened to his idea to use flag labels instead of labels that totally wrap around gears:

> I filled out a form for a bankable idea. If it passes, you get ten bucks. I gave two options [worth $20]. [The engineers] didn't accept my idea, so I started talking to the inspector. I did my own study [which showed] it would have saved time. So I went around [the engineers]—went to the purchaser directly to learn the cost for a label half as long. [After several rounds of communication] the engineer finally gave his approval. So it got implemented. But I never got the $20.

To Sean, the meaning of this episode was:

> If people try to go through [official] channels [it won't work]. . . . Individuals think you can just hand over an idea. But you can't. We also need to be able to talk to engineers. The only reason I didn't talk to the engineer myself is they wouldn't tell me who he was because I would of ripped his head off. It took six to eight months from the original idea to finally getting it in. The bankable system is still used—now the only problem is finding an engineer who has some time to do it. I came up with a tooling idea—an engineer has to draw it up. We have five or six team engineers. You get to know which ones deal with which gears. They are usually receptive but look like "Oh God, another thing to do!"

Our analysis extends Sean's own. The excerpt relates how his experience endowed the company slogans (e.g., "bankable idea"), stated intentions (e.g., "employee empowerment"), and principles of organization (e.g., teamwork among employees in different roles) with meanings which took into account, but also departed from, company meanings. The process of running company concepts through the mill of social interaction yielded Sean's own meanings of the company's terms and the social order to which they referred. Literacy played a powerful role in this social process. Sean mentioned many communication events entailing literacy. It is important to note, though, that these events—work with classes, designs, the quality manual, forms for bankable ideas, and maintenance orders—combined skills in reading and writing with other communication skills (e.g., speaking and listening) and knowledge about company social structure and economics. Thus, to understand Sean's application of literacy to production teamwork requires attention to the interlocking of many kinds of skills and knowledge.

We have seen that teamwork in production entails multiple skills to coordinate work on the line, maintain smooth interpersonal relationships, and negotiate production processes both with peers and with individuals of higher status. Written communication is often used for accomplishing these ends.

*Teamwork in Meetings.* Collaboration to analyze and improve work processes was a common aim of meetings. Literacy practices had a high profile in these meetings; they were used to analyze, record, and suggest improvements in work processes. One type of work process meeting focused on the Failure Mode Effects Analysis (FMEA) described earlier. Individuals with various responsibilities for a product (design, production, assembly, quality control, etc.) followed an intricate procedure to trace and document their work. Together, they determined and described in writing the probabilities of production problems, their effects, and ways to prevent them.

Archie, the W808 Assembly team quality technician, described FMEA meetings:

> The main purpose is to get the point of view [of each person involved in producing a part]. Engineers always have done this but they have not included the manufacturers' and assemblers' knowledge. I could have done this whole FMEA myself and might have come out with the same thing, but there's always the chance you'd miss something. Irwin [a manufacturing employee], in the last meeting, raised details about the size of the hub rim I would have missed. I learned a lot in the meeting. The others probably did too . . . . The key to good teamwork is understanding. Respect. It's amazing what people can do if they are treated with respect.

Archie pointed to a specific pay-off that effective collaboration had offered the company: Because he was able hear others' points of view, a problem with a hub was avoided. Archie, and other interviewees knew that teamwork is no simple, monolithic skill. Thus, to describe the FMEA meeting, Archie found it necessary to articulate the philosophy behind his teamwork: "It's amazing what people can do if they are treated with respect."

In this episode, Archie's skills were tied to Irwin's, rather than residing in the head (or behavior) of one of the two men. Archie contributed to the pairs' shared expertise his recognition that Irwin comprehended the rim problem and his understanding that learning was the kernel of this meeting, indeed of teamwork in general. Archie believed that close attention to the fundamentals of good human relations ("understanding" and "respect") in which one listens and incorporates others' views into one's own yielded successful interaction. Thus, according to his account, he actively encouraged teamwork that fostered shared cognition which avoided problems.

*Teamwork in PFK Activities.* Like production and meetings, the PFK system rested on a high degree of collaboration in which workers used a variety of practices to develop, interpret, and pass on documents. In establishing the PFK system , employees from all levels of the firm's hierarchy had analyzed their tasks and suggested methods for assessing and documenting the separate skills involved. As the compensation system was being implemented, close collegiality with superiors and peers continued to be necessary for line workers to find their positions or advance in the system.

The case of Nate illustrates the close cooperation that characterized the efforts line workers made to handle the PFK system. This case is interesting for the cooperation between a worker and his team leader, Max. Nate admitted to Max that he felt threatened by the plant atmosphere charged with education concerns, specifically the demands to take literacy classes. Like several other workers with low skills, he charged the company with requiring too much education, that is, classes after work on top of classes and continual learning at work. Max described his own response: "Nate has asked me not to sign him up for too many classes. . . . It all came out. . . . He has the struggle of outside as well as inside classes." In addition, Max tried to design "a better learning environment" for Nate on the shop floor: You don't want to ever make him uncomfortable. . . . I'll never put him in a position he's apt to fail at . . . I don't dare give him written instructions."

Max's helpful attitude was not uncommon among team leaders. One of their responsibilities was to encourage individuals to develop programs which fit their own style and speed, for instance, study from workbooks rather than attend classes, advance at their own pace, and take classes more than once. Support among peers was also common. Later we see an example in an account of Anne teaching Charlotte how to keep records.

Nate and Max striving together to render the plant environment an effective educational setting for Nate is an example of team organization leading to educational alternatives for a worker who wanted very much to increase his literacy skills. At the same time the PFK system helped to open doors to literacy development, it constrained workers' choices in designing their education programs. Teams may have been nurturing (as the discussion of teamwork on the production line indicates), but their primary purpose was production, not learning.

*The Roles of Individuals in Teamwork.*   At times, teamwork for production, meetings, and the PFK system appeared to engage Hardy workers and their managers in seamless interaction in which they were almost unaware of their cooperation. However, many episodes recorded in the fieldnotes (including the line breakdown described earlier) revealed how deliberately individuals made investments in collective work. These investments often entailed developing and applying literacy skills in the context of plant life.

Hardy workers often maintained that the most taxing communication skills were cooperation and sensitivity to others' viewpoints. Teresa, a 26-year-old machine operator on the Rescue Winch Team, listed the skills which teamwork demanded of her personally:

> Phrasing things right; getting in a circle to solve problems; finding a way to agree; understanding the function of a job—how a part and the process [for making it] fit into the whole picture; getting a second opinion on what's wrong with a part; learning that it can't be *my* way—it's got to be *our* way; communication—blueprint reading, writing, reading the micrometer, doing basic math, proportions—for checking on a process sheet and detecting failure on the [assembly] line.

Teresa's expression of this interpersonal aspect of teamwork was enthusiastic and original. First, she analyzed the subtle abilities of effective teamwork: being able to perceive her own activity as part of the larger work process and having an attitude that "it can't be *my* way." Only then did she touch on more technical "blueprint reading, writing," and so forth. The way she listed these "communication skills" sounded like a recitation from the PFK notebook. Her emphasis on social relations as the kernel of teamwork ("getting a second opinion . . . learning that it can't be *my* way—it's got to be *our* way") was a common opinion at the plant. For Teresa, the demand for social skills was weighty enough that she took great pains to analyze them.

Individuals struggled to apply the principles of teamwork at work and at home. Will, an energetic Miscellaneous Hub team member to whom others looked for guidance, noted: "Some of the new skills do contribute to productivity, some *don't*. People have to *apply* the skills—it all comes from personal motivation." In this vein, Margaret of the 611-C Team referred several times to her attempts to solve problems the "Working Class way," that is, following the problem-solving manual used in a required course by that name. Several workers related attempts to extend their new teamwork skills into their domestic lives. One man claimed that the problem-solving techniques he had learned in class had kept his daughter from going to jail.

These accounts of individuals' teamwork efforts illustrate the richness of meanings that team participation held for all the workers who were interviewed. The literacy practices that were incumbent in teamwork also took on these rich meanings. Thus, to learn how to perform a simple literacy task in the abstract was less the challenge than to learn how to get along with others and apply the literacy task in real situations. The lesson for workplace literacy education is how to structure settings to engender teaching and learning for competence in such real situations.

Literacy was a fundamentally collaborative enterprise that served workers in their coordination of complex production processes. Just as a shared repertoire of literacy practices can propel teamwork, lack of such a shared repertoire can retard teamwork. On the one hand, when tasks are highly cooperative, one worker with an inadequate grasp of the practices can bring the whole group down. On the other hand, in such a situation, all the players have a built-in incentive—their own success—to teach the one who needs to learn. Thus, the relationships between teamwork and literacy spiral, as one influences the other to more or less success, depending on the dynamics of the particular situation. Opportunities to foster teamwork and literacy skills together (so that they spiral upward to improve performance) fluctuate with lines of power, communication styles, equipment design, work organization, and other factors. The key to workplace restructuring that encourages effective teamwork and literacy development lies in understanding the interplay among these factors.

## Literacy

The teamwork configuration and compensation system called for wide-ranging literacy practices in almost all work settings. The examples of literacy in this section depict the crucial role literacy played in the three major categories of activity which comprised work at Hardy. As a consequence of the emphasis on literacy skills in all three categories, literacy was a major element in the definition of competence. As Cook-Gumperz (1986) has discussed, literacy skills are not simply technical skills, but context-bound prescriptions for specific uses of written materials. Their mastery was essential for success at Hardy.

Figure 14.1 shows these categories of work activity and the emphasis on literacy in each category. The triangle representing the emphasis on literacy is narrow in the row representing production because literacy is relatively infrequent (but not unimportant) during production. The triangle widens in the row representing meetings because the frequency of literacy in work activities increases as activities become distant from production. The breadth of the triangle where it crosses Pay-for-Knowledge activities stands for the relatively great role of literacy in the assessment system.

Figure 14.1: Literacy Practices during Production Meetings and Pay-for-Knowledge Activities

☐ Categories of Work Activity  ■ Work-related Literacy Activities

| *Pay-for-Knowledge* Activities for Assessing and Acquiring Production-related Skills |
| *Meetings* about Production |
| *Production* of Automobile Accessories |

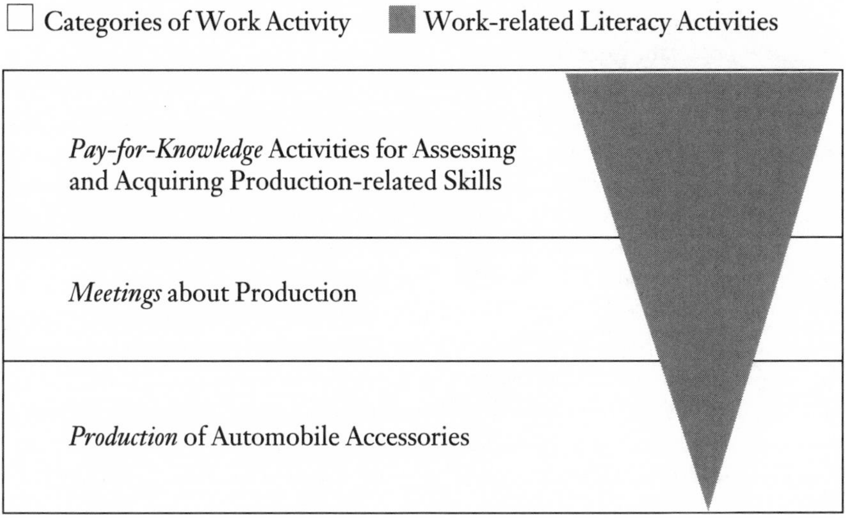

*Literacy in Production.* The data on Hardy indicate clearly that literacy was important to production. Workers who had been at Hardy before the introduction of product-centered teams and PFK reported that the restructuring had extended their responsibilities both on and off the production line. Some important literacy practices were routine, for example, tagging defective parts, reading and making labels (cf. Hull, this volume), and other similarly brief, but essential, tasks. Some members of each team usually had additional literacy tasks to take care of right near the line at the end of a shift, day, or week. These tasks, occurring during the five-minute clean-up period at the end of the shift, were a matter of recording parts produced and materials used. Examples were reading work orders and calculating and reporting the numbers of products produced. These ongoing routine communication tasks required workers to collect data from teammates, read many lines of fine print with technical vocabulary, calculate averages, and practice other literacy (and teamwork) skills.

Non-routine literacy tasks also were central to the production process. Anne, a member of the 611-C Team, created such a task for herself when she designed a dryer for the parts she assembled. She sought this challenge in order to eliminate a bottleneck that occurred because she had to wait for her parts to dry before she could assemble them. A portion of the sketch she gave Norm, the team tool design engineer, to get him to build or purchase the dryer for her is shown in Figure 14.2. Anne showed more initiative than some workers, but her request was not out of order. Norm frequently consulted with assemblers, demonstrating equipment and eliciting suggestions for improvements. Anne defined her job to include machine design. Although we can't know all the motivations behind Anne's decision to design the dryer, the episode does suggest that PFK incentives, a receptive engineer, and a production line problem, were among the strong situational factors. How workers tie existing literacy practices to innovative ends, and how they learn effective ways to do this, as Anne did, are important questions for grounding effective workplace literacy training.

Whether routine or unusual, literacy tasks were essential for performing Hardy production work. Most of these tasks required command of technical vocabulary; familiarity with specialized forms; ability to calculate, report, and read data about production; or other complex skills.

*Literacy in Meetings.* In all meetings observed for this study, participants referred to, and/or created, documents. As explained earlier, the company had added meetings to workers' jobs in the belief that communication among the workers who were involved in the multiple steps of producing the same product would lead them to build more and better parts. Written communications about the design and production steps were often the main subject of meetings. To understand the new work configuration, it is therefore important to examine the role of literacy in meetings. The sole aim of one type of meeting, called "work process meetings" was to create and interpret technical documents describing the way parts were made. In this regard, a work process meeting in which Judy, Steve, and Ethan analyzed Judy's production work was typical. Judy was a 41-year-old assembler whose production job was to work alone (as a "cell" within the 611-C Team) to build four types of hubs. The other participants, Ethan and Steve, were engineers. Judy's task at the

Figure 14.2: Anne's Design for a Dryer

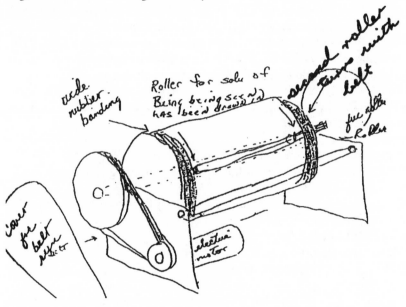

work process meeting was to help write process-control instructions (required by the automobile manufacturer who bought the products from Hardy). These were detailed instructions for making one of "her" hub types, the 470A.

Before coming to the meeting, Judy created and collected documents to bring with her. First she jotted a list of the names and numbers of machines she used to assemble the 470A hub. Then she searched the cabinet in her assembly area for other relevant sheets. This was a task in itself, for the cabinet held the paperwork of another cell as well as her own: notebooks, books, print-outs, and other sheets, including statistical analyses she had created pertaining to each of "her" hubs. From the cabinet she extracted minutes of the last meeting about her cell; a list of processes required on each type of hub she assembled; the old process-control instructions and materials list for the 470A hub; and the process-control instructions for another of "her" hubs, the model for rewriting the instructions for the 470A.

At the meeting, Judy collaborated with Ethan and Steve to create new process-control instructions. Steve opened the meeting by reviewing their list of tasks and getting Judy's opinion on a number of questions: What would be the best sequence of agenda items? Was the due date realistic? Which secretary would type their document? When would the team leader have time to take photos? What sorts of diagrams would be inserted? Then the three participants delved into "writing" the instructions. Actually, they created new instructions by editing the recently rewritten instructions for a different hub, the 480, to render a representation of the assembly process for the 470A. (The same writing strategy occurred in other work-process meetings.)

The following dialogue shows that Judy was an authority on her assembly procedures. Together, she and Ethan negotiated the description of the actual assembly process by referring to her experience as well as the factory's written work process instructions:

Ethan: Wait a minute. You can't do that with this [hub]. [Judy demonstrated with the actual hub casement and spring on the table that it could be done.]
Ethan: [reading the old process instructions] Put the spring down lady! [laughs]
Judy: O.K. but we *had* to do this first.
Ethan: [reads her the sequence as *written*]
Judy: [reasserting the order of *actual* assembly] I do them at the same time.
Ethan: Well it says here [on the written description]. . . . So let's reword this [to represent the procedure Judy uses].

Both Ethan and Judy implicitly acknowledged her decisive role in the meeting. At first Ethan tried to hurry her by saying, "I gotta get out of here pretty quick!" and "Are we almost done with the process?" Judy's calm response was, "I'm gonna lock the door." When Judy had figured out which of two parts they were supposed to write about, Ethan quipped, "Go ahead, make up my mind for me." Judy's directions did not mean that Ethan always had a passive role. It was he who decided that Judy should scrawl pencil edits on process instructions for the 480 hub and materials list. When they needed extra copies to edit, he was the one who dashed out to photocopy them. In other meetings for writing about work processes, a similar specialization tended to occur: Line workers provided knowledge about that work while engineers and team leaders contributed technical expertise about creating documents—formatting, wording, editing, and instructions for the secretary.

At the end of the meeting Judy gathered her own notes and written products of the group's collective work. These included: a seven-item list of things to do or get someone else to do (e.g., reminding the team leader that the group was waiting for him to take photos of assembly equipment to insert in the process control instructions); a copy of the 480 process control instructions which had been edited to become the 470A process control instructions; an old materials list, edited to represent the materials currently being used to assemble the 470A; and a book she planned to "go through at home" to find machine numbers to insert in process-control instructions which had been written previously.

Judy's participation in this meeting illustrated the considerable literacy, teamwork, and organizational skills which manufacturing workers routinely applied in co-producing a document about their work on the line. Although the literacy and teamwork practiced at meetings did not directly produce hubs, they strongly influenced hub production. The literacy task before Judy, Ethan, and Steve was to use existing documents, past experience, and trials with equipment in the room to create the required instructions. "Writing" is too simple a word to describe this complex interaction, for the process of creation included editing, copying, composing, and correcting text. Moreover, document creation was only one facet of the agenda. The pair needed to educate each other in a variety of matters as they proceeded. For instance, Judy told Ethan how the part was built before they could represent the process on paper, and Ethan informed Judy about the secretary's requirements. This interactive socialization, part and parcel of the literacy practice, suggests that individuals learning discrete skills are not fully preparing for the kind of work and learning that was the hallmark of Hardy meetings.

The detailed description of a particular meeting illustrates how attention to detail is necessary to unravel the relationships between literacy practices and their contexts. Meetings varied widely across the plant, even when they were of the same general type, for example, team meetings. The sole focus of Judy's meeting with the engineers, like other work process meetings, was to create and interpret technical documents. In contrast, most team meetings emphasized oral team problem solving and interpersonal relations. Meetings varied within types as well, but the socialization of participants in literacy practices was a part of each.

*Literacy in PFK Activities.*   Just as literacy practices occurred simultaneously with production and meetings, literacy was endemic to PFK activities. But, in a neat twist, PFK was not just a way to measure and gain literacy skills for production and meetings; the compensation system became a set of literacy tasks in itself. These tasks required one to apply advanced literacy skills in order to determine one's position and advance in the system.

An example is the way a worker applied literacy skills to "get PFK skills signed off." On the morning of the observation, Kim had just been hired in a permanent position on the 611-C Team. She left her work station to get her PFK assessment sheet from her locker and showed it to Claire, her informal mentor for learning how to steer through the PFK system. Claire asked whether a certain skill was in Block One or Block Two. When Kim didn't know the answer, Claire directed her to get a copy of the PFK notebook from the team leader, Bob. Regarding another skill Kim wanted to get signed off, Claire said, "Josh [the company trainer] will do it." Claire quizzed Kim about a third skill, discovering that Kim knew how to build a certain winch but not how to box it. "Can you get this signed off?," Claire probed. "I can ask," Kim responded hopefully. Claire told her to call someone from the team that made the winch. The pair discussed which individual to call. Claire pointed out the list of plant phone numbers under the phone near their assembly line. Kim decided, "Nah, I'll do it during break!"

Thus, individually and collaboratively, Kim and Claire used the PFK notebook, phone number list, and skills sheet to fulfill PFK procedures. In this illustration of literacy socialization, Kim and Claire were coupling literacy with other communication media—face-to-face interaction and the telephone. The exchange sheds light on the effects that the PFK incentive system had on learning: The two workers responded by developing a mentor/novice relationship in which they used literacy, in this case not so much to develop new skills for production or meetings as to certify Kim's credentials in the assessment system itself.

### Discussion

The perspective on literacy development employed in this research integrates two views that were helpful for understanding the significance and embeddedness of literacy in a work environment organized around teams. One is the overarching view of *literacy as cultural practices* that are inextricable from workplace social settings. When an institution like Hardy organizes workers into teams, links teamwork skills to literacy development, and structures incentives accompanied by learning opportunities to advance teamwork and literacy skills, it promotes patterns of distributed cognition in literacy practices. The other view looks at *teaching and learning literacy as pervasive aspects of social interaction* through which people share and formulate literacy practices and their meanings.

Indicating the importance of literacy, as well as its situated nature, Table 14.2 shows a range of literacy practices associated with each of the three categories of work activity—production, meetings, and PFK activities. (The display does not indicate salience, frequency, or duration of these practices.) The practices, performed by individuals and groups, were key tasks in Hardy manufacturing jobs, and many were learned in part as they were performed.

Table 14.2: Literacy Practices in the Three Main Categories of Work Activity

**1. Literacy Practices in Production**

| | |
|---|---|
| checking off parts on pick list | tagging defective parts |
| blueprint reading | reading and making labels |
| reading micrometer | recording parts produced and materials used |
| basic math, e.g., proportions | |
| checking on a process sheet | designing machine to dry parts |
| solving problems following method in manual | following instructions to set up machine for production |
| | filling out time card |

**2. Literacy Practices in Meetings**

| | |
|---|---|
| developing recording system for tracking bar size | reading work process control instructions |
| FMEA (Failure Mode Effects Analysis) | writing list of things to do |
| writing work process-control instructions | looking up machine numbers in book (at home) |
| statistical analysis of production processes | |

**3. Literacy Practices in PFK activities**

| | |
|---|---|
| literacy classes | filling out skills sheet |
| designing education program with team manager | reading problem solving course material |
| looking up information in PFK notebook | studying (at home and during breaks) |
| reading phone number | |

Our study offers the following implications for workplace literacy education:

The emphasis on team production can substantially increase the demand for literacy skills. The new responsibility for making decisions, coordinating work, and monitoring quality calls on workers to develop and employ a wide variety of literacy practices. Not only does teamwork expand the ways in which workers communicate; it also introduces many areas of knowledge about which they must communicate. Thus the growing demand is not just for basic skills abstracted from the contexts of their use, but for a complex set of understandings and abilities that necessitate practice, guidance, and reflection as well as continual communication about the skills themselves. These demands are prodigious, as evidenced by Hardy workers' struggles to meet them and the management's attempts to help them do so.

Team organization can open doors to new means of literacy development. Teams are environments with great potential for supporting workers' attempts to meet the new demands for learning. Careful structuring of goals, space, time, and tasks is necessary to create the kind of collaboration that binds coworkers together for effective on-the-job teaching and learning. Hardy workers' construction of instructional principles and practices suggests that long-term working relationships and support for collegiality encourage workers to share their expertise.

Incentives and support for meeting new skill requirements can encourage workers to accept and create learning opportunities. Following a "high performance" production model, manufacturing workers engage in literacy practices that are more diverse and sophisticated than is usual under a Tayloristic model. We have seen how Hardy workers plan and improve production processes, design equipment, and troubleshoot problems with both products and workers. In carrying out these responsibilities they have to use and further develop their capabilities in interacting with peers, engineers, and managers (inside as well as outside the company). Not only because success on the job depends on literacy learning, but also because they deem educational achievement as worthy in itself and as an avenue to self-respect, workers tend to welcome and extend opportunities to improve their skills. As a consequence, they actively enhance the educational aspect of the work environment by analyzing, assessing, and improving their own and others' skills and by teaching skills to others.

Learning opportunities can be a burden as well a benefit for employees. Our data suggest that the educational requirements of PFK helped some workers develop skills they found worthwhile in their work and personal lives. At least some of these individuals, however, felt that the costs, in terms of time demands and psychological pressures, were greater than the company had a right to exact from them. These costs of company-sponsored education might by reduced by carefully constructing learning opportunities to provide all employees: (1) the support they need for successful participation, and (2) alternative ways to meet their learning goals.

A company which restructures work to include incentives for learning may take on many functions of an education institution. Work and learning in a company affect and are affected by the definitions of work, education, and literacy in the full context of workers' lives. Just as schools have been powerful in defining literacy practices and determining kinds and levels of literacy competence in settings throughout society (Cook-Gumperz, 1986), companies that design education programs will shape the concept of literacy in many settings. Therefore, the education which is emerging in the new arena studied here—workplace teams—has broad implications for education internal and external to the workplace. Team-based workplace education can be a crucible for innovative instructional approaches both in workplaces and other education settings. Project-oriented and hands-on approaches in particular may be refined for workers learning skills through application and adapted to school settings where adults are learning skills.

Although work settings with team organization hold advantages for applied learning, from the point of view of society and the individual, workplaces have inherent limits as education institutions. Companies' aims and activities, in education as in all spheres, are largely determined by marketplace demands for efficiency, productivity, and quality in providing a product or service. The literacy needs of the larger society and its members, however, are much broader than the needs of one firm. Many Hardy workers, whether or not they believed that their employer's education requirements improved their work or had beneficial "side effects" on their personal lives, identified education needs that were not met by opportunities that Hardy offered. These personal educational needs were not restricted to degrees. Some workers aspired to take courses of their own choosing, on their own schedule. For some the goal of learning was self-fulfillment, family needs, or expanded participation in society; for others the goal was recognition for learning. While workplace-centered education may inadvertently answer some of these needs, most workplaces do not make it their business to do so. Therefore, the advantages of literacy education in workplaces should not blind us to the fact that the main purpose of these institutions is not to provide a broad literacy education. Awareness of this fact reminds us to view workplace education in relation to the wider adult education system and to continue to work for education reforms in workplaces and other education institutions that benefit learners and their communities.

# Note

1. This name and the names of all individuals, teams, and products are pseudonyms. This chapter is an abridged version of an article that appeared in *Reading Research Quarterly* (Hart-Landsberg & Reder, 1995). Some of this preliminary research at Hardy has been described elsewhere in conjunction with research on another setting which structured incentives for learning (Reder, Hart-Landsberg, Schwab, & Wikelund, 1991).

# References

Agar, M. H. (1986). *Speaking of ethnography*. Beverly Hills, CA: Sage.

Balfanz, R. (1991). Local knowledge, academic skills, and individual productivity: An alternative view. *Educational Policy, 5*(4), 343–370.

Best, M. H. (1990). *The new competition: Institutions of industrial restructuring*. Cambridge, MA: Polity Press.

Cook-Gumperz, J. (Ed). (1986). *The social construction of literacy*. Cambridge, England: Cambridge University Press.

Daniels, H. A. (1983). *Famous last words: The American language crisis reconsidered*. Carbondale, IL: Southern Illinois University Press.

Darrah, C. N. (1992). Workplace skills in context. *Human Organization, 51*(3), 274–283.

Engestrom, Y. (1991). Developmental work research: A paradigm in practice. *Quarterly Newsletter of the Laboratory of Comparative Human Cognition, 13*(4), 79–80.

Engestrom, Y., & Middleton, D. (Eds.). (in press). *Communities of practice: Cognition and communication at work*. Cambridge, England: Cambridge University Press.

Ferdman, B., Weber, R. M., & Ramirez, A. G. (Eds.). (1994). *Literacy across languages and cultures*. Albany NY: SUNY Press.

Fingeret, A. (1983). Social network: A new perspective on independence and adult illiterates. *Adult Education Quarterly, 33*, 133–146.

Geertz, C. (1973). *The interpretation of cultures*. New York: Basic Books.

Goody, J. (Ed.). (1968). *Literacy in traditional societies*. London: Cambridge University Press.

Hart-Landsberg, S., & Reder, S. (1995). Teamwork and literacy: Teaching and learning at Hardy Industries. *Reading Research Quarterly, 30*(4), 1016–1052.

Gowen, S. G. (1992). *The politics of workplace literacy: A case study.* New York: Teachers College Press.

Heath, S. B. (1983). *Ways with words: Language, life and work in communities and classrooms.* Cambridge, England: Cambridge University Press.

Hutchins, E., & Klausen, T. (in press). Distributed cognition in an airline cockpit. In Y. Engestrom & D. Middleton (Eds.), *Communities of practice: Cognition and communication at work.* Cambridge, England: Cambridge University Press.

Jenkins, G. D. Jr., Ledford, G. E. Jr., Gupta, N., & Doty, D. H. (1992). *Skill-based pay: Practices, payoffs, pitfalls and prescriptions.* Scottsdale, AZ: American Compensation Association.

Lave, J., & Wenger, E. (1991). *Situated learning: Legitimate peripheral participation.* Cambridge, England: Cambridge University Press.

Reder, S. M. (1987). Comparative aspects of functional literacy development: Three ethnic American communities. In D. A. Wagner (Ed.), *The future of literacy in a changing world* (pp. 250–270). Oxford, england: Pergamon Press.

Reder, S. M. (1992). Getting the message across: Cultural factors in the intergenerational transfer of cognitive skills. In T. Sticht, B. McDonald, and M. Beeler, (Eds.), *The intergenerational transfer of cognitive skills* (pp. 204–228). Newark, DE: Ablex.

Reder, S.M. (1994). Practice-engagement theory: A sociocultural approach to literacy across languages and cultures. In R. M. Weber, B. Ferdman, & A. Ramirez (Eds.), *Literacy across languages and cultures* (pp. 33–74). Albany, NY: SUNY Press.

Reder, S.M., & Green, K. R. (1983). Contrasting patterns of literacy in an Alaska fishing village. *International Journal of the Sociology of Language, 42,* 9–39.

Reder, S.M., Hart-Landsberg, S., Schwab, R. G., & Wikelund, K. R. (1991). *Literacy development: Transitions, opportunities and participation.* Philadelphia: National Center on Adult Literacy, University of Pennsylvania.

381

Reder, S.M., & Schwab, R. G. (1989). The communicative economy of the workgroup: Multi-channel genres of communication. *Office: Technology and People, 4,* 177–198.

Schultz, K. (1992). *Training for basic skills or educating workers? Changing conceptions of workplace education programs.* Berkeley, CA: National Center for Research on Vocational Education, University of California.

Scribner, S. (1984). Studying working intelligence. In J. Lave & B. Rogoff (Eds.), *Everyday cognition: Its development in social context* (pp. 9–40). Cambridge, MA: Harvard University Press.

Scribner, S., & Sachs, P. (1990). *A study of on-the-job training* (Technical Report No. 13). New York: National Center on Education and Employment, Teachers College, Columbia University.

Scribner, S., & Sachs, P. (1991, February). *Knowledge acquisition at work* (Technical Report No. 22, with L. DiBello and J. Kindred). New York: Institute on Education and the Economy, Teachers College, Columbia University.

Shaiken, H. (in press). Experience and the collective nature of skill. In Y. Engestrom & D. Middleton (Eds.), *Communities of practice: Cognition and communication at work.* Cambridge, England: Cambridge University Press

Shuman, A. (1983). Collaborative literacy in an urban multiethnic neighborhood. *International Journal of the Sociology of Language, 42,* 69–81.

Suchman, L. (in press). Constituting shared workspaces. In Y. Engestrom & D. Middleton (Eds.), *Communities of practice: Cognition and communication at work.* Cambridge, England: Cambridge University Press.

# List of Contributors

**Carol Bartlett** has been involved in workplace literacy and adult literacy programs working with marginalized people in all areas of literacy. She is currently the Literacy Educator at Georgia State University and coordinator of the Teaching Assistant Programs at Georgia Institute of Technology. She has extensive experience in secondary and postsecondary educational systems.

**Marisa Castellano** is a doctoral candidate in the Graduate School of Education at the University of California, Berkeley. Her dissertation examines the various types of competence (e.g., mathematical, physical, rhetorical) women need to succeed in the skilled trades. Her interests include working women and the work opportunities of youth who neither drop out nor go to college. Castellano uses anthropological and sociolinguistic methods to explore these issues. She is affiliated with the Institute for Research on Learning in Palo Alto, California.

**Jenny Cook-Gumperz** is professor of education at the University of California, Santa Barbara. A sociologist and sociolinguist, Cook-Gumperz is well known for her work on literacy theory and the social context of children's language learning. She is author of the *Social Construction of Literacy*.

**Debby D'Amico** is the deputy director of education and training at the Consortium for Worker Education, an organization comprised of 30 member New York City labor unions. She was formerly coordinator of research on publicly funded literacy programs in New York City at the Literacy Assistance Center, and has published reports and articles on workplace literacy, assessment in adult education, access to adult education programs among African-Americans, and the purposes and goals of adult learners. A report on staffing of adult education programs and an article about education policy for dislocated workers and public assistance recipients are in press. She has also

383

written on issues of class, race, and gener as these affect pedagogy and economic development.

**Charles Darrah** is associate professor in the Department of Anthropology at San Jose State University. His articles on work and workplaces have been published in *Human Organization* and *Work and Occupations*, and he recently completed the book *Learning and Work: An Exploration in Industrial Ethnography* (Garland Publishing, 1996). He is currently studying issues of identity and community in a sample of "high-tech" Silicon Valley companies.

**Sheryl Greenwood Gowen** is associate professor in the Department of Learning Support Programs in the College of Arts and Sciences at Georgia State University. Her research interests include gender and equity issues in literacy, access to higher education, and teaching in postsecondary institutions. Her publications include *The Politics of Workplace Literacy: A Case Study*. She is currently working on an edited volume of essays on the social and economic issues surrounding women and literacy.

**W. Norton Grubb** is a professor at the School of Education, the University of California, Berkeley. He is also a site director for the National Center for Research in Vocational Education, which has supported some of his investigations of education and job training programs. Most recently, he edited a two-volume work on the integration of academic and vocational education entitled *Education through Occupations in American High Schools*, published by Teachers College Press in spring 1995; and he is the author of forthcoming books on the sub-baccalaureate labor forces and on teaching in community colleges. His general interests include the role of schooling and training in labor markets; the flows of students into and through postsecondary education; the nature of teaching and the effects of policy and other social forces; and social policy toward children and youth. He received a Ph.D. in economics from Harvard University in 1975.

**Karolyn Hanna** is a professor of nursing at Santa Barbara City College, Santa Barbara, California. An author of articles in various nursing journals, she has worked as a registered nurse at several hospitals and has taught nursing at Imperial Valley College, California; Creighton University, Omaha, Nebraska; and Barnes Hospital School of Nursing, St. Louis Missouri. At present she is a graduate student in the Educational Psychology Department, School of Education, at the University of California at Santa Barbara.

**Sylvia Hart-Landsberg** is a research associate in the Science and Mathematics Education Program at the Northwest Regional Educational Laboratory in Portland, Oregon. Her research has focused on social organization, communication, and learning in school and work settings. Among her works are studies of literacy programs for children and adults, hospital secretaries' efforts to "learn the ropes" of their jobs, and elementary and secondary teachers' teamwork as well as their uses of advanced technologies. Currently she is writing about resources for learning science and mathematics.

**Glynda Hull** is associate professor of education and director of the College Writing Programs at the University of California, Berkeley. She has written about the teaching of writing, technology, and workplace literacy. Her most recent research is a study of the literacy requirements of two electronics factories in the Silicon Valley of northern California.

**David Jolliffe** is associate professor of English and director of Writing Programs at Depaul University in Chicago. He is co-author of *Assessing Writers' Knowledge and Processes of Composing* and *Scenarios for Teaching Writing*, contributing editor of *Writing in Academic Disciplines* and *Rhetoric: Concepts, Definitions, Boundaries*, and author of *Writing, Teaching, and Learning: Incorporating Writing Throughout the Curriculum*. In the 1970s, he worked as a drag and a pot digger at Ormet Aluminum Corporation and as a kiln worker at Corning Glass Company.

**Mark Jury** is a doctoral candidate in education at the University of California, Berkeley. A former high school English teacher, his research interests include language and literacy issues in work settings.

**Judy Kalman** is a researcher at the Departamento de Investigaciones Educativas, Centro de Investigaciones y Estudioes Avazados (DIE-CINVES-TAV) in Mexico City. She has published papers in English and Spanish on literacy practices from both a theoretical and applied perspective. She contributed to *Literacy and Other Forms of Mediated Action* and recently completed *La Educación de Adultos: Estado del Arte, Hacia una estrategie Alfabetizadora para México*, a policy statement on adult literacy and basic education in Mexico. A book about public scribes in Mexico and their literacy practices is forthcoming from Hampton Press.

**Kay M. Losey** is assistant professor of English and assistant director of the Writing Program at the University of North Carolina at Chapel Hill. Her research focuses on the teaching of writing to non-mainstream adults. Her forthcoming works include "Mexican American Students and Classroom Interaction: An Overview and Critique" to appear in *Review of Educational Research* and *"Listen to the Silences": Mexican American Interaction in the Composition Classroom and the Community* to be published by Ablex.

**Juliet Merrifield** is Director of the Center for Literacy Studies at the University of Tennessee, Knoxville, and an adjunct faculty member in the College of Education. Since 1989 she has conducted research, program, curriculum, policy, and staff development with literacy programs in Tennessee and the southern Appalachian region. She is a principal author of *Life at the Margins: Everyday Literacy Among Diverse Adults*, to be published by Teachers College Press. A native of Britain, she has a doctorate from Oxford University. Before coming to the University of Tennessee, Dr. Merrifield was Co-director of Research for the Highlander Research and Education Center, a non-formal learning center which has been working for social justice in Appalachia and the South for over sixty years.

**Stephen Reder** is a member of the faculty in the Psychology Department at Portland State University. His research interests include cultural factors in literacy development and educational outcomes; the relationships among information technologies, the social organization of work and patterns of workplace communication; and the ways in which differences in communicative activitties are constitutive of broader patterns of social differentiation.

**Emily Schnee** is an adult educator. She has worked for the Consortium for Worker Education since 1989 as a teacher, staff developer, and curriculum developer. She currently teaches ESL and writing to immigrant workers and coordinates a family literacy project. She has an M.A. in International Educational Development from Columbia University Teachers College and worked for several years in Nicaragua in popular health education and adult literacy.

**Katherine Schultz** is assistant professor in the Department of Educational Development at the University of Delaware. A former teacher and principal, she now teaches courses in teacher education, language development, ethnographic research methods, and theoretical perspectives on literacy. She is currently conducting qualitative research with urban adolescent females on their transition from school to work, with a particular focus on their literacy practices.

**Oren Ziv** is a doctoral student in Education in Language and Literacy at the University of California, Berkeley. His research concentrates on the role of language and literacy in the productive relations of the workplace. In particular, he studies the changing technologies of work from a social-cultural perspective. Ziv has worked as a writer and manager with the computer industry for over ten years.

# Index

INDEX